The A to Z
of Methodism

Edited by
Charles Yrigoyen Jr.
Susan E. Warrick

The A to Z Guide Series, No. 42

The Scarecrow Press, Inc.
Lanham • Toronto • Plymouth, UK
2009

Published by Scarecrow Press, Inc.
A wholly owned subsidiary of
The Rowman & Littlefield Publishing Group, Inc.
4501 Forbes Boulevard, Suite 200, Lanham, Maryland 20706
http://www.scarecrowpress.com

Estover Road, Plymouth PL6 7PY, United Kingdom

British Library Cataloguing in Publication Information Available

Library of Congress Cataloging-in-Publication Data

The hardback version of this book was cataloged by the Library of Congress as
follows:

Historical dictionary of Methodism / edited by Charles Yrigoyen, Jr. and Susan E.
Warrick.— 2nd ed.
    p. cm. — (Historical dictionaries of religions, philosophies, and movements ;
no. 57)
    Includes bibliographical references.
    1. Methodist Church—Dictionaries. 2. Methodist Church—Biography—
Dictionaries. I. Yrigoyen, Charles, 1937– II. Warrick, Susan E. (Susan Eltscher),
1957– III. Series.
    BX8211.H57 2005
    287'.03—dc22   2004024402

ISBN 978-0-8108-6825-0 (pbk. : alk. paper)
ISBN 978-0-8108-6341-5 (ebook)

Printed in the United States of America

Contents

Editor's Foreword

Not yet three centuries old, Methodism is one of the more recent religious communions. From the outset, it has been one of the more vigorous. In an amazingly short time, it spread from original societies in the British Isles to North America and then to other parts of the British empire. From there, because of active evangelism, it has been carried to many countries around the world. Meanwhile, membership has continued to rise. Given its relative tolerance and many far-flung centers, Methodism has generated numerous denominations, all part of the same family if often distinctive in significant ways. Today, through the World Methodist Council, the churches, and their members, Methodism plays an important role in the ecumenical movement and, through its many social and charitable activities, in world affairs.

The first edition was already an important addition to the literature on Methodism, coming more than two decades after any predecessor, and this second edition another decade later should be even more warmly welcomed. As before, it includes, in one handy volume, information on numerous prominent figures, from founders and leaders to others who have made notable contributions to the church and wider world. Entries on events, doctrines, and activities make Methodism what it is. And now there are substantial surveys of Methodism in different regions: the United States and Great Britain, but also Canada, Europe, Africa, Asia, Latin America, the Middle East, and the Pacific. The introduction tells us something of the geographic spread and present scope. The progress over a busy and fruitful period from the beginnings to the present day is summed up in a helpful chronology. An excellent bibliography directs readers to further sources on persons, places, events, doctrines, and whatever may especially interest them.

This second edition of the *Historical Dictionary of Methodism* is the result of sustained efforts by over 60 authors, 25 or so more than before.

They are all specialists in their particular fields and all have presented a multitude of subjects clearly and concisely. They include academics and administrators, pastors, and theologians. However, there had to be some control post, to see that all the bases were covered and the work kept moving along. This function was ably provided by Charles Yrigoyen, Jr. and Susan E. Warrick, respectively, general secretary and former assistant general secretary of the General Commission on Archives and History of The United Methodist Church, who, in addition, produced many entries themselves. I am certain that the efforts of this impressive team will be greatly appreciated by the Methodist community and beyond.

John Woronoff
Series Editor

Preface to the Second Edition

In 2003 Methodists around the world celebrated the 300th anniversary of the birth of their founder, John Wesley. In partnership with his brother Charles, John was an outstanding leader of the 18th-century Evangelical Revival in England. The Wesleys, ordained priests in the Church of England, set about to reform their nation and church by proclaiming God's grace in both word and deed. The movement which they founded ultimately gave birth to more than 300 Methodist denominations in 140 nations. These churches in Africa, Asia, Central and South America, Europe, the Middle East, North America, the Pacific Islands, and elsewhere number approximately 39,000,000 members with an even larger constituency, making Methodism one of the largest bodies in world Protestantism.

As we claimed in the first edition of the *Historical Dictionary of Methodism*, this reference work seeks to provide basic information about some of the most important personalities, ideas, events, and locations in the origin and development of Methodism. The focus of the first edition was mainly North America and Great Britain. This edition, approximately one-third larger than the first, includes new articles on North America and Great Britain as well as other parts of the world, e.g., Africa, Asia, Central and South America, Europe, and the Pacific Islands. Very difficult decisions have been made concerning subjects to include or omit. The bibliography at the end of the volume gives an indication of the vast literature on the Wesleys and the history of Methodism.

We remain grateful to the superb corps of theologians and historians who have assisted in the production of this volume. Special thanks is expressed to John A. Vickers, Natalie K. Watson, and the Editorial Committee of Epworth Press for permission to use in revised form some of the articles in the splendid *A Dictionary of Methodism in Britain and*

Ireland (2000). Finally, we offer our appreciation of Jon Woronoff, Series Editor, for inviting us to edit this new edition, and to the staff of Scarecrow Press whose encouragement and cooperation have been indispensable.

Charles Yrigoyen, Jr. and Susan E. Warrick

Acronyms

ABCFM	American Board of Commissioners for Foreign Missions
AME	African Methodist Episcopal Church
AMEZ	African Methodist Episcopal Zion Church
CIEMAL	Concilio Iglesias Evangélicas Metodistas de América Latina
CME	Christian [or Colored] Methodist Episcopal Church
COSMOS	General Conference Commission on Structure of Methodism Overseas
EA	Evangelical Association
EC	Evangelical Church
EUB	Evangelical United Brethren
GBGM	General Board of Global Ministries
IEMELIF	Iglesia Evangélica Metodista en las Islas Filipinas
MC	The Methodist Church
MCCA	The Methodist Church of the Caribbean and the Americas
MEC	Methodist Episcopal Church
MECS	Methodist Episcopal Church, South
MP	Methodist Protestant
NCC	National Council of the Churches of Christ in the USA
UB	United Brethren in Christ
UMC	The United Methodist Church
WCC	World Council of Churches
WCTU	Woman's Christian Temperance Union
WFMS	Woman's Foreign Missionary Society
WHMS	Woman's Home Missionary Society
WMC	World Methodist Council
YMCA	Young Men's Christian Association
YWCA	Young Women's Christian Association

Chronology

1703 John Wesley born.

1707 Charles Wesley born.

1709 Wesley saved from Epworth rectory fire.

1714 Wesley enters Charterhouse School, London. George Whitefield born.

1720 Wesley enters Christ Church, Oxford.

1725 Wesley ordained deacon.

1728 Wesley ordained priest.

1729 Charles Wesley forms Holy Club at Oxford.

1735 Samuel Wesley, rector of Epworth, dies. George Whitefield converted. John and Charles Wesley embark for Georgia.

1736 John Wesley forms fellowship societies in Georgia. Charles Wesley returns to England.

1737 Wesley publishes *A Collection of Psalms and Hymn*s in Charleston, South Carolina.

1738 George Whitefield sails for Georgia. Wesley lands in England from Georgia. Wesley and Peter Böhler form the Fetter Lane religious society. Charles Wesley's transforming experience (May 21). John Wesley's Aldersgate experience (May 24). Wesley visits Moravians in Germany.

1739 Wesley began field-preaching in Bristol. Wesley holds first service in the Foundery, London.

1741 Wesley accepts Thomas Maxfield as his first "son in the gospel" (full-time itinerant lay preacher).

1742 Wesley organizes society class at Bristol and issues quarterly tickets to members. Susanna Wesley dies at the Foundery, London.

1743 First English-Welsh Methodist Association meets under chairmanship of George Whitefield. Wesley publishes *The Nature, Design, and General Rules of the United Societies.*

1744 Wesley calls first Methodist Conference, at the Foundery, London.

1745 Francis Asbury born.

1747 Wesley's first visit to Ireland.

1749 Charles Wesley marries Sarah Gwynne.

1751 John Wesley marries Mary Vazeille.

1752 Howell Harris establishes community at Trevecka, Wales. First Irish Conference, at Limerick. Philip William Otterbein comes to America as minister of German Reformed congregation, Lancaster, Pennsylvania.

1755 Wesley publishes *Explanatory Notes upon the New Testament.*

1756 John William Fletcher ordained.

1759 Methodist chapel opens at Newbiggin-in-Teesdale, England, apparently oldest Methodist chapel in world in continuous use for weekly worship.

1760 Philip and Margaret Embury, Paul and Barbara Heck, arrive in New York from County Limerick, Ireland.

1766 New York Methodist society begun by Philip Embury, at Barbara Heck's urging.

1767 Captain Thomas Webb consolidates Methodism in New York and Philadelphia.

1768 Selina, Countess of Huntingdon, opens college at Trevecka, Wales. Wesley Chapel (John Street Church), New York, opens.

1769 Hannah Ball begins Sunday School at High Wycombe. Richard Boardman and Joseph Pilmore sail to America as Wesley's authorized itinerant preachers. Old St. George's Chapel, Philadelphia, dedicated.

1770 English Conference attacks Calvinism, sparking controversy in which John Fletcher champions Wesley with *Checks to Antinomianism.* George Whitefield dies at Newburyport, Massachusetts, on his seventh visit to America.

1771 Francis Asbury sails for America.

1773 First Methodist Conference in America, in St. George's, Philadelphia. William Watters accepted, first native-born American Methodist itinerant preacher.

1774 Lovely Lane Chapel, Baltimore, built. Otterbein becomes pastor of new "German Evangelical Reformed Church" in Baltimore.

1777 Richard Allen converted.

1778 Wesley begins *Arminian Magazine.* Wesley's Chapel, City Road, London, opens.

1779 William Black converted, founder of Methodism in Nova Scotia.

1780 Wesley publishes A *Collection of Hymns for the Use of the People called Methodists.*

1783 Robert Carr Brackenbury pioneers Methodism in the Channel Islands, whence it spreads to France.

1784 Wesley's Deed of Declaration secures legal recognition for the annual conference as the governing body of British Methodism. Wesley ordains Richard Whatcoat and Thomas Vasey as preachers for America and commissions Thomas Coke to ordain others. Methodist Episcopal Church is organized at the "Christmas Conference," Baltimore, Maryland. Francis Asbury ordained by Coke, Otterbein, and probably Whatcoat and Vasey.

1786 Thomas Coke lands in West Indies.

1787 Cokesbury College opens at Abingdon, Maryland. Free African Society formed in Philadelphia, the beginnings of African Methodist Episcopal Church.

1788 Charles Wesley dies.

1789 Otterbein organizes first Annual Conference of his followers. Methodist Book Concern begun in Philadelphia under John Dickins.

1790 American Methodists take over British work in Canada.

1791 John Wesley dies. British Methodism divided into districts. France made a separate circuit of British Methodism.

1792 First quadrennial General Conference of American Methodism. James O'Kelly leads first major schism in American Methodism, forming Republican Methodist Church, later the Christian Church.

1794 Beginnings of camp meeting movement at Rehoboth, North Carolina.

1796 Beginnings of group in New York which culminates in the organization of the African Methodist Episcopal Zion Church. Jacob Albright begins preaching with a Methodist Episcopal exhorter's license.

1800 Wesleyan Methodist missionaries sent to Wales. Jacob Albright forms three classes among the Germans in Pennsylvania. Philip William Otterbein and Martin Boehm found The United Brethren in Christ and are elected its first bishops.

1803 First conference of Albright's followers held.

1806 Methodism introduced into South Africa.

1807 First English camp meeting, on Mow Cop.

1808 Jacob Albright dies.

1809 First Discipline and catechism of Albright's followers (*Evangelische Gemeinschaft*) printed.

1810 Adam Clarke begins his commentary on New Testament (3 vols.) and Old Testament (5 vols.). First Evangelical (and first German) camp meeting held in the United States.

1811 William Clowes and Hugh Bourne unite their followers and take the name "Primitive Methodists" in 1812. First ordained Wesleyan missionary to Sierra Leone.

1812 First Methodist class meeting and service in Australia.

1813 Wesleyan Methodist Missionary Auxiliary Societies formed. Thomas Coke launches mission to Ceylon. Philip William Otterbein ordains Christian Newcomer. Philip William Otterbein dies.

1814 Thomas Coke dies, is buried in Indian Ocean.

1815 First society of Bible Christians formed. Samuel Leigh arrives as first Wesleyan missionary in Australia. First General Conference of United Brethren in Christ formed and first *Discipline* approved.

1816 Francis Asbury dies. African Methodist Episcopal Church formed, Richard Allen chosen bishop. First General Conference of Evangelical Association convenes. Barnabas Shaw goes as Wesleyan missionary to South Africa.

1817 Methodist mission begun on Indian mainland. First church and first publishing house of Evangelicals built at New Berlin, Pennsylvania.

1818 American *Methodist Magazine* begins publication.

1819 Missionary societies organized in New York and Philadelphia.

1820 Nathan Bangs becomes editor and general book steward of the Methodist Book Concern. First United Brethren Sunday School held at Croydon, Indiana. African Methodist Episcopal Zion Church organized in New York. English Wesleyan Methodists begin mission to Gambia.

1822 Daniel Coker organizes Methodist Society for freed slaves en route to Liberia. Methodist work begins in Tonga.

1823 *Zion's Herald* begins publication, first Methodist weekly newspaper. Richard Watson begins publication of *Theological Institutes.*

1824 *Child's Magazine* (later *Kiddies' Magazine*) begun by Wesleyan Methodists in England. African Methodist Episcopal work begun in Haiti and the Dominican Republic.

1826 Joseph Rayner Stephens begins mission in Sweden. *Christian Advocate* begun by Nathan Bangs in New York.

1828 Methodist work begins in Samoa.

1829 Primitive Methodists begin mission to the United States.

1830   Methodist Protestant Church organized in America.

1833   Melville Cox begins first American Methodist foreign mission, to Liberia.

1834   United Brethren Publishing House formed. *Religious Telescope* begun by United Brethren.

1835   First British Methodist weekly newspaper, *The Watchman* (ceased 1884). First Methodist mission in South America begun, to Brazil. Nicholas Snethen publishes *Lay Representation*. William Nast converted. Mission to Fiji Islands begun. Phoebe Palmer institutes a weekly prayer meeting in her home.

1836   *Der Christliche Botschafter* begun by Evangelical Association.

1838   Thomas Birch Freeman lands at Cape Coast, pioneering missions in West Africa, especially in Ghana.

1839   Missions begun in Switzerland.

1840   Newbury Biblical Institute founded, Newbury, Vermont, first American Methodist seminary, ancestor of Boston University School of Theology (1868).

1841   *The Ladies' Repository*, the first Methodist periodical for women, begins publication.

1842   First Methodist church built in Argentina.

1843   T. B. Freeman begins missions in Dahomey and Togo. Orange Scott and others, favoring the abolition of slavery, withdraw from the Methodist Episcopal Church to form the Wesleyan Methodist Church.

1844   The Methodist Episcopal Church is divided by the Plan of Separation.

1845   Methodist Episcopal Church, South, is organized in Louisville. Olaf Gustaf Hedstrom opens Swedish mission in ship *John Wesley* (also known as *Bethel Ship*) in New York harbor.

1846   First quadrennial General Conference of the Methodist Episcopal Church, South.

1847   Judson Dwight Collins establishes mission in China.

1849 Ludwig S. Jacoby establishes a German Methodist mission in Bremen.

1852 First French Methodist Conference.

1853 First British ordained missionaries go to China. *London Quarterly Review* begins publication. Ole Peter Petersen is ordained by the Methodist Episcopal Church and assigned to Methodist missions in Norway.

1855 Australasian Conference formed. Methodism introduced to Hawaii. United Brethren missionaries go to Sierra Leone.

1856 American Methodist missions begun in India by Dr. and Mrs. William Butler.

1858 Women's Missionary Auxiliary begun in England.

1859 First Methodist Episcopal society organized in Denmark.

1860 Mission to Italy launched from British Methodism. Free Methodist Church formed in United States.

1861 United Methodist Free Churches begin a mission to Kenya.

1865 Evangelical Mission to Switzerland formed.

1866 Methodist Episcopal Church forms Freedmen's Aid Society. Methodist Episcopal Church, South, adopts lay representation in General and Annual Conferences. Helenor M. Davison is ordained a deacon by the Indiana Conference of the Methodist Protestant Church, probably the first ordained woman in the Methodist tradition.

1867 Wilberforce University in Wilberforce, Ohio, opened by African Methodist Episcopal Church. Missions established in Brazil by Methodist Episcopal Church, South.

1868 Evangelical mission to France.

1869 Methodist Episcopal Church founds the Woman's Foreign Missionary Society. United Brethren Mission to Germany.

1870 Colored Methodist Episcopal Church organized. Methodist preaching begins in Austria.

1871 First English missionary assigned to Portugal.

1872   Laymen received into General Conference of the Methodist Episcopal Church.

1873   Mission begun in Mexico. Mission in Japan by both American and Canadian Methodists.

1874   The Woman's Christian Temperance Union is formed; Annie Wittenmyer is its first president and Frances Willard is chosen corresponding secretary.

1875   First Methodist service in New Guinea. Evangelical Mission to Japan. Cape May Commission declares that the Methodist Episcopal Church and Methodist Episcopal Church, South, are coeval branches of Methodist Episcopal Church founded in 1784.

1876   Methodist Episcopal mission officially recognized as an independent denomination in Sweden.

1877   Bishop William Taylor introduces Methodism into Chile and Peru.

1879   Bishop James M. Thoburn begins Methodist Episcopal work in Burma.

1880   Anna Howard Shaw and Anna Oliver are denied ordination by the General Conference of the Methodist Episcopal Church; Shaw is later ordained by the Methodist Protestant Church.

1881   First Methodist Ecumenical Conference, London.

1882   South African Conference founded.

1884   Methodist Episcopal Church begins mission in Korea. The African Methodist Episcopal General Conference approves licensing women as local preachers, but limits them to evangelistic work.

1885   Bishop William Taylor begins missions in Angola and Congo. Bishop James M. Thoburn begins missions in Singapore and Malaysia.

1886   Swiss Methodism becomes Annual Conference of the Methodist Episcopal Church.

1887   Army chaplain J. H. Bateson begins British Methodist work in Burma. Isabella Thoburn founds the first Christian woman's college in Asia (Lucknow, India).

1888 Bishop William Taylor takes over work of Congregational Church in Mozambique for the Methodist Episcopal Church. Deaconess work is given official standing by the Methodist Episcopal General Conference.

1889 United Brethren mission in China. Ella Niswonger becomes the first woman ordained in the United Brethren Church. Eugenia St. John is ordained an elder by the Kansas Annual Conference of the Methodist Protestant Church. Epworth League founded in the United States. Church of United Brethren in Christ (Old Constitution) splits from parent body.

1891 Methodism introduced into Rhodesia. Second Ecumenical Methodist Conference, in Washington, D.C.

1893 Primitive Methodists begin missionary work in eastern Nigeria.

1894 The United Evangelical Church divides from The Evangelical Association.

1895 The Methodist Episcopal Church, South, begins missions in Korea.

1897 British and American missions in Germany merge.

1898 African Methodist Episcopal women form Woman's Home and Foreign Missionary Societies. United Brethren begin mission in Japan.

1899 Bishop James M. Thoburn begins mission in the Philippines. United Brethren mission begun in Puerto Rico. Methodism established in Cuba by the Methodist Episcopal Church, South.

1900 Methodism introduced into Hungary by a German Methodist preacher. Evangelical mission begun in China. A Lay Conference established, parallel to the Annual Conference of clergy, in the Methodist Episcopal Church; women are granted "equal laity rights."

1901 Third Ecumenical Methodist Conference, London. United Brethren begin missions in Philippines. Ella Niswonger (United Brethren) is elected the first woman clergy delegate to a General Conference in the Wesleyan tradition.

1902 Methodist mission begun in Borneo.

1904 Women are given laity rights and admitted to the Methodist Episcopal General Conference as delegates.

1905 Methodism introduced into Panama. Methodist missions begun in Java and Sumatra. United Brethren missions in Germany transferred to the Methodist Episcopal Church.

1907 Japan Methodist Church is formed from the missions of American and Canadian Methodists. United Methodist Church in England formed from the Methodist New Connexion, the Bible Christians, and the United Methodist Free Churches. Canadian United Brethren join Congregationalists.

1908 American Methodist Manifesto on Social Questions prepared (Social Creed of the Churches). Evangelical Mission begun in Riga, Latvia. Mission to Manchuria begun by the Methodist Episcopal Church, South.

1910 New Zealand becomes conference independent of Australia.

1911 Southern Congo Conference of the African Methodist Episcopal Church established. Bishop Walter R. Lambuth of the Methodist Episcopal Church, South, begins work in Central Congo. Fourth Ecumenical Methodist Conference, Toronto.

1920 Methodist Episcopal Church begins work in the Dominican Republic. The local preacher's license, the first step to ordained ministry, is officially extended to women in the Methodist Episcopal Book of Discipline.

1921 Baltic and Slavic mission formed from work begun by the Methodist Episcopal Church in Lithuania (1904), Latvia (1912), and Estonia (1921). Fifth Ecumenical Methodist Conference, London.

1922 Belgian Mission begun by Methodist Episcopal Church, South. Czechoslovak Mission begun by Methodist Episcopal Church, South. Poland-Danzig Mission begun by Methodist Episcopal Church, South. The Evangelical Church is formed from The United Evangelical Church and The Evangelical Association.

1924 Methodist Episcopal women are given limited clergy rights.

1925 Canadian Methodist Church joins Congregationalists and Presbyterians to form The United Church of Canada.

1927   The Methodist Church of South Africa is constituted by an Act of Parliament.

1930   Korean Methodist Church is formed from the missions of the Methodist Episcopal Church and the Methodist Episcopal Church, South. Methodist Church of Brazil becomes autonomous (self-governing). Methodist Church in Mexico becomes autonomous.

1931   Sixth Ecumenical Methodist Conference, Atlanta, Georgia.

1932   The Methodist Church (England) is formed by union of the Wesleyan Methodists, the Primitive Methodists, and the United Methodists.

1939   Methodist Church (USA) is formed from the union of the Methodist Episcopal Church, the Methodist Episcopal Church, South, and the Methodist Protestant Church. Georgia Harkness becomes the first female professor of theology at an American Methodist seminary (Garrett Biblical Institute).

1940   The French Methodist Conference is united with the Église Réformée de France.

1941   The Japanese Methodist Church becomes part of the new Church of Christ in Japan.

1946   Dr. John R. Mott is awarded the Nobel Peace Prize. Evangelical United Brethren Church is formed by union of The Evangelical Church and The Church of the United Brethren in Christ. The Revised Standard Version of the New Testament is published.

1947   Seventh Ecumenical Methodist Conference, Springfield, Massachusetts.

1948   World Council of Churches is organized.

1950   National Council of Churches of Christ in the USA is organized.

1951   Eighth Ecumenical Methodist Conference, Oxford, organizes standing committees and officially adopts name "World Methodist Council."

1952   Revised Standard Version of the Old Testament is published.

1953   Methodist Church in Taiwan organized.

1956 Ninth World Methodist Conference, Lake Junaluska, North Carolina. World Federation of Methodist Women formed. Women in The Methodist Church win full clergy rights.

1961 Methodist Church of Ghana becomes autonomous. Tenth World Methodist Conference, Oslo, Norway.

1962 Methodist Church of Nigeria becomes autonomous. Evangelical Methodist Church of Italy becomes autonomous.

1963 Methodist Church of Ceylon becomes autonomous.

1964 Methodist Church of Upper Burma becomes autonomous. Methodist Church of Indonesia becomes autonomous.

1965 Methodist Church of Lower Burma becomes autonomous. Methodist Church in Zambia unites with two others to form United Church of Zambia.

1966 Eleventh World Methodist Conference, London, England.

1967 Methodist Church of Sierra Leone becomes autonomous. Methodist–Roman Catholic dialogues begin.

1968 Methodist Church of Kenya becomes autonomous. Methodist Church of the Caribbean and the Americas becomes autonomous. The Methodist Church and The Evangelical United Brethren merge to form The United Methodist Church. Methodist Church of Malaysia-Singapore becomes autonomous.

1969 Methodist Church of Cuba becomes autonomous. Methodist Church of Pakistan becomes autonomous. Methodist Church of Chile becomes autonomous. Methodist Church of Argentina becomes autonomous. Belgian Annual Conference becomes part of the Protestant Church of Belgium.

1971 Twelfth World Methodist Conference, Denver, Colorado.

1973 European Methodist Council established. CIEMAL founded in Santiago, Chile.

1974 Formal commencement of *The Bicentennial Edition of the Works of John Wesley* held at Drew University, Madison, New Jersey.

1976 Thirteenth World Methodist Conference, Dublin, Ireland.

1977 Annual Methodist Peace Award initiated by World Methodist Council.

1980 Marjorie Matthews is elected a bishop of The United Methodist Church, the first woman in any major Protestant denomination to hold the office.

1981 Fourteenth World Methodist Conference, Honolulu, Hawaii.

1983 British Methodism publishes new hymnal, *Hymns and Psalms.*

1984 American Methodist bicentennial. African Methodist Episcopal Church publishes *Bicentennial Hymnal.*

1985 Methodist-Reformed conversations initiated.

1986 Fifteenth World Methodist Conference, Nairobi, Kenya.

1989 New Revised Standard Version of the Bible is published. *The United Methodist Hymnal* is published. Free Methodists publish *The Hymnal for Worship and Celebration.*

1991 Sixteenth World Methodist Conference, Singapore.

1992 *The United Methodist Book of Worship* is published. Africa University opens in Old Mutare, Zimbabwe. Methodist-Anglican conversations begin. Puerto Rico Methodist Church becomes autonomous.

1996 Seventeenth World Methodist Conference, Rio de Janeiro, Brazil. African Methodist Episcopal Church, Zion, celebrates its bicentennial, publishes new hymnal, *The African Methodist Episcopal Zion Hymnal.*

1998 World Council of Churches assembly in Harare, Zimbabwe.

2000 Eighteenth World Methodist Conference, Brighton, England.

2003 300th anniversary of John Wesley's birth.

2004 The Protestant Methodist Church of Ivory Coast, Africa, joins The United Methodist Church.

2006 Nineteenth World Methodist Conference scheduled for Seoul, Korea.

A Brief History of Methodism

by Frank Baker
Revised by the editors for this edition

The millions of warm-hearted people throughout the world who look to John and Charles Wesley as their spiritual pioneers still remember that in 1739 John Wesley had proclaimed prophetically, "I look upon all the world as my parish." This was written by the priest of the Church of England after he had led a frustrating mission to British immigrants and Native Americans in Georgia, been stirred up to his own spiritual shortcomings by Moravian refugees, and returned to England. Here on May 24, 1738, under the influence of Peter Böhler, another Moravian, John Wesley altered his allegiance from stern religious discipline as God's way of salvation to simple faith in Christ and declared, "I felt my heart strangely warmed. I felt I did trust in Christ, Christ alone for salvation, and an assurance was given me that he had taken away my sins, even mine, and saved *me* from the law of sin and death." Less than three weeks later he made a pilgrimage to the Moravians in Germany, seeking (as he replied when asked why he went to Herrnhut) "to see the place where the Christians live."

Returned to England, John Wesley began to preach salvation by faith, now from personal experience and with new spiritual power. The churches in general were not ready for this, and on April 2, 1739, Wesley ushered in an evangelical revolution by agreeing to preach in the open air in Bristol.

The Wesleys gathered their multiplying followers into "societies" for Christian fellowship, striving to keep them within the Church of England community. However, they refused to turn them away provided they avoided moral evil, sought to do all the good in their power, and attended the means of spiritual grace in one genuine evangelical group or another, which usually meant welcoming people increasingly nicknamed "Methodists."

Although he strove at first to enroll ordained clergy as colleagues, in 1741 John Wesley deliberately began to accept the assistance of trained laymen as his "sons in the gospel" who proliferated so rapidly that he was enabled to raise Methodist societies throughout the British Isles. In 1769 Wesley sent two of his experienced preachers to train and organize along British lines the societies which had sprung up in Maryland, New York, and Philadelphia, of whom Francis Asbury became the acknowledged leader. With the birth of the United States, Wesley unsuccessfully tried to secure ordained evangelical clergy for his American societies, or the ordination of some of his own preachers.

Eventually in 1784 he authorized (and reordained) Dr. Thomas Coke to lead a small delegation to launch the Methodist Episcopal Church, with Asbury ordained as a second "bishop"—though Wesley strongly preferred the term "superintendent," soon discarded by his American followers. This formed the first Methodist *Church*.

By his death in 1791, therefore, Wesley had two major denominations springing from his evangelical leadership: those in Britain with something like an interwoven Presbyterian organization, which he termed a "connexion," and those in America whose organization was Episcopalian, with three orders of ministry: deacons, elders (rather than "priests" or "presbyters"), and bishops. In 1791 the British Methodist Conference listed a total membership in Europe of 72,476 and the Methodist Episcopal Church in America, 64,146, though these statistics were inevitably only an approximation. "Europe" really implied the British Isles.

Wales had developed its own form of Calvinistic Methodism under the leadership of Howell Harris (a layman) who began his evangelism there in 1735. The first English-Welsh Methodist Association assembled under the leadership of George Whitefield (an ordained priest), John Wesley's former pupil at Oxford and Calvinist in outlook, who had taken over Wesley's American mission and continued to tour both America and Wales, as well as England and Scotland. To the general public Whitefield was the main target of anti-Methodist satire.

Charles Wesley was the chief pioneer in Ireland, taking over from his brother John in 1747. The Irish warmed to the straightforward evangelism of the Methodists and multiplied rapidly, eventually furnishing many leaders for American Methodism.

Scotland did not resonate to John Wesley as eagerly as it did to Whitefield, but from 1751 onward, Wesley built up solid societies in the major cities. The Isle of Man became a phenomenal hotbed of Methodism under the evangelism of John Crook (Wesley's lay itinerant preacher) from 1775 onward.

Sporadic evangelizing visits to the Channel Islands from 1783, including that of John Wesley and Thomas Coke in 1787, had minor success, nurturing both English and French-speaking societies. In 1791 Methodism trickled over thence into France. Most of Methodism planted in Europe after Wesley's death, however, sprang from America.

METHODISM AFTER WESLEY

Both in the British Isles and in the United States a similar kind of development took place during the following two centuries. During the 18th century there was steady growth out from the original centers, and some missionary activity. During the first half of the 19th century there was more growth, more missionary activity, but also some internal policy divisions; during the second half, growth, together with occasional reunions, and many more missionary ventures from the bewildering number of Methodist and Methodist-related churches (especially from those in the USA), now scattered over every continent.

The 20th century witnessed more reunions, more ecumenical fellowship, some unions with other denominations, and some national unions between Methodist-related "missionary" churches from different countries and Methodist denominations. It is not unrealistic, indeed, to speak of the Methodist missionary melting-pot. The global results are admirably documented in the handbook, *World Methodist Council Handbook of Information, 2002–2006, revised edition* (Clark Communications, 2003), describing the Methodist and Methodist-related churches organized in 125 countries with 39,000,000 members and a constituency of over 74,000,000. Before attempting to summarize the contemporary amalgam in the World Methodist Council, however, it seems wise to sketch the continuing history after Wesley in the "home countries" of Britain and the USA.

Wesley's followers, whether in Britain or in America, never split from their parent body because of disagreement over Wesley's basic insistence upon proclaiming salvation by faith, though there were divisions in America because of a lowered emphasis upon Christian perfection, or holiness.

British Isles

In 1797 in England, however, Alexander Kilham led an agitation to secure more democracy in organization, which led to the Methodist New Connexion. Hugh Bourne in the Potteries and William Clowes in Hull sought to revive open-air evangelism, especially in the American form of camp meetings, and united in 1811 to form the Primitive Methodist Connexion. William O'Bryan's overeager evangelism in Cornwall and Devon led to his expulsion and the formation in 1819 of the Bible Christians. They accepted women as itinerant preachers, as later did the Primitive Methodists. The Protestant Methodists were formed in Leeds in 1828 because they felt that the installation of an organ would disrupt the spontaneity of their worship, and the Wesleyan Methodist Association in 1835 opposed a college for theological education.

Unrest in many forms was in the air. In 1848 several reformers were expelled from the Wesleyan Church in Brixton, London, including Catherine Mumford, recently converted, "the mother of the Salvation Army," who in 1855 married William Booth, another expelled reformer, who for a time served as a revivalist with the Methodist New Connexion. He became his wife's right hand in the Christian Revivalist Association, which in 1877 took the title The Salvation Army. Egged on by an anonymous pamphlet campaign against Wesleyan ministerial autocracy, in 1849 the reform movement developed into such a landslide that it split the Wesleyan Methodist Church in two.

The tide began to turn. In 1857 many of the reformers came together in the United Methodist Free Churches. These joined forces with the Methodist New Connexion and the Bible Christians in 1907 to form the United Methodist Church. In 1932 this church reunited with the Wesleyan Methodist Church and the Primitive Methodists to form the Methodist Church. Remaining outside this reunion was a small group of Independent Methodist Churches (formed in 1806), with no paid ministry, and the small Wesleyan Reform Union, organized in 1859.

The Primitive Wesleyan Methodists in Ireland were organized in 1818 by Adam Averell, an ordained deacon of the Church of Ireland, who nevertheless sought communion administered by Methodist preachers rather than the parish clergy. The disestablishment of the Irish church in 1869 paved the way for their reunion in 1879 with the parent body, which was then renamed the *Methodist Church in Ireland*. The Irish Conference remained independent of the British Conference but with somewhat ambiguous vestigial links at the presidential level.

ACROSS THE ATLANTIC

Even during Wesley's lifetime two west Atlantic communities with loyalties to their mother country found themselves increasingly coming under the oversight of the Methodist Episcopal Church of the United States.

Canada

Those in "British North America" were centered from 1785 in the circuits of Newfoundland and Nova Scotia. Laurence Coughlan, an Irishman who went to Newfoundland in 1765, in 1776 published an account of his labors there. William Black, a Yorkshireman, began preaching in Nova Scotia in 1779. James Evans from Hull devised a printed syllabic language for the Cree Indians in the northern territories.

Preachers from both Britain and America, representing their varied denominations, expanded the work in Canada, struggled for generations to achieve unity, and at last in 1884, from what had been five separate Methodist denominations, formed The Methodist Church of Canada. In 1925 they joined most of the Presbyterians and the few Congregationalists to form The United Church of Canada—supported by a very active Canadian Methodist Historical Society.

Caribbean

The other west Atlantic area during Wesley's day was that in Antigua, which, through the indefatigable energy of Thomas Coke from 1786 onward, spread to other islands in the West Indies and was regarded as

Britain's first "Overseas Mission." In 1758 Nathaniel Gilbert of Antigua brought his family to London where Wesley baptized two of his black slaves.

In 1778 Wesley sent out John Baxter, a Chatham shipwright and lay pioneer who became Wesley's full-time preacher to the Caribs. The stations organized over the years by the Wesleyan Methodist Missionary Society became autonomous in 1967 as The Methodist Church in the Caribbean and the Americas, one of the founding members in 1973 of the Caribbean Conference of Churches. They join many other groups from American Methodism in several ecumenical ventures. The World Methodist Council now lists approximately 20 groups of islands and 20 distinct Methodist entities.

United States

The huge distances in the United States naturally led to Methodism there being subdivided into many separate conferences, with Bishops Asbury and Coke itinerating among them. They were soon aided by additional bishops, especially as Coke himself shuttled between America and England and became the chief proponent of British missions to the Caribs in the West Indies and also to Africa and Asia.

Within the Methodist Episcopal Church itself divisions arose, especially with the growing self-consciousness of the blacks among them, many of whom were officeholders. Richard Allen had long been a respected preacher at St. George's Church in Philadelphia and its black offshoot, Bethel, when in 1799 Bishop Asbury ordained him deacon. In 1816 Allen gathered together a group of black leaders to form the African Methodist Episcopal Church, and they elected him their first bishop. In 1829 a similar outgrowth from the John Street Methodist Episcopal Church in New York City led to the formation of the African Methodist Episcopal Church, Zion.

The church suffered from other internal problems, as well as being greatly perplexed by antislavery agitation. For many years there was agitation for more democracy in organization, focusing on the elimination of the powerful office of bishop. Some expelled members formed a society of "Associated Methodist Reformers" who in 1830 adopted a new constitution, published in Baltimore, in which they took the name, The Methodist Protestant Church.

At the General Conference of 1844 the northern delegates accepted a "Plan of Separation" from those of the South, where the fact that emancipation was legally forbidden had jeopardized the position of a bishop whose wife owned slaves. This most devastating split (mainly, but not solely, over the issue of slavery) led to the formation of the Methodist Episcopal Church, South, which held its first General Conference in 1846.

In 1870 a third black denomination hived off from the Methodist Episcopal Church, South, taking the title, Colored Methodist Episcopal Church, renamed in 1956 *Christian Methodist Episcopal Church*. Many blacks nevertheless remained with the parent Methodist Episcopal Church and developed responsible positions within that body.

In 1939 the three major Methodist denominations in the USA—the Methodist Episcopal Church; the Methodist Episcopal Church, South; and the Methodist Protestant Church—reunited as *The Methodist Church*, remaining an episcopalian body with about 8,000,000 members. Among the terms of the union was the formation of a Judicial Council and the grouping into five regional jurisdictional conferences to meet quadrennially, as well as a sixth "central" jurisdictional conference to incorporate the black conferences. In 1968 all jurisdictions were integrated during a union with the Evangelical United Brethren (which church had culminated in 1946 from a series of unions between Methodist-related churches having German origins), forming The United Methodist Church.

There are also a number of less numerical churches in the United States affiliated with the World Methodist Council. In 1829 English Primitive Methodists from Hull and Tunstall established missions in New York and Philadelphia. In 1840 they separated from their home conference as The Primitive Methodist Church. This spread to Canada where they merged with other Methodist bodies in 1884.

The Wesleyan Methodist Church of the United States was formed in 1843 with a strong emphasis on holiness, although for many its opposition to slavery was the main attraction. Upon union in 1968 with The Pilgrim Holiness Church (itself formed in 1897 and passing through unions with other holiness churches) its title was simplified to The Wesleyan Church.

The Free Methodist Church was founded in 1860 in New York State by Benjamin T. Roberts, mainly to recapture an emphasis on holiness and enthusiastic worship. There is an offshoot in Canada which remains distinct from the United Church of Canada, as does the offshoot of The Wesleyan Church.

After negotiations with many holiness groups having strong sympathies with Wesley's teachings, but disavowing any major emphasis upon "speaking with tongues," the Church of the Nazarene was organized in 1908. It now has half a million members in the USA and Canada and almost as many in dozens of mission fields on every continent.

Also affiliated with the World Methodist Council are several quite small Methodist-related churches in the USA: the African Union First Colored Methodist Protestant Church which dates from 1813 but has passed through several changes of title; the Allegheny Wesleyan Methodist Connection; the Bible Protestant Church, extremely conservative; the Congregational Methodist Church, strongly conservative; the Evangelical Methodist Church, ultra-fundamentalist; Fundamental Methodist Church, Inc., formed in 1948; Holiness Methodist Church formed in 1909; Missionary Methodist Church of America formed in 1913 from the Wesleyan Methodist Church of the United States; Reformed Methodist Union Episcopal Church formed in 1885 from the African Methodist Episcopal Church; Reformed Zion Union Apostolic Church formed in 1869 from the African Methodist Episcopal Zion Church; Southern Methodist Church formed in 1934 from the Methodist Episcopal Church, South; Union American Methodist Episcopal Church formed in 1850.

A WORLDWIDE COMMUNITY

We have traced in outline the histories of the parent body of Methodism in the British Isles and of its much more prolific daughter church in the United States. Already we have seen something of the missionary urge from both sides of the Atlantic and have realized that Wesley's evangelical enthusiasm, even during his own lifetime, was developing into a worldwide community. This was dramatized and forwarded by the beginning of the decennial World Methodist Conferences in 1881 and the quinquennial World Methodist Councils from 1951.

It is impossible in this brief article to relate in detail the stories behind all the members of this great Methodist family, especially as many of them have merged or are merging their Methodist identity in the greater Church of Christ Universal. What we propose now, however, is to move eastward around the globe, adding to what we have already said about America and the Caribbean to Latin America, then moving from the British Isles to the remainder of Europe, and thence to Africa, Asia, and Australasia.

Latin America

From the United States Methodism moved in 1873 to Mexico where it united in 1930 to form the flourishing autonomous Iglesia Metodista de Mexico with six episcopal areas. Mexican Methodism, like Methodism in most of South America, saw John Wesley as a prototype of liberation theology because of his close ties with the poor and oppressed.

There are also strong autonomous Methodist churches in Argentina, Bolivia, Brazil (founded in 1836 and now supporting a missionary conference in the northeast as well as six regular conferences), Ecuador, Paraguay, Peru, and Uruguay, as well as mission churches elsewhere (established especially by the Church of the Nazarene). In Chile Methodism became autonomous in 1969 but has close ecumenical links with pentecostal and holiness groups with Methodist backgrounds.

In South America there is a total membership of 1,150,000 and a Methodist community of 2,750,000. The total Methodist-related membership in Central America and the Caribbean was 502,000 in 2003, with a community of 992,000.

European Continent

On the continent of Europe Methodism was relatively unsuccessful until the middle of the 19th century, and even then the predecessors of the episcopal United Methodist Church in America was the pioneer or dominant church in Austria (where the British had begun work in 1870), Bulgaria, Czechoslovakia, Denmark, Estonia, Finland, Germany, Hungary, Norway, Poland, Russia, Sweden, Switzerland, and Yugoslavia. The United Protestant Church of Belgium also had its roots in The United Methodist Church of the USA.

The tiny beginnings of French Methodism from England in 1791 were revived by the creation of an autonomous conference under

Charles Cook in 1852, but in 1939 this became part of the French Reformed Church, except for a few who continued as the Union of Evangelical Methodist Churches. The small group in the Netherlands came from the Church of the Nazarene.

A British mission in Italy was begun in 1861 and joined by an American mission in 1870. From 1878 Roman Catholicism claimed to be the state religion and others were barely tolerated. Nevertheless the Methodist witness from both Britain and the USA remains strong in Italy, even in Rome.

In 1811, during the Peninsular War, Methodism in Portugal was fostered by class meetings held by soldiers in the Duke of Wellington's army. A Cornish layman began a class meeting in 1853. The first missionary was sent to Oporto in 1871 from which the British work has developed with ecumenical activities and an increasing likelihood of autonomy.

Methodism in Spain developed from the British soldiers in Gibraltar from 1792, though organized evangelism began its slow progress with William H. Rule in 1832, later paralleled by American work organized in 1920 as the Spanish Methodist Mission. Driven underground during revolution and civil war, the various missions were reorganized in 1945 in the new Evangelical Church of Spain.

Africa

The British-based Methodist Church of South Africa is easily the largest on the continent, with a million and a quarter members and a community twice that size. It began from the evangelism of George Middlemiss, a British soldier, in 1806.

There are also other major Methodist communities stemming from both British and various combinations of American churches in Ghana, Nigeria, and Zaire. In Livingstone's area, which became Northern Rhodesia and then independent Zambia in 1964, Methodism begun by the British Primitive Methodists and Wesleyan Methodists was united in 1932, and in 1965 became part of the United Church of Zambia, leaving four small Methodist groups independent.

In Zimbabwe (formerly Rhodesia) Methodist union is still being sought. The first African bishop of The United Methodist Church there, Abel T. Muzorewa, became the first black prime minister of Zimbabwe. That church's first Africa University was opened at Mutare in 1992.

Although it is impracticable to name all the countries or missionary societies, an exception should be made in one of the oldest civilizations, Egypt. Here in 1968 the Free Methodist Church united with the Methodist-related Holiness Movement Church of Canada to form a Methodist movement with a healthy community of 30,000. The Church of the Nazarene also has a small church here, as they do in Israel, Jordan, Lebanon, and Syria, and also in 17 other African countries, the largest being in South Africa and Mozambique. Altogether in Africa there is a Methodist community of over 19,000,000 in 33 countries, whose missionary enterprise is shared by dozens of sponsoring societies, mainly from the USA. Church membership stands at 9 million.

Asia

Methodist membership in Asia now numbers 10 million members, with a community of some 19,000,000, possibly a larger proportion on this continent stemming from Britain than from the USA. The father of Methodist missions, Thomas Coke, died at sea on his way to Ceylon (now Sri Lanka), where the Methodist Church became autonomous in 1964. Thence the Methodist Church spread to South India to form part of The Church of South India (1947), while the founding efforts of William Butler of the Methodist Episcopal Church formed part of The Church of North India (1969). Other American Methodist components still work in both areas.

Pakistan is a predominantly Muslim republic formed from India in 1947. Here in 1970 the United Church of Pakistan incorporated 60,000 United Methodists into this 200,000-member union.

In Buddhist Burma, now Myanmar, missionary work began from the USA in 1873 and from Britain in 1887. Both became autonomous in 1965, but they still remain independent of each other. The smaller American body (in Lower Myanmar) also spread into Malaysia and Singapore, and their church in Indonesia became autonomous as Gereja Methodist Indonesia.

In Japan both Canadian and American Methodist missionaries began their successful evangelism in 1873. In 1907 the Japan Methodist Church was organized at Aoyama Gakuin University, Tokyo, a highly influential institution founded by the Methodist Episcopal Church in 1874. In 1941 most of the Japanese Methodists joined with other

Protestants to form Kyodan, The United Church of Christ in Japan, although when World War II ended in 1945 some smaller Protestant and Methodist-related bodies withdrew. Kyodan in return sends out lay missionaries to other parts of the world, both East and West. The same is true of the autonomous Korean Methodist Church, springing from American Methodism in 1884, which now has 1,322,000 members with over 100 lay missionaries proclaiming the gospel in 43 different countries. This tradition of lay missionaries is also true of the Korean Evangelical Church whose teaching on holiness is also rooted in American Methodism.

The Philippines also constitutes an evangelical stronghold with American rootage, the Evangelical Methodist Church in the Philippines being an indigenous off-shoot of the Methodist Episcopal Church formed in 1909, which, with two other churches, The United Methodist Church and The United Church of Christ (partly Methodist), and the Free Methodist and the Wesleyan Churches, comprise a total community of 2,500,000 with 1,300,000 members.

In China the American Methodists celebrated their centenary in 1947. Within the following few years, especially in 1950 when Christian missionaries were ejected, the 250,000 Methodist disciples in mission from both America and Britain (1851) were in turmoil. Many were officially transferred to Taiwan and Hong Kong, but many went underground and relied on lay leadership. Both in China and Hong Kong the Methodist Church had come to rely on the "three-self church—self-governing, self-supporting, self-propagating." Since 1980, thousands of new Protestant churches have been opened, and Chinese Methodists are eager for overseas Methodists to worship with them but not for denominational proselytization.

Australasia

Methodist membership in Australasia is 1,500,000 with a total community of about 2,500,000. The first missionary sent out to Australia by the Wesleyan Conference was Samuel Leigh who landed in Sydney in 1815 with the hope that this would form the springboard for evangelism also in New Zealand and the Pacific islands. In 1902, after the incorporation of other British Methodist churches in 1896, The Methodist Church of Australasia was formed. From this in 1913 The Methodist

Church in New Zealand sprung, joined by the Primitive Methodists, and also accepting responsibility for the work in the Western Solomons. In 1983 the New Zealanders made a firm commitment to secure partnership with the Maoris, and thus implement the Treaty of Waitangi made with them by Queen Victoria in 1840. In 1977 the Australian Methodists entered into an ecumenical union with Congregational and Presbyterian churches in Australia under a carefully chosen title, The Uniting Church in Australia, with a community of over 1,300,000.

The Methodist Church in Fiji grew from its British Wesleyan roots in 1835 to become a strongly spiritual multiracial church with a community of 600,000. The Methodist Church of Samoa achieved independence in 1964 from The Methodist Church of Australasia and seeks to be an evangelical missionary church, even with a small membership of 35,000.

After initial failures the Australian missionaries to Tonga met great encouragement from the king of Tonga who acknowledged Christianity by taking the name George Tupou I and later becoming a Methodist local preacher. Queen Tupou Salote (1918–1965) and her sons continued this strong British Methodist tradition though their title, Free Wesleyan Church, denotes freedom from any link with Australia.

In 1968 The United Church of Papua, New Guinea, and the Solomon Islands took over four areas begun by the inspiration of George Brown from 1871 onward, a largely Methodist community of 1,000,000.

John Wesley (1703–1791), Anglican clergyman and Methodist founder.
Used by permission of the General Commission on Archives and History of
The United Methodist Church, Madison, New Jersey, USA.

Charles Wesley (1707–1788), Anglican clergyman and Methodist founder.
Used by permission of the General Commission on Archives and History of The United Methodist Church, Madison, New Jersey, USA.

Francis Asbury (1745–1816), early American Methodist leader and bishop. Used by permission of the General Commission on Archives and History of The United Methodist Church, Madison, New Jersey, USA.

*Richard Allen (1760–1831), founder and bishop of the
African Methodist Episcopal Church.
Used by permission of the General Commission on Archives and History of
The United Methodist Church, Madison, New Jersey, USA.*

Barbara Ruckle Heck (1734–1804), leader in founding American Methodism. Used by permission of the General Commission on Archives and History of The United Methodist Church, Madison, New Jersey, USA.

Marjorie Swank Matthews (1916–1986), first female Methodist bishop. Used by permission of the General Commission on Archives and History of The United Methodist Church, Madison, New Jersey, USA.

United Methodist Uniting Conference, 1968, Dallas, Texas, USA.
Used by permission of the General Commission on Archives and History of The
United Methodist Church, Madison, New Jersey, USA.

E. Stanley Jones (1884–1973), American missionary to India.
Used by permission of the General Commission on Archives and History of
The United Methodist Church, Madison, New Jersey, USA.

Francis Asbury's ordination, Baltimore, Maryland, USA, 1784.
Used by permission of the General Commission on Archives and History of The
United Methodist Church, Madison, New Jersey, USA.

19th-century American Methodist circuit rider.
Used by permission of the General Commission on Archives and History of The
United Methodist Church, Madison, New Jersey, USA.

MRTHODIST CAMP MEETING.

19th-century American Methodist camp meeting.
Used by permission of the General Commission on Archives and History of The United Methodist Church, Madison,
New Jersey, USA.

Methodist Episcopal Church camp meeting, Quesa, Angola, 1926.
Used by permission of the General Commission on Archives and History of The United Methodist Church, Madison, New Jersey, USA.

Methodist mission medical class, Bareilly, India, c. 1870.
Used by permission of the General Commission on Archives and History of
The United Methodist Church, Madison, New Jersey, USA.

Mary Johnston Hospital, Manila, Philippines, 1950.
Used by permission of the General Commission on Archives and History of The United Methodist
Church, Madison, New Jersey, USA.

Clopton School, Shanghai, China, c. 1880s.
Used by permission of the General Commission on Archives and History of The United Methodist Church, Madison, New Jersey, USA.

The Dictionary

– A –

ABORTION refers to stopping human fetal development. This stoppage may occur naturally (spontaneous abortion, miscarriage), or it may be induced. Throughout history, induced abortion has been practiced, often by crude means and not infrequently causing the woman's death (*see* WOMEN). Early Christians opposed abortion on the grounds that it was contraception: interfering with the natural reproductive process. Later, as conception came to be better understood, many Christians opposed abortion as an unjustifiable taking of life. Until the early 1970s, most USA states prohibited abortion, except to save the mother's life. But the sexual-liberation and feminist movements of the 1960s advanced the argument that a woman has the right to decide what happens in and to her body. Then, in 1973, the USA Supreme Court ruled (*Roe v. Wade*) that because the Fourteenth Amendment to the USA Constitution protects privacy, a woman has a qualified right to terminate her pregnancy. This ruling polarized American opinion, with proponents of legal abortion being styled Pro-Choice and opponents taking the label Pro-Life. The **United Methodist Church (UMC)**, in its Social Principles, stakes out middle ground, saying, "In continuity with past Christian teaching, we recognize tragic conflicts of life with life that may justify abortion, and in such cases we support the legal option of abortion under proper medical procedures."

John G. McEllhenney

AFRICA. Methodism gained a foothold in Africa in the 19th century with the arrival of European and American missionaries, and the missionary enterprise was enhanced by the conversion of Africans who

1

became the core of indigenous leadership. Missionary outreach in Africa was further encouraged by the World Missionary Conference in Edinburgh, Scotland, in 1910. What follows is an overview of the continent of Africa. The discussion is divided into West, Central, North, East, and Southern Africa.

In West Africa, British Wesleyans began missionary work in The Gambia in 1821. These early missionaries, like many that followed, were debilitated by the climate. Furthermore, Protestant **missions** faced strong opposition from Islam, the dominant religion. In 2004, total Methodist Church membership was about 2,500, but the church is more influential than its size. In addition to pastoral work, The Methodist Church in Gambia operates several primary schools and medical clinics in addition to other ministries which serve the wider community.

A Methodist presence in Sierra Leone was established as early as 1792, although British Methodists did not send missionaries until 1811 (*see* BRITISH METHODISM). Many of the earliest Methodists were freed slaves. Various Methodist churches are active in Sierra Leone, including The United Methodist Church (**UMC**), African Methodist Episcopal Church (**AME**), West African Methodist Church, **Wesleyan Church**, and Methodist Church of Sierra Leone. The latter sponsors primary and secondary schools, and medical work, including a hospital where nurses and community health workers are trained. The church became autonomous in 1967. The UMC became autonomous in 1973 and is a member of the West Africa Central **Conference** of its denomination. The church sponsors schools and health clinics as well as community development programs. There are more churches planted along the coast among the Creoles than in the hinterland.

Liberia is the oldest independent state in West Africa. Methodism began there in 1822 and the first church was constructed in 1825. The first Methodist Episcopal Church (**MEC**) missionary, **Melville Cox**, arrived in 1833 and an annual conference was organized the following year. Methodism was strengthened in 1853 when several Liberian ministerial candidates were ordained **deacons** and **elders**. During his service as missionary bishop for Africa (1884–1896), **William Taylor** fortified the Liberian mission. He introduced the principle of financial autonomy and under his direction work was established in many places across the country. An outstanding result of Methodist work was the establishment of two schools in Monrovia, the College of West Africa, founded in 1839, and the Gbarnga School of Theology. The UMC also maintains the Ganta Medical Center, which includes a hospital, leprosarium, and school of nursing. In addition to The United Methodist Church, which is the largest of the Methodist bodies, other Methodist denominations organized in Liberia include the AME, African Methodist Episcopal Zion Church (**AMEZ**), Christian Methodist Episcopal Church (**CME**), and Wesleyan Church, as well as the Church of the Nazarene.

British Methodists began a mission in Ghana, formerly the Gold Coast, in 1835 when Joseph Dunwell arrived to work among the Fantes, some of whom were already Christians. Thomas Birch Freeman was instrumental in expanding the missionary outreach of the church among both the Fantes and the Ashanti. By 1913, the Ashanti Mission had been well established and had 26,000 baptized members. The chiefs were friendly to missionaries and invited them to send teachers and evangelists to the villages. Methodist missions placed a great emphasis on **education** and were instrumental in the establishment of a number of schools and colleges. A number of medical facilities are operated under Methodist sponsorship. The largest Methodist denomination is the Methodist Church Ghana, which numbered more than 1,000,000 members in 2004.

Mission work in the Ivory Coast was inaugurated in 1924 by British Methodists, although William Wade ("Prophet") Harris, a Liberian who was raised under Methodist influence, preached widely and successfully in the country between 1914 and 1915. Thousands were converted under Harris's ministry. He organized groups of new Christians, encouraged them to build chapels, and appointed pastors to guide and instruct new converts. Harris was arrested in 1918 by French authorities who suspected that his followers would become a dangerous political party. Following his arrest, nothing further was heard of Harris, although the movement he led survived and Methodists built on his success. Many of the churches organized by Harris joined the Methodists while some preferred to remain independent. The Protestant Methodist Church is the largest Methodist body with a membership in 2004 of approximately 1,500,000.

Nigeria is one of the largest and most populous nations in Africa. While the southern and eastern parts of the country have a Christian majority, the northern regions are predominantly Muslim. Methodist mission work began with the establishment of the mission at Abeokuta and Badagry in 1842 under the leadership of Thomas Birch Freeman. **Primitive Methodists** initiated significant ministry in northern and eastern Nigeria when in 1893 missionaries Ben and Fairley Showell arrived. As in other African nations, the church has been deeply involved in educational and medical institutions. In 1976 an episcopal form of church government was introduced providing for a patriarch, archbishops, and bishops. The Methodist Church, Nigeria, is the largest Methodist body with 1,500,000 members in 2004 followed by The UMC with approximately 200,000 members.

The next to consider is Central Africa. There is not a strong Methodist presence in this area except for the Republic of Congo. There were scattered attempts to establish Methodism in some of the countries in Central Africa, but most of these endeavors could not be sustained.

In 1885, the year after being elected MEC missionary bishop for Africa, William Taylor established his headquarters in Luanda, Angola, with 40 assistants who had expertise in **evangelism**, agriculture, translation, and printing. He proposed that a series of self-supporting mission stations be established from which Methodism was to spread across the nation. Although his plan was not fully realized, the MEC created effective mission outposts. Following Taylor's retirement in 1896, the MEC Board of Foreign Missions assumed the work and the Congo Mission Conference was organized by Bishop **Joseph C. Hartzell** with Angola as one of its districts. The Angola Annual Conference was constituted in 1940. In 2004, there were 150,000 United Methodists in Angola's two annual conferences.

Christianity in the Congo owes much to David Livingstone, the pioneer missionary who made Europe and America aware of the great potential of missions along the Congo River. Methodist presence in the Congo began as early as 1885, but virtually disappeared until it was revived by MEC missionary **John M. Springer**, who established the first mission station in 1911. Four years later, Joseph Hartzell formally organized the Congo Mission Conference. Meanwhile, in 1911 the **MECS** began work north of Katanga under Bishop **Walter R.**

Lambuth. Both the northern and southern Methodist work included the formation of schools, colleges, hospitals, and clinics. Congo's major Methodist bodies are The UMC with approximately 1,200,000 members and the **Free Methodist Church** with a membership of 53,000.

Christianity was present in North Africa from its earlier years. The Coptic church remained stronger than other groups although it lacked a zeal for evangelism. Methodism membership in this area is insignificant although its influence is far greater than its numbers.

Methodist work in Tunisia commenced in 1908 under Joseph Hartzell. Its growth has been unusually slow due to the Muslim influence in the area. The church is oriented toward serving English-speaking foreign workers and not the indigenous population. The government of Tunisia is not well disposed toward Christianity. As a result, direct evangelism is very difficult.

The MEC began work in Algeria in 1909 under the direction of Joseph C. Hartzell. The mission established medical work, an educational program, and evangelistic outreach, and the North Africa Provisional Conference was organized in 1928. By 1962, Methodists reported eight places of worship and a membership of approximately 400. It conceded, however, that the work was difficult as direct evangelism was discouraged. In Tunisia and Algeria there are approximately 1,000 UMC members under the direction of a European bishop.

East Africa is the next to be considered. Methodism was introduced to Kenya by the British **United Methodist Free Churches** in 1862. Thomas Wakefield was the pioneer missionary who established work in Ribe, Mazeras, Jomvu, Golbanti, and Lamu. In 1884, W. H. During, an African from Sierra Leone, opened work along the Tana River. Reginald T. Worthington instituted missions in Meru in 1912. In addition to evangelism, the mission work included educational, medical, and agricultural dimensions. Kenya Methodism became an autonomous church in January 1967. In 2004, the Methodist Church in Kenya numbered more than 300,000 members who worshipped in more than 1,000 congregations.

John Wesley Haley, Free Methodist missionary, established work in Rwanda and Burundi beginning in 1935. Both countries are composed of two main ethnic groups, the Hutu (about 80% of the population) and the Tutsi. Violence between the two in recent times has created turmoil, especially in Rwanda, making church work difficult. The Free Methodist Church remains strong in both countries, but The UMC is larger in Burundi with more than 100,000 members in 2004.

Southern Africa is the last area. Ndevu Mashaba, converted in a British Wesleyan Mission while a miner in South Africa, is responsible for the origins of Methodism in Mozambique in 1885. Methodism grew under Mashaba whose work was directed by Wesleyan Methodist missionary George Weavind. MEC bishops William Taylor and Joseph Hartzell were responsible for enlarging the Methodist presence in the country and an MEC Mission Conference was formed in 1920. Free Methodist mission work began in 1885 under the pioneering leadership of G. Henry Agnew. In 2004, The UMC was the largest denomination with more than 150,000 members, followed by the Church of the Nazarene with more than 45,000.

Methodism entered Zimbabwe, formerly Southern Rhodesia, in 1891 in response to an appeal by Cecil Rhodes. Wesleyan Methodist missionaries Owen Watkins and Isaac Shimmin originated and developed the earliest ministry. Several mission stations were opened in the years following. The ministry was greatly impeded by the Matabele revolt in 1894 and 1896. Joseph Hartzell initiated a ministry for the MEC in 1897 when the British South Africa Company was transferring its administrative center from Umtali to Beira. The MEC organized in areas around Umtali and opened schools, hospitals, and clinics, and engaged in evangelistic outreach. Methodism is significantly represented in Zimbabwe by several denominations, the largest of which are the Methodist Church of Zimbabwe (112,000 members) and The UMC (95,000 members). Africa University in Old Mutare opened in 1992 under international UMC sponsorship.

Two missionary societies, both from Britain, were responsible for the origins of Methodism in Zambia (Northern Rhodesia): the Primitive Methodists in 1890 among the Mashukulumbwe and the Wesleyan Methodists in 1912. The work of the two societies was merged in 1932 and later joined in the formation of the United Church of Zambia, the largest Methodist and Protestant denomination in the country with 630,000 members. The AME Church began its Zambian mission in 1930 and in 2004 was the second largest Methodist body with 43,000 members.

Methodism in South Africa owes its origins to British soldiers who occupied the Cape in 1806. Wesleyan Methodist missionary Barnabas Shaw was dispatched to South Africa in 1816 and established a successful mission at Leliefontein. Other mission stations were established through the assistance of local evangelists. In 1820, another British Wesleyan Methodist missionary, William Shaw, arrived and within four years opened a series of mission locations, including Natal and Delagoa Bay. In addition to establishing congregations, educational and medical work was central to the ministry. Methodism was strengthened through the work of William Taylor who arrived in 1866 and conducted meetings in Cape Town, Port Elizabeth, and Vitenhagen. In 2004, the largest Methodist denomination in the country, the Methodist Church of Southern Africa, counted approximately 735,000 members. Eight other Methodist denominations are also organized in the country, but are considerably smaller.

The London Missionary Society and the Wesleyan Methodist Mission Society ministered to the Namagua in the northern Cape Province. However, they ceded their work to the Rhenish Missionary Society. The Rhenish society was able to extend its ministry into the southern part of Namibia. The only Methodist group that has sustained work in Namibia is the AME in the Herero Reserves. Four thousand members of the Evangelical Lutheran church joined the AME. Under their leadership new congregations have been planted, thus expanding Methodist ministry in Namibia. The Methodist Church in Southern Africa has also extended its jurisdiction to Namibia thereby adding to the Methodist presence. In 2004, the total membership of the Methodist churches was about 5,000.

Zablon Nthamburi

AFRICAN METHODIST EPISCOPAL CHURCH (AME). The AME grew out of the Free African Society (FAS), which **Richard Allen**, Absalom Jones, and others established in Philadelphia in 1787. When officials at St. George's **MEC** pulled blacks off their knees while praying, FAS members discovered just how far American Methodists would go to enforce racial discrimination against

African Americans. Hence, these members of St. George's made plans to transform their mutual aid society into an African congregation. Although most wanted to affiliate with the Protestant Episcopal Church, Allen led a small group who resolved to remain Methodists. In 1794 Bethel AME was dedicated with Allen as pastor. To establish Bethel's independence from interfering white Methodists, Allen, a former Delaware slave, successfully sued in the Pennsylvania courts in 1807 and 1815 for the right of his congregation to exist as an independent institution. Because black Methodists in other middle Atlantic communities encountered racism and desired religious autonomy, Allen called them to meet in Philadelphia to form a new Wesleyan denomination, the AME.

The geographical spread of the AME prior to the Civil War was mainly restricted to the Northeast and Midwest. Major congregations were established in Philadelphia, New York City, Boston, Pittsburgh, Baltimore, Washington, D.C., Cincinnati, Chicago, Detroit, and other large cities. Numerous northern communities also gained a substantial AME presence. Remarkably, the slave states of Maryland, Kentucky, Missouri, Louisiana, and, for a few years, South Carolina, became additional locations for AME congregations. The denomination reached the Pacific Coast in the early 1850s with churches in Stockton, Sacramento, San Francisco, and other places in California. Moreover, Bishop Richard Allen sent missionaries to Haiti in 1824, while in 1840 Bishop Morris Brown established the **Canada** Annual **Conference**.

The most significant era of denominational development occurred during the Civil War and Reconstruction. Oftentimes with the permission of Union army officials AME clergy moved into the states of the collapsing Confederacy to pull newly freed slaves into their denomination. "I Seek My Brethren," the title of an often repeated sermon that Theophilus G. Steward preached in South Carolina, became a clarion call to evangelize fellow blacks in Georgia, Florida, Alabama, Texas, and many other parts of the South. Hence, in 1880 AME membership reached 400,000 because of its rapid spread below the Mason-Dixon line. When Bishop **Henry M. Turner** pushed African Methodism across the Atlantic into Liberia and Sierra Leone in 1891 and into South Africa in 1896, the AME now laid claim to adherents on two continents (*see* AFRICA).

While the AME is doctrinally Methodist, clergy, scholars, and laypersons have written important works that demonstrate the distinctive theology and praxis that have defined this Wesleyan body. Bishop Benjamin W. Arnett, in an address to the 1893 World's Parliament of Religions, reminded the audience of the presence of blacks in the formation of Christianity. Bishop Benjamin T. Tanner wrote in 1895 in *The Color of Solomon-What?* that biblical scholars wrongly portrayed the son of David as a white man. In the post–civil rights era theologians **James H. Cone**, Cecil W. Cone, and Jacqueline Grant who came out of the AME tradition critiqued Eurocentric Christianity and African-American churches for their shortcomings in fully impacting the plight of those oppressed by racism, sexism, and economic disadvantage.

In 2000, the AME included over 3,300,000 members, 8,000 ministers, and 6,200 congregations in the USA, and congregations in more than 30 nations. Twenty bishops and nine general officers comprised the leadership of the denomination.

Dennis C. Dickerson

AFRICAN METHODIST EPISCOPAL ZION CHURCH (AMEZ). **James Varick** and other progenitors of the AMEZ withdrew from **John Street MEC** in New York City in 1796 to protest the racial discrimination white parishioners imposed upon them. Restrictions placed upon black preachers were among the grievances that motivated these Wesleyan blacks to incorporate in 1801 as an autonomous congregation. Their desire to sever all ties with the **MEC** and to decline affiliation with **Richard Allen's AME** moved Varick, Christopher Rush, Abraham Thompson, and others to found the AMEZ in 1820. In 1821 black Methodist societies in New York City, Long Island, New Haven, Philadelphia, and Easton, Pennsylvania, agreed to establish a new Wesleyan body. In 1822 and 1826, respectively, James Varick was elected and reelected the first bishop/superintendent of the AMEZ. Varick's 14 successors bore the title of superintendent and submitted to quadrennial elections. The **General Conference** of 1868 eliminated the superintendency in favor of a lifetime bishopric.

While Southern **slavery** restricted the AMEZ to the Northeast during the antebellum period, the denomination rapidly pushed into the former Confederacy even before the Civil War ended. The evangelistic efforts of James Walker Hood were particularly pivotal. He arrived in North Carolina in 1864 and drew black Methodists in New Bern, Wilmington, Fayetteville, and Charlotte into the denomination. These successes laid the foundation for phenomenal AMEZ growth in the state. Consequently, Hood was elevated to the **episcopacy** in 1872. Bishop Joseph Jackson Clinton, the prelate who assigned Hood to North Carolina, sent numerous other clergy into other parts of the South. Their efforts allowed Clinton to organize the Louisiana, Virginia, South Carolina, and Alabama Annual Conferences.

When Andrew Cartwright, a North Carolina pastor, arrived in Brewerville, Liberia, in 1876, the AMEZ venture in **Africa** commenced. By 1880 three congregations had been established in that West African nation. The denomination spread to Ghana when the West Gold Coast and the East Gold Coast Annual Conferences were established in 1909 and 1910, respectively. The Nigeria Annual Conference followed in 1928. Bishop Enoch B. Rochester convened the first South Africa Annual Conference in 1994, and shortly thereafter he received into the denomination 45 congregations in Malawi and Mozambique. Growth in Jamaica happened because the United Holy Church in 1966 merged into the denomination. The organization of the London-Birmingham Annual Conference brought the AMEZ into England in 1971.

Bishops Alexander Walters and Stephen Gill Spottswood became two of the most important African-American leaders to emerge out of the denomination. Walters, elected to the episcopacy in 1892, headed the National Afro-American Council between 1898 through 1907. During the presidential election of 1912 Walters gave crucial support to Woodrow Wilson. Spottswood became a bishop in 1952 and served in several important offices in the National Association for the Advancement of Colored People. He was president of the Washington, D.C., branch, was elevated to the national board in 1951, and a decade later he was elected chairman. He stirred national attention in 1970 when he criticized President Richard M. Nixon for undermining the nation's commitment to civil rights for African Americans.

By 2000, the AMEZ had more than 1,500,000 members and 12 bishops who presided in episcopal districts in the USA, the

Caribbean (*see* LATIN AMERICA AND THE CARIBBEAN), England, India (*see* ASIA), and Africa. The denomination supports several educational institutions, including Livingstone College and Hood Theological Seminary in Salisbury, North Carolina. *The Star of Zion*, the *AME Zion Quarterly Review*, and the *Missionary Seer* are the principal publications.

Dennis C. Dickerson

AIKENHEAD, ELIZABETH HANNAH DIMSDALE (ca. 1863–November 23, 1945), Methodist evangelist, was born in Minden, **Canada** West. As a young woman Elizabeth taught school. When she was about 20 she showed signs of consumption, and for her health went to teach in the more northerly Muskoka region. Her father, visiting her, discovered there was no church nearby and began to preach. As he departed for home, he announced that she would fill his engagements. She began to preach and before she left the area she had nearly 100 converts ready for church membership.

At its meeting in 1885, Toronto **Conference** appointed her a conference evangelist. Her sister Gertrude also began to do evangelistic work and over the next several years the two labored sometimes together, sometimes separately. Other young **women** also began to lead **revivals**, but Elizabeth, a pioneer in the work, was the most prominent. She criss-crossed Ontario and met with great success.

In 1891, she married James Robert Aikenhead, a newly ordained Methodist minister. Elizabeth continued some evangelistic work even after her husband's retirement as a minister of The United Church of Canada in 1928. During her final years, declining health brought her labors to an end.

Marilyn Färdig Whiteley

ALBANIA. *See* EUROPE.

ALBRIGHT, JACOB (May 1, 1759–May 18, 1808), evangelical preacher, founder and first bishop of the **EA**, made his contribution to Christianity in a brief 12-year ministry. The son of German immigrants was born near Pottstown, Pennsylvania, into a family affiliated with the Lutheran church. At age 17 he served in the local militia during the American Revolution. In 1785 he married Catherine Cope and settled on land in Lancaster County, where he farmed and had a profitable business as a tile maker.

Although Albright attended a Lutheran church, he showed little interest in religion until the death of several of his children in an epidemic (1790) seemed like divine punishment for his indifference. In spiritual turmoil, he turned to three devout Christians: the German Reformed minister who conducted the children's funerals, a neighbor associated with the pietistic movement of **Philip William Otterbein** and **Martin Boehm**, and a Methodist **lay preacher** on a nearby farm. Finally able to move beyond the wrath of God, Albright in **repentance** found forgiveness and redemption. He also found spiritual fellowship at a Methodist class meeting, which he joined (*see* SOCIETIES, CLASSES, AND BANDS). In that context he learned a disciplined spiritual lifestyle and eventually was licensed as an exhorter or lay preacher.

Now able to testify to his personal faith and **experience**, he gradually overcame personal doubts that he was not educated enough to preach. His newfound discipline of Bible study, extended meditation and **prayer**, and strict morality that led to rigorous **fasting** and other austerities evidenced his deepening commitment. Ultimately, in October 1796 he began to travel as a German-speaking evangelical preacher. In his ministry Albright proclaimed biblical **salvation** but also condemned the gambling, drunkenness, and cheating habits of many Germans. Often this aroused angry, dangerous opposition, even bodily harm, and he earned a reputation as a religious fanatic. His emphasis on personal holiness as evidence of **faith** reflected the Methodist influence, and it attracted intensely loyal converts as well as opposition.

After four years of preaching (1796–1800), Albright realized he needed some organization to nurture his followers. In 1800 he created three Methodist-style classes of converted people in diverse areas of southeastern Pennsylvania. At a general meeting of lay leaders and lay preachers of his movement (November 5, 1803) Albright was elected to the office of **elder**, received an official license, and two lay preachers ordained him by placing their hands on his head (*see* ORDINATION). This is regarded as the formal beginning of the EA, although that name was not adopted until the first **General Conference** in 1816. In November 1807 Albright presided at the first regular annual conference, which elected him bishop and authorized him to prepare a book of church rules or **Discipline** for the society. **George Miller** was also chosen elder, possibly because of Albright's worsening health. Exhausted by tuberculosis and his itinerant preaching, he died at the home of a friend in spring 1808, six months after becoming bishop and 17 days after his 49th birthday.

Donald K. Gorrell

ALDERSGATE EXPERIENCE. Aldersgate Sunday is still commemorated in May, with events taking place at Bristol, London, and elsewhere on May 21 and 24, featuring a remembrance of the heartwarming experiences of **conversion** or renewal that Charles and John Wesley respectively, had on those dates in or near Aldersgate Street in London in 1738. The reading heard by John of the passage from Luther's *Preface to the Romans* at "about a quarter before nine" the evening of May 24 came at the culmination of a period of spiritual turmoil following the unsuccessful time in Georgia. Conversations with **Peter Böhler**, a Moravian (*see* MORAVIANS), on his desire for **faith** led to the moment when John felt the gift of faith was his. This gave him an **assurance** of **salvation** and allowed him to move on in his spiritual pilgrimage to work with the societies he formed and the people he encountered in open-air **preaching**. A new confidence was born in the experience, which confirmed his call to ministry and gave him fresh heart for the evangelistic tasks ahead in mission and service to all God's creatures. Charles captured this feeling in the hymn written on the days of May 23–24, 1738:

> Outcasts of men, to you I call,
> Harlots and publicans and thieves
> He spreads his arms t'embrace you all
> Sinners alone his grace receives:
> No need of him the righteous have;
> He came the lost to seek and save.

Such an experience is still central to Methodist understanding and belief.

Tim Macquiban

ALGERIA. *See* AFRICA.

ALLEN, RICHARD (February 14, 1760–March 26, 1831), founder of the **AME**, was born into **slavery** in Philadelphia, Pennsylvania. His slave master sold Allen, his parents, and siblings to Stokely Sturgis of Kent County, Delaware. When financial difficulties caused Sturgis to sell away Allen's mother and some siblings, he and his brother resolved to purchase freedom for themselves. Allen was converted in 1777 by an itinerant Methodist minister. After his manumission in 1783, Allen became a traveling Methodist preacher who ultimately settled in Philadelphia in 1785.

His affiliation with St. George's **MEC** allowed him to preach to blacks at special worship services. Allen, Absalom Jones, and others in 1787 also formed the Free African Society (FAS), a religious mutual aid society. After whites at St. George's became increasingly uncomfortable with the congregation's significant black membership, church officials physically accosted some of Allen's followers while they prayed in the sanctuary. Although they left St. George's, Allen and other FAS members could not agree about what denominational form their organization should take. While most of them preferred the Protestant Episcopal Church, Allen and a few others remained with the Wesleyan faith. Hence, he established the Bethel AME in 1794. When white Methodists sought jurisdiction over the congregation, Allen successfully sued in the Pennsylvania courts in 1807 and in 1815 to gain legal recognition of Bethel's independence. In 1816 he called together Wesleyan blacks in the mid-Atlantic states and they formed the AME. When Daniel Coker, leader of the Baltimore group, declined the **episcopacy**, Allen became the denomination's first bishop.

During Allen's episcopacy the New York Annual **Conference** and the Western Annual Conference (Pittsburgh and Ohio) were established. He also received black Methodists in Charleston, South Carolina, into the AME. In 1820, when one of the local preachers, Denmark Vesey, was accused and subsequently executed for planning a slave insurrection, Allen gave sanctuary in Philadelphia to Morris Brown, the leader of the disbanded Charleston AME constituents. In 1824, Allen sent emissaries to spread the denomination to Haiti.

Allen produced several literary works, including an AME **Discipline** in 1817 and three hymnals in 1801, 1808, and 1818. His autobiography was *The Life Experience and Gospel Labors of Rt. Rev. Richard Allen, An Address to those who keep slaves, and a Narrative of the Proceedings of the Colored People During the Awful Calamity in Philadelphia, in the year 1793; and a Refutation of Some Censures Thrown Upon Them in Some Publications.*

As an African-American leader Allen organized opposition to the American Colonization Society. Although he supported the organization when it was founded in 1817, Allen eventually denounced efforts to resettle free blacks in **Africa**. Allen also presided over the first national Negro convention, which met in 1830 in Philadelphia's Bethel AME. He was elected president and the group was named "The American Society of Free Persons of Colour, for Improving Their Condition in the United States; for Purchasing Lands; and for the Establishing of a Settlement in Upper **Canada**." The date of Allen's first marriage, to Flora, is unknown. Apparently, she left him widowed. His second marriage to Sarah (d.1849) in ca. 1800 produced six children: Richard, Jr., James, John, Peter, Sarah, and Ann.

Dennis C. Dickerson

ALLEN, YOUNG JOHN (January 3, 1836–May 30, 1907), **MECS** missionary to China, arrived in Shanghai with his wife, Mary Houston, on July 13, 1860 (*see* ASIA). The Civil War cut off all support from the Board of Missions, so Allen became headmaster of an Anglo-Chinese School and also worked for the Educational, Editorial, and Translation Department of the Chinese government. During these years, as acting superintendent of the mission, he also preached almost daily and itinerated whenever possible. When the new superintendent, J. W. Lambuth, arrived in 1865, Allen remained an unpaid missionary, living on his secular salaries to help the struggling MECS. In 1881, he became superintendent of the China mission and was salaried at last. Allen was the first president of the Anglo-Chinese University, 1885–1895 (later merged with Soochow University). He was the founder, with **Laura Askew Haygood**, of the McTyeire Home and School (1892), and helped establish the Methodist Press. He founded and edited (1868–1907) the influential *Review of the Times*, the first Chinese-language newspaper of world events, which made him the best-known foreigner in China. He died in Shanghai. The Allens had nine children, six of whom survived infancy.

Susan E. Warrick

AMES, JESSIE DANIEL (November 2, 1883–February 21, 1972), suffrage leader, anti-lynching crusader, and interracial movement leader, was born in Palestine, Texas. Widowed in 1914, Ames entered Texas politics in 1915 through the National American Woman Suffrage Association, League of Women Voters, and Democratic Party, motivated by huge inequities in the legal and social positions of **women** and men. Interracial work as director of the Texas Interracial Commission (1922–1929) led to a position as director of Women's Work (1929–1937), then general field secretary (1937–1944) of the Commission on Interracial Cooperation supervising interracial work in 13 southern states. Ames worked closely with **MECS** leaders of the Woman's Missionary Society (1925–1939) and the **MC** Woman's Division of Christian Service (1940–1944). Ames founded the Association of Southern Women for the Prevention of Lynching (1930–1942). With Methodist leaders Bertha Newell, **Mary McLeod Bethune**, and **Dorothy Tilly**, Ames organized an ecumenical, yet substantially Methodist women's movement in the South that reduced lynchings by changing local attitudes and state laws. She was a catalyst behind the formation of the Southern Regional Council. Retiring to Tryon, North Carolina, Ames served as secretary of Christian Social Relations of the Western North Carolina **Conference** Woman's Society of Christian Service (MC).

Alice G. Knotts

ANDREW, JAMES OSGOOD (May 3, 1796–March 2, 1871), bishop who played a central role in the **MEC** division over the **slavery** controversy of the 19th century. Elected bishop in 1832, his service included most of the southeastern **conferences**. After the death of his first wife, Ann Amelia McFarlane, Andrew inherited her slave. Although Georgia state law forbade slaveowners from freeing their slaves, he declared that the girl was free to leave the state whenever due arrangements for her support could be made. When his second wife, Leonora Greenwood, inherited slaves from her first husband in 1844, Andrew made careful legal arrangements to renounce their ownership and to secure them to his wife. The controversy over slavery came to a head at the 1844 MEC **General Conference** in Louisville. Lengthy debate followed, with northern **antislavery** delegates commanding a majority in the conference. Southern delegates prevented Bishop Andrew from acting on his offer to resign from his episcopal office. A resolution was adopted by the conference that requested Bishop Andrew to cease exercising his episcopal functions. Southern protest against the resolution argued that Bishop Andrew had violated no church law. As a result, the plan of separation for the two branches of the church (MEC and **MECS**) was implemented. Bishop Andrew remained active in the latter body.

J. Steven O'Malley

ANGOLA. *See* AFRICA.

ANTIGUA. *See* LATIN AMERICA AND CARIBBEAN.

ANTINOMIANISM. One of the earliest uses of the term antinomianism, from the Greek *anti* (against) + *nomos* (law), is found in Luther's assessment of the theological emphases of Johann Agricola and his followers. During the 18th century, **John Wesley** criticized the major tenets of antinomianism which had surfaced in England, namely: 1) that Christ abolished the moral law, 2) that believers are not obliged to use the means of **grace**, and 3) that preachers ought not to exhort to good works. The first phase of Wesley's polemic dealt with the teachings of two **Moravians**, Philip Molther, who had undermined the means of grace in the name of **faith**, and Count Zinzendorf, whose 1741 dialogue with Wesley resurfaced in the latter's *A Dialogue between an Antinomian and His Friend* (1745). The second phase responded to the seeds of antinomianism that were growing within Methodism itself through the work of William Cudworth, against whom Wesley wrote *A Second Dialogue between an Antinomian and His Friend* (1745), and through the theological antics of Thomas Maxfield and James Relly, to whom Wesley directed his

Blow at the Root (1762). Beyond this, Wesley criticized the Calvinistic tendency (**Countess of Huntingdon**, Walter Shirley, and Richard Hill), to stress the imputed righteousness of Christ to the detriment of real, imparted, holiness. However, the principal argument in this last phase was offered not by Wesley but by **John Fletcher** in his celebrated *Checks against Antinomianism.*

Kenneth J. Collins

ANTISLAVERY MOVEMENT in 19th-century America was significantly influenced by various streams of American Methodism. **John Wesley** opposed **slavery** in the British West Indies, and the early leaders of American Methodism, including **Francis Asbury**, were also forthright in their opposition to slavery among Methodists. Similar opposition was shared by the early **UB** and **EA**. Among the first antislavery organizations was the American Colonization Society (1817), which paid slave owners to release their slaves so that they could emigrate to West Africa. The racial motives for this colonization program offended many African Americans. **Richard Allen,** founding bishop of the **AME**, rejected colonization, as did William Lloyd Garrison (1805–1879), the prominent white antislavery journalist. By the 1830s, the call for the "immediate emancipation" of all slaves was gaining ground in the North. The abolitionists not only opposed the southern defenders of slavery, but also more moderate reform efforts, such as colonization. Theodore Weld, a convert of the evangelist Charles G. Finney, sounded the call for immediate abolition as an expression of Christian repentance in 1833. That year he joined with Garrison to form the American Anti-Slavery Society. A leading abolitionist in the **MEC** was **Orange Scott**, whose disillusionment with his church's compromising stance led him to organize a secessionist body, the Wesleyan Methodist Connection (1843) (*See* WESLEYAN CHURCH). Growing polarization over slavery in the MEC resulted in its division in 1844 along the same lines that would later divide the states at the outbreak of the Civil War.

J. Steven O'Malley

APPENZELLER, HENRY GERHARD (February 1, 1858–June 11, 1902), **MEC** missionary pastor and educator, was born in Souderton, Pennsylvania, of a Lutheran family with roots in Germany and Switzerland. He was converted in a Presbyterian **revival** meeting and joined the MEC in 1879. In December 1884 he married Ella Dodge. After graduation from Franklin and Marshall College, Pennsylvania, and Drew Theological Seminary, New Jersey (1885), he was ordained in San Francisco immediately prior to sailing to Korea (*see* ASIA). He became a member of the Newark **Conference**, and a year later the Philadelphia Conference. He was appointed assistant superintendent of the Korea Mission and later was superintendent, pastor, and principal of Pai Chai Haktang, traveling throughout Korea. He was a member of the Permanent Bible Committee, president of the Korean Religious Tract Society, and coeditor of *Korean Repository*. He died traveling aboard a Japanese steamer that sank.

Barbara E. Campbell

ARGENTINA. *See* LATIN AMERICA AND CARIBBEAN.

ARMINIUS, JACOBUS (October 10, 1560–October 19, 1609), Dutch preacher and controversialist, who after studies in Holland and Switzerland in the Reformed tradition, exercised his ministry in Amsterdam until his appointment as professor of theology at Leiden University in 1602. There he increasingly fell into disputes with his fellow professor, Gomarus, particularly on the doctrine of predestination. After his death in 1609, his disciples produced the *Remonstrance* (1610), which stressed human freedom and **free will** more than divine **grace**; God willed all to be saved and not merely the chosen. Splits developed in the Calvinist-dominated Dutch church, culminating in the Synod of Dort (1617–1619), where supporters of Arminius (Remonstrants) were condemned in an attempt to preserve national unity. The work of Arminius was widely read and disseminated throughout Europe. His influence on English church life, through Archbishop Laud, the Cambridge Platonists, and the Latitudinarians, was considerable. **John Wesley**, through his reading of Grotius, an admirer of Arminius, was a convinced Arminian in his opposition to Calvinist predestination. This led him into disputes and a pamphlet war with others of the Evangelical Revival on the subject, notably **Howell Harris** and **George Whitefield**.

Tim Macquiban

ARTICLES OF RELIGION are concise statements of doctrine that are officially approved by a denomination and thus provide established standards of belief (*regula fidei*) for that denomination, which then function as a measure of the correctness or orthodoxy of theological statements that might be made within that group.

In the Church of England, the Thirty-Nine Articles of Religion have provided the standards of doctrine since the time of Elizabeth I. These brief doctrinal paragraphs are not a creed, but historically have functioned as the basis upon which doctrinal uniformity could be enforced within the church. These articles were the measure of orthodoxy within the Church of England during Wesley's time. He always claimed that Methodist **preaching** was consistent with those articles, as well as with the Book of Common Prayer and the Book of Homilies

When, in the 1770s, some of Wesley's associates, especially Joseph Benson and **John Fletcher**, began to propose the formation of the Wesleyan movement into the Methodist Church of England, a daughter organization of the established church, they suggested certain documents as suitable ecclesial foundations, including a "rectified" version of the articles. Wesley did not approve this suggestion at that time. But with the conclusion of the American Revolution in 1784, Wesley sent to the New World a scheme for establishing Methodism in America as a church, and provided for the new church a set of **doctrinal standards** in the form of Twenty-Four Articles of Religion adapted from the Church of England's Thirty-Nine Articles. He omitted several of the British articles and revised others, with special concern for those with Calvinist content. Among those he omitted was one regarding obedience to the monarch (now inappropriate for the new country). The Americans added one appropriate to their new context, regarding the rulers of the USA, making a total of Twenty-Five Articles of Religion. By their acceptance at the **Christmas Conference** in 1784, they became the "established standards of doctrine" for the **MEC**: the measure of doctrinal orthodoxy in matters of church trial for doctrinal heresy in the succeeding generations, especially for protection against Socinianism, Arianism, and Unitarianism.

The Articles of Religion were constitutionally protected in 1808 by the First Restrictive Rule, which stated that the **General Conference** could not "revoke, alter, or change" them. About the same time, the Methodist Church in Great Britain debated the possibility of adopting some similar set of articles for the "security of their doctrines," but finally rejected the proposed documents by **Adam Clarke, Thomas Coke**, and Joseph Benson. In the late 19th century, several suggestions to revise the articles were proposed in the MEC, but none were adopted.

Several Methodist bodies that developed from or parallel to American Methodism, including the **EA**, adopted or adapted the same set of Wesleyan articles as their standards of doctrine. The Twenty-Five Articles of Religion currently are among the doctrinal standards (with the Confession of Faith from the former **EUB** tradition, which is similar in format and content) of the **UMC**.

Richard P. Heitzenrater

ASBURY, FRANCIS (August 20/21, 1745–March 31, 1816), pioneer bishop of the **MEC**, was born in Handsworth, England. His boyhood home in Great Barr still stands. He proved an able pupil, but at the age of 13 was apprenticed to a chape-maker, John Griffin (not to the blacksmith Foxall, as surmised by F. W. Briggs). Under his mother's influence he became a Methodist, serving in succession as class leader (*see* SOCIETIES, CLASSES, AND BANDS) and local preacher before being called out as an itinerant in 1767.

At the Bristol **Conference** in 1771, Asbury responded to Wesley's appeal for preachers to go out to America. He landed in Philadelphia on October 27 and was soon making his influence felt both there and in New York. Concerned that the two preachers, **Joseph Pilmore** and **Richard Boardman**, were city-bound, he insisted that the principle of **itineracy** should be observed and was soon traveling farther and farther afield. He was equally concerned that Methodist discipline should be applied.

During the Revolutionary War, Asbury was the only preacher of British origin to remain at his post, despite being forced into hiding at the home of Judge Thomas White in Delaware. Despite the shortage of episcopally ordained clergy in the later stages of the war, he strongly opposed moves by the southern preachers to ordain one another and administer the **sacraments** and appealed to Wesley for help.

At the **Christmas Conference** of 1784, on Wesley's authority and (at Asbury's own insistence) with the unanimous approval of the other itinerants, **Thomas Coke** ordained him **deacon, elder**, and "superintendent" (later changed to the more biblical "bishop").

Largely singled-handed, he led the newly formed MEC through its formative years. His relationship with his fellow bishop, Coke, was an uneasy one. Coke was a British citizen and only an occasional visitor. Both to Asbury and to the American Methodists generally, he represented Wesley's desire to maintain remote control over the American church. Neither Wesley nor Coke knew America or had the trust of the American Methodists as Asbury did. In the interests of the growing work he was prepared to defy the dictates of "old daddy Wesley" if they were inappropriate to the American situation.

His leadership did not go entirely unchallenged, for example, by William Hammett and **James O'Kelly**. His proposed council of senior preachers in place of the **General Conference** was defeated as seeming too autocratic. Despite his reservations about Coke's ambitious plans for **Cokesbury College**, he was one with Wesley in his concern for **education** and actively encouraged the founding of schools.

With no home of his own and remaining unmarried, Asbury was always in the saddle and is said to have traveled a quarter of a million miles through rugged terrain and in all weather, preaching incessantly. His journal is a day-to-day chronicle of hardship and unstinted service. He died still in harness, struggling against sickness and fatigue to reach Baltimore for the General Conference. In 1854 his body was removed to the Bishops' Lot in Mount Olivet Cemetery, Baltimore.

John A. Vickers

ASIA. The story of Methodism in Asia begins with **Thomas Coke** and the British East India Company. The company, founded in 1600 to develop trade with India and the Far East, had long prohibited missionary activity in India, fearing the unsettling effects of foreign religious influences. In 1813, under pressure from Parliament, the prohibition was lifted, and Coke immediately organized a party of Wesleyan missionaries, bound for Ceylon (Sri Lanka), Java, and India. Coke died on board ship, but his compatriots anchored in Sri Lanka. By 1819 the mission they founded was large enough to be divided into two districts.

The programs and institutions developed by these first missionaries would be duplicated throughout Asia over the next 150 years. Chief among these were schools for all ages. **Education** met several needs: missionaries taught people to read the Bible and trained them in Christian principles; they provided more general education, otherwise unavailable to the poor and to girls; and, crucially, they trained those who would become pastors, doctors, teachers, and administrators. Mission presses supported educational ventures and produced millions of pages of Christian literature in vernacular languages. Medicine was an equally important mission emphasis. Through clinics and hospitals, missionaries often provided the only medical care for **women** and the poor. Local authorities often welcomed schools and hospitals, since they provided services the government could not. Reform often followed education, and it was Western missionaries who were most vocally opposed to such practices as foot-binding in China and suttee in India. Social changes were sometimes welcomed and sometimes viewed with tremendous hostility by nationalist groups.

In Sri Lanka, missionaries founded colleges and industrial schools, provided medical care, and trained Bible women. A trend toward indigenous leadership was accelerated by the evacuation of missionaries during World War II, and in 1964, the British Methodist **Conference** transferred full authority to an autonomous Sri Lanka Conference. As of 2004 the Methodist Church had 15,500 members.

Coke's dream was fulfilled in 1817 when James Lynch established the first mission on the Indian mainland, in Madras. British Methodists were initially concentrated in south India, which spared the mission from the worst effects of the national uprising (Sepoy Mutiny) in 1857. Eventually, the mission moved west into Bangalore and northwest into Hyderabad State. In Bombay, Wesleyans first worked with British troops, then moved outward through the efforts of a Hindu convert, Samuel Mahator. It was not until the 1880s that the mission had any success as far north as Calcutta, and at the same time efforts in the Lucknow area (northwest of Calcutta) began bearing fruit.

Despite this, British Wesleyan work remained strongest in south India. In 1947 the (United) Church of South India was formed, composed of the Presbyterian, Anglican, and British Wesleyan Methodist **missions**. The Methodists contributed some 175,000 members to this new church, along with a much larger worshipping community. British Wesleyan churches in northern India (about 4,000 members at the time), remained in the British church.

The first American missionaries to India were William and Clementina Rowe Butler of the **MEC**, who arrived in Calcutta in September 1856. **William Butler** had been James Lynch's assistant in Ireland after Lynch's retirement from India, and after emigrating to the United States, the Butlers volunteered to serve as the denomination's first missionaries to India. After narrowly escaping the Sepoy Mutiny, the Butlers made their headquarters in Bareilly and Lucknow. It was through the efforts of Clementina Rowe Butler that the Woman's Foreign Missionary Society of the MEC was organized in 1869 and sent its pioneer missionaries, **Clara Swain** and **Isabella Thoburn**. Clara Swain Hospital, founded in Bareilly in 1874, was the first women's hospital in Asia, and Isabella Thoburn College in Lucknow was the first college for women in Asia. The women's missionary societies of Methodism brought "women's work for women" to Asia, initiating a quiet revolution in women's status.

In 1864, the MEC organized the North India Conference, with three districts, six schools, 10 chapels, two orphanages, and a mission press that would become the dominant Christian press in India. Most significantly, four Indian ministers were ordained and received into conference membership. **James Thoburn** headed the mission after the Butlers return to America in 1865, and greatly expanded its territory. In this he was aided by the evangelist bishop **William Taylor**, whose four years in India drew people of all castes into Methodism.

In 1884, the MEC General Conference approved the formation of Central Conferences in foreign mission fields with more than one annual conference or mission. The Central Conference of Southern Asia was organized in 1885, including India (as well as present-day Myanmar and Pakistan), Malaya, and the Dutch East Indies; Sarawak and the Philippines joined later. The 1930 Central Conference elected

Jashvant Rao Chitambar as its first Indian bishop. By the 1960s, the conference was administering two colleges, supporting two interdenominational seminaries, and operating hundreds of primary, secondary, and training schools, 18 hospitals, numerous clinics and health centers, and the venerable publishing house in Lucknow.

India was the first foreign mission field of the **Free Methodist Church**, which in 1885 assumed the support of a faith mission established in 1881. In 1922, the mission established a hospital and boarding school in Umri in Maharashtra Province, and Union Biblical Seminary in Yeotmal began as an outgrowth of the Free Methodist Bible School. American Wesleyans (*see* WESLEYAN CHURCH) came to India in 1910, establishing schools and clinics around Pardi and Sanjan, about 100 miles north of Bombay. Central India was also the first mission field of the Church of the Nazarene, beginning in 1898. By the 1930s, most mission leadership was indigenous.

By 2004, there were eight Methodist-related denominations in India: Church of South India (2,800,000 members), Church of North India (1,250,000), Methodist Church in India (600,000), Church of the Nazarene (49,000), Wesleyan Methodist Church of India (27,000), Wesleyan Church (7,000), **AME** (5,000), and Free Methodist Church (4,200).

Pakistan, part of the British Crown Colony of India until 1947, was inaugurated as a republic in 1956. The first Methodist presence in the region dates from William Taylor's preaching in 1874. At the time of partition, there were 27 members of the annual conference and some 25,000 Methodists, along with a number of schools. The Methodist Church in Pakistan became autonomous in 1969, and joined several Protestant denominations in 1970 to form The Church of Pakistan, which in 2004 had 1,500,000 members. The Methodist Church had 13,300 members and the Wesleyan Church had 4,200.

China became a viable Protestant mission field in 1842, when the Treaty of Nanking opened several port cities to foreign residence. As in India, education, medicine, and interdenominational cooperation marked Methodist missions. The MEC sent its first missionaries, **Moses White** and **Judson Dwight Collins**, to Foochow (Fuzhou) on the south China coast in 1847. **Robert Samuel Maclay** joined the mission the following year and led the mission for the next 20 years, expanding to the west, north, and south. By 1939, the MEC had eight annual conferences.

The **MECS** entered China in 1848, focusing on the regions around Shanghai and Soochow (Suzhou). **Young J. Allen** arrived in 1860, bringing his considerable energies to the mission press. The MECS established Soochow University, founded mission stations throughout Kiangsu (Jiangsu) and Chekiang (Zhejiang) provinces, and cooperated in the union Nanking (Nanjing) Theological Seminary. An **MP** mission was established in Kaigan. In 1940, the MEC, MECS, and MP missions united to form The Methodist Church in China.

In 1889, **UB** missionaries Austia Patterson and Lillian Shaffner opened a day school for girls and a street chapel in Canton (Guangzhou). They were soon joined by others, including Regina Bigler, the legendary "Beloved Physician of South China." The United Evangelical Church (UEC), which broke away from the **EA** in 1894, selected China as its first foreign mission field. In 1900, its missionaries arrived in Hunan and shortly opened a street chapel and a dispensary. When the UEC merged with the EA in 1922 to form the **EC**, work continued in Hunan, which was becoming increasingly hazardous due to rising nationalism. When the UB joined the Church of Christ in China in 1919, the EC mission remained separate until after the 1946 EUB merger. Free Methodists entered the Honan (Henan) province in 1905, headed by Clara Leffingwell. The Church of the Nazarene began work in North China in 1914.

The first British Methodist missionaries arrived in Canton (Guangzhou), South China, in 1853. By 1860, they had moved into the Hupeh (Hubei) and Hunan provinces of Central China, where David Hill began his extensive career. Besides cooperating in several union colleges and theological schools in Guangzhou and Wuchang (Heilongjiang), the Wesleyans founded hospitals, nursing schools, middle schools, and city churches, as well as undertaking significant work among rural populations. The **Methodist New Connexion** sent missionaries to Tientsin (Tianjin) in 1860, and the **United Methodist Free Churches** mission began in Chekian (Zhejiang) Province in 1864. **Bible Christian** missionaries settled in 1883 in southwestern China, and particularly worked among the aboriginal tribes of Yunnan (Yunlong) and Kweichow (Guizhou). Denominational mergers in 1907 and 1932 (*see* BRITISH METHODISM) led to mergers of mission programs, but British and American Methodist efforts toward further unity were thwarted by World War II and the Communist Revolution.

Canadian Methodist missionaries came to China under the leadership of MEC missionary Virgil Hart, entering Szechuan (Sichuan) Province in 1892. The Canadian mission's main centers were in Chungking (Chongquing) and Chengtu (Chengdu). They were active in West China Union University and West China Theological College. By 1934, they had joined the Church of Christ in China (*see* CANADA).

Despite the disruptions of World War II, there were some 1,000,000 Protestant communicants in China by 1949. After the Communist takeover that year, missionaries were expelled, most church activities were banned, and all mission schools and hospitals were taken over by the government. During the 1960s, violence by the Red Guards against all religious activity finished what the revolution had begun. As of 2004, there were three Methodist bodies in China: the Chinese Methodist Church (20,000 worshippers), the Church of the Nazarene (300), and the Magnolia (Wesleyan) community (150). In Hong Kong, the Church of Christ in China numbered 27,000 members; the Methodist Church, 12,000; Free Methodists, 2,100; and the Church of the Nazarene, 250. In the Republic of China (Taiwan), the Free Methodist Church had 12,000 worshippers. The Church of the Nazarene had 1,800 members and the Methodist Church (organized in 1953), 2,500.

In Korea, centuries of conflict with its neighbors resulted in strict antiforeign policies, but an 1882 commercial treaty with the United States opened the door to American missions. MEC missionary Robert Maclay (then in Japan) received permission from the Korean government to engage in limited mission activity. The first MEC missionaries, **Henry G. Appenzeller**, W. B. Scranton, and Mrs. M.F. Scranton, arrived in 1885. Two years later, the first Korean Methodist church was founded, at Chung-Dong. The MECS sent its first missionaries in 1895 in response to a request by Korean Methodist Yoon Chi-ho. By 1900, antiforeign feeling was diminishing, and Koreans began responding in large numbers to mission activity. Combined MEC/MECS church membership grew from 1,199 in 1900 to 13,333 in 1910. An autonomous Korean Methodist Church, combining both northern and southern Methodist missions, was organized in 1930.

Methodists and Presbyterians were the dominant mission groups in Korea until after the Korean War, and participated in a number of joint ventures, including the Christian Literature Society, a radio station and a chaplaincy program. **Ewha University** is only the most wellknown of a number of union educational ventures.

The Church of the Nazarene in Korea is the largest non-U.S. body of that denomination. Work began in the early 20th century through the efforts of Japanese missionaries and Korean converts, ultimately supported by American missionaries.

In the 1930s and during World War II, Methodists were active in resistance movements against Japanese occupation, leading to numerous arrests of clergy and laity. All contact with Western missionaries was broken. In 1945, with division into North and South, Methodists lost half their churches, along with many schools and hospitals. As far as is known, all church activities in North Korea ceased. The Communist invasion of South Korea in 1950, followed by the Korean War, brought much destruction of property and personnel. The church continued to grow, however, numbering some 71,000 members by 1967. Movements such as Seven Thousand Churches and Two Million Church Members led to dramatic growth by the 1990s.

As of 2004, church memberships were as follows: Korean Methodist Church, 1,300,000 members; Evangelical Church, 350,000; Church of the Nazarene, 19,000; the Free Methodist Church, 4,200; Wesleyan Church, 600. There was also a Methodist Church in North Korea with 500 members.

Foreigners were banned from Japan until Commodore Matthew Perry forcibly opened the country to Western trade in 1854. In 1873, after a centuries' long prohibition of Christianity was lifted, the first Methodist missionaries entered the country, led by the veteran MEC China missionary Robert Maclay. In 1878, the mission ordained Yoitsu Honda, the first Japanese Methodist pastor. Six years later, the first annual conference in Japan was organized with 19 Japanese preachers.

Japan was the first foreign mission field of the Methodist Church of Canada, which in 1873 sent two missionary couples to Tokyo. The following year, the first Methodist baptism in Japan took place at the home of Canadian missionary George Cochran. The EC General

Conference voted in 1875 to open a mission in Japan, and later that year sent three missionaries to Tokyo. The first MP missionary, Harriet G. Brittain, arrived in Yokohama in 1880, and the first MP church organized outside the United States was founded in Yokohama in 1887. The MECS established its presence in Japan in 1886, with the transfer of three couples from its China mission, including **Walter Russell Lambuth**. The UB sent its first missionaries to Japan in 1898, focusing its efforts around Tokyo and Kyoto. In 1931, full responsibility for the UB annual conference in Japan was transferred to Japanese leadership.

Free Methodist mission work was carried on in the 1890s by a Japanese convert, Teikichi Kawabe, who founded what was at one time Free Methodism's largest church, in Osaka. By 1903, American missionaries had come to assist Kawabe. Predecessors of the Church of the Nazarene supported missionaries in Japan by 1901, with formal oversight beginning in 1914.

The threads of Methodism began to unite in 1907 with the formation of the Japan Methodist Church, the first national Methodist denomination to grow out of the modern missions movement. The new church united the MEC, the MECS, and the Canadian Methodist Church, and Yoitsu Honda was elected its first bishop. In November 1941, The United Church of Christ was formed, uniting nearly all Japanese Methodists. After World War II, some bodies, including the Free Methodists, withdrew to work independently, but the United Church remained the largest Protestant body in Japan.

As in other countries, education at all levels was a primary means of mission outreach. Scores of schools were founded by Methodist missions; among the best known is Aoyama Gakuin University, founded in 1874 in Tokyo by the MEC. Methodist social service institutions, most founded before World War II, played valuable roles in Japan's postwar recovery. As of 2004, church membership stood as follows: United Church of Christ, 206,000; Wesleyan Church (Immanuel General Mission), 12,000; Wesleyan Church, 600; Free Methodist Church, 2,500; and Church of the Nazarene, 4,600. The Methodist Church (Okinawa) had 1,400 members.

Malaysia (then including Singapore) became a Methodist mission field in 1885, when William F. Oldham and James Thoburn established work in Singapore under the auspices of the MEC South India

Annual Conference. Two years later, the Woman's Foreign Missionary Society appointed Sophia Blackmore, who served the mission for 40 years. Methodism in Malaysia centered on education, with many thousands of pupils. The mission became the Malaysia Annual Conference in 1902, and a separate Chinese conference was formed in 1948. Singapore became an independent country in 1965. In 1969, the Methodist Church of Malaysia and Singapore was constituted as an autonomous church, with Dr. Yap Kim Hao its first bishop. As of 2004, church membership in Malaysia stood at 143,000, with 30,000 in Singapore.

Methodism came to Indonesia in the person of Hong Tean, a Chinese student from Malaya, who in 1904 established a school in Medan, Sumatra. MEC missionaries working in Singapore and Malaysia launched missions in Java and Bogor, later expanding to Jakarta, Medan, and West Borneo. In 1919, the Netherlands Indies Mission Conference was formed, and in 1921, Lamsana Manurung became the first ordained Indonesian Methodist. In 1964, the Methodist Church of Indonesia became autonomous. A breakaway group formed the Free Methodist Church of Indonesia. By the 1990s, a strong relationship had developed between the Methodist Church of Indonesia and the Korean Methodist Church, with the latter financing a number of Indonesian church building projects. As of 2004, the Methodist Church of Indonesia had 119,000 members; the Church of the Nazarene, 3,100; and the Free Methodist Church, 1,100.

Protestantism was banned in the Philippines during the centuries when it was a Spanish possession. This ended with the 1898 American victory in its war with Spain, and the following year James Thoburn, then MEC bishop for India and southern Asia, arrived to establish a mission. In 1900, Thoburn ordained Nicholas Zamora as the first Filipino Methodist preacher, and the first American missionaries arrived in 1910. Mission emphases were student work, hospitals and medical services, and education, including a number of ecumenical ventures.

In 1901, the first UB missionaries began work in the northwestern part of Luzon, which eventually became the strongest foreign mission of that denomination. Free Methodist and Nazarene missionaries started work on Mindanao and Bunawan, respectively, in 1949.

In 1908, the Philippine Islands Annual Conference was organized, and the following year the Iglesia Evangélica Metodista en las Islas Filipinas (IEMELIF) was formed as part of a nationalist schism led by Nicolas Zamora. In 1948 a portion of the IEMELIF joined the new United Church of Christ in the Philippines, which also included the EUB church. Methodism in all its expressions emerged intact from the chaos of World War II, and in 2004 there were six Methodist-related bodies in the Philippines: The United Church of Christ (900,000 members), the United Methodist Church (296,000), the Evangelical Methodist Church (45,000), the Wesleyan Church (including Indonesia, 29,000), the Church of the Nazarene (14,000), and the Free Methodist Church (11,200).

A Methodist presence in Burma (Myanmar) began in 1879 with a church founded by James Thoburn and F. E. Goodwin, who were both serving in India and came to Yangon (Rangoon) at the request of Christian sympathizers. Within three years, the MEC Woman's Foreign Mission Society had sent its first missionary, Ellen Warner, who established a school, soon followed by an orphanage. Initial contact was with English-speakers, but mission work soon broadened to include the Chinese, starting with a Chinese Methodist evangelist from Canada who arrived in Yangon in 1895. Anglo-Chinese schools for boys and girls soon followed. In the 1950s, the mission moved northward, establishing Chinese churches in northern Myanmar. James Thoburn inaugurated work among Indians in Burma, opening a boys' school in 1883, followed by schools and missions for various Indian language groups. The first British Wesleyan missionaries arrived in Mandalay in 1887, led by Army chaplain J. H. Bateson, and focused their efforts in Upper Myanmar, including mission schools and a home for lepers.

World War II scattered the churches, but some missionaries returned after the war. The Methodist Church of the Union of Burma became autonomous in 1964, mission schools and properties were nationalized by 1965, and all foreign missionaries had gone by 1966. As of 2004, the Methodist Church of Upper Myanmar had 14,600 members; the Methodist Church of Lower Myanmar, 2,100; the Wesleyan Church, 8,000; the Church of the Nazarene, 1,400; and the Free Methodist Church, 1,000.

Susan E. Warrick

ASSURANCE, CHRISTIAN. Christian assurance is a primary mark of Wesleyan theology and spirituality. It asserts the personal experience of consciously living in God's love, being immediately aware of one's reconciliation with God. This is assurance of present **salvation**, not assurance of final salvation. It includes, however, full conviction of perseverance.

The key scriptural grounding of the teaching is Romans 8:15–17. When disciples of Christ Jesus call God "Father" it is the Spirit (*see* HOLY SPIRIT) of God bearing witness with their spirit that they are the children of God, and if children then inheritors of God and fellow inheritors with Christ, the Son of God. Thus, assurance of salvation is normal for Christians. In fact, in the early period following their 1738 evangelical awakening, **John** and **Charles Wesley** taught that assurance was essential to genuine Christian **experience**. They moderated this view to acknowledge that periods of doubt and "dark nights of the soul," while not to be rejoiced in, do occur in the life of discipleship. Still, assurance is the ordinary privilege of the disciple of Christ Jesus.

The doctrine of assurance is not unique to Wesleyanism in the post–New Testament Christian tradition. As an Anglican **John Wesley** was strongly influenced by the Greek language theologians of Christian antiquity. He cited the great Alexandrians Clement and Origen, Ignatius of Antioch, Polycarp of Smyrna, and the martyr Romanus as illustrative of the general acceptance of this teaching in the pre-Nicene church. Anglicans were very unsympathetic to the medieval and post-Reformation **Roman Catholic Church**, but there too Wesley found persons such as Bernard of Clairvaux, Francis of Assisi, John of the Cross, Teresa of Avila, and François de Fénélon as examples of "heart religion," disciples who lived joyously in the humble confidence Christian assurance brings. While the Wesleyan interpretation of assurance was often seen as distinguishing, even separating, them from other Protestants, the doctrine is also found in Martin Luther, Philip Melancthon, John Calvin, **Jacob Arminius**, and the Westminster Confession.

Christian personal experience of the assurance of being reconciled with God must be distinguished from individualism or subjectivism. Private experience is not the sole, or even primary, criterion for establishing Christian truth. A danger for Christian life is that assurance may be replaced by its counterfeit, arrogance. Wesley warned that individual feeling is the least reliable guide for Christian experience. Christian assurance is, first, a scripture doctrine. Second, it has the testimony of unbroken Christian tradition.

Furthermore, authentic Christian assurance is experienced only in the body of Christ, the church. The Bible knows no holiness but social holiness, Wesley insisted. Christian experience is personal, that is, it is the experience of an individual in community. Christian life is life together. Corporateness is integral to Christian discipleship. In addition to the canons of scripture, tradition, and reason, another test of the validity of personal experience is the experience of those with whom we enjoy Christian conversation and fellowship.

Christian assurance is one of the consequences of the witness of the **Holy Spirit** with the person's spirit that that person is a child of God. One is first aware of it by the witness of one's own spirit. But this chronological primacy of human awareness is not the cause of assurance. Its cause is the action of the triune God on our soul. The Holy Spirit attests the gift that the Loving Parent offers through the Son. Though we are aware of it first, the witness of our own spirit is a response to the witness of God's Spirit that we are reconciled members of the family of God.

All this adds up to a personal direct testimony of the Spirit in the heart of a person, an inward impression on the soul, the witness of the Spirit with my spirit that I am a child of God.

There is a question regarding how Wesley defined the terms heart, soul, spirit, and mind. By modern standards he did not define them strictly. Wesley's usage parallels that of the Bible. Heart is the broadest concept of the four. The heart is a physical organ but also the seat of the emotions, intellect, will, and moral life. The word heart connotes our deepest interior personhood. In the New Testament, soul and spirit were so similar as to sometimes be used synonymously. Paul's use of spirit in Romans 8:9–17 and I Corinthians 2:9–16 elevates this term to prominence as the designation for that part of us which makes it possible for God's Spirit to dwell in us. Mind, obviously the intellectual capacity of humans, can also be used to indicate the whole personality, the character, the interior person. In the Bible each of these words is employed at times to designate the deepest, most sublime part of humanness.

It remains to comment on the personal nature of the relationship between God and persons. Relationships between persons may change. Friends and family members grow closer or more distant as they nurture or neglect one another. We live together moment by moment. How we treat one another moment by moment determines the progress of our relationships.

The same is true for the divine/human relationship. In Wesleyan spirituality Christian assurance is dependent upon continuous living in the means of **grace**. Assurance is assurance of present salvation, not of final salvation. God will always remain faithful, but we may not.

This is no cause for despair. We can never be in a situation or condition where God's **grace** is not at work (Psalm 139; Romans 8:35–39). When we come with **faith** to the means of grace we are where God has promised to be. So, moment by moment, living joyously in Christian assurance, we may be fully convinced that we shall persevere.

Charles Wesley gave the church a hymn prayer to the Holy Spirit, the Spirit of faith. The Spirit is petitioned to show the strength of Jesus' name: "the grace which all may find, the saving power impart, and testify to humankind, and speak in every heart." All who receive this living faith have the witness in themselves and consciously believe.

It is altogether owing to the concept of who God is that Wesleyan theology and spirituality assert that Christian assurance is an ordinary privilege of a disciple of Jesus Christ. *See also* CHRISTIAN EXPERIENCE; DOCTRINAL STANDARDS; WITNESS OF THE SPIRIT.

Charles W. Brockwell, Jr.

ATONEMENT. The atonement is the work of Christ that reconciles God and sinful humanity. In contrast to the **Trinity** and the Incarnation, the doctrine of the atonement was not defined by the councils of the early church. Over the centuries, many theories of atonement have been proposed. The more influential of these, and a representative of each, include the following: the dramatic theory (Irenaeus), Christ's triumph over the powers of evil; satisfaction (Anselm), the discharge of the debt which sinful human beings owe to God; the exemplarist theory (Abelard), the display of God's love, which spurs the transformation of personality; and the governmental theory (Grotius), the affirmation of universal moral order.

Wesley's concept of atonement includes ideas of satisfaction, his primary emphasis, and exemplarism. These are correlated with his doctrines of **justification** and **sanctification**. Christ's fulfillment of the law and his death upon the cross satisfy the requirements of divine justice. Satisfaction, in turn, is the basis upon which the forgiveness of sin rests. The beginning of sanctification or inward renewal accompanies justification. The believer is expected to grow in **grace,** taking the life of Christ as his or her pattern. Here an exemplarist note is sounded.

The thirty-first of the Church of England's **Articles of Religion** avows "Christ's satisfaction, for all the sins of the whole world." Wesley repeated this language in Article 20 of the Twenty-Four Articles that he transmitted to the **MEC** in 1784.

During the 19th century, Methodist theologians continued to affirm the concept of satisfaction. The work of the British Methodist Richard Watson illustrates this point. His *Theological Institutes* was a standard theological source for two-thirds of the century. In time, however, the idea of satisfaction became the subject of criticism. The transfer of the guilt of sin, and the penalty for it, from the sinful individual to Jesus Christ is, critics said, illogical and unethical. The governmental theory was seen as an attractive alternative. The British theologian, **William Burt Pope**, and the southern Methodist, Thomas O. Summers, combined satisfaction and governmental conceptions of atonement. In 1879, John Wiley of Drew Theological School, New Jersey, published his governmental theory. He was both praised and criticized for it.

Theological diversity has characterized 20th-century Methodism. Exemplarist concepts of atonement were popular among "evangelical liberals." The Boston theologian Henry C. Sheldon inclined toward this view and Albert C. Knudson explicitly endorsed it. During the 1930s and 1940s, another trend emerged. The European "theology of crisis" came to influence certain Methodist theologians. They stressed the "objective" character of the atonement. For example, the British scholar **Vincent Taylor** emphasized the sacrifice that Christ offered to the Father, while retaining elements of the exemplarist and governmental theories. The Drew theologian, Edwin Lewis, presented a dramatic theory of the atonement. Both the **MC** and the **UMC** reaffirmed Article 20 of Wesley's **Articles of Religion**. The UMC **General Conference** created theological study commissions in 1968 and 1984. The reports of these commissions emphasized the incarnation of God in Christ and paid relatively little attention to the atonement. *See also* DOCTRINAL STANDARDS.

John C. English

AUSTRALIA. Following exploration of the eastern coast of Australia, a British penal settlement was established at Sydney Cove in 1788. Initially, Anglican chaplains directed the colony's religious life. However, in 1812, Thomas Bowden and John Hosking, Wesleyan schoolmasters, began meetings in their homes, which marked the beginning of Australian Methodism. Realizing the need for a qualified preacher, they requested the Methodist Missionary Society of England to send a missionary to serve the 20,000 people in the colony. In response, **Samuel Leigh** arrived in August 1815. In 1817, he opened the first Wesleyan Chapel in New South Wales, at Castlereagh.

Wesleyan Methodism came to Hobart Town in 1820 and, by 1823, with more ministers sent to Sydney, missions were established in **New Zealand** (1821), Tonga (1822), Samoa (1835) and Fiji (1835) (*see* TONGA, FIJI, SAMOA). On the mainland the church took root in Fremantle (1830), Adelaide (1836), Melbourne (1837), and Brisbane (1847), notably with laymen, their class meetings (*see* SOCIETIES, CLASSES, AND BANDS) and preaching playing important roles. Towns were proliferating and the 1850s gold rush further increased immigration. Methodism gained particularly from the influx of Cornish miners.

To this point the church had developed under the auspices of the Missionary Society in England. However, given the difficulty of managing the expanding denomination from such a distance, the society granted the Australian Wesleyan Methodists autonomy as a "distinct but affiliated" connexion (1854). The first Australasian **Conference**, held at Sydney in January 1855, consisted of missionaries in Australasia, Van Diemen's Land (Tasmania), New Zealand, the Islands (Tonga) and Fiji. Full autonomy was granted in 1873. The church's governmental structure now included four annual conferences, representing the six colonies, New Zealand and the Islands, and a triennial **General Conference**. In 1875, a provision allowed for equal representation of ministers and laymen at both annual and general conferences.

By the 1860s, most of the smaller Methodist bodies, which had originated in Britain—**Primitive Methodists, Bible Christians, Methodist New Connexion**, and **United Methodist Free Churches**—had migrated to Australia. The British Wesleyan Church remained the largest by far. A union of these several branches was consummated in 1902 and Methodism became one throughout the Commonwealth of Australia and New Zealand, under the name of "The Methodist Church of Australasia." At that time the membership was approximately 10 percent of Australia's population.

To a large extent, throughout the 19th century, the church owed its dynamism to lay people—class leaders, local preachers, **Sunday school** teachers. The supply of ministers depended largely upon the migration of ordained men from England. Increasingly, however, ministerial training became the responsibility of Australian theological colleges. Although an order of deaconesses was established in 1935 (*see* DEACONESS MOVEMENT), the **ordination** of **women** was not debated until 1966, with the first woman being ordained in 1969.

During the 1860s, the church was energized by visiting evangelists, particularly **William "California" Taylor**. Such campaigns inspired tent missions and local **revivals** and church membership increased considerably during this period. Later, the church's organization included several **mission** departments. Central Missions provided specialized ministries and service agencies in the major cities. Home Mission departments supported marginal and developing areas, while the Federal Inland Mission (1926) served the needs of people living in the "outback."

The 19th century saw attempts to evangelize Australian Aborigines, but with slight effect due to limited conceptions of their language and culture. In later years, welfare and educational programs were introduced and support offered to Aboriginal claims to tribal lands and sites. More successful were the early missions to the Maori of New Zealand and to the Samoans, Tongans, and Fijians. The Overseas Mission Department also began work in New Britain (1875), New Guinea (1891), the Solomon Islands (1902), and India (1907). World War II in the Pacific devastated numbers of mission stations. However, in 1950, Methodist missionaries joined others in serving in the Papuan highlands, the last part of the Pacific to be reached by missions.

Following the government's withdrawal of funding from denominational schools in the 1870s, the church established fee-paying institutions. In most states, tertiary colleges, some related to universities, provided training for ministry and also nurtured lay students for key community roles. From the 1920s, Young People's Departments exercised an important educational influence as they supported Sunday schools and youth groups through publications, visitations, summer schools, and camps. In the early decades of the 20th century, Conference Social Service departments expressed concerns about the liquor traffic, gambling, and the misuse of Sunday. These themes were, in part, replaced by debates on pacifism (*see* WAR AND PEACE), racism, industrial relations, housing, poverty, and other social issues. Concern was also reflected in the church's building hospitals, nursing homes, and institutions for the care of children.

In 1977, following 75 years of conversation, the Congregational, Presbyterian, and Methodist churches in Australia formed The Uniting Church in Australia. The Methodist members voted overwhelmingly in favor of union. Although cherishing their Methodist heritage, they offered that heritage to a new church, so reflecting **John Wesley**'s "catholicity of spirit."

Lawrence D. McIntosh

AUSTRIA. *See* EUROPE.

– B –

BAKER, FRANK (April 15, 1910–October 11, 1999), one of the two preeminent Wesley scholars of his generation (the other being **Albert Outler**), was born in Kingston-upon-Hull, England. Educated at London (B.A.), Manchester (B.D.), and Nottingham (Ph.D.) universities, he was ordained in the British Methodist Church in 1937 and served various **circuit**s until 1959. The following year, he joined the faculty of Duke Divinity School, Durham, North Carolina, and taught English church history until his retirement in 1980. Baker collected Wesleyana and Methodistica (15,000 items), wrote or edited 30 books, and published more than 200 articles. He dealt with key figures associated with Methodism (**John Wesley, Charles Wesley, William Grimshaw, Thomas Webb,** William Law) and offered major assessments of the Methodist movement, notably *John Wesley and the Church of England* (1970) and *From Wesley to Asbury: Studies in Early American Methodism* (1976). He was the first editor-in-chief of the Oxford, then Abingdon edition of the *Works of John Wesley,* himself preparing the first two *Letters* volumes (1980, 1982); and contributed 80 entries to the *Encyclopedia of World Methodism* (1974). Just before his death, the Baker Methodist Research Center was established in his honor at Duke Divinity School. Baker married Ellen Eliza (Nellie) Levitt in 1937. They had two daughters and a son.

John G. McEllhenney

BALL, HANNAH (1733–1792) was a leader in the Methodist society at High Wycombe in Buckinghamshire (*see* SOCIETIES, CLASSES, AND BANDS). She was active in visitation to the sick, backsliders, and prisoners, seeking to minister to their spiritual needs as well as addressing their physical concerns. Ball was an effective communicator who often spoke in class meetings and worship services. She also preached as an itinerant, although surviving historical records are not sufficient to determine how extensive this ministry was. Many letters were exchanged between **John Wesley** and Ball. Clearly Wesley had great respect for this woman whose opinions he often sought. Trusting her judgment, he utilized her to evaluate some of his preachers and even to counsel with them in order to improve their effectiveness. Ball is best known for her work in the earliest establishment of **Sunday schools**. She probably began the first such school in 1769 in High Wycombe (11 years before Robert Raikes's more famous effort in Gloucester). Her pupils were children from poor families and she taught them basic knowledge and practical skills as well as providing religious instruction. Ball's lengthy journal of her spiritual life is extant, but offers little information about the external events of her career.

Gayle Carlton Felton

BANGS, NATHAN (May 2, 1778–May 4, 1862), missionary advocate, book agent, and the **MEC**'s most prominent second-generation historian, was born in Stratford, Connecticut, and migrated with his family to Delaware County, New York. He taught school there and near Niagara Falls, where he experienced **conversion** in 1799, joined the local Methodist society (*see* SOCIETIES, CLASSES, AND BANDS), and began preaching in 1801. Ordained in 1804, he served as a missionary in western **Canada** (near Detroit) and then in Quebec. He married in 1806 and by 1808 returned to appointments in the USA. In 1820 he became agent of the Methodist Book Concern, a post he held for over 20 years, putting it on a strong footing and variously editing *The Christian Advocate*, *The Methodist Magazine*, and *The Quarterly Review*. Meanwhile, he had also begun his own writing, culminating in his four-volume *History of the Methodist Episcopal Church* (1838–1841), the standard denominational history for a quarter century. In 1819 he helped organized what became the church's Missionary Society, which he served as treasurer and corresponding secretary. After a brief stint as president of Wesleyan University, he lost denominational favor by urging compromise on the **slavery** issue for the sake of a unified church. Bangs finished his career preaching in New York City, where he became a ministerial leader of **Phoebe Palmer**'s weekly holiness meetings.

Charles Wallace, Jr.

BAPTISM is one of two **sacraments** celebrated in Methodism as signs and means of God's **grace**. Persons of any age may be baptized, but, in accord with the historical practice of most of the Christian church, Methodism has always advocated baptism of the infant children of Christian families. Sprinkling, pouring, and immersion are accepted as equally valid modes of administering water. Baptisms are appropriately performed only by ordained persons and, unless circumstances demand, only in the presence of a worshipping congregation.

The sacrament is considered valid if water is administered in the name of the Triune God. Baptism has been a requirement for church membership since the early 1800s, but Methodists have always insisted that, in spite of its importance, the sacrament is neither essential nor sufficient for **salvation**.

John Wesley's understanding is articulated most thoroughly in his *Treatise on Baptism*. He vigorously defended the baptism of infants and explained the five major benefits which were received: cleansing of the guilt of **original sin**, entry into covenant with God, admission into the church, regeneration, and becoming heirs of the divine kingdom. Wesley contended that the merits of the atoning death of Christ were applied to a person in baptism so that, "In the ordinary way, there is no other means of entering into the Church or into heaven." God, however, is not limited to working through baptism, although it is a means of divine grace given to be used by the church. In his sermons, Wesley insisted that while persons had been spiritually reborn in baptism, that grace was usually lost as they mature and they must, through **repentance** and **faith**, receive another experience of forgiveness and regeneration. The grace of baptism is not an end, but a crucial part of the lifelong process of salvation.

The tendency in American Methodism has been to place less emphasis upon the grace of God available in the sacraments and more on the necessity of the human response of **conversion** and faith. Baptism continued to be practiced throughout the time when Methodism was characterized by **camp meetings** and **revivalism**, but the understanding of its meaning was modified. In controversies with other denominational groups, Methodists strongly defended the baptism of infants and the use of modes other than immersion. As a more optimistic view of human nature developed in American culture, infant baptism ceased to be seen as an antidote for the effects of original sin and was cited instead as the emblem of the divine kingdom into which innocent infants were born. By the 1950s, infant baptism was understood largely as a ceremony of dedication focused on pledges of parental responsibility. Adult baptism was seen as the occasion when a person joined the church.

Since that point, Methodism has been moving toward recovery of the significance of baptism as an act of God through the church. The ritual in the 1989 UMC hymnal evinces this renewed appreciation of the meaning of sacrament and of the role of baptismal grace in the process of salvation.

Gayle Carlton Felton

BARRATT'S CHAPEL, near Frederica, Delaware, is where in November 1784 **Thomas Coke** and **Francis Asbury** projected the organizing **Christmas Conference** and celebrated **baptism** and holy communion (*see* EUCHARIST). Philip Barratt, **Freeborn Garrettson**'s prominent convert, deeded land for this chapel erected by early Methodists where Asbury frequently preached to crowds near Drawbridge. Begun in May 1780, by the November quarterly meeting 1,000–2,000 people jammed the 42 × 48 foot edifice which Asbury called "a heavy house to preach in," yet full of God's sanctifying grace. The high pulpit, removed in 1841, almost concealed the preacher except from those in the unfinished galleries. In 1826 pews replaced puncheon benches. A vestry room, added later, housed the cemetery sexton. The fateful 1784 meeting of Coke, Asbury, and **Richard Whatcoat** set Methodism's course when Asbury refused appointment as superintendent unless elected, effectively ending Wesley's direction of the American church. Later, membership decline brought maintenance problems, although crowds attended special celebrations. After church closure in 1958, the **conference** erected a curator's house/museum, now exclusively an archives/museum. Barratt's Chapel is a **UMC** Heritage Landmark.

Edwin Schell

BAUERNFEIND, SUSAN (November 25, 1870–October 27, 1945), **EA** missionary to Japan, was born in Holden, Minnesota, to Matthias and Mary Anna (Keller) Bauernfeind. She was a graduate of North-Western (now North Central) College, Naperville, Illinois, where she trained to become an educator. Her attendance at the Student Volunteer Movement conference in February 1894 apparently confirmed her calling to the overseas mission field. Bauernfeind was the first missionary sent out by the Woman's Missionary Society of the EA. She arrived in Tokyo in October 1900 (*see* ASIA). In 1904 she began to organize the Bible Women's Training School, which had over 300 students by 1925. She also assisted in the founding of the Japan branch of the Women's Missionary Society. The circumstances that preceded World War II forced Bauernfeind to return to the USA in 1941. Her love for the USA, the land of her birth, and Japan, the land of her mission, made this a very difficult time. She was honored for her effective ministry with a doctorate conferred by Westmar College, Iowa, in 1937. Her death occurred in Naperville, Illinois, and she was buried in Keyon, Minnesota.

Charles Yrigoyen, Jr.

BELGIUM. *See* EUROPE.

BENNETT, BELLE HARRIS (December 3, 1852–July 20, 1922), missionary society organizer, prominent **MECS** churchwoman, and founder of two schools, was born near Richmond, Kentucky, and raised in a culture of privilege and aristocracy. Bennett never married or received a salary. In 1875 she experienced a **revival** and began to integrate Bible study, prayer, and work. From 1887–1892 she raised funds to open Scarritt Bible and Training School debt free in Kansas City, Missouri. Providing theological education for missionaries and deaconesses (*see* DEACONESS MOVEMENT), the school relocated to Nashville in 1924 as Scarritt College for Christian Workers. Bennett was elected to the Central Committee of the Woman's Parsonage and Home Mission Society (MECS) in 1892. She fulfilled her sister's dream of providing education for Kentucky's mountain children, founding Sue Bennett Memorial School in London, Kentucky, in 1897. Bennett served as president of the Woman's Home Missionary Society (1896–1910) and as president of the successor Woman's Missionary Council (WMC), 1910–1922. During Bennett's tenure the WMC founded Paine College Annex for women (**CME**, Augusta, Georgia) in 1901, launched Bethlehem community centers (1913), and opposed lynching (1913). Male controls regulating **women**'s mission work led the WMC to form a women's **laity rights** movement. Illness prevented Bennett, the first woman MECS delegate to **General Conference**, from attending in 1922.

Alice G. Knotts

BERMUDA. *See* LATIN AMERICA AND CARIBBEAN.

BETHUNE, MARY MCLEOD (July 10, 1875–May 18, 1955), Methodist educator, was born in South Carolina to former slaves. The 15th of 17 children, she was the first to receive formal education, first at a local Presbyterian mission school, then at Scotia Seminary in Concord, North Carolina. Following graduation in 1894, she attended what is now Moody Bible Institute, Chicago, to prepare for a career as a foreign missionary. When she applied to the Presbyterian mission board, she was told there were no openings for black missionaries in **Africa**, a crushing disappointment. However, she soon turned her energies toward teaching. She eventually moved to Daytona Beach, Florida, where she founded the Daytona Literary and Industrial School for Negro Girls (1904), now Bethune-Cookman College (UMC). Bethune became nationally famous through her work with the National Association of Colored Women. She established the National Council of Negro Women (NCNW) in 1935, uniting the major black women's associations. She advised Eleanor Roosevelt on civil rights issues, and in 1936 became the head of Negro Affairs in the National Youth Administration (NYA). That same year she organized the Federal Council on Negro Affairs (FDR's "Black Cabinet"). A delegate to four **MEC General Conferences**, she adamantly opposed the formation of the Central Jurisdiction in 1939. She married Albert Bethune (d.1918) in 1897. They had one son, Albert McLeod. She died at her home on the Bethune-Cookman campus, now a UMC Heritage Landmark.

Susan E. Warrick

BIBLE. Methodists have always shared with other Christians a high regard for the Bible as the primary source on which they base their understanding and practice of the Christian faith. **John Wesley's** respect for scripture is found throughout his writings, especially in his sermons. He referred to himself as *homo unius libri* (a man of one book, i.e., the Bible), though he read widely in many disciplines. His *Explanatory Notes Upon the New Testament* (1755), a commentary on scripture, were considered **doctrinal standards** for Methodists in both Britain and America. Articles 5 and 6 of the **Articles of Religion** that Wesley sent to America in 1784 set forth his views on the significance of the Bible and designate the 39 books of the Old Testament and the 27 books of the New Testament as canonical for Christians. Present-day Methodists hold differing views on the authority and interpretation of the Bible, but it retains a place of preeminence for spiritual growth and study.

Charles Yrigoyen, Jr.

BIBLE CHRISTIANS. Founded in 1815 by **William O'Bryan**, a Wesleyan Methodist local preacher turned self-appointed evangelist working in the vicinity of the Wesleyan Stratton Mission in northeast Cornwall, England. Expelled (for the second time) from membership in the St. Austell **Circuit** and failing to gain the approval of the Superintendent of the Stratton Mission for his local evangelizing, on October 1, 1815, he established an independent circuit based in Week St. Mary, where the whole society joined with him (*see* SOCIETIES, CLASSES, AND BANDS). Soon afterward he formed new classes at Launcells and at Shebbear across the Devon border. This was at Lake Farm, home of the Thorne family, who joined him en masse. The new denomination was still unnamed, but soon became known as the "Bible Christians," to which O'Bryan himself sometimes prefixed the adjective "Arminian" (dropped after 1819) (*see* ARMINIUS, JACOBUS). They were also popularly known as "Bryanites."

Circuits were soon formed and a quarterly meeting was held on January 1, 1816. The first **conference** was held in 1819 at Launceston. The movement was not a breakaway from Wesleyanism, but, like the **Primitive Methodist** movement, an attempt to return to its roots. O'Bryan himself said that **John Wesley** was "ever near" him. The Bible Christian "Rules of Society" were closely modelled on John Wesley's **General Rules**, and when a monthly magazine was begun in 1822 it was, like Wesley's, called the *Arminian Magazine*. As an evangelical mission, the movement followed the Wesleyan model, reflected the form of the contemporary Cornish **revivals** and was, in many ways, an outreach of the "Great Revival" of 1814. O'Bryan's small army of itinerant preachers, most of them young men and **women**, went everywhere, usually on foot, to engage in open-air **preaching**, form societies, and eventually build chapels. In this way the movement took root in Cornwall and the West Country and, by 1825, had been transplanted from there, though on a smaller scale, to Kent and London, along the south coast, to the Channel Islands and South Wales, and was beginning to follow West Country migrants to the north of England. Increasingly, the major figure during this period of expansion was James Thorne, who eventually led the denomination.

When O'Bryan left the Bible Christians in 1829 he was accompanied by two of the preachers and a few hundred members, who reverted to the name Arminian Bible Christians. The denomination's spread overseas began with O'Bryan's emigration to **Canada** in 1831 and reached the USA in 1845. Back home, in 1907 the Bible Christian Church, with over 32,000 members, joined with the **Methodist New Connexion** and **United Methodist Free Churches** to form the United Methodist Church.

Thomas Shaw

BIOMEDICAL ETHICS. From the beginning, Christians have pondered whether they should to do all that God has given them the ability to do. Are some things possible but contrary to the divine will revealed in nature and the **Bible**? Shaving was once denounced because God created men and women with hair on their bodies. Opponents of using the cowpox virus to vaccinate against smallpox declared that it would "animalize" humans. Using drugs to render childbirth "painless" was held to be contrary to Genesis 3:16.

Debates about whether it is good to do all that humans are capable of doing became front-page news during the closing third of the 20th century. Artificial hearts, organs transplanted from animals into humans, in vitro fertilization, mapping the human genome, altering DNA in plants, animals, and humans in order to correct disorders or to introduce more desirable characteristics, news reports in 2004 that South Korean scientists had successfully cloned the first human embryo—all became subjects of intense debate.

As a result, United Methodists added new categories such as "Medical Experimentation" and "Genetic Technology" to their Social Principles (*see* SOCIAL CREED). The 1988 **General Conference** authorized the General Board of Church and Society to form a bioethics task force, composed of scientists, educators, health professionals, ethicists, theologians, a social worker, a lawyer, and a farmer. This group's report was adopted by the 1992 General Conference, then adopted as revised by the 2000 conference and printed in the denomination's *Book of Resolutions*. Beginning with general theological principles, the statement "New Developments in Genetic Science" raises the broad question of whether, with all the knowledge that researchers have, they have sufficient information to foresee all the consequences of what biotechnology can accomplish. Should the basic building blocks of human life, considering the lack of perfect prescience, be tampered with? Also, given limited resources, should vast sums be spent on projects of benefit to the few, when the many lack basic medical care? Finally, the UMC, in its *Book of Discipline* (*see* DISCIPLINE), specifically opposes "the cloning of humans and the genetic manipulation of the gender of an unborn child."

John G. McEllhenney

BISHOP. *See* EPISCOPACY.

BLACK, WILLIAM (November 10, 1760–September 8, 1834), Methodist minister, was born in Huddersfield, England. He immigrated with his family to Nova Scotia in 1775 (*see* CANADA). In 1779, he attended religious meetings held in the homes of Yorkshire Methodist settlers, and was converted. He began preaching in 1781. On February 17, 1784, he married Mary Gay in Cumberland County, Nova Scotia. Black recognized the need for more preachers in this time of loyalist immigration. In September 1784 he set out for the USA to ask for help from Methodists there. His appeal led to the appointment of two missionaries to Nova Scotia. In 1789, he was named general superintendent for eastern British North America. The progress of the church was slow, however. Unable to obtain more missionaries from the USA, Black left for England in 1799 to appeal to the British Wesleyan **Conference**. He returned a year later with four preachers. "Bishop" Black continued to oversee Methodism in the region until 1812, when poor health forced him to retire. On July 29, 1828, he married Martha Calkin in Liverpool, Nova Scotia. When he died in Halifax, Black was widely regarded as the "Father of Methodism" in the Maritimes.

Marilyn Färdig Whiteley

BLAND, SALEM GOLDSWORTH (August 25, 1859–February 7, 1950), Methodist (later United Church of Canada) minister and author, was born in Lachute, Quebec (*see* CANADA). His father, Henry Flesher Bland, was a prominent Methodist clergyman. Salem Bland began his ministry in 1880, serving congregations in the St. Lawrence and Ottawa valleys, and taking an active part in sabbath and **temperance** reform. Increasingly, however, he became convinced of the broader social implications of Christianity. In 1903, Bland joined the faculty of Wesley College, Winnipeg. Popular as a preacher and public speaker, he was an advocate of various social reform endeavors. Following his controversial dismissal from the college in 1917, he spent the next two years as a lecturer and a columnist for the *Grain Grower's Guide*. Bland returned to the pulpit in 1919 in Toronto. The following year he published *The New Christianity*, a **social gospel** analysis of what he saw as the contemporary crisis. Bland was not stationed with a congregation after 1923, but remained active as a lecturer and preacher, and as a journalist for the *Toronto Star*. Long an advocate of a third political party in Canada, he helped form the Co-operative Commonwealth Federation in the 1930s. He died in Toronto.

Marilyn Färdig Whiteley

BOARDMAN, RICHARD (1738–1782), British Methodist itinerant, was one of the first two volunteers for the work in America, commissioned by **John Wesley** at the Leeds **Conference** in 1769. Together with **Joseph Pilmore**, he probably landed on October 21, 1769, at Gloucester Point, New Jersey. As Wesley's assistant in America, he traveled to New York, leaving Pilmore to do the work in Philadelphia. The two men exchanged appointments frequently, sometimes in the coldest months of the year. Little is known of his work in America which, for the most part, was confined to New York and Philadelphia. **Francis Asbury**, who joined the itinerants in 1771, prodded him into reaching out beyond the two cities, and in spring 1772 he traveled to Boston, where he formed a short-lived Methodist society (*see* SOCIETIES, CLASSES, AND BANDS). His name is not mentioned in the Minutes of the Conference of 1773, held in St. George's Meeting House, Philadelphia, and presided over by Wesley's new assistant, **Thomas Rankin**, although he was probably present. In January 1774, possibly because of the changing political situation, he sailed with Pilmore for En-

gland, where he served in **Ireland** under Wesley until his death at Cork in 1782.
He was buried in St. Fin Barre's Cathedral.

Frederick E. Maser

BOEHM, HENRY (June 8, 1775–December 29, 1875), born the son of Martin and Eve [Steiner] in Lancaster County, Pennsylvania, traveled with Bishop **Francis Asbury** and attained the century mark still preaching. **Robert Strawbridge, Francis Asbury**, and **Philip William Otterbein** were welcomed by his sometime Mennonite preacher father (*see* BOEHM, MARTIN) who was later a founding **UB** bishop. His mother early joined a Methodist class (*see* SOCIETIES, CLASSES, AND BANDS), and Boehm's Methodist Chapel was erected on their land in 1791 and is now a **UMC** Heritage Landmark. Converted under Methodists in 1793 and impressed with the spiritual power and discipline at the 1800 **MEC General Conference**, Henry joined the Philadelphia **Conference** in 1801. As a bilingual preacher, he superintended and financed a German **Discipline** in 1807. While serving as Asbury's companion from 1808 to 1813, he preached in German in 14 states and received book monies at annual conferences. As the bishop's executor, Boehm distributed Bibles to 400 Asbury namesakes. He nursed Bishop **Richard Whatcoat** and **Jesse Lee** during their last illnesses, presided over three districts, and was pastor in the Philadelphia and New Jersey Conferences before settling on Staten Island, New York, in 1837 with his wife, Sarah Hill, and four children. His *Reminiscences* include characterizations of many Methodist leaders and a description of his gala Newark Conference centennial birthday celebration on June 8, 1875.

Edwin Schell

BOEHM, MARTIN (November 30, 1725–March 23, 1812), Mennonite preacher and co-bishop with Philip William Otterbein at the founding of the **UB**, was the youngest son of a German immigrant family in Lancaster County, Pennsylvania. Reared in the Mennonite faith of his parents, Martin married Eve Steiner in 1753. They had eight children.

About 1758 his Mennonite congregation chose him by lot to be a minister, which created a spiritual crisis because he lacked **assurance** of his own **salvation** and had no message to proclaim. His agony climaxed one day while plowing, when God provided the needed assurance of salvation and he experienced the joy of regeneration. From that point he was increasingly effective as an evangelical preacher. Among Mennonites he advanced to full pastoral standing with the title of bishop, but he preached to other Germans as well and a Boehm Revival resulted. At a mass meeting in Isaac Long's barn in Lancaster County (ca. 1767) one of those present was German Reformed pastor **Philip William Otterbein**, who afterward embraced Boehm and exclaimed "*Wir sind brüder* (We are brothers)." A common evangelical faith united their hearts and made them colleagues.

Boehm's evangelistic style, doctrine, and association with Christians of other traditions led the Mennonite Church to excommunicate him (ca.1775). Entrusting his farm to eldest son Jacob, Martin became a full-time itinerant evangelist among Germans in Pennsylvania, Maryland, and Virginia. During succeeding decades Boehm and Otterbein guided an informal pietistic ministry that transcended denominational distinctions. Eventually, 13 preachers at a **conference** in Frederick County, Maryland, organized themselves into a society called the UB (September 25, 1800) and elected Otterbein and Boehm as bishops (*see* EPISCOPACY). Neither exercised much leadership after 1805 because of advanced age. **Christian Newcomer** succeeded Boehm as bishop and basically shaped the church the founders inspired. According to Newcomer's journal, the last time Boehm and Otterbein met was March 1810 at **Francis Asbury**'s lodgings in Baltimore, to negotiate whether their society should unite with the MEC in its German-speaking ministry.

As easily as Boehm could be both Mennonite and associate with Christians of other traditions, he fellowshipped with Methodists while leading the UB. About 1775 a Methodist class meeting was organized at his home, in which his wife and children participated (*see* SOCIETIES, CLASSES, AND BANDS). In 1791 a parcel of Boehm family land was donated to the Methodist conference and Boehm's Chapel was erected on it. Although Martin did not formally join, he had special status that enabled him to worship there when home and was one of its trustees. Boehm's youngest son, **Henry**, became a prominent Methodist preacher and traveling companion of Bishop Asbury. Two weeks after Martin died, Asbury preached the funeral sermon of his friend at Boehm's Chapel, where his body was buried, praising him as a man plain in dress and manner but patriarchal in importance.

Donald K. Gorrell

BÖHLER, PETER (December 31, 1712–April 27, 1775), Moravian pastor who was spiritual mentor to **John** and **Charles Wesley** in early 1738. Born in Frankfurt-am-Main, Germany, and educated at the University of Jena, he was raised a Lutheran. In 1731 he experienced a religious **conversion** and three years later joined the Moravian Church (Unitas Fratrum). He was shortly thereafter ordained as a Moravian minister by Bishop David Nitschmann. On his way to America in 1738, he went to England, where he met the recently returned Wesleys, with whom he had many conversations on the nature of saving **faith**. Böhler's teaching on "**justification** by faith alone" was instrumental in the Wesleys' spiritual pilgrimage leading to their own experience of **assurance** of **salvation** in May 1738. However, subsequent differences over several related issues, such as "quietism," led to a split between the English **Moravians** and the Wesleys, a conflict that helped shape much of **John Wesley**'s theological development during the following decade. Böhler also was a founder of the Fetter Lane Society at John Hutton's house on May 1, 1738, attended by John Wesley, who later considered this small religious society to be a significant step ("third rise") in the early development of Methodism. *See also* MORAVIANS; SOCIETIES, CLASSES, AND BANDS.

Richard P. Heitzenrater

BOOK OF DISCIPLINE. *See* DISCIPLINE.

BOOTH, CATHERINE MUMFORD (January 17, 1829–October 8, 1890), co-founder of the **Salvation Army**, was born in Derbyshire, England. In 1855, she married **William Booth**, a licensed preacher in the **Methodist New Connexion**. Conflict with the church over the Booths' desire for freedom for **evangelism** versus the confinement of an assigned **circuit** led to their leaving the Connexion. In 1865 they began mission work on London's east side, which became the Salvation Army in 1878. Catherine's involvement with the English meetings for the promotion of holiness led by American Methodist lay-revivalist **Phoebe Palmer** encouraged her to take up her own preaching ministry and to become an advocate of equal rights for **women** in church and society. Among other more devotional works, she wrote a book in defense of women preachers. Her genuine concern for people combined with her strong will and moral purpose made her a major player in the life and growth of the Salvation Army. She bore eight children, all of whom took their own places of service and leadership either within the army (two as generals) or in other Christian organizations. Her reasoned yet passionate approach to the administration of the army often balanced William Booth's more acerbic and hurried manners.

Melvin E. Dieter

BOOTH, WILLIAM (April 10, 1829–August 20, 1912), co-founder of the **Salvation Army**, was born in Nottingham, England. Converted at the age of 15, he quickly became involved in Methodist **evangelism**. In 1855, he married Catherine Mumford (*see* BOOTH, CATHERINE). Together they founded the Christian Mission in London in 1865, having severed relations with the **Methodist New Connexion** in 1861 because of differences over the time he devoted to evangelism. With the organization of his work as a "Salvation Army" in 1878, his ministry of saving souls and caring for their physical and social welfare spread rapidly around the world. Booth utilized a multiplicity of agencies and means to advance his cause against social evils such as drunkenness, gambling, and prostitution that were depriving the poor of basic resources for life, welfare, and dignity. In 1890 he outlined some of the army's philosophy of social reform in his book *In Darkest England and the Way Out*. His use of street evangelism supported by brass bands whose tunes often sounded little different from those sung in nearby saloons brought abuse and arrest to many early Salvationists. But their persistent concern for people in desperate personal and social circumstances overcame such opposition and won General Booth and his Salvation Army worldwide respect.

Melvin E. Dieter

BOSANQUET, MARY (Mrs. John Fletcher) (September 1, 1739–December 9, 1815) met with opposition from her well-to-do family because of her religious inclinations and left home at 22, taking lodgings in London. She joined the London society (*see* SOCIETIES, CLASSES, AND BANDS) and became involved in the great Methodist **revival** there in 1761–1762. In 1762, she went to live in her own house in Leytonstone, where, with Sarah Crosby and Sarah Ryan, she established a Christian community and began "to exhort, and to read and expound the scriptures." In June 1768, partly for financial reasons, the community moved to Cross Hall near Leeds. Mary corresponded with **John Wesley**, consulting him about her call to preach. Although **women** preachers were not then permitted among the Methodists, he admitted that she had an "extra-ordinary call," but stopped short of agreeing to her becoming an itinerant preacher (*see* PREACHING). On November 12, 1781, she married the Rev. **John Fletcher** of Madeley and they exercised what was effectively a joint ministry. To avoid giving local offense, Mary "spoke" regularly in the Madeley tithe barn. After her husband's death, she continued her work in Madeley, acting as an unofficial curate to his successor.

E. Dorothy Graham

BOURNE, HUGH (April 3, 1772–October 11, 1852), carpenter and co-founder with **William Clowes** of the **Primitive Methodist** Connection, was born at Ford Heys Farm, Stoke-on-Trent, Staffordshire, England, moving to Bemersley in 1788. Converted in 1799 as a result of reading Wesley's sermons and the writings of **John Fletcher**, he was involved with the **revivalism** sweeping Cheshire and Staffordshire in the 1800s. Harriseahead and other societies grew and the Wesleyan **Conference** became alarmed at such unlicensed preaching, the links with independent Methodist groups, the presence of **Lorenzo Dow**, and the open-air **camp meetings** of 1808. His followers, the Camp Meeting Methodists, and those of Clowes joined together forming a society called the Primitive Methodists in 1811–1812, of which Bourne became general superintendent. The connection grew rapidly in the 1820s and spread into Cumbria, Yorkshire, and the East Midlands. Bourne acted as its administrator and editor until 1842, writing its history (1823, 1835) and compiling its hymnbooks (1809, 1821, 1824), from the Bemersley headquarters in Tunstall, helped by his brother James. He went on a mission to the USA in 1844 and died in 1852. He is buried at Englesea Brook, where there is museum of Primitive Methodism.

Tim Macquiban

BRAZIL. *See* LATIN AMERICA AND CARIBBEAN.

BRESEE, PHINEAS FRANKLIN (December 31, 1838–November 13, 1915), **MEC** minister and founder of the Church of the Nazarene, was born in Franklin, New York. Bresee was converted in a Methodist "protracted meeting" in 1856. Moving to Iowa in 1857, Bresee soon received full ordination and embarked on 25 years of successful service throughout Iowa. In 1883, embarrassed and bankrupt from his involvement in a failed mining company, Bresee moved to Los Angeles and assumed the prestigious pastorate of Los Angeles First MEC. Here, influential laypersons were already urging a greater stress on the necessity of entire **sanctification**. Bresee soon joined them. In 1895 Bresee and J. P. Widney founded the Church of the Nazarene. Appalled by the extravagance which accompanied Methodism's upward mobility, they proposed plain buildings, located near the poor. Bresee vigorously promoted the work, both personally and through the movement's official paper, *The Nazarene Messenger*. A Bible college was started in Los Angeles in 1902 and missionaries were sent to India in 1907 (*see* ASIA). In 1908, the movement became national with the merger of the holiness Church of Christ and the **pentecostal** Church of the Nazarene at Pilot Point, Texas. Bresee became general superintendent and held the position until his death. *See also* HOLINESS MOVEMENT.

Dale H. Simmons

BRIGGS, WILLIAM (September 1836–November 5, 1922), Methodist minister and publisher, was born in Banbridge, **Ireland**. When he was six, his family moved to Liverpool, England, and there he received an education intended to prepare him for a business career. When he was 22, however, he felt called to enter the Methodist ministry. He immigrated to **Canada**, and was received on probation as a preacher in 1859. In 1863 he was ordained in the Wesleyan Church, and in 1865 he married Rosalie Marion Clarke. He served a number of charges in Quebec and Ontario, moving in 1876 to the important pulpit of Metropolitan Church in Toronto. In 1879, Briggs was chosen book steward for his denomination. His executive abilities served the church well. During the 40 years he headed the Book Room, he broadened its scope, making it one of the largest publishing houses in Canada. He was elected president of Toronto **Conference** in 1882, and was a member of every **General Conference** during his active ministry. William Briggs retired in 1919. Following the death of his wife in 1920, he moved to Port Credit to live with his son, Alfred W. Briggs. He died there two years later.

Marilyn Färdig Whiteley

BRIGHTMAN, EDGAR SHEFFIELD (September 20, 1884–February 25, 1953) was an educator and philosopher of religion. He received two degrees from Brown University, Rhode Island, and the STB and Ph.D. from Boston University. Having taught at Nebraska Wesleyan (1912–15) and Wesleyan University, Connecticut, Brightman joined the graduate faculty at Boston. He was named Borden Parker Bowne Professor of Philosophy in 1925. Brightman served as president of the National Association of Biblical Instructors and of the eastern division of the American Philosophical Association. He was an ordained **elder** of the **MEC**. Brightman advocated a personal idealism which, in his judgment, best accounts for the full range of human experience. Philosophy must be open-ended, though, since it must reckon with continuous change, both in nature and in history. Brightman is best known for his concept of the finite God and his analysis of moral and physical evil. God is supreme value and supremely creative. In effecting his purposes, however, God is limited by "The Eternally Given," a passive element within his very being. Brightman wrote 200 articles or more and 14 books, including *The Problem of God*, *The Spiritual Life*, *Nature and Value*, and the lectures which he delivered at Harvard, Vanderbilt, and Southern Methodist universities. *Person and Reality* was published posthumously.

John C. English

BRITISH METHODISM. The Methodist Church in Britain was formed in 1932 by the union of the **Wesleyan Methodist Church**, the Primitive Methodist Church (*see* PRIMITIVE METHODISTS [BRITISH]) and the United Methodist Church under the provisions of the Methodist Church Act of 1929 (amended by a second act in 1976). Two smaller denominations, Independent Methodism and the Wesleyan Reform Union, remained separate.

The original Methodist movement was part of the wider Evangelical **Revival** of the early 18th century. **John Wesley** was one among a number of its influential figures. In his lifetime there were tensions, notably between the Calvinistic and the Arminian (*see* ARMINIUS, JACOBUS) wings of the Revival. The growth and continuance of the "Wesleyan" part of the movement owed much to his pastoral and administrative gifts and the organization he bequeathed to his successors.

After Wesley's death in 1791, tensions within Wesleyanism led to breakaway movements, such as the **Methodist New Connexion** (1797), and to new outbreaks of evangelical fervor, notably the Primitive Methodists (1811) and **Bible Christians** (1815). The Wesleyan Connexion in the early 19th century remained, politically and ecclesiastically, more conservative than its offshoots, continuing to see itself in relation to the Church of England, rather than to the Nonconformist (or Free) Churches. During the same period, protest against what was perceived as the growing autocracy of the Wesleyan ministry came to a head in several reforming movements which were consolidated into the **United Methodist Free Churches** in 1857. By the end of the century, this divisive trend had been reversed and, in 1907, the New Connexion and United Methodist Free Churches, together with the Bible Christians, came together as the United Methodist Church. The way was opened for the further union of 1932.

Wesley drew on various precedents in developing an organization for his "connexion" of societies. The societies themselves owed much to the Anglican religious societies of the late 17th century and Wesley saw their relationship to the parish church as similar to the Moravian concept of *ecclesiolae in ecclesia*. New patterns of spiritual life and pastoral oversight developed. The class meeting began as a financial expedient, but soon became a primary means of nurturing and, when necessary, disciplining society members (*see* SO-

CIETIES, CLASSES, AND BANDS). Alongside the **preaching** service the **love feast**, the **watch-night** services, and the annual renewal of a covenant with God became and remained features of Methodist spiritual life. Wesley's insistence on "**field preaching**" and on regular attendance at Holy Communion (*see* EUCHARIST), together with his warnings against the spiritual danger of growing affluence, met with rather less enthusiasm.

It had been no part of Wesley's original intention to launch a new denomination, though the pressure of events pushed him in that direction. As early as 1746, he began grouping the societies in "**circuits**" (or "rounds") in which lay itinerants (forerunners of the later ordained ministry) were stationed under a Superintendent (originally known as the "Assistant"). Only after his death, in 1791, were the circuits themselves grouped into Districts, each under the leadership of a District Chairman. This organizational pattern was largely adopted by the non-Wesleyan branches. In the 19th century connexional Committees were set up to deal with particular Methodist activities, such as home missions and ministerial training. In 1932, these became Departments, which in turn, in the restructuring of the 1970s, were reorganized into seven "Divisions." Finally, in 1996, a single "Connexional Team," led by four "Co-ordinating Secretaries" replaced the earlier structures.

As early as 1744, Wesley met in conference with some of his clerical and lay supporters. This became an annual event and gradually assumed a more formal aspect. In 1784, Wesley gave it legal status and authority by means of his Deed of Declaration. The laity, though holding an increasing variety of offices, had no place in the Wesleyan Conference until 1878, and **women** representatives were not admitted until 1911. In these matters, the other branches of Methodism were well in advance of the parent body.

In his closing years, Wesley ordained a few of his full-time preachers, first for the work overseas, then for Scotland, and, in 1788, for England. A few sporadic **ordination**s followed his death, but from 1792 until 1836 ordination was abandoned in favor of "reception into full connexion." From 1836 ordination was into a single presbyteral ministry, into which women were not admitted until 1974.

When Wesley died in 1791, there were 58,218 British Methodists, excluding those in **Ireland**. Despite substantial losses during the height of the Reform agitation of the 1850s, Wesleyan membership reached a peak of 498,464 in 1911 and then began a steady decline. The total membership of the newly formed Methodist Church in 1932 was 769,101. By the beginning of the 21st century, the total had dropped to 333,000.

John A. Vickers

BROWN, GEORGE (January 29, 1792–October 25, 1871), largely self-educated **MP** leader, was born in Virginia of early Maryland Methodist parents, soldiered, was converted, and joined the Baltimore **Conference** in 1816. As a **presiding elder** by 1823, and aroused by conference rejection of reformers, he secretly circulated *Mutual Rights* papers to laity and in 1828 joined the new MP in Pittsburgh. While Ohio MP Conference president, he united "Reform Methodists" besides winning many "old church" people to MP principles. Widely sought as preacher, organizer, and president, Brown traveled 7,000 miles annually and was a **General Conference** leader (1834–1854). His wife, Eliza Jackson, and five children suffered frequent moves and impoverishment. He deprecated church silence against **slavery** and foresaw the 1858 MP rift while heading floundering Madison College (Pennsylvania). Remaining with the North and West in the split, he presided at several conventions 1860–1871. Despite failing to unite all nonepiscopal Methodists, he compiled a Union Hymnal. In 1860 he told former Pittsburgh colleagues the MP would accept bishops if the **MEC** allowed lay representation. Settled in Springfield, Ohio, as the able *Western Methodist Protestant* editor, he continued preaching despite illness and published *Recollections of an Itinerant Life* and *The Lady Preacher*.

Edwin Schell

BUCKLEY, JAMES MONROE (December 16, 1836–February 8, 1920), influential **MEC** pastor and editor, was born in Rahway, New Jersey. While attending Wesleyan University in Connecticut, he recognized a call to ministry and was ordained in the New Hampshire Annual **Conference** (MEC) in 1859. From 1863 to 1866, he was pastor of Central MEC in Detroit, Michigan. In 1866, he was transferred into the New York East Annual Conference, where he served appointments in Brooklyn and Stamford, Connecticut, until 1880, when he was named editor of the *New York Christian Advocate*. He published a number of books, including *A History of Methodism in the United States*, the influential *Constitutional and Parliamentary History of the MEC*, and such treatises as *The Wrong and Peril of Woman Suffrage* and *Theory and Practice of Foreign Missions*. Buckley was instrumental in the foundation of the Methodist Episcopal Hospital in Brooklyn in 1881, the first MEC hospital. Buckley served as president of its board for 35 years (1881–1916). He was an influential member of every **General Conference** of the MEC from 1872 to 1912. He was a delegate to the Ecumenical Methodist Conferences in London, 1881; Washington, D.C., 1891; and Toronto, 1911 (*see* WORLD METHODIST CONFERENCES).

Edwin E. Sylvest, Jr.

BULGARIA. *See* EUROPE.

BUNTING, JABEZ (May 13, 1779–June 16, 1858), the architect of the Wesleyan Methodist Church, was a more representative figure than the crude dictator vilified by his opponents. Born in Manchester, the son of a radical tailor, he studied medicine there under Dr. Thomas Percival. His **circuit** ministry was spent mainly in the north. After 1832, he resided in London as the first secretary and mastermind of the Wesleyan Methodist Missionary Society and, from 1835, president of the Hoxton Theological Institution. He was secretary of the **Conference** in 1814–1819 and 1824–1827 and connexional editor, 1821–1824. He was four times president of Conference (1820, 1828, 1836, and 1844).

Bunting was the epitome of "high Methodism," which stressed the Connexion, the national, and the international (including foreign missions). He gave much-needed leadership, not only for ministers but also for wealthy and articulate laymen. The "Liverpool Minutes" of 1820, responding to a decline in membership, was his work. He promoted the election of younger ministers (including himself) to Wesley's "Legal Hundred" conference corporation, the annual Pastoral Address, the right to memorialize Conference, the place of laymen on key committees, the proper training of ministers and their **ordination** by laying-on of hands. He saw Methodism as an independent body between Church and Dissent. Though often typecast as a Tory, he supported Catholic Emancipation in 1829 and, in the 1840s, allied himself with evangelical Dissenters in opposition to several parliamentary measures. Later he championed Methodist day schools.

When defending the supremacy of Conference, he declared that "Methodism was as much opposed to democracy as to sin" (*Nottingham Review*, December 14, 1827). His policies provoked opposition leading to the secession of Protestant Methodists (1828) and the Wesleyan Association (1835), and finally to the "Fly Sheets," pamphlets that were highly critical of Bunting and which led to further defections from the Wesleyans.

Bunting received an M.A. from Aberdeen and a D.D. from Wesleyan University, Connecticut (USA). Before his death he declared that he had sought to be a true Methodist, an Evangelical Arminian (*see* ARMINIUS, JACOBUS), as in his classic sermon, "**Justification** by Faith" (1812). *See also* BRITISH METHODISM.

John Munsey Turner

BURMA. *See* ASIA.

BURNS, NELSON (March 22, 1834–June 14, 1904), Methodist minister, holiness preacher, author, and editor, was born in Niagara, Upper **Canada**. After receiving a B.A. from University College, Toronto, in 1857, he became a teacher and then a high school principal. He was received on trial by the Wesleyan Methodist Church in 1863 and ordained in 1866. At 14 Burns had read **Phoebe Palmer**'s *Faith and Its Effects* and experienced **sanctification**. After he entered the ministry he became known as a holiness preacher (*see* HOLINESS MOVEMENT). His holiness specialty deviated enough from the mainstream of his denomination so that, in 1868, he was forced to resign his pastorate. The next year he participated in the formation of the Canadian Holiness Association and became its president. He edited the group's monthly *Expositor of Holiness*. In 1889, he published *Divine Guidance, or The Holy Spirit* in which he maintained that no Christian accepting God's absolute will could make regrettable mistakes. Burns was charged with heresy and, in 1894, at a meeting of the Guelph **Conference,** he was deposed from the ministry. The

Canadian Holiness Association continued to hold meetings and conventions, and Burns remained its president until his death.

Marilyn Färdig Whiteley

BURUNDI. *See* AFRICA.

BURWASH, NATHANAEL (July 25, 1839–March 30, 1918), Methodist minister and university chancellor, was born at St. Andrew's, Quebec, and raised in Baltimore, Ontario (*see* CANADA). He attended Victoria College in Cobourg, Ontario, graduating in 1859. In 1864, he was ordained a Methodist minister, and, in 1868, he married Mary Proctor. Burwash began teaching natural science at Victoria College in 1867. Particularly interested in the education of ministers, he prepared himself at Garrett Biblical Institute in Illinois for teaching theology if Victoria established a theological faculty. When such a faculty was formally organized in 1873, Burwash became its dean. In 1887, Burwash was appointed president and chancellor of Victoria. He had been one of the chief architects of a plan for university federation, and it was under Burwash's leadership that Victoria moved from Cobourg to open in Toronto in 1892. In the controversies that occurred during his tenure, he supported those who advanced the views of higher criticism. As president of the subcommittee on doctrine, he played an influential role in the preparation for church union which took place in 1925. After his retirement in 1913, Burwash continued to teach theology until his death.

Marilyn Färdig Whiteley

BUTLER, WILLIAM (January 30, 1818–August 18, 1899) founded **MEC missions** in India and Mexico. He emigrated from **Ireland** to America in 1850 with his second wife, Julia Lewis, and three sons. After Julia's death he married Clementina Rowe. They had two daughters. Clementina Rowe Butler instigated the formation of the WFMS (MEC) in 1869. In 1856, after several years of ministry in Massachusetts, the Butlers were chosen by Bishop **Matthew Simpson** to begin a mission in India. The mission officially opened in Bareilly in August 1858, and within three years Butler and his fellow workers had established nine mission stations. He resigned from the mission in 1864 and returned to pastorates in the New England **Conference**. In December 1872, Bishop Simpson asked the Butlers to begin a mission in Mexico. Butler was strong-willed and impatient, and his independent oversight of mission finances led to a recall by the Board of Missions in April 1878. He resigned in December 1878 and returned to the pastorate. In later years he traveled to India, the Holy Land, and Mexico, and wrote three books about India and Mexico. He died in the Missionary Rest Home, Old Orchard, Maine. *See also* ASIA; LATIN AMERICA AND THE CARIBBEAN.

Susan E. Warrick

– C –

CAMP MEETING MOVEMENT. The camp meeting has become one of the most productive institutions of Christianity. Immediate antecedents include Scottish "Holy Fairs," **field preaching** by **George Whitefield** and the **Wesleys**, and the "outdoor church" on the American frontier. Founded by southern Methodists no later than 1794, pioneer Methodist **circuit** rider John McGee probably carried the idea from Carolina to Kentucky. There the camp meeting fueled the fires of the Great Revival, and gained international fame at Cane Ridge in 1801. This outdoor **revival** festival quickly became an institution, and by 1820 Methodists were holding 500 encampments per year, some at permanent sites. Tremendous changes occurred after 1850, including the founding of permanent black encampments, the building of camp meeting resorts, and the development of holiness, **temperance**, and women's camp meetings; **Chautauqua**, Prophecy and Bible Conferences; Christian assembly grounds, and the family camping movement. Methodism contributed heavily to this institution, and continues to invest with strong commitment to camping programs for all ages, leisure ministries, and the development of conference and retreat centers. Moreover, hundreds of "old-time" camp meetings are still held each year, and at these places of spiritual renewal Methodists by the thousands continue to find renewed commitment to Jesus Christ.

Kenneth O. Brown

CANADA. The Methodist movement entered what is now Canada from two areas—the British Isles and the United States—and missionary preachers came to the new land over many years. Thus, in Canada the followers of **John Wesley** were divided into many strands that were only united in the latter part of the 19th century.

The first preacher to bring the Methodist message was **Laurence Coughlan**, who came to Newfoundland in 1766. Although a priest of the Church of England, he had worked in England and in his native **Ireland** as a Wesleyan. He remained only briefly in Newfoundland, but a few Methodist classes continued after his departure (*see* SOCI-ETIES, CLASSES, AND BANDS). During the 1770s, Methodists from Yorkshire settled near what is now the border of Nova Scotia and New Brunswick, and a **revival** began as they met together. Among those converted was **William Black** who became a preacher and was instrumental in organizing Methodism in eastern Canada. The movement was bolstered by loyalist Methodists who arrived following the American Revolution. The Maritime Methodists came under the supervision of the British **Wesleyan Methodist Church**. In 1855, the work was organized as the Wesleyan Methodist **Conference** of Eastern British America.

Loyalist settlers such as Paul and **Barbara Heck** also brought Methodism to Upper Canada (Ontario), especially to the eastern part of Lake Ontario and the upper St. Lawrence River. Preachers came from the United States, and **William Losee** organized a class meeting at Hay Bay in 1791. These Methodists were connected to the **Methodist Episcopal Church**. The situation grew more complex, however, after the War of 1812 when suspicion arose that the Methodists were "pro-American," and some missionaries arrived from Britain. In 1820, an agreement was reached whereby the British Wesleyans were given authority for Lower Canada (Quebec), and the Methodist Episcopals for Upper Canada. In 1928, the latter group severed their American connections. Tensions continued, however, and after 1834 there were two Methodist denominations in the area, the Wesleyan Methodist Church in Canada and the Methodist Episcopal Church in Canada. In addition, English immigration brought three more evangelical groups: **Primitive Methodists**, **Bible Christian** Church, and **Methodist New Connexion**.

This confusion of Methodist denominations was finally settled by two unions. The first, in 1874, brought together the Wesleyan Methodist Church, the Conference of Eastern British America, and the New Connexion Church to form the Methodist Church of Canada. Ten years later, in 1884, this group joined with the Primitive Methodist Church, the Bible Christian Church, and the Methodist Episcopal Church in Canada to form the Methodist Church (Canada, Newfoundland, Bermuda), the largest denomination in the country. These unions ended the rivalry that had drained the energy of the separate groups and allowed the denomination to focus on the settlement of newly opened western lands, and on mission work. It continued the earlier **missions** among Canadian Indians, and opened missions in Japan (1873) and in West China (1892) (*see* ASIA).

The settlement of the vast western lands provided a challenge to the Methodist Church, which considered itself the most "Canadian" of the country's denominations. The church attempted to minister to the needs of the settlers from the eastern part of the nation, and to "Christianize" and "Canadianize" the large numbers of non–Anglo-Saxon immigrants. This latter challenge helped to ally many in the denomination with the **social gospel**. The church as an organization and many of its individual members were active in the movement to bring about prohibition.

In 1902, a Presbyterian delegate to the Methodist **General Conference** proposed a union of the two denominations. The denominations entered into conversations in which the Congregationalists also participated. By 1910, the three national bodies had approved a Basis of Union. Then churchwide plebiscites were held and eventually the Presbyterians held an every member vote. Finally on June 10, 1925, The United Church of Canada came into being. It was made up of the Methodist and Congregational churches, and approximately 70 percent of the Presbyterians.

There were other churches with a Wesleyan heritage that did not join in the unions of 1874 and 1884, and in the union that formed The United Church of Canada. They include the Free Methodist Church and the British Methodist Episcopal Church.

Marilyn Färdig Whiteley

CANDLER, WARREN AKIN (August 23, 1857–September 25, 1941), **MECS** bishop, was born in Villa Rica, Georgia. In 1875, Candler graduated from Emory College and was admitted to the North Georgia **Conference** (MECS). Advancements came rapidly. He was a pastor (1875–1886), then assistant editor of the Nashville *Christian Advocate*, and from 1888 president of his alma mater. Elected bishop in 1898, he served until 1934. Candler was a wordsmith and pulpit power in a time when memorable homiletical oratory was expected of MECS leaders. **Missions** and **education** were the other major emphases of his ministry. Candler College in Havana, Cuba, was named for him and his brother Asa G. Candler (1899). When Emory College moved from Oxford, Georgia, to Atlanta, Bishop Candler served as its chancellor (1914–1921). The university's school of theology was named for him in 1915. Theologically, ecclesially, and politically Candler was deeply conservative. He did not favor church involvement in politics. He fought Methodist reunification, but when it came in 1939 Candler equally strongly disapproved of any who left the new **MC**. Asa G. Candler, developer of the soft drink Coca-Cola, provided major funding, especially for his brother's educational ministry. His $1,000,000 gift was the key to establishing an MECS university in Atlanta. Candler and Nettie Cartwright married in 1877 and had five children. Candler wrote many articles and ten books. His signature theological volumes are *Christus Auctor* (1900) and *The Christ and the Creed* (1927). He died in Atlanta and is buried at Oxford, Georgia.

Charles W. Brockwell, Jr.

CANNON, WILLIAM RAGSDALE (April 5, 1916–May 11, 1997), a leader in Methodist and ecumenical organizations, was born in Chattanooga, Tennessee, but grew up in Dalton, Georgia. Educated at the University of Georgia (B.A.) and Yale (B.D., Ph.D.), he was ordained **elder** in the **MC** in 1942 and pastored churches in Georgia until 1944, when he joined the faculty of Candler School of Theology at Emory University, Atlanta, Georgia. He taught church history, then served as dean from 1953 to 1968, when he was elected a bishop of the **UMC** (*see* EPISCOPACY). Before his retirement in 1984, Cannon headed the Raleigh (1968), Richmond (1970), Atlanta (1972), and Raleigh (1980) episcopal areas. As a leader in Methodism, he was elected to the presidium of the **World Methodist Council** (1976), served as an editor of the Oxford, then Abingdon edition of the *Works of John Wesley*, authored *The Theology of John Wesley* (1946), and was one of the founders (1994) of the "Confessing Movement," a group calling the UMC to return to an "orthodox Trinitarian **faith**." Ecumenically, Cannon was a delegate to three assemblies of the **World Council of Churches** (1961, 1968, 1975), an observer at the Second Vatican Council (1965), and a participant in Roman Catholic–Methodist dialogue (1966–1993). He was a lifelong bachelor. *See also* ECUMENISM.

John G. McEllhenney

CAPERS, WILLIAM (January 26, 1790–January 29, 1855), missionary, was born at the Bullhead Swamp Plantation, St. Thomas Parish, South Carolina. After college and studying law, he was admitted to the South Carolina Annual **Conference** (MEC) in 1808. Capers founded and served the Asbury Mission to the Lower Creek Indians, Fort Mitchell, Alabama, from 1821 to 1824. As **presiding elder** (1827–1830) he founded the first slave **missions** and developed an oral catechism for their use. Transferring to the Georgia Conference in 1834, Capers was pastor in Savannah, Georgia, supervising the slave missions on nearby islands. Returning to the South Carolina Conference he taught and became editor of the *Southern Christian Advocate*. The 1840 **General Conference** appointed him superintendent of the southern division of the mission work of the church. After the 1844 General Conference, Capers supported the controversial bishop **James O. Andrew**. With the formation of the **MECS** Capers was elected bishop in 1846. His biographer, Wightman, observed, "He was one of the master spirits of the second generation of southern Methodists; a worthy successor of [Francis] Asbury." Capers died in Anderson, South Carolina, and is buried in Columbia, South Carolina.

Robert Drew Simpson

CARIBBEAN. *See* LATIN AMERICA AND THE CARIBBEAN.

CARMAN, ALBERT (June 27, 1833–November 3, 1917), bishop, was born in Upper **Canada** and graduated from Victoria College in 1855. In 1857, he was named professor of mathematics at Belleville Seminary (Ontario), a newly organized MEC school. The following year, he was appointed principal. The school thrived during his tenure, becoming Albert University in 1866. Carman was ordained a **deacon** in 1859 and an **elder** in 1863. He became a bishop of the Canada MEC in 1874. He was a leader in the negotiations that led to Methodist union in 1884, and was general superintendent of the Methodist Church of Canada until 1914, when he was relieved of his duties and named general superintendent emeritus. A prolific writer in the denominational press, he also wrote The *Guiding Eye or The Holy Spirit's Guidance of the Believer.* He was a strong supporter of higher education and of **missions** in western Canada and beyond, helping to found the Methodist Church of Japan in 1905.

Susan E. Warrick

CARTMELL, MARTHA J. (December 14, 1845–March 20, 1945), missionary, was born in Hamilton, **Canada** West. She studied at the Wesleyan Female College in Hamilton and at the Toronto Normal School, and became a teacher. Long interested in foreign **mission** work, Cartmell was present at the meeting in 1880 when the Methodist **women** of Hamilton formed the denomination's first Branch Missionary Society and became its recording secretary. At a meeting the following year she put forth the motion that a denominationwide Woman's Missionary Society (WMS) be organized. This national group resolved to support a missionary in Japan (*see* ASIA). Cartmell took on that pioneering task, arriving in Tokyo in 1883. She organized a school for Japanese girls and the Toyo Eiwa Jo Gakko welcomed its first students in 1884. Cartmell became ill and returned to Canada in 1887.

In 1890, she accepted another assignment with the WMS, this time at a rescue home in Victoria, British Columbia. Two years later she returned to Japan as an evangelist. In 1896, her health once more forced her return to Canada and after two more years in Victoria she retired. She remained active in the WMS, and attended the 50th anniversary of its founding.

Marilyn Färdig Whiteley

CASE, WILLIAM (August 27, 1780–October 19, 1855), pioneer preacher, was admitted on trial to the **MEC** New York Annual **Conference** in 1805. His first assignment was the Bay of Quinte **circuit**

in Upper **Canada**, where he was junior preacher to **Henry Ryan**. He was subsequently assigned to other circuits in Canada, Michigan, and New York. In 1810, he was named **presiding elder** of the Cayuga District in the new Genesee Conference (New York). Five years later he became presiding elder of the Upper Canada District. In 1821 Case was assigned to a new conference committee on Indian **missions**. His interest and involvement in Indian missions became the primary focus of his ministry, although he remained presiding elder. Case worked for the formation of a separate Canada Conference, and when it was organized in 1824, he became its secretary. When the conference became independent in 1828, he was elected conference president and named superintendent of Indian missions and schools. He resigned the presidency in 1833 to devote his full attention to missions, and became general missionary to the Indian tribes. From 1837 until 1851 he served as superintendent of the Alderville mission and of the Manual Labor School he established at the mission.

Susan E. Warrick

CENTRAL AMERICA. *See* LATIN AMERICA AND THE CARIBBEAN.

CHANNEL ISLANDS. *See* EUROPE.

CHAUTAUQUA INSTITUTION was founded in 1874 by **John H. Vincent** and Lewis Miller as the Chautauqua Sunday School Teachers Assembly. Miller was a Methodist layman and a trustee of the Chautauqua Camp Ground at Fairpoint (later Chautauqua), New York, site of the assembly. Initially a two-week teacher training course, the assembly quickly became a full eight-week summer school with classes, concerts, and lectures. Its popularity reflected a widespread desire for self-improvement, and "chautauquas" soon appeared across the country, offering popular education and cultural enrichment. By 1900, there were at least 400 permanent chautauqua assemblies in the USA, constituting the most influential movement in popular education in the nation's history. In the early 1900s, the permanent assemblies were supplemented by temporary "tent chautauquas," which traveled to small towns offering lectures and entertainments. In 1878, Vincent brought self-improvement into the home with the Chautauqua Literary and Scientific Circle (CLSC), a four-year correspondence course for adults. At least 10,000 circles were organized during the first 20 years of the CLSC, mostly in rural communities. In 1902 the original assembly was chartered as Chautauqua Institution, which continues to provide educational and cultural opportunities for thousands of visitors each year.

Susan E. Warrick

CHECOTE, SAMUEL (1819–September 3, 1884) was one of the most significant leaders of the Creek people, especially in the post–Civil War era. Checote was born in 1819 in the Chattahoochee Valley, Alabama, and attended Asbury Manual Labor School (*see* CAPERS, WILLIAM) when he was nine years old. In 1829, the lives of his family and other Creeks were disrupted by removal to the Indian Territory. There Checote came into contact with missionary John Harrell and became a Methodist. In 1835 and 1844, the Lower Creek council forbade most Christian missionary activities, and Checote successfully appealed to the chief to rescind the ban. In 1852, Checote was admitted on trial to the Indian Mission **Conference** of the **MECS**, and in 1854, he was admitted in full connection. His ministry eventually included service as a **presiding elder** and the founding of local churches. His ministry was interrupted by military service as lieutenant colonel of the first Creek regiment to fight for the South in the Civil War. After the war he was elected principal chief of the Creek Nation in 1869, 1872, and 1879. He worked to unify Upper and Lower Creek factions, opposed federal efforts to annul treaties, and encouraged education.

Bruce David Forbes

CHICAGO TRAINING SCHOOL officially opened its doors October 20, 1885, in a rented house at 19 West Park Avenue. With the approval of the **MEC** Rock River **Conference**, **Lucy Rider Meyer** volunteered her service as principal, a position she held until 1917. Training in Bible, church history, and basic medicine became standard requirements for **women** entering home and foreign missionary work. In 1886, the Chicago Training School moved to a four-story building at 114 Dearborn Avenue. As part of their education, the students made evangelistic and social service calls to people living in the nearby tenement neighborhoods. A free dispensary, started in the subbasement, grew into Wesley Hospital. Within two years of its founding, visiting work gained increased significance in the training school curriculum, prompting Meyer to revive the deaconess office (*see* DEACONESS MOVEMENT). With generous contributions from Chicagoan Norman Wait Harris, the training school moved to large, impressive quarters at 4949 Indiana Avenue in 1895. Thereafter, CTS established itself as the premier midwestern female training school with enrollment peaking at 248 students in 1912. World War I, the fundamentalist challenge, and increasing academic standards undermined the school's vitality. Enrollment plummeted in 1918 to 82, leading to the admission of male students. The Great Depression, a changing neighborhood, and declining enrollment sealed the 1934 decision to affiliate with Garrett Biblical Institute in Evanston, Illinois.

Mary Agnes Dougherty

CHILE. *See* LATIN AMERICA AND THE CARIBBEAN.

CHINA. *See* ASIA.

CHOWN, SAMUEL DWIGHT (April 11, 1853–January 30, 1933), **social gospel** leader, was born in Kingston, Ontario, **Canada**. After his discharge from military service, he worked in the family's hardware business. In 1874 the Wesleyan Methodist Church accepted him on probation. He attended Victoria College, 1876–1877, and was ordained in 1879. Chown's early pastoral experience in Ontario was coupled with leadership in **temperance** work at the **conference** level. From 1894 to 1902, he held pastorates in Toronto and became active in denominational administration. In 1902, Chown was elected first general secretary of the new Department of Temperance and Moral Reform, a position he held until 1910. During those years he also actively participated in the movement toward union of the Presbyterian, Methodist, and Congregational churches of Canada. In 1910, he was elected co-general superintendent (with **Albert Carman**) of the Methodist Church of Canada. After Carman's retirement in 1914, Chown led the church through continuing negotiations that in 1925 resulted in the union of the three denominations. Although he retired in 1926, he remained active in the church he had helped to create. He died in Toronto.

Susan E. Warrick

CHRISTIAN ASSURANCE. *See* ASSURANCE, CHRISTIAN.

CHRISTIAN EXPERIENCE. *See* EXPERIENCE, CHRISTIAN.

CHRISTIAN METHODIST EPISCOPAL CHURCH is an African-American body of American Methodism that was originally organized under the name Colored Methodist Episcopal Church.

At the beginning of the Civil War, the **MECS** had approximately 207,000 African-American members. By the war's end this number had dwindled to 78,000. There was dissatisfaction among the African-American membership with the MECS. In 1866, the African-American membership petitioned the **General Conference** to separate and form their own independent denomination.

At the next meeting of the MECS General Conference in 1870, legislation was passed which turned some church property over to the African Americans and five annual **conferences** were formed to become the nucleus of the new denomination. In December 1870, the first General Conference of the CME was held in Jackson, Tennessee. It was presided over by MECS bishops Robert Paine and Holland N. McTyeire. The organization adopted the name Colored Methodist Episcopal Church, established committees, adopted a **Discipline**, created nine annual conferences, and elected **William Henry Miles** and Richard H. Vanderhorst bishops.

By 1874, there were 15 annual conferences, 600 traveling preachers, and 75,000 members. The 1874 General Conference began planning a seminary where its clergy could be educated. In the mid-1880s the denomination began to take on more structure. The church organized its denominational work into various departments. Financial constraints were always a concern and it was hoped that the new organization would help the denomination be more efficient in carrying out its missions.

In 1886 the following schools were organized: Paine College in Augusta, Georgia; Lane College in Jackson, Tennessee; Phillips College (which later became Texas College) in Tyler, Texas; and Haygood

Seminary in Washington, Arkansas. **Education** continued to be of concern for the denomination. The ministerial course of study was reviewed and revised during this period and again at the turn of the century. The involvement of **women** in the denomination reached a new status with the creation of the Woman's Missionary Council. This council has been involved with **missions** and educational concerns both within the USA and abroad.

At the 1954 General Conference, the denomination voted to change its name to the Christian Methodist Episcopal Church, which took effect in January 1956.

The CME continues to be active in education. In addition to the schools mentioned above it began Miles College in Birmingham, Alabama; Mississippi Industrial College at Holly Springs, Mississippi; and Phillips School of Theology in Atlanta, Georgia (part of the Interdenominational Theological Seminary). It has been active in pan-Methodist movements and in several ecumenical settings. It has continued to challenge the church and the nation to address racism and other injustices.

L. Dale Patterson

CHRISTIAN PERFECTION stands, in **John Wesley**'s words, as "the grand depositum which God has lodged with the people called Methodists." He referred to **repentance** as "the porch of religion," **faith** as "the door," and perfection, or holiness, as "religion itself." God, he thought, had created Methodism to propagate this doctrine. Wesley equated true religion and Christian perfection, only slightly changing his definition over the decades: (1734) "I take religion to be . . . a renewal of our minds in the image of God . . . a still-increasing conformity of heart and life to the pattern of our most holy Redeemer" (1746). We define "religion itself" as "the loving God with all our heart, and our neighbor as ourselves, and in that love abstaining from all evil, and doing all possible good to all." Summarizing his position in 1767, Wesley wrote, "By perfection I mean the humble, gentle, patient love of God, and our neighbor, ruling our tempers, words, and actions." Perfected souls commit no deliberate sin. However, because they "dwell in a shattered body," they experience temptations and make mistakes "in things not essential to **salvation**."

Some mistakes, Wesley conceded, "accidentally flow from" pure love itself. This love renders one unsuspicious, ready to believe the best of women and men, and therefore susceptible to acting as if some persons are better than they are.

Wesley called on scripture, tradition, reason, and experience to support the doctrine of Christian perfection. His biblical texts pointed to perfection (Matthew 5:42; Philippians 3:12; Hebrews 6:1), cleansing (Ezekiel 36:25; II Corinthians 7:1), entire **sanctification** (II Thessalonians 5:23–24), and loving God (Deuteronomy 6:5; Matthew 22:37). Using as his evidence the Prayer for Purity of Heart, Wesley argued that Christian perfection accorded well with the traditions of the Church of England: "Cleanse the thoughts of our hearts by the inspiration of thy Holy Spirit, that we may perfectly love thee." Wesley reasoned, reflecting on Matthew 25:29, that we lose whatever we have if we fail to improve it. Therefore, when we cease to go on toward perfection, we slip backward into, at best, a lower order of Christians. Talking with believers, Wesley discovered that their experience confirmed the doctrine he preached. He examined five men and six women at Rotherham in 1759, agreeing with them in their belief that they were "saved from sin." They felt "nothing but love."

As Wesley formulated the doctrine of Christian perfection, he uncovered the foundational principle of his theology: the interaction of the divine and human initiatives. "Whatever grace we receive," Wesley maintained, "it is a free gift from" Christ. But we must prepare ourselves to receive it. Elizabeth Vandome's experience epitomized Wesley's theology: "I wrestled on till the Lord broke in upon my soul like the sun in his glory." Questers for perfection bear the responsibility of making windows in their souls. These are created by keeping all God's commandments, by taking up one's cross daily, and by praying, studying the Bible, **fasting**, attending **worship**, and partaking of the Lord's Supper (*see* EUCHARIST). This window-making continues until God sheds the light of perfect love on the soul. Then it goes on in the expectation that God will pour in more light.

Wesley articulated this interplay of the divine and human initiatives with particular clarity in 1787. The person justified by God's **grace** receives the choice of "walking in the higher or the lower path." The **Holy Spirit** "incites" this newly justified person "to choose the narrowest path in the narrow way, to aspire after the heights and depths of holiness, after the entire image of God." Freedom to decide belongs to the believer, however. He or she may neglect the Spirit's offer and decline "into the lower order of Christians." This order saunters along in "a good way," and "finds mercy in the close of life, through the blood of the covenant."

When Wesley's doctrine of Christian perfection crossed the Atlantic to America, it lost many of its nuances. Debate tended to concentrate on whether perfection was an instantaneous or gradual blessing. Wesley thought it was both. Perfection, which occurs in an instant, "is constantly both preceded and followed by a gradual work." American preachers found it almost impossible in the emotionally charged atmosphere of American **camp meetings**, where people expected to "feel" religion, to explain to seekers that they might still be perplexed and in anguish after they had been delivered from sin. Wesley noted that "the mind itself may be deeply distressed while the heart cleaves to God by perfect love."

It was hard to send a person home from a camp meeting with the Wesleyan insistence that the "perfect Christian" must become "more perfect" in love and demonstrate this by setting slaves free. So by the 1830s American Methodists had shelved what Wesley had termed their "grand depositum." When the doctrine of Christian perfection reappeared in the 1850s, it became the baptism of the Holy Spirit. This doctrine focused on the independent work of the Holy Spirit, while Wesley's Christian perfection focused on the work of Christ applied by the Spirit to the believer. By 1874, Daniel Steele was appealing to his Methodist brethren to "cease to discuss the subtleties and endless questions arising from entire sanctification or Christian Perfection and all cry mightily to God for the baptism of the Holy Spirit." This baptism bestowed the powers of prophecy, healing, and, later in its development, speaking in tongues.

Persons who substituted the baptism of the Holy Spirit for Wesley's doctrine of Christian perfection left Methodism and established the holiness and **pentecostal** movements. Meanwhile, in mainstream Methodism, a few leaders began to proclaim the social dimension of Christian perfection. C. W. Barnes wrote in 1912: "This is the 'new sanctification,' the redemption of society, the cleansing of the social order from all sin." This **social gospel** interpretation of Christian perfection never became dominant, however.

The 1952 **MC** Episcopal Address adumbrated an individualistic understanding of perfection, which characterized the relatively rare 20th-century affirmations of the doctrine: "It is our faith that the fundamental change wrought in the individual be regeneration is a dynamic process which by growth in grace moves toward 'mature manhood, to the measure of the stature of the fullness of Christ.'" *See also* DOCTRINAL STANDARDS.

John G. McEllhenney

CHRISTMAS CONFERENCE. At the direction of **John Wesley**, the American Methodist preachers created a new church, the **MEC** in America, at a conference held in Baltimore, Maryland, during the 1784 Christmas season. Before this Christmas Conference, American Methodism mirrored Wesley's understanding of British Methodism as a supplement to the Church of England. Wesley admonished his followers to participate in Prayer Book **worship** in Anglican churches, to receive **baptism** and the Lord's Supper (*see* EUCHARIST) from Anglican priests, and to adhere to the Anglican standards of Christian doctrine (*see* DOCTRINAL STANDARDS).

When most Anglican priests returned to England during the American Revolution, American Methodists lacked sacramental worship. Some preachers responded by ordaining themselves (*see* ORDINATION). The majority objected and asked **Francis Asbury** to write Wesley for guidance. Wesley responded with a letter dated September 10, 1784, in which he sent liturgies for Sunday worship and the sacraments, a hymnal, **Articles of Religion**, and a plan for ordaining **deacon**s and **elder**s (called priests in the Church of England). Wesley ordained **Richard Whatcoat** and **Thomas Vasey** elders and sent them with **Thomas Coke**, whom he appointed **superintendent**, to carry his instructions, which amounted to the constitution of a new church, to America.

Coke met Asbury in Delaware and informed him of Wesley's actions, including the choice of Asbury to serve as joint superintendent with Coke. Asbury insisted on putting the matter to the vote of the American Methodist preachers, who were summoned to gather in **Lovely Lane** Chapel, Baltimore, at Christmas 1784. The preachers adopted Wesley's plan and elected Asbury joint superintendent with

Coke, who then, assisted by others, ordained Asbury. Understanding the office of superintendent to be similar to that of bishop, the Christmas Conference named the new denomination the MEC in America. The conference selected elders for ordination, appointed missionaries to **Canada** and the Caribbean (*see* LATIN AMERICA AND THE CARIBBEAN), proposed a college (*see* EDUCATION), and wrote a ban on owning slaves into the new church's rules (*see* ANTISLAVERY MOVEMENT).

John G. McEllhenney

CIEMAL. Concilio Iglesias Evangélicas Metodistas de América Latina, also known as the Council of Evangelical Methodist Churches in Latin America, was founded February 2, 1969, and helps autonomous and nonautonomous Latin American and Caribbean Methodist churches collaborate and support each other. CIEMAL is united in its historical and doctrinal Methodist heritage and its recognition of the authority of scripture, the **Articles of Religion**, the sermons of **John Wesley**, and the **General Rules**. CIEMAL includes Methodist churches of Chile, Argentina, Brazil, Uruguay, Peru, Bolivia, Costa Rica, Panama, Cuba, the Caribbean (includes Belize, Honduras, and Guianas), Mexico, the United Methodist Church in Equador, the Evangelical Church in the Dominican Republic, and the Evangelical National Primitive Methodist Church in Guatemala. CIEMAL relates to Methodist churches in Colombia, Nicaragua, Venezuela, Puerto Rico, and with Methodists Associated Representing the Cause of Hispanic Americans (MARCHA) in the USA. CIEMAL's program agency, the Commission for Mission and Testimony, bears witness to God's love for needy and marginalized persons in nations where half of the people live in poverty due to oppressive forces of colonialism and neocolonialism. CIEMAL enhances the search for the identity, indigenization, and contextualization of Latin American and Caribbean Methodism and is committed to the liberation of Latin American people, starting with the poor. *See also* LATIN AMERICA AND THE CARIBBEAN.

Alice G. Knotts

CIRCUIT. The Methodist use of this term originated with **John Wesley**. In his time it referred to two or more Methodist societies joined together for pastoral supervision. **British Methodism** and its related churches continue to use the term and utilize a circuit plan in which several local churches are grouped together, served by several ministers, one of whom is appointed **superintendent** minister. Until recently American Methodism employed the circuit system to designate two or more **preaching** places or local churches. In its earlier days the preacher appointed to a circuit was known as a circuit rider since he traveled among his preaching places by horse. The term is rarely used in American Methodism today. Two or more churches served by one pastor are usually designated a pastoral charge. *See also* ITINERACY; SOCIETIES, CLASSES, AND BANDS.

Charles Yrigoyen, Jr.

CLARKE, ADAM (1760–August 26,1832), early **British Methodist** leader, was born in County Londonderry, **Ireland**. Clarke's ministry had a profound impact on Methodism throughout Britain and in America. He became a Methodist in 1779 and **John Wesley** appointed him as an itinerant preacher in 1782. In 1783, he was received into full connection by the **Conference** at Bristol. Clarke served **circuits** throughout the British Isles, including appointments on the Channel Islands, the Shetland Islands, and Dublin. Methodist concern for the needs of the poor and disadvantaged was evidenced in Clarke's role as founder of the Dublin branch of the Stranger's Friend Society, and in his efforts to establish schools for poor children. A skilled linguist and biblical scholar, he was active in the British and Foreign Bible Societies. Clarke's multivolume commentary on the Bible became the standard for the course of study for the preparation of itinerant ministers in Britain and America. John Wesley cautioned Clarke concerning his rejection of the catholic Christian doctrine of the eternal Sonship of Christ, but Clarke was never censured for his theological independence (*see* DOCTRINAL STANDARDS).

Edwin E. Sylvest, Jr.

CLOWES, WILLIAM (March 12, 1780–March 2, 1851), son of a Tunstall, England, potter, was converted in 1805, spent some time distributing Bibles and tracts, and became a Wesleyan class leader.

He attended the **camp meeting** on Mow Cop on May 31, 1807. He preached during the second camp meeting and was placed on the Burslem Wesleyan plan as a preacher on trial. Although he was expelled from Wesleyan membership in 1810, he continued to preach. He and his followers joined forces with those of **Hugh Bourne** and J. Steele, and his name appeared as preacher no. 5 on the handwritten **preaching** plan for Tunstall in 1811. J. Nixon and Thomas Woodnorth gave him financial support, enabling him to extend his travels into nearby counties, establishing many societies (*see* SOCIETIES, CLASSES, AND BANDS). In 1819, he reached Hull, which became the center from which he extended his travels as far as London and Cornwall until his retirement in 1844. His name is linked with that of Hugh Bourne as a founder of the **Primitive Methodist** Connexion and he was president of the **Conference** for three successive years, 1844–1846. Part of the tension between him and Bourne was that, unlike Bourne, he was a powerful and persuasive preacher. He had lived a wild and dissipated life before his **conversion**, but thereafter revealed a gentle and generous character. A more traditional Methodist than Bourne, he contributed significantly to the rapid growth of the Primitive Methodist movement by his success as an evangelist.

William Leary

COKE, THOMAS (September 28, 1747–May 2, 1814), close associate of **John Wesley** and bishop of the **MEC**, was born in Brecon, South Wales. He went to Jesus College, Oxford, in 1764, was ordained priest in 1772, and in 1775 obtained a doctorate in civil law. During a curacy at South Petherton, Somerset, his Methodist tendencies made him increasingly unpopular in the parish. John Wesley met him at Kingston St. Mary in August 1776 and sent him back to his parish with renewed zeal. But the following spring local opposition came to a head and he was driven out. From then on Coke associated openly with the Methodists. Wesley found him an invaluable assistant. For some years they alternated in visiting **Ireland** and presiding over the Irish **Conference**.

These were turbulent years for the British connexion and Coke became Wesley's troubleshooter, especially in disputes over the chapels at Birstall, Dewsbury, and North Shields. For his pains he was suspected of being an upstart intruder, eager to step into Wesley's shoes.

In particular, for his part in drawing up the Deed of Declaration (1784), Coke was condemned by those preachers who found themselves omitted from the "Legal Hundred."

Charles Wesley resented his role in the connexion, especially when Charles learned in 1784 that John Wesley had secretly "ordained" him for America, suspecting him of enticing his brother into schism. Meanwhile, armed with Wesley's authority, Coke sailed for America. At the **Christmas Conference** in Baltimore, **Francis Asbury** was ordained as joint **superintendent** with Coke (*see* EPISCO-PACY), and the **MEC** was established. Coke's enthusiasm and his realistic appraisal of the American scene in the aftermath of political independence led him to go further than Wesley's intentions for American Methodism. Nevertheless, in the main he followed the blueprint given him by Wesley. He made eight more visits to America before his marriage in 1805 confined him to England.

In England, Coke is remembered as the founder of foreign **missions**. His first abortive venture was a "Plan of the Society for the Establishment of Missions among the Heathens" (1783). In 1786, with Wesley's support, his "Address to the Pious and Benevolent" proposed missions not only in the **Caribbean** and British North America but also in the Channel Islands and the remoter parts of Scotland. He was almost the sole administrator and supporter of the resulting missions until official responsibility was accepted by the Conference by the appointment of a missionary committee in 1804.

Although the itinerants were determined that after Wesley's death that there should be no further "king in Israel," Coke was twice elected to the presidency, in 1797 and 1805. Despite his active and peripatetic existence, he managed to produce several substantial works, including a six-volume *Commentary on the Bible* (1801–1807) and a *History of the West Indies* (1808–1811). With Henry Moore he wrote the authorized biography of John Wesley (1792). A collected edition of his journals was published in 1816. He died at sea on his way to launch a mission in India and Ceylon (*see* ASIA). *See also* BRITISH METHODISM.

John A. Vickers

COKESBURY COLLEGE was located in Abingdon, Maryland. As early as 1780 **Francis Asbury** discussed with **John Dickins** the possibility of establishing a school for the children of Methodist preachers. The **Christmas Conference**, the organizational **conference** of the **MEC**, responded in 1784 to these dreams by establishing Cokesbury College, combining the names of its first bishops within the school's name. Founded as a college, according to the wishes of **Thomas Coke**, it never achieved that level of **education**, so it served as an academy, Asbury's preference from the beginning. Although a Board of Trustees governed the college, Asbury served as its ex officio president and was largely responsible for soliciting its funds, a difficult and constantly trying task. Serving the children of Methodist preachers, orphans, and children of "our competent friends," the school's disciplined regimen was patterned after that of Wesley's Kingswood School. It combined traditional academic training (English, Latin, Greek, Philosophy) with "recreation" that taught gardening and several trades seeking to produce knowledgeable well-rounded persons who would be "rational scriptural Christians." The college building burned in 1795, leading Coke to reestablish the school in Baltimore, where, unfortunately, it burned again within the year. In its short history Methodism's first college trained at least one USA senator and other clergy and lay leaders.

Robert C. Monk

COLLINS, JUDSON DWIGHT (February 2, 1822–May 13, 1852), first **MEC** missionary to China, was born in Wayne County, New York. He was named for Baptist missionary Adoniram Judson, and was one of four sons who entered the ministry. The family moved to Michigan, where he graduated in the first class of the University of Michigan in 1845. Two months later he became professor of "Natural and Moral Science" at Wesleyan Seminary (now Albion College). The following year he was received on trial in the Michigan **Conference** (MEC). He felt called to missionary service in China even before the church established a mission (*see* ASIA). Money was found, and Bishop Edmund S. Janes appointed him the first missionary. He sailed to Foochow with Jane and **Moses White** in 1847, staying three years and seven months. Soon after arrival he founded a school for boys and a **Sunday school**. On the advice of his doctor he returned to the USA for health reasons in 1851, hoping to return to China for further work. He died the following year.

Barbara Campbell

COLOMBIA. *See* LATIN AMERICA AND THE CARIBBEAN.

COMMUNION, HOLY. *See* EUCHARIST.

CONE, JAMES HAL (August 5, 1938–), theologian and educator, professor at Union Theological Seminary in New York City since 1969. Cone provided a theological interpretation of Black Power, a movement that originated in the late 1960s in response to violent resistance to African-American claims for equal rights. In contrast to the nonviolent resistance that characterized the early phases of the civil rights movement, Black Power advocates argued for the use of violence in self-defense and to secure justice. In his first important work, *Black Theology and Black Power* (1969), Cone argued that God cannot be conceived as a neutral judge who stands above all such social conflicts. In the context of the struggle for liberation, Christians must acknowledge that God is black. Cone has subsequently become one of the leading interpreters of **liberation theology** in North America. He also has written on African-American religion and culture (*Black Spirituals and the Blues*, 1972) and the African-American role in American public life (*Malcolm and Martin and America*, 1991). Cone was educated at Philander Smith College, Garrett Theological Seminary, and Northwestern University. He is a member of the **AME**.

Robin W. Lovin

CONFERENCE. John Wesley instituted the conference as a major feature of Methodist structure. He convened and presided over the first conference of his preachers in London in 1744. Wesley met annually thereafter to confer with his preachers until his death. These meetings consisted of **worship**, discussions about doctrine and **discipline**, and the appointment of the preachers to their places of ministry. **British Methodism** continues to meet annually in conference with a similar agenda. Voting members are duly elected or are persons who hold the most important denominational offices. Ministers and laity are equally represented in conference. American Methodists generally adopted Wesley's conference system. Their first conference was held in 1773 in Philadelphia, Pennsylvania. The **UMC**, the largest Methodist denomination in the United States, is structured in a connectional system of conferences, the most important of which are the charge conference (one or more local churches), an annual conference (a geographical grouping of clergy and laity representatives who meet annually), a jurisdictional or central conference, and a **general conference** (delegates elected by annual conferences who meet every four years). Other Methodist churches historically related to the UMC or its predecessors have a more or less similar conference structure. In most of the Methodist churches qualified clergy and properly elected laity are equally represented and are entitled to vote.

Charles Yrigoyen, Jr.

CONGO. *See* AFRICA.

CONVERSION, OR NEW BIRTH. These terms signify the transformation that occurs in the life of the believer when the saving work of Jesus Christ is personally appropriated by **faith**. Conversion emphasizes the role of the human will in effecting the "turning about" from a life enslaved to sin and death to a Christ-centered life. New Birth emphasizes the divine agency in effecting this transformation. The latter term is more characteristic of biblical and apostolic usage.

Methodism emerged as part of a larger revival within Protestant Christianity and emphasized the possibility and urgency of personal new birth in Jesus Christ as the defining mark of one's existence as a Christian. This doctrine had long been submerged under the reigning sacerdotal views of Christian initiation that were represented by **Roman Catholicism** and by the sacramental and ecclesial authority of the Protestant state churches of Europe.

The centrality of the new birth in the early Methodist revival was seen by **John Wesley** to be the recovery of a primary emphasis within the apostolic church. This is especially apparent in the Johannine tradition. Jesus explained to Nicodemus (John 3) that the new birth by the Spirit of God (*see* HOLY SPIRIT) is entry into life eternal. Paul spoke of this transformation in summary fashion with the words, "If anyone is in Christ, he is a new creation; the old has passed away, behold, the new has come" (II Corinthians 5:17). In Pauline theology, regeneration presupposes that all persons are sinners from birth and leads to the elimination of the power of conscious sin and the reign of Christ's perfect love in the heart.

For Wesley, all persons are invited to share in the new birth by virtue of Christ's atoning death and resurrection for all, but everyone must respond to this provision if it is to be personally appropriated. Such response is for Wesley the preventing or drawing work of **grace** (John 1:9) within the context of the community of faith. The parameters of that community were established by Wesley in his **General Rules**.

In the **UMC** context, any discussion of the new birth also needs to take into consideration the thought of **Philip William Otterbein**. Given his Reformed Pietist context, Otterbein characteristically located regeneration as one aspect in the larger "order of **salvation**" that began with God's purposes in externally grounding his redemptive kingdom within history through the Incarnation of the Son and proceeded to his internal planting of that kingdom within the lives of the reborn. For Otterbein, "conversion" is a more generic term, referring to the entire phase that begins with the personal summons of the sinner by the word and the Spirit, and that includes **justification** as well as regeneration (the new birth) and full **sanctification**.

The other principal United Methodist founder, **Jacob Albright**, made the new birth the focus of his revival preaching among the nominal German church groups of late-18th-century Pennsylvania.

Thus, Wesley's understanding of the new birth needs to be seen as part of a larger historical milieu of Christian renewal and also as part of a larger understanding of the plan of salvation that was to be normative for the serious member of a Methodist class (*see* SOCIETIES, CLASSES, AND BANDS).

For John Wesley and the early Methodists, the new birth was emphasized to counteract the lifeless formalism that prevailed in Anglican **worship**, as seen in his sermon, "The New Birth." His appeal was that nominal Anglicans not rely on that "broken reed" (i.e., "I was once baptized") and consider instead the urgent now, "Are you now born again?" This means, "Is the spirit now bearing witness with your spirit, that you are a child of God?" (see WITNESS OF THE SPIRIT). For Wesley, the new birth is signified in one's **baptism**, but it must be personally appropriated and visibly manifested in daily practice. The new birth, or regeneration, is to be correlated with justification, or pardon, which is to be appropriated instantaneously as a gift of faith. Pardon implies a relational change of status of the forgiven sinner before a forgiving God, for the sake of Christ's atoning death. However, regeneration, or the new birth, implies an actual change in the believer, whereby imparted grace begins a transforming work that proceeds as sanctification in Christ through the indwelling Holy Spirit. The goal of this transformation, which begins with the new birth, is **Christian perfection**, which results in choice (Romans 3:23). Its extrinsic basis is the sacrificial death of Christ (I Corinthians 15:2–3; I Peter 1:17–23). As the convicting and converting work of the Holy Spirit, it is called the "washing of regeneration" (Titus 3:5), a phrase which probably should also be read in a baptismal context. However, the indispensable basis of the new birth is personal faith in Christ (I Corinthians 15:2; John 6:12–13).

In reaction to the one-sided sacerdotal understanding of the new birth in medieval Roman Catholicism, the Protestant reformers sought to reappropriate the biblical witness concerning this doctrine. Their interpretation was guided by Luther's redefinition of saving grace as personal and relational, as God's "good will" toward sinners rather than as a sacrifice mediated through the agency of its priests.

Regeneration is the personal result of one's discovery and appropriation, through the proclaimed word of the gospel, of the gift of Christ's imputed righteousness (Romans 1:16–17), which frees one from divine condemnation. It also denotes the relational change that occurs for the believer in the **sacrament** of baptism. For Luther, to live as a regenerated person is to live in remembrance of one's baptism. For Calvin, equal weight is given to regeneration and justification as the twin "benefits" of the believer who is personally united to Christ through the ministry of the word of God and the sacraments of baptism and the Lord's Supper (see EUCHARIST). The English **Puritans**, who were Calvinists, understood regeneration to be the defining mark of divine election that entailed for the elect the mandate to "prove" his/her election by working to establish the theocratic kingdom of God within the English culture. In the free church tradition, beginning with the Anabaptists and including later the Baptists and others, the new birth is almost exclusively identified with the ordinance of believer's baptism that signifies a radical separation from the "fallen" order of the present world and a commitment to obedience as Christ's disciple. *See also* DOCTRINAL STANDARDS; NEW BIRTH.

J. Steven O'Malley

COOPER, EZEKIEL (1763–1847), early Methodist preacher, was born into a nominally Anglican family in Caroline County on Maryland's eastern shore. A serious youth, Cooper experienced "divine impressions," but received no spiritual direction until age 13, when **Freeborn Garrettson** preached near his home, finally converting and joining a Methodist society five years later (*see* SOCIETIES, CLASSES, AND BANDS). Recovery from an illness confirmed his call to preach, and he responded to **Francis Asbury**'s invitation that he "travel" in late 1784. He itinerated in a number of appointments between Boston and Charleston before succeeding **John Dickins** as book steward in 1798, first in Philadelphia and then, from 1804 until his resignation in 1808, in New York City. In addition to preaching and editing, Cooper earned a reputation for theological dispute, contending against Deism, predestination, and Episcopal attacks on the validity of Methodist **ordination**. In the **General Conference**s of 1808–1820 (excepting 1816, during a seven-year period in which he had "located"), he unsuccessfully advocated the election of **presiding elders**. From 1821–1824 he also wrote pseudonymous pieces favoring lay delegates to **conference**, providing a template for the **MP** Constitution and **Discipline** at the end of the decade. However, he remained with the **MEC**, serving out his ministry from 1821 on in various capacities, albeit on "supernumerary" status, in and around Philadelphia.

Charles Wallace, Jr.

COUGHLAN, LAURENCE (d.1784), preacher and missionary, was born in **Ireland**. Reared a Catholic, he was converted to Methodism in 1753. Two years later he became a preacher, serving in Ireland and England. Although he was a zealous preacher he was uneducated, and when, in 1764, he had himself ordained by Erasmus, who claimed to be a Greek Orthodox bishop, **John Wesley** was angry because he did not consider Coughlan worthy (*see* ORDINATION). In 1765, Newfoundland residents requested a Protestant minister, and Coughlan was recommended if he could be ordained within the Church of England. This was done and he arrived in Newfoundland in 1766. He served as priest of the Church of England, but at the same time worked toward an evangelical awakening. Finally a **revival** broke out and spread vigorously. Methodist societies were established (*see* SOCIETIES, CLASSES, AND BANDS) and a chapel was erected at Blackhead. Coughlan came into conflict with some of the residents, however, and he left Newfoundland in 1773, resigning his mission after he reached England. His career during the rest of his life is obscure and Methodism in Newfoundland waned during the years after Coughlan's departure. Yet to him goes the distinction of bringing the first Methodist **preaching** to what is now **Canada**.

Marilyn Färdig Whiteley

COUNTESS OF HUNTINGDON. *See* HUNTINGDON, COUNTESS OF.

COX, MELVILLE BEVERIDGE (November 9, 1799–July 21, 1833), the first foreign missionary commissioned by the **MEC** Missionary Society, was born in Hallowell, Maine, and received on trial in the New England **Conference** in 1822. In May 1825, Cox contracted tuberculosis and traveled south for his health. He settled in Baltimore, and married Ellen Cromwell in 1828. After her death in 1830, Cox joined the Virginia Conference, but was not healthy enough to preach full time. He turned instead to the mission field, hoping to go to South America. However, the bishops asked him to go to Liberia, and he sailed from Norfolk on November 6, 1832 (*See* AFRICA). He arrived in Monrovia March 8, 1833, and purchased the headquarters of the defunct Basle Mission. On April 12, Cox fell ill with "African fever" (malaria). Death soon followed, but in his few months in Liberia, Cox conducted a **camp meeting** (probably the first in Africa), organized a **Sunday school**, established the MEC in Liberia, and mapped out a detailed mission strategy. Cox wrote his own epitaph. He told a friend that if he died in Liberia, the friend should write on his gravestone, "Let a thousand fall before Africa be given up."

Susan E. Warrick

CREIGHTON, WILLIAM BLACK (July 20, 1864–October 30, 1946), minister and editor, was born on a farm at Dorchester, Ontario, Canada. In 1890, he graduated in arts from Victoria University, and became a Methodist probationer. Four years later, he graduated in divinity from the same school, and was ordained. He married Laura Harvie on September 11, 1895. Creighton began his ministry in the pastorate, but, in 1900, he joined the staff of *The Christian Guardian* as assistant editor. Six years later, he became its editor. He remained in that position until the time of church union in 1925, and then served as editor of *The New Outlook*, the paper of the new United Church of Canada, until he retired in 1937. After his retirement, he continued writing, and was correspondent for the Religious News Service of New York until a few months before his death in Toronto in 1946. Creighton could express strong convictions, but, as one observer stated, he was "by disposition and intellect disqualified" for religious controversy: "Always he heard the other side." His breadth of view served his church well during a crucial period as Methodists prepared for and then entered church union.

Marilyn Färdig Whiteley

CROSBY, FANNY (March 24, 1820–February 12, 1915), gospel hymn writer, was born Frances Jane Crosby in Putnam County, New York. Blinded at six weeks by an improper treatment for an eye infection, she was nevertheless a very active child. While a student at the New York Institution for the Blind (New York City) 1835–1843, she became a minor celebrity as a poet. Her first book of poetry was published in 1844. After graduation, she taught at the school until 1858. She began putting her verse to **music** in 1851, and was writing hymns by the mid-1860s. Crosby wrote as many as 9,000 hymns. Two of her most famous collaborators were **Ira D. Sankey** and William H. Doane. She was the premier hymnist of the gospel song period (ca. 1870–1920), writing in a popular style that spoke to the emotions. She made frequent public appearances, was active in a ministry to railroad workers and in city rescue missions, and supported the **temperance** movement. Raised a Presbyterian, she converted to Methodism in 1850. In 1858, she married Alexander Van Alstyne, a fellow teacher. He died in 1902. They had one child who died in infancy. Fanny Crosby died in Bridgeport, Connecticut, where she is buried.

Susan E. Warrick

CROSBY, THOMAS (1840–January 13, 1914), missionary, was born in Pickering, Yorkshire, England. At 16, he immigrated with his family to **Canada**, eventually settling in Woodstock, Ontario. It was there that he was converted, and he found himself drawn toward missionary work. He responded to an appeal for volunteers for Indian work in British Columbia, and began the work that he later described in two books, *Among the Ankomenums*, and *Up and Down the Pacific Coast*. A few years later Crosby married Emma Douse, daughter of a Methodist minister. They spent most of their missionary careers based at Port Simpson, British Columbia, but Crosby's work was not limited to that place. Using a steamer, "Glad Tidings," he took the gospel to countless bays and coves up and down the Pacific coast. Crosby was elected president of the British Columbia **Conference** in 1897, and was moved to Victoria at that time. In 1906, while on missionary deputation work in the East, his health broke down. He recovered sufficiently to return home, and spent the remaining seven years of his life in retirement.

Marilyn Färdig Whiteley

CZECHOSLOVAKIA. *See* EUROPE.

– D –

DEACON. The Greek word *diakonos* is used a number of times in the New Testament to describe a servant ministry which may have included **women**. By the beginning of the second century several sources refer to deacons as a recognizable group of ministers distinct from **elders**/presbyters and bishops when they too emerge as a separate ministry. Like bishops and presbyters their **ordination** was by prayer and the imposition of hands. Deacons were given liturgical functions (to preach, to perform the marriage ceremony, to bury the dead, and to assist at the **eucharist** by reading the gospel, leading the prayers of the people, preparing the elements of bread and wine, and helping distribute communion) as well as pastoral duties (oversight of the church's finances and care for the poor and the sick). In the Middle Ages, the diaconate became no more than a probationary period for candidates for the presbyterate, increasingly of brief duration, and their traditional pastoral and liturgical functions were commonly exercised by presbyters.

John Wesley ordained a few of his preachers deacons prior to becoming elders beginning in 1784. Methodist deacons in America followed the diminished role of Catholic and Anglican deacons in the Post-Reformation period. The pressures of urbanization and industrialization led Methodists in the late 19th century to admit women to an order of **deaconess**, a special permanent diaconate. Missionary pressures led many autonomous churches overseas in the early 20th century to abandon transitional deacons as serving no useful purpose as in the Korean Methodist Church (1930). Ecumenical pressure in the late 20th century promoted a reformed, lifelong, service-driven, world-oriented diaconate (*see* ECUMENISM). After 1996, persons on the way to becoming elders in the **UMC** were no longer ordained deacon first. A new, permanent order of deacon emerged. As ordained servants of Christ in the world, deacons proclaim, witness to, and do the work of compassion, justice, and reconciliation. Although responsible for their own employment and nonitinerant, their places of service are subject to episcopal appointment. British Methodists adopted a revived permanent diaconate in 1993.

Kenneth E. Rowe

DEACONESS MOVEMENT. The New Testament concept of deaconess work was revived in 1833 by the German pastor Theodor Fliedner at Kaiserwerth on the Rhine. Industrialization in America and Europe, with its insatiable demand for cheap labor, created serious urban problems, and eventually led Protestantism to notice the temporal as well as the spiritual needs of the urban poor. The idea that deaconesses could supply the mother element in the church made more credible the idea of revising the female diaconate, a ministry of service historically and scripturally traceable to the apostolic church. **Lucy Rider Meyer**, principal of the **Chicago Training School** for City, Home, and Foreign Missions, was not the only American Methodist voice speaking about the need for deaconesses, but she was one to act on her convictions. On April 13, 1887, she proposed to the school's Executive Committee that several **women** remain on after term's end in May, to concentrate on house-to-house visiting among Chicago's immigrants. That fall, a few of the women chose to continue their work. They moved to 17 West Erie Street, calling their residence a deaconess home. In May 1888, **General Conference**, acting on memorials from the Bengal Conference (India) and Rock River Conference (Illinois), recognized the office of deaconess in the **MEC**. Between 1888 and 1908, the deaconess office was established in all the predecessors of the **UMC**.

In England, **Thomas B. Stephenson** founded the Wesley Deaconess Order (Wesleyan Methodist Church) in 1890, with headquarters at Mewburn House, Bonner Road, London. The next year, Thomas J. Cope founded a similar order with the **United Methodist Free Churches**, and in 1895 J. Flanagan established a Sisters' Settlement to serve the **Primitive Methodist Church**.

Mary Agnes Dougherty and Susan E. Warrick

DENMARK. *See* EUROPE.

DICKEY, SARAH ANN (April 25, 1838–January 23, 1904), **UB** educator of freedmen, was born near Dayton, Ohio. She attended school and received a teacher's certificate (1857) despite indifferent relatives. From 1857 to 1863, she taught in country schools near Dayton. She joined the UB in 1858. Rejected for missionary service in Sierra Leone, she taught for two years in a UB freedmen's school in Vicksburg, Mississippi, which determined her life work. In 1869, she graduated from Mt. Holyoke Female Seminary and returned to Mississippi, where she taught in the American Missionary Association freedmen's school and a black public school. In 1875, she opened Mt. Hermon Female Seminary, a nonsectarian boarding school for black girls at Clinton. After her death the school was taken over by the American Missionary Association, and finally closed in 1924. In

1896, she was ordained a UB minister. She died in Clinton, Mississippi, eight years later and was buried on the school grounds.

Barbara E. Campbell

DICKINS, JOHN (August 24, 1747–September 27, 1798), editor, publisher, and **MEC** minister, was born in London. Possibly educated at London and Eton College, he came to America before 1774. He was converted in Virginia and became a traveling preacher in the Methodist movement in 1777. In 1780 he was forced to locate because his voice was gone. He married Elizabeth Yancey, and, in 1783, **Francis Asbury** persuaded him to enter the **itineracy** again, placing him at **John Street Chapel,** New York. Mrs. Dickins was the first woman to live in a Methodist parsonage in America. He was the first to welcome **Thomas Coke** to America when he arrived in 1784 with Wesley's plan for American Methodism. He attended the **Christmas Conference** of 1784 and was elected a **deacon.** He made the motion to name the new church the MEC in America. In 1786, he prepared its first **Discipline.** In 1789 he was appointed to St. George's MEC, Philadelphia, where he founded the MEC book business, becoming the first book editor of the MEC. He used £125 of his own money to begin the business, publishing 114,000 books and pamphlets before his death from yellow fever.

Frederick E. Maser

DISCIPLINE. When in 1753 **John Wesley** published his *Complete English Dictionary* he did not include the word "discipline," no more than did Samuel Johnson in his massive two-volume work in 1755. Perhaps part of the reason was that this was a word seldom used and difficult to define. In his second edition (1764) Wesley used four words, "strictness, instruction, correction, order," of which the first word represented the expected mind-set of the early Methodists, the fourth underlined churchmanship. As an Anglican clergyman in Georgia he was subject to William Beveridge's *Codex Canonum*, the collection of apostolic canons and decrees of General Councils which set the rules for the Greek Church, which Wesley twice used in September 1736, including a complaint about irregular procedures: "Oh discipline! Where art thou to be found? Not in England, or (as yet) in

America." In neither sense did Wesley use this word frequently. In his journal for August 17, 1750, however, the context shows that already he was also thinking of the Methodist societies as subject to ecclesiastical as well as personal discipline: "Through all Cornwall I find the societies have suffered great loss from want of discipline. Wisely said the ancients, 'The soul and body make a man; the spirit and discipline make a Christian.'" Wesley used the same quotation in his sermon, "The Late Work of God in North America" (1778), "Those who were more or less affected by Mr. Whitefield's (see WHITEFIELD, GEORGE) preaching had no discipline at all. . . . They were formed into no societies. They had no Christian connection with each other." This was one of his constant complaints in the British Isles, too: "I advise Mr. Cole to instruct the next preachers in the nature of the case, and to encourage them to persist in the whole Methodist discipline" (1786). He had written to **Thomas Rankin** in July 1774, when the British ties with American Methodism were fraying, "In yours of May the 30th you give me an agreeable account of your little Conference at Philadelphia. I think b[rother] Shadford and you desire no novelties, but love good old Methodist Discipline as well as Doctrine" (see SHADFORD, GEORGE).

Personal discipline remained strongly enforced during Wesley's lifetime by the **General Rules** of the Methodist societies, first published in 1743, and regularly handed out and explained to each new member. These were simply summarized as "doing no harm . . . , doing good of every possible sort . . . attending upon all the ordinances of God." If after admonishment and trial "he repent not, he hath no more place among us." Even more insistent were the rules of the intimate single sex "band societies." See SOCIETIES, CLASSES, AND BANDS.

As the Methodists grew more numerous and widespread, personal discipline, so important for the good standing of the societies, became stabilized by a form of ecclesiastical discipline, the ordering of the societies by Wesley's "assistants" and "helpers," their own training and rules and stationing in **circuits**, and movement around their circuits; the marshalling of other laymen and (especially!) **women**. This was done at the annual **conferences** begun by Wesley in 1744, which were subdivided from 1749 into subsidiary quarterly meetings of the circuits. The conferences periodically summarized their decisions in occasional "Large" *Minutes.* The most significant of these was that of 1780. Upon this was based three-quarters of the polity of the newly created American Methodist Church of 1785. It bore a similar title, but had the subtitle, "composing a Form of Discipline." From 1787 this became *A Form of Discipline for the Ministers, Preachers, and Members of the Methodist Episcopal Church in America.* The subsequent story of its quadrennial changes demonstrates the history of the denomination and its divisions and reunions. *See also* DOCTRINAL STANDARDS.

Frank Baker

DISCIPLINE. *See* Discipline.

DIVORCE. Although **John Wesley** and his wife, **Mary Vazeille Wesley**, lived separately for roughly 24 of the 30 years they were married, divorce was not an option. Scripture was clear: "What God has joined together, let no one separate" (Mt 19:6, Mk 10:9). Centuries of Christian tradition, as well as the canons of Wesley's own Church of England, refused to countenance divorce. This opposition carried over into American Methodism, whose earliest *Disciplines* do not even mention divorce and provide no guidelines for solemnizing the **marriage**s of divorced persons.

During the second half of the 19th century, churches in the **UMC** tradition acknowledged the growing reality of divorce and established rules for pastors asked to officiate at weddings of divorced persons. In 1877, the **UB General Conference** declared that ministers "should not solemnize the marriage of persons who have been divorced for any offense other than adultery." The **MECS** permitted the solemnization of the marriage of divorcees only if the divorced person was the "innocent party," the one not guilty of extramarital sexual activity (Mt 19:9). When the **MC** was founded in 1939, the general phrase, "other vicious conditions," was added to adultery as justifiable reasons for a divorce and for officiating at the marriage of "innocent" divorced persons.

The UMC recognizes in its *Book of Discipline* that a married couple may be "estranged beyond reconciliation." In such instances, "divorce is a regrettable alternative," yet the legal fact of divorce does not dissolve "other covenantal relationships resulting from the marriage," such as "the nurture and support of children." "Divorce," the

UMC's Social Principles (*see* SOCIAL CREED) continue, "does not preclude a new marriage." This applies to clergy as well as laity; the UMC has divorced and remarried pastors, district **superintendents**, and bishops—something unthinkable as recently as 1950.

John G. McEllhenney

DOBSON, HUGH WESLEY (March 4, 1879–June 5, 1956), minister, was born in Molesworth, Huron County, Ontario, **Canada**, but later moved with his family to Manitoba. In 1901, he was received on probation for the Methodist ministry. He earned both the B.A. and B.D. degrees at Wesley College in Winnipeg, Manitoba, and was ordained in 1906. In 1908, he married Edythe Thomas. Dobson's only pastorate after ordination was at Grenfell, Saskatchewan. From 1911 to 1914, he taught at Regina College in Regina, Saskatchewan, holding the newly created Chair of Biology and Human Relations. Then in 1914 he became Western Field Secretary of the Department of Evangelism and Social Service of the Methodist Church. Following church union in 1925, he remained in a similar position in the United Church of Canada, moving from Regina to Victoria, British Columbia, in 1926. He served as president of British Columbia **Conference** in 1941–1942. As field secretary for the western provinces, Dobson gave vigorous and informed leadership in the areas of **temperance** and family and social welfare, including health care and social hygiene. He retired in June of 1949, but continued to work part-time until March 1951. He died in Vancouver.

Marilyn Färdig Whiteley

DOCTRINAL STANDARDS. Methodism has been reluctant to frame its basic doctrinal beliefs in a confessional formula such as one finds in the Lutheran, Reformed, and Anglican traditions. The Wesleys maintained that they preached and taught the scriptural doctrines contained in the "Thirty-Nine Articles" of the Church of England as well as its *Homilies* and *Book of Common Prayer*. The Model Deed (1763) which **John Wesley** devised for his meetinghouses and chapels did specify, however, that those who preached in those places should preach the doctrines found in his four volumes of sermons and *Explanatory Notes upon the New Testament*, thereby establishing doctrinal standards. Furthermore, in 1784, when Wesley sent his **worship** book to America, *The Sunday Service of the Methodists in North America. With Other Occasional Services*, to guide the liturgical life of the newly formed **MEC**, it contained his revision of the Church of England's "Thirty-Nine Articles," which he had revised to Twenty-Four Articles of Religion. American Methodists added one article to Wesley's twenty-four, which recognized the legitimacy of the federal and state governments of the USA. Wesley's sermons, New Testament *Notes*, and the articles remain important doctrinal standards for Methodism in the USA. The sermons and *Notes* are more or less highly regarded among Methodists elsewhere in the world. The **UMC** lists all three as "Doctrinal Standards" in its *Book of Discipline* and adds a fourth standard, the Confession of Faith of the former **EUB**. Some consider these doctrinal standards merely important historical documents, while others view them as parameters within which Methodist preaching and teaching should take place. *See also* DISCIPLINE.

Charles Yrigoyen, Jr.

DOMINICAN REPUBLIC. *See* LATIN AMERICA AND THE CARIBBEAN.

DORSEY, DENNIS B. (December 28,1799–March 18,1860), American preacher who was instrumental in the creation of the **MP**, was born in Baltimore County, Maryland, but reared in Brooke County, Virginia. Following his **conversion** in 1817, he joined the Baltimore **Conference** (MEC) in 1820 and served in Loudon, Mahoning, East Wheeling, Huntington, Bedford, and Harford **Circuits**. In April 1827 the Baltimore Conference brought Dorsey to trial for circulating "an improper periodical work," *Mutual Rights*, advocating lay representation in the church and opposing the **episcopacy**. He was not appointed. One year later he failed to appear at conference and was expelled. For two years, starting in September 1828, he edited and published the *Mutual Rights and Christian Intelligencer* and during this time studied medicine, graduating from the Washington Medical College of Baltimore in 1831. In 1828, he helped to organize the Associated Methodist Churches, which became the MP in 1830. He moved to Wheeling, West Virginia, and gave up itinerating to practice medicine in 1832. He served as president of the Pittsburgh Conference in 1834, and as pastor of Sixth Street Church, Cincinnati, in 1854. He died at his son's home in Fairmont, West Virginia.

Robert J. Williams

DOW, LORENZO (October 16, 1777–February 2, 1834) was a well-known evangelist, and **PEGGY HOLCOMB DOW** (1780–January 6, 1820), was a prototypical preacher's wife. Lorenzo Dow was born and raised in Coventry, Connecticut. There he had a dramatic evangelical **conversion**, united with the local Methodist society (*see* SOCIETIES, CLASSES, AND BANDS), and began to preach. Much to the consternation of **MEC** superiors, Lorenzo became a maverick Methodist who itinerated wherever the Spirit led him. Despite continuous opposition both within and without the church, he was responsible for thousands of conversions to Christ (and subsequent accessions to Methodism) in the USA, **Ireland**, and England. In the latter country, Lorenzo's promotion of **camp meetings** was partially responsible for the formation of the **Primitive Methodist** Church. Lorenzo consciously cultivated a popular perception of himself as an "eccentric," evidenced by his unusual dress, bizarre actions, reputed clairvoyance, and histrionic preaching. He colorfully narrated his exploits in a popular autobiographical journal. Later editions of Lorenzo's journal also included the journal of his first wife, Peggy Holcomb Dow. Peggy's account narrated the "vicissitudes" and privations of her life as the "rib" of an itinerant preacher. Historian Leonard Sweet views Peggy Dow as the archetypal example of a woman who sacrificed her own identity on behalf of her husband's vocation.

Douglas M. Strong

DREISBACH, JOHN (June 5, 1789–August 20, 1871), **EA** minister, was born in Union County, Pennsylvania. Dreisbach was converted in 1806 and received a license to preach the following year from **Jacob Albright**, founder of the EA. Dreisbach began his career as a traveling minister in Pennsylvania and in 1814 was elected the first **presiding elder** in the church. In his early years Dreisbach frequently traveled with Albright. From 1820 to 1831 Dreisbach served as publishing agent for the denomination. In 1831, he moved his family to

Ohio, but due to recurring illness was able to preach only intermittently during the next 23 years. At the **General Conference** of 1854, Dreisbach was elected editor of the church's English newspaper, the *Evangelical Messenger*. He had to resign this position three years later due to poor health. In addition to his regular ministry, Dreisbach helped compile the EA's first hymnal in 1817. In later years he became a prolific writer of original hymns. Dreisbach also had an interest in politics, serving two years in the Pennsylvania legislature. Although he became unable to actively engage in ministry, Dreisbach was revered in his later years as one of the important early leaders of the church.

Daryl M. Elliott

DRESS. John Wesley included plainness of dress among the ways Methodists could give evidence of their full commitment to a life of love. He argued for cheap, clean, simple linen or woolen apparel by pointing to biblical texts such as I Timothy 2:9–10 and I Peter 3:3–4. Using those passages as his grounding, Wesley reflected on human experience and concluded that expensive clothes puff up their wearers, promote vanity, incite anger, inflame lust, retard the pursuit of holiness, and steal from God and the poor. "Every shilling," Wesley wrote in 1786, "which you needlessly spend on your apparel is in effect stolen from God and the poor." American Methodists underscored Wesley's counsel. At the 1784 **Christmas Conference**, they asked, "Should we insist on the rules concerning dress?" "By all means," they replied. "This is no time to give any encouragement to superfluity of apparel." They discouraged the wearing of gold jewelry, silk and velvet, glaring colors, wigs, and curled hair. In 1800, **Nathan Bangs**, later a prominent MEC leader, experienced **conversion**. Immediately he had the ruffles taken from his shirt and the long cue from his hair. During the ensuing decades, American Methodists progressively conformed themselves, in Wesley's words, to "that tyrant of fools, fashion."

John G. McEllhenney

DRINKHOUSE, EDWARD JACOB (March 26, 1830–April 18, 1903), editor and historian, was a longtime pastor in the Maryland **Conference**

of the **MP**. In the 1850s, he served charges in Potomac, Cumberland, and Baltimore, Maryland, and in Harper's Ferry and Jefferson, Virginia (now West Virginia). He later filled prominent MP pulpits in Philadelphia (First Church) and Washington, D.C. (Ninth Street). He was a representative to the MP **General Conference** for six successive sessions. In 1875, Drinkhouse became editor of the denominational newspaper, the *MP*, an appointed position that he held with distinction for 18 years until his retirement. Drinkhouse did much to establish a firm ecclesiastical identity for the second generation of MPs. He accomplished this through his role as an effective editor of the paper and by his authorship of a two-volume chronicle of the rise and development of the denomination, *History of Methodist Reform*, the most comprehensive historical account ever written about the MP. Drinkhouse is buried in Oak Hill cemetery in Washington, D.C.

Douglas M. Strong

– E –

ECUADOR. *See* LATIN AMERICA AND THE CARIBBEAN.

ECUMENISM is the striving to overcome divisions that separate Christian churches and Christian persons from one another through dialogue, joint action, councils of churches, and efforts toward unification. The word comes from the Greek word *oikoumene,* which means literally the "whole inhabited earth." In a broader sense, ecumenism is the concern for whatever divides the human community. However, it does not usually include interfaith or interreligious dialogue or programs. In 1951, the **WCC** used ecumenical "to describe everything that relates to the whole task of the whole church to bring the gospel to the whole world." Christian unity is understood as a gift to be received and to be made visible. Jesus prayed for the oneness of all Christians in John 17. Current expressions of ecumenism on a worldwide basis include the WCC, organized in 1948 as a commingling of the Faith and Order and Life and Work movements and joined later by the International Missionary Council, and the **WMC** comprising more than 70 churches in the Wesleyan tradition from more than 90 countries. There are numerous regional and national councils of churches. In the USA four Methodist churches, the **AME, AMEZ, CME,** and **UMC,** join with five other communions in the Consultation on Church Union (proposed in 1962 by Presbyterian Eugene Carson Blake). In Great Britain several Methodist bodies reunited in 1932 but efforts at Methodist–Anglican reunion have not been successful as of 2004, although conversations between the two continue.

Robert J. Williams

EDUCATION is the process through which human groups impart knowledge and skills that enable persons to preserve valued memories and solve new problems. In its earliest form, prior to the development of writing, education consisted primarily of learning by memory the stories of a people, their history, and their heroes. The texts that became the Hebrew scriptures were no doubt passed on in this way for many generations before they were written. By the time of Jesus, an educator or teacher who knew the precepts of the law of Moses and could teach others to follow them had a well-established role in Jewish life. Jesus was seen as such a person by his contemporaries, who often called him by the title "rabbi," which means "teacher." Jesus, however, taught in ways that did not simply follow the letter of the law. He challenged his hearers to think about what God truly requires, even when that contradicts what the law has taught (Matthew 5:17–48). This critical skill, which gives the ability to rethink customary practices in light of both their original purpose and contemporary needs, is also part of education, along with the preservation of the heritage of the past.

   In Christianity, education has always encompassed a good deal more than the minimal requirements of preserving the traditions of the faith. Early Christian writers and teachers, including Jerome, Clement of Alexandria, and Augustine were well educated in Greek and Latin culture, and when the institutions of Roman learning largely disappeared from Western Europe, Christian monks kept alive not only the religious knowledge but also the law and the science of their day. By the 13th century, newly founded universities began to spread learning more broadly, but literacy was still largely confined to those educated for the clergy. The invention of printing made reading more accessible, and Protestantism encouraged all people to read and understand the Bible for themselves.

Methodism sought to care for a broad range of needs among the working people who became its members. This included their needs for basic education. Wesley provided abridged versions of religious classics for the education of Methodists, and Methodists in North America quickly established a publishing house as part of their organization as a distinct religious denomination. **Sunday schools**, providing elementary education for children who could not otherwise attend school, became common in England and the USA. As Methodists spread across the North American continent, they organized schools and colleges everywhere they went. The growth of public elementary and secondary education largely supplanted the Methodist schools, but institutions of higher education flourished. In the late 19th century, Methodist missionaries carried the same educational impulse to other parts of the world.

During the 20th century, Methodist educational initiatives concentrated on teaching materials for religious education in the churches, developing an extensive knowledge of the Bible and skills for Christian living among both children and adults. Methodist interest in higher education continues in several hundred Methodist-affiliated colleges, universities, and seminaries worldwide, including Africa University, at Old Mutare, Zimbabwe, which opened in 1992.

Robin W. Lovin

ELDER. In origin a Latin word translating the Greek term, *presbyteros*, meaning "elder" which is used in parts of the New Testament to refer to certain individuals within primitive Christian communities. Exactly who these people were is not clear. Were they simply those who were elder in years, or those who were older in conversion, or were they a specific group elected in some way to take leadership or form a governing body? In the earliest Christian communities the term presbyter is used interchangeably with bishops. By the early second century many local churches seemed to be governed by a council of presbyters/elders and only slowly did the office of bishop emerge everywhere as distinct and superior to that of the presbyters, who became an advisory council to the bishop in pastoral and administrative functions. By the third century bishops began delegating to a presbyter presidency at **baptisms** and **eucharists**. Nevertheless even in the fourth century many presbyters still assisted their bishops liturgically, and it was not until later that presbyters were normally the sole pastor of a church and hence its regular liturgical president. Not until presbyters assumed most of the bishop's former liturgical functions were they described as priests.

At the Reformation the Church of England and some Lutheran churches continued to use the designation "priest" for the presbyter, but most other churches including the Methodists rejected "priest" and "presbyter" as having unacceptable sacerdotal connotations and returned to the term "elder." In 1784 **John Wesley** ordained a few of his preachers **deacons** prior to their becoming elders. This practice was quickly abandoned in Britain but retained in American Methodism until 1996. After 1996, elders in the **UMC** are no longer ordained deacons first. Following completion of formal preparation, the order of elder is conferred first by the vote of the clergy members of the Annual Conference and then by the formal rite of **ordination** with the laying on of hands by a bishop and other elders. As ministers of word, sacrament, and order, elders are itinerant and subject to episcopal appointment. **Women** were granted full clergy rights in 1956. *See also* EPISCOPACY; PRESIDING ELDER.

Kenneth E. Rowe

EL SALVADOR. *See* LATIN AMERICA AND THE CARIBBEAN.

EMBURY, PHILIP (September 29, 1728–ca. 1773), one of the lay founders of American Methodism, was born in **Ireland** to a family of Palatine Germans who had immigrated there early in the century. Schooled in German and English and apprenticed as a carpenter, he was converted by Methodists in late 1752 and became a class leader (*see* SOCIETIES, CLASSES, AND BANDS) and local preacher. In 1760, with his new wife and a handful of others, Embury sailed to New York, where he set himself up as a schoolmaster and joined Trinity Lutheran Church in lower Manhattan, remaining active there through 1766. That year, responding to his cousin **Barbara Heck's** fear that their immigrant community would "all go to hell together" (she had observed a group of them playing cards), Embury reclaimed his Methodism and set up a small class. Soon a rigging loft was hired for meetings, quickly followed by the construction of their own Wesley Chapel on **John Street** in 1768. Embury not only helped build it but also preached the first sermon and served as trustee and treasurer. In 1770, Embury moved upstate to Washington County, where he founded another Methodist society, but within a few years died suddenly from a mowing injury. His remains were moved from their unmarked farm grave to the town of Ashgrove in 1832.

Charles Wallace, Jr.

EMORY, JOHN (April 11, 1789–December 16, 1835), **MEC** pastor, editor, and bishop, was born in Spaniard's Neck, Queen Anne County, Maryland. He trained for a career in law, graduating from Washington College in 1804 and was admitted to the bar in 1808. Following an experience of saving grace he resolved to shift from law to ministry and became a class leader (*see* SOCIETIES, CLASSES, AND BANDS), exhorter, and local preacher, joining the Philadelphia **Conference** in 1810. In 1818, he was transferred to the Baltimore Conference and served Foundry Church in Washington and subsequently churches in Annapolis, Hagerstown, and Baltimore. At the 1816 **General Conference**, he favored the election of **presiding elders**. Emory's support for this in 1820 prevented his election to General Conference in 1824. He served as assistant book agent to **Nathan Bangs** and then as book agent, editing and contributing many articles to *The Methodist Magazine*. He edited several works including the first American edition of Wesley's *Works*. He opposed the reformers who organized the **MP** by writing *The Defence of Our Fathers*. He assisted in the formation of Wesleyan University and served as president of the Board of Trustees of Dickinson College. After his election as bishop in 1832, he opposed the abolitionist ministers in the New England and New Hampshire Conferences. He died near Reisterstown, Maryland and is buried in Mt. Olivet Cemetery, Baltimore.

Robert J. Williams

ENDICOTT, JAMES (May 8, 1865–March 9, 1954), minister and missionary, was born in Devonshire, England. At 17, he immigrated with his family to Ontario, **Canada**. Soon he became a probationer for the Methodist ministry, and did church work in Ontario and Western Canada before he began theological studies at Wesley College in Winnipeg, Manitoba. In 1893, Endicott was ordained and married Sarah Diamond of Lucan, Ontario. Endicott sailed with his bride for China to serve in the recently opened West China Methodist mission (*see* ASIA). There he gave leadership especially in church publishing and **education**. He returned to Canada in 1910. In 1912, Endicott became field secretary of the Missionary Society of the Methodist Church, and the following year he was elected general secretary of foreign missions. After church union in 1925, he served as secretary of the Board of Missions of the United Church of Canada until his retirement in 1937. His first wife died in 1925, and he married Marietta Wilson McIrvine in 1930. Endicott became the second moderator of the United Church in 1926, and during part of his two-year term he toured foreign **missions** explaining the new church to those in the field. He participated in the Foreign Missions Conference of North America and in the International Missionary Council. Endicott died in Toronto.

Marilyn Färdig Whiteley

ENGLAND. *See* BRITISH METHODISM.

ENGLISH, DONALD (July 20, 1930–August 28, 1998), an evangelical conservative in his InterVarsity Fellowship days, restored evangelicalism to Methodist leadership through an irenical and mediating realism. He was theology tutor at Hartley Victoria College and Wesley College, Bristol, England, 1972–1982, and general secretary of the Home Mission Division, 1982–1995. He was the only minister since the union of 1932 to be elected twice as president of the Conference (1978,1990). He was Moderator of the Free Church Federal Council in 1986 and chair of the **World Methodist Council** Executive Committee, 1991–1996. The author of many books relating Christianity to modern society, he was a noted biblical expositor and preacher at many conferences.

Gordon S. Wakefield

ENTHUSIASM. John Wesley and his Methodist followers were often accused by their opponents of displaying "enthusiasm," an accusation they consistently rejected. In modern usage Methodists surely welcome such a description as it denotes energy and zeal! An explanation of such different responses is found in the changing meanings of enthusiasm over the intervening 200 years, yet in both periods the experiences that called forth the word remain central to Methodist tradition.

In its Greek origins the word denoted "possession" by the divine. Plato refers to poets, mystics, and philosophers as having enthusiasm and means thereby that they were "inspired" by the divine. Christians through history retained such an understanding although often struggling over its exact application. Determining the reliability and truthfulness of claims to divine inspiration is difficult at best. With the renewal of new "prophesies" and appeals to direct inspiration, Protestant reformers identified the term with radical individualistic Christian groups spawned by the Reformation. In such cases spiritual "possession" was judged as leading to false doctrine manifesting itself in many aberrations in **worship** and daily life.

Seventeenth-century English **Puritan** reforms often attracted comparisons with the earlier radical movements and were judged to be "enthusiasm." Englishmen, including the moderate Puritans, found claims of inspiration for unusual doctrines and outbreaks of distinctive emotional and spiritual zeal to be highly questionable. They were often judged enthusiastic and abhorrent. By Wesley's period the word had taken on a meaning that in modern understanding would be better expressed as "fanaticism."

Wesley's conviction that one directly experiences God's presence in **conversion, assurance,** perfection of love (*see* CHRISTIAN PERFECTION), and Christian fellowship drew the label of "enthusiasm" from many of his detractors. The zeal and excitement of Methodist meetings wherein the phenomenon of an unusual "spiritual" presence was experienced contributed to such labeling.

Accusations grew vehement enough that Wesley chose to answer them in "The Nature of Enthusiasm," a sermon clarifying his understanding of the word. The sermon suggests that among his contemporaries those who claim an active **faith** will be falsely labeled with enthusiasm, "if you aim at the religion of the heart, if you talk of righteousness and peace and joy in the Holy Ghost." Nevertheless, he proposed that if the word is to carry the meaning of fanatic or madman then it could properly be applied to many, for example, those who imagine they have the **grace** of God but fail to display it in their lives, those who claim special "gifts" from God, those who suppose that God "dictates the very words they speak," those who claim to speak for God without studying His word, those who take pride in a special relation to God, along with others.

Appropriating enthusiasm to describe false and prideful Christianity, Wesley in the sermon adroitly defended a true faith animated by God's active presence. The evangelical movement's achievements perhaps helped change the meaning of the word so that we may embrace again a proper sense of God's lively empowerment of a zestful, energetic Christian life when we speak of enthusiasm.

Robert C. Monk

ENVIRONMENTALISM. Scientific investigation of the natural world fascinated **John Wesley**. This fascination motivated him to produce a general-reader digest of the best research, titled *A Survey of the Wisdom of God in the Creation* (1775). He was not merely a popularizer of science, however; he was a theologian of the relationship between humans and their environment. Wesley believed that the "dominion" over nature given by God to men and women (Genesis 1:26) was meant to be a God-like management; that sin often downgraded this caring role into an exploiting one; that one way **salvation** becomes visible is through actions recognizing that Christ is "the life of everything that lives in any kind or degree," specifically, vegetables and animals (Sermon 77, "Spiritual Worship," II.3). Therefore Wesley admonished his preachers to be merciful to their horses, gently riding them and personally overseeing their care at the end of a journey. He also declared that loving parents forbid their children "to hurt or give pain to anything that has life" (Sermon 95, "On the Education of Children," §25).

The **UMC** reiterated Wesley's assertion that human beings are managers, not exploiters, of creation during the last third of the 20th century by placing "The Natural World" first in the enumeration of Social Principles in the *Book of Discipline* (*see* DISCIPLINE; SOCIAL CREED). It begins: "All creation is the Lord's, and we are responsible for the ways in which we use and abuse it" — following which are paragraphs dealing with "Water, Air, Soil, Minerals, Plants," "Energy

Resources Utilization," "Animal Life," "Space," "Science and Technology," and "Food Safety." Also there is a roughly 50-page section in the UMC's *Book of Resolutions* dealing with "The Natural World," which is subheaded "Environment/Energy." Some of this environmental concern was inspired by *Silent Spring* (1962), a book written by American marine biologist Rachel Carson (1907–1964) that sensitized many to their polluted environment. The major inspiration for theological environmentalism, however, was Wesley's fundamental insight that God has endowed human beings with sufficient intelligence to comprehend and defend the divine purposes disclosed in all created things.

John G. McEllhenney

EPISCOPACY is the ecclesiastical practice of most American Methodist denominations in utilizing bishops for presidential, sacerdotal, appointive, and other functions. Although subsequently eschewed by British Methodism, episcopacy was effectually originated by **John Wesley** in *The Sunday Service* of 1784 and his appointing **Thomas Coke** and **Francis Asbury** as **superintendent**s for America. Asbury's demurral unless the preachers elected him thwarted Wesley's continuing authority as underscored in 1787 by **conference** refusal to elect **Richard Whatcoat** superintendent and their adopting the title bishop. The 1784 **Christmas Conference** organized the **MEC,** affirmed Coke, and ordained Asbury. The preachers thereby retained sole control of conference membership and **ordination** while bishops exercised unlimited appointive power despite **James O'Kelly**'s schism. From 1792 preachers gained legislative power in quadrennial **General Conference**s.

Philip William Otterbein and **Martin Boehm** were named **UB** bishops in 1800. UBs evolved the term *episcopacy*, as did reinstituted **EA** bishops from 1839. The first black bishops were **AME Richard Allen** in 1816 and MEC Francis Burns for Liberia (1856). Nonepiscopal **MP** and **Wesleyan Methodist** Churches emerged from *Mutual Rights* and **antislavery** struggles in 1828–1830 and 1843, respectively. From 1845 MECS bishops wielded power as equals at General Conference. Old Constitution UBs departed over doctrinal issues in 1889. (*See* UNITED BRETHREN IN CHRIST, [OLD CONSTITUTION]. Recrimination and episcopal egos fragmented the EA from 1894 to 1922.

The service of the 538 **UMC** episcopal leaders from 1784 to 2003 ranged from a month to 53 years by **MC** Herbert Welch (1862–1969). Cities sought residential bishops, including Philadelphia, Oxford, Georgia, and Baltimore, where UBs built a bishop's residence, which is now mandated in each UMC episcopal area. Before jet travel, national and worldwide presidential duties prolonged bishops' absences from home.

Many bishops plucked from pastoral, publishing, or educational roles gladly sought or accepted election but **Wilbur Fisk** and **E. Stanley Jones** declined and **L. L. Hamline** later resigned (1852). Church trials exonerated James Cannon (**MECS**) but unfrocked Anton Bast (**MEC**).

Once missionary bishops were inferiors but now UMC Central Conference bishops preside over general agencies or the Council of Bishops. USA black MEC bishops date from 1920 while the 1939 MC union provided two MP bishops. **Women** arrived in 1980 with **Marjorie Matthews** and African-American Leontine Kelly in 1984. In 2003, 11 women, 14 African Americans, one Asian, and two Hispanic bishops served USA areas. Central Conference bishops include 11 Africans, four Europeans, and three Asians.

Episcopal duties include pastoral, celebrative, teaching, and executive tasks as well as ecumenical, civic, programmatic, visionary, and worldwide responsibilities. *See also* PRESIDING ELDER.

Edwin Schell

ESCHATOLOGY. The term eschatology, derived from the Greek word *eschatos*, refers to the doctrine of "the last things," such as death, the intermediate state, the second coming of Christ, the judgment, and the final consummation. Considering the question of death and the intermediate state, **John Wesley** affirmed the immortality of the soul (as well as the future resurrection of the body), denied the reality of purgatory, and made a distinction between hell (the receptacle of the damned) and hades (the receptacle of all separate spirits), and also between paradise (the antechamber of heaven) and heaven itself. In terms of the judgment itself, Wesley rejected the **Roman Catholic** notion of two judgments: a particular one at death and a later one at the consummation of things. However, similar to Catholicism, Wesley affirmed the reality of hell and noted that the punishments of the damned include *poena damni* (punishment of loss) and *poena sensus* (punishment of sense), though his emphasis was clearly on eternal life as both a present and a future reality. Gradations in heaven (Wesley listed three) will correspond to our "inward holiness, our works, and our sufferings." After the judgment, the heavens will pass away and the earth and all its works will be burnt up to prepare for the new creation in which even natural evil will be overcome.

Kenneth J. Collins

ESTONIA. *See* EUROPE.

ETHICS. *See* BIOMEDICAL ETHICS.

EUCHARIST is another name for the **sacrament** that has more commonly been called Holy Communion or the Lord's Supper. The term "Eucharist" comes from the Greek word for "thanksgiving" and is particularly appropriate for the celebratory mood evoked in the current UMC ritual. As opposed to **baptism,** which is received only once, Eucharist is an infinitely repeatable means through which divine **grace** is conveyed for converting, sustaining, and sanctifying God's people. The essence of the Eucharist is the fourfold action of taking the bread and wine, giving thanks to God for the gifts of creation and **salvation,** breaking the bread, and distributing the elements to be shared. Although laypersons can assist in the distribution, celebrants are to be ordained **elders** (exceptions are granted for unordained persons who are appointed to charges).

Eucharistic observances were a vital part of the evangelical movement that became Methodism. In a time when the Anglican Church offered the sacrament infrequently, **John Wesley** exhorted his followers to partake of communion as often as possible. He believed that the Eucharist was a powerful vehicle of divine grace upon which growth in holiness was dependent. (See his sermons, "The Means of **Grace**" and "The Duty of Constant Communion.") Wesley himself usually communed several times each week. The Wesleyan theology of Eucharist was most thoroughly expressed in the 166 *Hymns on the Lord's Supper*, published by John and Charles. In the organization of this work, five concepts of the Eucharist are developed. First, a memorial, not simply an intellectual recalling, but an *anamnesis* in which the death of Christ is made real and its benefits immediately accessible. Second, a sign and means of grace in which the presence of Christ is real and active. Third, a pledge of heaven by which believers receive a foretaste of the eternal fellowship of the saints. Fourth, a commemorative sacrifice, not repeated, but re-presented to God. Fifth, a sacrificial commitment of the believer in love and loyalty to Christ.

Wesley's "**Sunday Service**" ritual for the Eucharist was soon revised, shortened, and simplified by American Methodists. Celebration of the sacrament could not be weekly, as Wesley had recommended, because of the shortage of ordained elders. Instead, **camp meetings** and especially quarterly meetings on a charge, when the **presiding elder** came to preach and conduct business, were sacramental occasions. Methodists understood the Lord's Supper almost exclusively as a memorial recalling the death of Christ. They prided themselves on the "open table," in contrast to the Baptist practice of close communion. In the second half of the 20th century, Methodism began to recover the service of Word and Table as the normative order of **worship** for each Sunday. The ritual finalized in the 1989 UMC hymnal, after 17 years of trial and revision, is patterned largely on the practice of the early Christian church. Its mood is more celebratory than penitential. The intinction mode of communing is becoming increasingly popular. In accord with the recommendation in the baptismal ritual, most congregations commune baptized children.

Gayle Carlton Felton

EUROPE. Methodism in continental Europe has both a British and an American background. Both will be discussed, beginning with the British tradition. Knowledge about Methodism spread at an early stage to the European continent. However, even those who gladly spread news about the evangelical revival in Britain did not necessarily rejoice at the arrival of Methodist preachers in their own country. On the Continent, state churches dominated the scene and free churches struggled to find their place. In the beginning, Methodist presence on the Continent was dominated by three factors: private initiatives that were followed by officially sent missionaries; Methodists from Britain and not from the USA; the aim to renew state churches and not to build up a separate free church.

Gibraltar and the Channel Islands were British territories that became bridgeheads for Methodist outreach to two regions on the Continent. Soldiers brought Methodism to Gibraltar as early as 1769. They built a chapel long before a missionary was sent in 1804. From Gibraltar attempts were made to distribute **Bibles** in Catholic Spain despite legal prohibitions. After the Spanish Revolution of 1868, regular visits to several cities became possible. Ministry developed particularly well in Barcelona and from there to the Balearic Islands. From Gibraltar contacts were also established in Portugal, where a missionary was stationed in the northern city of Porto in 1871. On the Iberian Peninsula, schools became the most important Methodist institutions.

Methodism in Gibraltar is still linked to the British Methodist **Conference**. In 1955, the Spanish Methodists joined the Evangelical Church, a union of several Protestant bodies. In 2000, the united church had about 3,000 members. In Portugal, the Methodists became autonomous in 1996 and numbered about 1,500 professing members in 2000.

In 1775, Methodism came to the Channel Islands via Newfoundland, and developed an English and French ministry. Fifteen years later, a Methodist tradesman from Guernsey drew attention to spiritual needs in France. In 1791, **Thomas Coke** visited, hoping to establish Methodism in early revolutionary France, and designated a missionary to Normandy. Lasting effects only came with a new missionary in 1818. He formed Methodist societies within the Reformed Church (*see* SOCIETIES, CLASSES, AND BANDS). A religious revival among the French attracted many to Wesleyan Arminianism (*see* ARMINIUS, JACOBUS). Methodism developed best around Nîmes in the southeast. It spread to Protestant minorities in other cities as well as to the French-speaking part of Switzerland (1840–1900). French Methodism was among the first British mission fields to become an annual conference on its own (1852). It tried to maintain a role in bringing renewal to the Reformed Church as well as forming a church of its own. Under British pressure it entered a union with the Reformed Church in 1935. A small minority remained independent. In 2000, this united church had about 300 professing members and negotiations about joining the Switzerland/France annual conference of **UMC** were in progress.

For a short period, British Methodists ministered in Sweden (1826–1842) at the initial request of a British engineer. One of the missionaries, George Scott (1804–1874), had a strong impact on later leaders of free churches and on the establishment of societies for welfare and revival within the Lutheran state church. Because of his criticism of the spiritual life of the state church, Scott came under attack and was forced to leave the country. No new missionary was appointed to replace him.

For some decades British Methodists worked in Germany (1830–1897) and from there in Austria (1870–1897). As in other European work, the German initiative came from a layperson. The work began within the state church at a time when the establishment of dissenting churches was not allowed. Later a seminary and a deaconess training institution were established (*see* DEACONESS MOVEMENT). In 1870 a preacher was sent to Vienna, Austria. Several times, there were talks about uniting with one of the American branches of Methodism. In 1897, the British work in Germany and Austria (about 30 preachers and 2,400 professing members) became affiliated with the **MEC**.

The mission to Italy in 1861 was initiated by the British Wesleyan Methodist Missionary Society. Well-trained and liberally minded clergy were leaving the Roman Catholic Church. Some joined Protestant churches, including the Methodists. In 1871, **British Methodism** was the first Protestant denomination to open **worship** services in Rome. With the fascist government in the 1920s all Protestants came under pressure. Discussions between the British and the USA branches of Methodism in Italy finally led to the integration of the British into the American branch after World War II. The Methodist Church in Italy became autonomous from Britain in 1962. A process of federation with the Waldensian Church began in the late 1970s. In 2000, there were approximately 2,500 professing members in the Methodist Church.

Together with the British and the Irish Conferences, the autonomous or united churches in Portugal, Spain, and Italy belong to the **World Methodist Council** and to the European Methodist Council. The latter was established in 1993 to unite European Methodists who traced their origins to the British and American traditions.

Methodism in continental Europe also traces its origins to the USA. Several American Methodist churches began **missions** in Europe. The most widespread was undertaken by the MEC. It was fostered by two important factors: migration from Europe to the USA which grew to more than a million people per year toward the end of the 19th century; domestic foreign-language missions within the USA, especially among Danish/Norwegian, Swedish, and German-speaking immigrants. Up to the 1920s, these domestic missions in the USA counted more members than their respective language groups in Europe. Two German-speaking churches in the Methodist tradition, the **EA** (later **EC**) and the **UB**, also opened mission fields in German-speaking Europe. The history of their unions was different on the European continent from what happened in the USA. The **MECS** was the last major Methodist denomination to come to Europe, which it did after World War I.

In 1946, the EA and UB united to become the **EUB** and in 1968 the EUB joined the **MC** to form UMC. In the last decades of the 20th century, other Methodist churches have opened small missions in several European countries. Some of these missions have reached out to countries without any former Methodist presence. From the Korean Methodist Church missionaries have been sent to Kazakhstan, Kirghizia, Romania, and Tajikistan. Methodist Holiness churches have established missions such as the Church of the Nazarene to the Netherlands and the **Free Methodist Church** to Greece.

What follows is limited to the UMC and is organized according to its structure at the beginning of the 21st century. The first to be considered is the Central Conference of northern Europe and Eurasia. Geographically and historically, the area of Northern Europe and Eurasia is best subdivided into Scandinavia, the Baltic states, and Russia/Eurasia.

The first outreach from an American branch of Methodism to Scandinavia came by seamen and was not an organized mission endeavor. It was linked to the seamen's mission (Bethel Ship) in New York City, where immigrants arrived. Converts of the Bethel Ship mission were either immigrants or seamen returning to their native countries. Thus, laymen took Methodist testimonies back to Norway (1849), Sweden (in the early 1850s), Denmark (1857), and Finland (1859). The first missionaries were sent years later: to Norway in

1853, to Denmark in 1858, to Sweden in 1866–1867, and to Finland in 1883. The Bethel Ship mission was a proponent of **Phoebe Palmer**'s holiness message. In Scandinavia this message, with its optimistic conviction of the change brought about by God's **grace** in human life, collided with a Lutheranism which stressed the depth of sin clinging to all human beings. Methodism spread along the southern coastlines. The northern part of Scandinavia, sparsely populated, was only reached by Methodism toward the end of the 19th century. Around 1900, Sweden had the largest Methodist community on the Continent (over 15,000 adult members), but numbers began to decline shortly thereafter. In Norway, Thomas Ball Barratt (1862–1940), a Methodist pastor, was among the most convinced followers of the new Pentecostal revival in the early 20th century (*see* PENTECOSTALISM). He finally left the church and became an evangelist who influenced many leaders of the Pentecostal revival in Scandinavia. The drop in membership in Norway was important, but new evangelistic efforts helped to reverse the trend even before World War I. In Denmark, one of the pastors, Anton Bast (1867–1937), developed a strong social and diaconal program with Central Missions in several large cities, especially Copenhagen. He won the admiration and support of the royal family. In 1920, he became bishop of the newly created Central Conference of Northern Europe. Shortly after, he was accused before civil courts for misuse of church funds when he was a director of the Central Mission. He was finally forced to resign in 1927. The long legal battle involving Bast paralyzed Danish Methodism for decades.

Scandinavian Methodists were among the first on the Continent to send missionaries overseas. Foreign mission was a high priority during the first half of the 20th century. In 1949, there were almost 100 Scandinavian Methodists serving as foreign missionaries. At that time, there were 11,600 Methodists (professing members) in Sweden, 8,600 in Norway, 3,300 in Denmark, and 2,100 in Finland. Numbers have continued to decline. By 2000, there were 4,000 in Sweden, 5,000 in Norway, 1,400 in Denmark, and 1,300 in Finland.

In the Baltic states, Methodism arrived from the east (St. Petersburg and the Russian Empire) and from the west (the German Empire) when the Baltic still belonged to the Russian Empire. The MEC sent preachers to Lithuania in 1905, to Estonia in 1907, and to Latvia in

1911. The EA had contact with Latvia as early as 1908 and sent its first preacher from Germany in 1911. After World War I, the Baltic states became independent. Both churches continued their ministries with steady growth until World War II. With the Russian occupation, the Methodist presence was destroyed in Latvia and Lithuania, and only survived in Estonia amidst hardship and persecution. After political change, Methodism grew again in 1991 in Latvia and in 1995 in Lithuania. In 2000, there were around 2,000 professing members in Estonia, 500 in Latvia, and 300 in Lithuania.

The Central Conference also covers Eurasia (Russia and the other countries of the former Soviet Union). Beginnings of the work in Russia go back to the 19th century. From the Grand Duchy of Finland, which was governed by the Russian czar, MEC preachers went to St. Petersburg in 1889. The ministry covered five different languages and expanded to the Baltics. After the October Revolution of 1917, a **deaconess** was the only missionary remaining in St. Petersburg. In the early 1920s, the Methodist bishop of Central Europe developed a holistic proposal for a religious, educational, and agricultural program in cooperation with the Russian Orthodox Church, but failed because of fear of supporting Bolshevism. The Methodist work in St. Petersburg was terminated in the 1930s. Archival documents of police trials finally helped to prove a Methodist presence in Russia and facilitated official registration with the Russian Federation more than 60 years later. After the fall of communism, there was a rebirth of Methodism. In 2000, there were more than 5,000 professing members in Russia, the Ukraine, and Moldova, and the work has since been divided into four Annual Conferences.

A second important area is the Germany Central Conference of UMC. The German-speaking Methodist mission has always extended beyond Germany even if the latter at times covered territory much larger than today. The mission of the British branch united with the MEC in 1897. The latter had begun its mission to Germany in 1848 in the seaport city of Bremen, where most of the emigrants left the country. It stretched out to major German cities and from there to the surrounding cities, towns, and rural areas. In Saxony, Methodism was begun by lay initiative in 1850 and was soon united with the official German mission. Two churches established in the USA by German immigrants, the UB and the EA, also opened mission work in Europe. The UB began its mission in 1869 and handed it over to the MEC in 1905. The EA opened a mission in Germany in 1850. It began in the south of Germany as a work within the state church. Following new dissenter laws, it slowly developed toward an independent free church.

The **holiness movement**, led by Robert P. and Hannah W. Smith, swept into Europe in the 1870s and strengthened Methodist outreach. Until 1914, the MEC and the EA had spread to most regions of Germany and often worked side by side (29,000 professing members in the MEC; 16,600 in the EA). In some regions the EA was about the same size as the MEC. The German Empire, which covered large territories in Central Europe, became the strongest Methodist mission field on the whole continent and continued to grow.

In 1938, German Methodists wanted to form a Central Conference for Germany and elect a German bishop. During the Hitler regime, they succeeded in maintaining most of their activities, although with limitations in youth and diaconal work, but they had no prophetic voice. They were not prepared to face a totalitarian government. Words and acts of support for Jews came from Methodists in other countries such as Belgium, Poland, and Czechoslovakia, or by personal initiatives of Methodists like the Swiss vice-consul in Budapest. After World War II, German Methodism again experienced a period of growth until the end of the 1950s. At the time of union between MC and EUB in 1968, the latter influenced the shape of the new UMC in Germany. From 1968 to 1992 a separate Central Conference existed for the eastern part of Germany, the former German Democratic Republic. In 2003, there were about 40,000 professing members in Germany.

The third area of UMC ministry is the Central Conference of Central and Southern Europe (Geneva Area), which includes countries that were left in Central Europe after the establishment of the Central Conference of Germany and the dissolution of the Central Conference of Western and Southern Europe (Paris Area) in the late 1930s. The latter had been created in the early 1920s when the MEC wanted to expand its mission to Roman Catholic and Eastern Orthodox countries and when the Congregationalist American Board of Commissioners for Foreign Missions (ABCFM) started its retreat in countries around the Mediterranean. The MEC centenary of missions in 1919 stimulated large mission projects, most of which had to be reduced a few years later because of the severe economic crisis. The period between the two world wars led European Methodism from euphoria to depression.

The MEC work in Italy collapsed under its heavy debts. What could be saved was handed over to the British branch of Methodism. In France the MEC had taken up a mission after the separation of church and state in 1905. It developed in regions where the British branch was not yet present and rapidly grew to equal size. However, it was also given up for financial reasons in the 1930s. The EA was the only Methodist denomination which maintained its presence in France, but it was limited to German-speaking people in the Alsace. After World War I, the MEC supported two schools in Spain until the civil war destroyed everything. In Macedonia Methodists took over the work of the ABCFM. The MEC had been present in northern Serbia (Voyvodina), mostly among German-speaking people, since 1900. From there, they spread to Hungary. In 1920, the government of Albania, a Muslim country, asked the MEC to help with instituting higher **education** in the country. What came out of the project is not known.

By far the oldest mission in the region was to Orthodox Bulgaria, where Methodists and the ABCFM started a cooperative effort in 1857–1858, the former to the north and the latter to the south. At that time, Bulgaria was still part of the Ottoman Empire (Muslim). In the early 1920s, Bulgaria seemed to become the center for spreading Methodism to the Balkans, but even the older mission fields were hardly surviving the economic crisis 10 years later. During the time of communism in the second half of the 20th century, Methodists continued their witness in Macedonia, Serbia, and Hungary, but in Bulgaria all Protestant churches came under heavy persecution. In 1989, three elderly Methodist pastors challenged the government in establishing again the UMC according to its own **Discipline**. The church has rapidly grown with the help of **lay preachers**.

In Switzerland the MEC has been present since 1856 and the EA since 1866. Both branches grew rapidly. In 1914, the former had 10,000 professing members and the latter 7,000 (with the Alsace). Peak growth was in the 1930s. As in Germany and Scandinavia, strong deaconess movements developed with hospitals and homes for elderly people. Many deaconesses were sent to serve in Central Europe and in Southern Europe. After the 1960s, social and diaconal work changed dramatically in personnel and in institutional structures. In Austria Methodist work always remained numerically small, but developed a strong ecumenical presence.

In 1920, the MECS developed a mission initiative to assist wartorn Belgium, Poland, and Czechoslovakia. Diaconal, educational, and religious work went hand-in-hand. During the economic crisis of the 1930s, the MECS wanted to close down all three fields, but strong resistance convinced them that their local churches would continue even without financial support. In Belgium, Methodists united with other Protestant churches in 1969 to form the Protestant Church of Belgium.

During the last decade of the 20th century, Methodist churches have grown in Central Europe and in Eastern Europe, whereas most in Western Europe have continued to decline in membership. In 2000, the Central Conference of Central and Southern Europe of the UMC incorporated the following Annual or Provisional Annual Conferences (with membership): Austria (1,200), Bulgaria (1,000), Czech Republic/Slovakia (1,300), Hungary (2,000), Macedonia/Serbia (3,000), Poland (2,500), and Switzerland/France (9,000).

Patrick Streiff

EVANGELICAL ASSOCIATION/EVANGELICAL CHURCH (EA). The EA had its beginnings in the great evangelical awakening that occurred among the Pennsylvania Germans during the late 18th century. One of those influenced by this movement was the Pennsylvania farmer, **Jacob Albright.** Although Albright originally became a Methodist lay preacher, during his itinerant travels he became associated with Germans of various denominations. Albright was highly respected by these like-minded Germans and they gradually gravitated to him for leadership. These persons were often referred to as "Albright's People." Without intending to form a new denomination, a meeting was held in 1807 near Kleinfeltersville, Pennsylvania, where this group officially adopted the name "The Newly-Formed Methodist **Conference.**" Albright was also elected to superintend this developing movement.

Following Albright's death in 1808, his successor, **George Miller,** prepared articles of faith and a **Discipline** for the church. In 1816, the organization held its first **General Conference** in New Berlin, Pennsylvania. Here the name EA was adopted as well as approval of a revised Discipline. The basis for a formal denomination had now been laid.

Originally, the EA had no formal episcopacy. Instead, the church relied on **presiding elders** for leadership. In 1839, however, the General Conference elected **John Seybert** to be the first bishop of the church. Seybert proved instrumental to the expansion and institutionalization of the young denomination.

Theologically, the EA was Wesleyan. In fact, the EA's articles of faith closely paralleled those of the Methodists (*see* ARTICLES OF RELIGION). However, after 1848 adherence to the doctrine of entire **sanctification** became controversial, and for nearly 25 years the dispute between the Reformed and the Wesleyan views on holiness created tension in the church.

Beginning at the General Conference of 1887, the EA entered a painful process of disintegration. Through a complex series of personality conflicts, misunderstandings, and mistreatment of fellow ministers, a division occurred throughout the church. One of the issues in question was the proper extent of episcopal powers. Finally, in 1894, after hope of unity had ended, the EA officially divided when the United Evangelical Church was formed in Naperville, Illinois. Although the split was bitter and painful, movement toward healing the rupture soon began. In 1922 the two churches finally reunited and adopted the name Evangelical Church. In 1934 formal talks began with the **UB** regarding uniting the two denominations. This merger was consummated at Johnstown, Pennsylvania, in 1946.

Daryl M. Elliott

EVANGELICAL CONGREGATIONAL CHURCH was legally established in 1928 after years of litigation denied its membership the right to continue using the name The United Evangelical Church. Headquarters for the 25,000-member denomination include a church center, publishing house, home for the aging, and theological seminary at Myerstown, Pennsylvania. The legal controversy resulted from the 1922 reunion of two branches of the former **EA** that had divided in the 1890s. A minority of the United Evangelical Church (1894–1922) sought to continue the beliefs and practices of that tradition and refused to be part of the union now called the EC, which retained the more Methodist polity of the original EA. Dissent centered in the East Pennsylvania Annual **Conference**, where 20,000 members continued to call themselves United Evangelicals until courts denied that right. A few congregations in Ohio and Illinois joined them. Calling themselves Evangelical Congregational conveyed historical connection with EA founder **Jacob Albright** and emphasis on congregational rights. Other distinctive features are limited tenure and power of bishops, increased power for laity, annual appointments by a Stationing Committee, more conservative Articles of Faith, and affiliation with the National Association of Evangelicals rather than the **NCC**.

Donald K. Gorrell

EVANGELICAL UNITED BRETHREN CHURCH (EUB) was created on November 16, 1946, at Johnstown, Pennsylvania, by the union of the **EC** and the **UB**. Both denominations had origins among German-speaking Americans but such ethnic ministry was no longer a priority and they negotiated the compromises needed to combine their similar heritages and resources for a new mission in the 20th century.

In structure this church was governed by **conference**s on three levels. The local conference of a congregation was the basic unit. It was represented at the annual conference level by a lay delegate and its minister. Annual conferences elected superintendents from among their clergy, and they supervised its work for four-year terms, and with the bishop they appointed ministers annually to churches. Attendees at quadrennial conferences selected an equal number of ministerial and lay delegates to the **General Conference**, which exercised the highest legislative, administrative, and judicial authority of the denomination.

Like its antecedents, the communion had a modified **episcopacy**. There were seven bishops elected by the General Conference from among the ordained **elder**s. They had no priestly power but supervised and administered the church for four-year terms, although they usually were reelected. While responsible for the entire denomination, each was the chief administrative officer of one of seven episcopal areas and the presiding officer over the annual conferences in that region. Bishops also served on the governing boards of all general agencies and institutions.

There was one order of ministry, the order of elder. Prospective ministers had to be recommended by a local conference and licensed by an annual conference, as well as fulfill stated requirements for professional training. After **ordination** elders were appointed annually, but over the years it became the practice functionally to be reappointed in longer pastorates. **Women** as well as men had been ordained since 1889 in the **UB** tradition, but not in the EC. Their status was quietly maintained in the united church and there were no recorded objections to isolated ordinations of women during the EUB years.

Theologically, the statement of faith of the merged denomination consisted of the affirmations each fellowship brought into the union. Neither contained novelties, but stood in the Arminian tradition of the Protestant Reformation (*see* ARMINIUS, JACOBUS). The 1962 General Conference revised the two declarations into a single Confession of Faith written in the living language of the times.

Committed to **ecumenism** throughout its history, the EUB actively participated in councils of churches at every level. In 1958 they responded to a proposed union with the **MC**, which led to a Plan of Union approved by both communions (November 1966). On April 23, 1968, at Dallas, Texas, delegates from both churches celebrated the birth of the **UMC**.

In 1968, the EUB had 750,000 members in 32 conferences in the USA and **Canada**, and 42,000 in six conferences abroad, plus **missions** in **Africa**, **Asia**, **Latin America**, and nine united churches overseas. There were seven colleges and three theological seminaries. General church headquarters were in Dayton, Ohio.

Donald K. Gorrell

EVANGELISM. The evangelical message and mission of Methodism was based on the climactic personal experience of **John Wesley**. He had been ordained and exercised a limited ministry as a devout Anglican priest, and had sailed as a missionary to the colony of Georgia. Dispirited, he returned to England and on January 24,

1738, he entered in his journal: "I went to America to convert the Indians; but Oh! who shall convert me? . . . [But] whoever sees me sees I *would* be a Christian." The example of the **Moravians** in Georgia had demonstrated his failure. Within a few weeks **Peter Böhler**, himself waiting for a passage to Georgia, showed him the way. Throwing overboard his former dependence upon his own righteousness and good works, he engaged in "continual prayer for . . . justifying, saving **faith**, a full reliance on the blood of Jesus Christ shed for *me*, a trust in him as *my* Christ, as *my* sole **justification, sanctification**, and redemption" (echoing Martin Luther). On May 24, 1738, in the Aldersgate religious society, while William Holland was reading from Luther's preface to Romans, the answer to his persistent prayers came: "About a quarter before nine, while he was describing the change which God works in the heart through faith in Christ, I felt my heart strangely warmed. I felt I did trust in Christ, Christ alone for **salvation**, and an **assurance** was given me that he had taken away *my* sins, even *mine*, and saved *me* from the law of sin and death" (*See* ALDERSGATE EXPERIENCE).

This was good news indeed, which he must share with others, and encourage them to share with the world. He had carefully prepared "A Sermon on Salvation by Faith," tried it out on a country congregation on Sunday, June 11, and later that same day delivered a public manifestation of his new gospel to St. Mary's, Oxford. His brother Charles learned the sermon by heart, preached it frequently, and was rewarded by many **conversions**. The brothers decided not to publish it, however, until John had returned from a three-month pilgrimage to the land of the Moravians to whom he owed his **new birth**. Having corrected the proofs of "Salvation by Faith," John turned to one of Charles's important discoveries, the Edwardian *Homilies*, first published in 1547, containing the sermons on the way of salvation of the martyred reforming archbishop Thomas Cranmer. Wesley abridged three of these for publication in Oxford in 1738, entitled *The Doctrine of Salvation, Faith, and Good Works. Extracted from the Homilies of the Church of England*. Thus he proved in thousands of published handouts that the Methodist evangelical **preaching** was not that of ranting "enthusiasts," but the solemn words of solid churchmen.

As more and more **lay preachers** rallied to Wesley's challenge to help him reform the Church of England from within, Wesley called them into **conference** with him. The major themes from 1744 to 1749 were "what to teach" and "how to teach," though these were in reality two aspects of the same subject, later summarized as "doctrinal Minutes." In effect Wesley debated with his junior colleagues the many aspects of human spiritual need and God's solutions for that need, thus summed up: 1. All persons have sinned and need salvation. 2. All persons may be saved from sin. 3. All persons may *know* that they are saved. 4. All persons may be saved to the uttermost. Ideally these positive statements came to be known by Methodists (in whatever varying terms) as "our doctrines." All Methodist preachers, through the centuries, through the nations, and through the denominations, are expected to proclaim them in their evangelism. *See also* DOCTRINAL STANDARDS.

Frank Baker

EVANS, JAMES (January 18, 1801–November 23, 1846) was born in Kingston upon Hull, England. In 1822, he came to **Canada** and became a teacher. He was converted at a Methodist **camp meeting** and in 1828 he accepted an appointment to the Methodist school for Indian children at Rice Lake.

In 1830, he became a probationer in the **MEC** (later the **Wesleyan Methodist Church**) and was ordained in 1833. He was appointed to the St. Clair mission and worked among the Ojibwas, devising an Ojibwa syllabary and translating hymns and scripture. In 1840, Evans went to Manitoba as a missionary, arriving at Norway House that August. He soon developed a syllabic alphabet for the Cree language and printed several works. While his missionary activity was successful, his work was hampered by difficulties including controversies with the Hudson's Bay Company and an accusation of inappropriate conduct with the native girls in his home. Regarding the charge, he was judged innocent but imprudent. He was invited to England to talk with the missionary society and died there of a heart attack. The difficulties of his later years have tended to obscure Evans's significant accomplishments, particularly the introduction of Cree syllabics.

Marilyn Färdig Whiteley

EWHA WOMAN'S UNIVERSITY, Seoul, Korea began May 31, 1886, as a class in the home of WFMS (MEC) missionary Mary F. Scranton. Originally called Ewha Haktang (School), its objective was to change society through the education of Korean **women**. Ewha means "pear flower" and was a symbol of royalty. School buildings were constructed on Chung Dong campus in 1900, and WFMS missionary Lula E. Frey founded Ewha College in 1910. The college was accredited in 1925 to become Ewha Woman's College, and moved to the Shin Cho site in 1935. The Japanese government changed Ewha to Kyung Sung Womans College (1943). Following liberation in 1945, it was the first college to apply for approval as a university and became Ewha Womans University. The first graduate school was started in 1950. **Helen Kim** was the first Korean president of Ewha College, 1939–1941, and of Ewha Woman's University, 1945–1961. Enrollment in 2003 exceeded 21,000 full-time students, with 14 colleges and 13 graduate schools. *See also* ASIA.

Barbara E. Campbell

EXPERIENCE, CHRISTIAN. John Wesley joined the mainstream of Christian belief by acknowledging that the faith experience must focus upon an awareness of Christ if it is to be called Christian. Other traditions, like Wesley's, pointed to scripture and reason as foundations for a knowledge of the faith. But central to Wesley's view is the appeal to experience as the bridge that allows one to know that the Christlike God, through scripture and reason, has witnessed to the spirit of the individual (*See* WITNESS OF THE SPIRIT). Using the biblical text, "The spirit itself beareth witness with our spirit, that we are the children of God" (Romans 8:16), Wesley declared in 1767, ". . . by 'testimony of the spirit' (*see* HOLY SPIRIT) I mean an inward impression of the soul, whereby the Spirit of God immediately and directly witnesses to my spirit that I am a child of God, that 'Jesus Christ hath loved me, and given himself for me;' that all my sins are blotted out, and I, even I am reconciled to God."(sermon, "The Witness of the Spirit, II"). **Albert Outler** offers a helpful and substantive interpretation of Wesley's view of experience: "It should be noted that by 'experience,' he normally means religious intuition, not perception or feelings in general. This distinction enables him to differentiate 'experience' from '**enthusiasm**,' and thus deny the charge that Methodists are enthusiasts." *See also* ASSURANCE, CHRISTIAN.

Robert Drew Simpson

EYNON, ELIZABETH DART (April 1792–January 13, 1857), **Bible Christian** preacher, was born in Marhamchurch, England. She joined the Wesleyan Methodist Church, but on October 9, 1815, she was one of the small company of women and men who met at Shebbear with **William O'Bryan** to form what came to be called the Bible Christian Church. The following year she became the group's first itinerant, under O'Bryan (*see* ITINERACY). She preached reluctantly at first, but her **preaching** was effective. She traveled mainly around Devon and Cornwall. She also preached in Wales and one of her converts there, John Hicks Eynon, became her husband on March 18, 1833. Early that May they set forth for Upper **Canada** as missionaries. They went to Cobourg, on the shores of Lake Ontario, and she preached her first sermon there on July 10, 1833. She and her husband often traveled separately on a 200-mile **circuit**, a strenuous life for both wife and husband. When John was ill for several months in 1839, Elizabeth took on his ministry while maintaining her own. In 1848, they went to England for a year, then returned to Cobourg, where Elizabeth, despite ill health, remained active in the church until her death.

Marilyn Färdig Whiteley

– F –

FAITH. The Methodist doctrine of faith stands in an evangelical, synergistic tradition of the mutual cooperation between divine initiative and human response in the awakening of saving faith in Christ. This tradition was shared by the apostolic fathers before Augustine, and by the English Reformers, most Pietists, and the evangelical Arminians (*see* ARMINIUS, JACOBUS). By contrast, the tradition of monergism asserts that God acts alone in creating saving faith in Christ within the life of the believer. This is largely the Augustinian tradition, which includes the mainline Protestant Reformers and, in our century, the neo-orthodox theology of Karl Barth (1886–1968). Both traditions have appealed to the writings of St. Paul as a biblical precedent for their positions.

The Pauline concept of faith as a personal union with Christ that results in a new, heart-centered incentive for moral obedience was at times perverted in an **antinomian** direction (Romans 6:1), especially in the Gentile context. Hence, the second century church began to emphasize "the Faith," or a body of authoritative teaching, as in Irenaeus's "Rule of Faith." This "objectifying" of faith was accelerated in the medieval era as personal faith became increasingly displaced by a devout assent to the sacerdotal authority of the **Roman Catholic** Church. The danger in this system was that faith could degenerate into a belief in the automatic efficacy of ritual observance.

An attempt to recover the Pauline conception of faith was undertaken by the Protestant Reformers. Martin Luther (1483–1546) arrived at a personal, relational concept of faith as trust in the course of his struggle against the late nominalist emphasis upon active righteousness. In his exposition of Romans 1:16–17, Luther perceived that righteousness is God's free gift in Jesus Christ, which is not a legal requirement for sinners to fulfill but rather a gift made available to them by faith. Hence, faith was now perceived to be the only condition acceptable to God whereby **grace** may be appropriated. This contrasts with the prevailing Roman Catholic position, which affirmed that faith is established only in conjunction with an accruing program of good works, whereby one's acceptance by God is progressively merited. Luther's insight into the nature of faith was also inseparable from his reformulation of the meaning of saving grace. Instead of grace being sacramental, it was now perceived as a wholly new, relational event that transforms one's standing before God. This event occurs only in the context of the hearing of the proclaimed word of God. Its message discloses God's unmerited gift of forgiveness to undeserving sinners, and for that reason it is called "good news."

For John Calvin (1509–1564), faith plays a somewhat less prominent role in **salvation**, since he taught that faith is merely the "bond" that the **Holy Spirit** employs to join the sinner substantially to Christ's divinity, which is disclosed in the hearing of the proclaimed word of God. For the Anabaptists, and for later Baptists, faith has the distinctive character of active obedience to Christ through the biblical injunction to discipleship, for which they were set apart by believers' **baptism**.

In the Anglican tradition, which was given definitive formulation by Thomas Cranmer in the Thirty-Nine Articles of Religion (1549 and 1552), faith and works are balanced in a distinctive manner. While **justification** by grace through faith is accorded primacy, good works are given recognition as a "secondary witness" to one's personal appropriation of saving grace. Hence, it may be said that personal salvation comes by faith "primarily," though not "solely." These points of balance are due to Cranmer's intent of forging an Anglican tradition that would comprehend both early Catholic and evangelical (Reformation) aspects.

In the period following the Reformation, the conception of saving faith was reduced to that of a cognitive assent to propositional truths, as contained in scripture and the Protestant creeds, rather than as personal trust in a living, present Savior. Under the influence of German **Pietism** in the 17th century, renewed emphasis was placed upon the personal, "trust" aspect of faith. Faith was linked to the **new birth**, interpreted as the personal, regenerative **experience** of the indwelling Christ. For the nonseparatist, church Pietists, it was to be an experience subsequent to and confirming one's infant baptism, the normative baptismal practice among Catholics and mainline Protestants alike. Pietists tended to place greater emphasis upon the imparted Christ "in us" as the object of saving faith, rather than upon the Christ who is mainly "for us," whereby the declaration of imputed righteousness is conveyed to the sinner.

Consistent with the Pietist renewal of "personal" faith, **John Wesley** proceeded from a "historical" faith, based on assent to Christian truths, to a personal, saving faith in Christ's pardoning grace, which culminated in his experience at **Aldersgate** on May 24, 1738. In Wesley's Arminian outlook (*see* ARMINIUS, JACOBUS), saving faith is first awakened through the inward operation of prevening grace (John 1:9), which enables the will, damaged as it is by sin, to respond to the ongoing activity of saving grace in Christ, by appropriating justifying grace (pardon) and sanctifying grace, that begins with pardon and proceeds, with the believer's cooperation, to the experience of **Christian perfection**. The latter state of grace is the gracious capacity to live in compliance with the love commandment. This many-faceted operation of grace is to be appropriated by saving faith, which, according to Wesley, is "not barely a speculative, rational thing, a cold, lifeless assent, a train of ideas in the head; but also a disposition of the heart, a full reliance on the blood of Christ; a trust in the merits of His life, death, and resurrection; a recumbrancy upon Him as our **atonement** and our life" (Sermon, "Salvation by Faith").

As an Arminian, Wesley recognized that saving faith can be lost, even as grace can be resisted. From the Moravian Pietists (see MORAVIANS) he learned not only that instantaneous **conversions** were still occurring, as in apostolic times, but also that one's faith in pardoning grace can be reinforced by personal **assurance** granted through the "**witness of the Spirit**" (Romans 8:16).

During the **holiness movement** of the 19th century, special emphasis was placed upon Christian holiness, inaugurated by the "baptism of the Holy Spirit," as the chief focus of personal faith in Christ.

Finally, from the Reformed Pietist heritage of **Philip William Otterbein**, UMC has inherited the insight that the focus of evangelical faith has both a personal and a larger historical reference. One's personal regeneration in Christ is to be seen as a strategic aspect of God's larger plan in securing the deliverance of human history from the bondage to evil through the advancing kingdom of Christ. The reign of the kingdom is to be within the hearts and mutual relationships of the reborn in Christ, who live as lights amid a generally godless world.

J. Steven O'Malley

FASTING is the practice of abstaining from food as a means of spiritual discipline. Fasting has been used since biblical times as an expression of penance, as preparation for decision, and as a help in discerning the will of God. Like all ascetical practices, fasting diverts attention from the ordinary business of attending to our human needs and desires and creates a space in which we can be more attentive to God. Jesus began his ministry by fasting in the wilderness (Luke 4:1–4), although he apparently did not observe fasts as strictly as the pharisees or the disciples of John the Baptist (Luke 5:33–35). Early Christian ascetics sometimes carried fasting to extremes, living for years on very small quantities of food. Protestant reformers, wary of attempts to win **justification** by works, rejected the more severe forms of fasting, but they regarded it as a discipline that all Christians should practice from time to time. **John Wesley** continued this discipline for his followers, and admonished his preachers to teach it by precept and example. Whole congregations or **conferences** of early Methodists would fast when they were troubled by disagreements or seeking guidance for a difficult decision.

Robin W. Lovin

FEMINISM, the advocacy of **women**'s rights, has been present in Methodism since its earliest days. **John Wesley** actively supported women as spiritual leaders. Feminism was closely linked with **laity rights,** civil rights, and the suffrage movement.

Paradoxically, feminism was fostered by the 19th-century notion of "woman's sphere," which asserted that women's natural arena is the home and the church (though not behind the pulpit and never usurping male authority). Women's activities were segregated and consequently somewhat autonomous. In church groups women felt connected to a larger sisterhood, spoke and prayed in public, and grew more willing to claim spiritual authority. In women's missionary organizations they gained experience administering programs and handling finances. Women missionaries, especially single women, were models of independence and capability (*see* MISSIONS).

Women claimed nearly all of the 19th century's important social issues as part of their sphere, among them **temperance,** moral reform, **antislavery, education,** and workers' rights, culminating in the suffrage movement. Leading reformers such as **Frances Willard** used the language of domesticity and sphere to advance political causes. The **Holiness Movement** likewise did not directly challenge the boundaries of sphere, but drew many women into positions of spiritual leadership (*see* PALMER, PHOEBE WORRALL).

As the restrictions of woman's sphere diminished, early concerns about the propriety of women speaking to "mixed public assemblies" gave way to the long campaign for clergy rights and female representation at every level of the church. Beginning in the 1880s, Methodist denominations slowly began to accept women into the ordained ministry. By the 21st century, dramatic societal changes had diminished the status of church women's organizations, but women continue their historic advocacy of women's and children's issues in every Methodist-related denomination in the world.

Susan E. Warrick

FIELD PREACHING, associated in the popular mind and especially in Anglican circles with dissent and political disaffection, was undertaken by the Wesleys with considerable reluctance. In April 1739, **George Whitefield** persuaded **John Wesley** to take over the open-air witness he had begun in Bristol and Kingswood. By the end of May, **Charles Wesley** too had overcome his misgivings. Field preaching became a major feature of Methodist outreach, attracting both popular attention and open hostility. In reply to Anglican critics, Wesley defended the practice on biblical grounds (Jesus' Sermon on the Mount and the injunction to "go out into the highways and hedges"), and denied that it was illegal. At first he advocated it only when no church was available, but at the **Conference** of 1747 he argued that it enabled him to reach many who would never enter a church: "We have always found a greater blessing in field-preaching than in any other **preaching** whatever." He admitted that while the novelty of open-air preaching aroused popular curiosity, it "rarely made any impression at all till the novelty of it was over." There was always some reluctance among the itinerants to follow Wesley's example, and the practice had largely died out among the Wesleyans by the time it was adopted by **Primitive Methodism** and **Bible Christians** early in the 19th century. In America, especially on the frontier, it was formalized in the **camp meeting**.

John A. Vickers

FIJI. *See* TONGA, FIJI, AND SAMOA.

FINLAND. *See* EUROPE.

FISK, WILBUR (August 31, 1792–February 22, 1839), first president of Wesleyan University, was born in Brattleboro, Vermont. Graduating with honors from Brown University, Fisk worked as a private tutor while beginning legal studies. However, a personal spiritual awakening ensued and he entered the ministry (1818), becoming the first college graduate to enter the Methodist **itineracy** in New England. In 1823, Fisk was appointed **presiding elder** of the Vermont district, and, in 1826, was elected principal of Wilbraham (Wesleyan) Academy. Poor health plagued Fisk throughout his life, leading him to decline election to the **MEC episcopacy** in 1828 and 1836. Beyond health concerns, Fisk rejected the latter offer out of his commitment to Wesleyan University, where he served as president from 1830 to his death in 1839. A strong advocate of the doctrine of perfect love (*see* CHRISTIAN PERFECTION), Fisk was noted for his personal piety, intellectual clearness, and tact in controversy. Although opposed to **slavery**, Fisk was offended by the practices of abolitionists and advocated colonization instead. In addition, Fisk spoke and wrote on behalf of **missions** and **temperance** and against Calvinism and Universalism. The first American Methodist theologian to achieve recognition outside of his denomination, Fisk's advocacy of **conference** educational societies led to the formation of the Methodist Board of **Education**.

Dale H. Simmons

FIVE POINTS MISSION was organized in 1850 by the Ladies' Home Missionary Society of the **MEC** in New York City in one of the most notorious slums in the USA. The mission soon outgrew its original rented quarters, and the society purchased an old brewery, infamous as the home of desperately poor squatters. The society tore down the ramshackle building and erected a mission house in 1853. "The Old Brewery" had a chapel, schoolrooms, baths, and 20 apartments. The mission had limited evangelistic success in the heavily Roman Catholic neighborhood. More effective were its social programs, which grew to include a **Sunday school** for adults and children, a day school, an employment agency, adoption services, and a kindergarten/nursery. Missionaries also regularly distributed food and clothing to the needy. The mission expanded through the 19th century and moved twice, first to Worth Street and then to Madison Street. The Chinese **UMC** in lower Manhattan now uses the latter site for its outreach programs. Another direct descendant of the Five Points Mission is the Camp and Retreat House at Olmsted (New York), founded in the early 20th century as the mission's summer camp for inner-city children.

Susan E. Warrick

FLETCHER, JOHN WILLIAM (September 12, 1729–August 14, 1785), leader of the Methodist movement in England and **John Wesley**'s designated successor, was born in Néyon, Switzerland. He was baptized Jean Guilliame de la Flechère. In 1752, Fletcher settled in England and was attracted to the message of Wesley's Methodism. Ordained a priest in the Church of England in March 1757, Fletcher became vicar of Madeley, Shropshire, in 1760, where he served until his death. From 1768 until 1771, he also acted as president of the **Countess of Huntingdon**'s college for the training of ministers at Trevecka near Brecon, though he supervised its work while pursuing his ministry at Madeley. Fletcher resigned his post at the college when it became clear that his Arminian views did not correlate with the Calvinist predestinarian theology that the countess favored. Fletcher's *Check's to Antinomianism* (1771) explicate the theological views of early Methodism and was one of its principal textbooks in both Britain and America. In 1781, Fletcher married **Mary Bosanquet**. Both were widely known in Methodist circles for their saintly lives. Since Fletcher predeceased Wesley, he never assumed the leadership of Methodism that Wesley intended for him. He is buried in the churchyard at Madeley.

Charles Yrigoyen, Jr.

FOSTER, RANDOLPH SINKS (February 22, 1820–May 1, 1903), pastor, professor, college president, and bishop, was born in the county jail in Williamsburg, Ohio (his father was the jailer). Foster studied briefly at Augusta College. Anxious to begin ministry, he dropped out of school and entered the Ohio **Conference** (MEC) on trial. Thus at 17 he became a **circuit** rider in the Ohio Valley. Realizing that he had made a mistake in leaving college, Foster embarked on an intensive program of self-education. He quickly gained a reputation as a scholarly defender of Wesleyanism through his controversies with Calvinists and his advocacy of entire **sanctification**. By age 30, he was being offered prestigious assignments, such as New York's fashionable Mulberry Street Church (1850–1852). A life-long advocate of the necessity of an educated clergy, Foster served as president of Northwestern University (1857–1860) and Drew University (1870–1873), where he also served as professor of systematic theology (1868–1873). Elected bishop in 1872, Foster's 24 years in that capacity were distinguished, yet controversial. For example, his semi-Swedenborgian views on the resurrection of the body and the afterlife resulted in heresy charges, while his writings along these lines enjoyed widespread popularity. Moreover, Foster's efforts at reuniting the **MEC** and the **MECS** strongly offended black membership.

Dale H. Simmons

FOWLER, CHARLES HENRY (August 11, 1837–March 20, 1908), **MEC** bishop, was born in Burford, Ontario, **Canada,** and moved with his family to Illinois in 1841. After graduating from Genesee College in 1859, he first considered law but, following a Christmas Eve **conversion,** entered Garrett Biblical Institute. He graduated in 1861, was received into the Rock River **Conference,** and successively served four churches in the Chicago area. He was engaged for a time to **Frances Willard** but later married Myra Hitchcock in 1868. Fowler toured eastern cities following the Chicago fire of 1871, raising funds for church and school restorations and enhancing his reputation as an orator. He was elected president of Northwestern University in 1872, followed by positions as editor of the *Christian Advocate* (1876–1880) and corresponding secretary of the MEC Missionary Society (1880–1884). He was elected bishop in 1884, residing thereafter in San Francisco, Minneapolis, Buffalo, and New York but presiding over conferences throughout the nation. Consistent with the nickname "whirlwind" given him in student days, he was known as a "man of action" whose activities ranged from campaigning for the presidential election of William McKinley, a Methodist layman, to involvement in the founding of numerous institutions, such as Peking and Nanking universities in China, Maclay College of Theology in California, Nebraska Wesleyan University, and the first Methodist church in St. Petersburg, Russia. His sister was **Jennie Fowler Willing**.

Bruce David Forbes

FRANCE. *See* EUROPE.

FREE METHODIST CHURCH, an evangelical denomination in the holiness tradition, was founded in Pekin, New York, in 1860. In the period just prior to the Civil War, the rising socioeconomic status of the **MEC** brought about a number of changes in ecclesiastical practice. Some people were disturbed by these changes. Specifically, they noticed that **worship** was less spontaneous and more formalized, participation in class meetings declined (*see* SOCIETIES, CLASSES, AND BANDS), **camp meetings** were replaced by summer resorts, carnivals and dances were used to raise money, organs and robed choirs provided **music** in place of congregational singing, members joined elitist secret societies (such as the Masons), and congregants arrayed themselves in fine clothing and jewelry instead of plain dress. Many persons missed the fervor and simplicity of the early Wesleyan revival. They were concerned that the emerging urban bourgeois culture of mid-19th-century Methodism neglected the poor and compromised **John Wesley**'s emphasis on holy living. Among the "Nazarites," as the reformers were nicknamed, the spiritual decline and worldliness of Methodism was symbolized most clearly by the church's accommodation to **slavery**, its de-emphasis on the doctrine of entire **sanctification**, and its frequent practice of renting pews in order to finance the construction of elaborate church edifices.

Two regions of the country became particularly agitated by these issues: the Rock River **Conference** in Illinois under the leadership of John Wesley Redfield and the Genesee Conference in upstate New York under the leadership of **Benjamin Titus Roberts**. For many years, Roberts attempted to establish a congregation with free pews for the urban poor of Buffalo. He also focused his ministry on the preaching of holiness and the need for greater democracy in church government, but was rebuffed in all of these efforts by a group of Genesee Conference clergy known as the "Buffalo Regency." In 1857, Roberts responded to his opponents by writing an article that attacked the practices of "New School Methodism." Soon thereafter, the regency orchestrated a successful attempt to expel him and several other Nazarites from the conference. The expelled ministers and sympathetic laymen organized the Free Methodist Church in 1860. The new name signified the central tenets of Free Methodism: free

seats in all meetinghouses, freedom from slavery, freedom from ecclesiastical authoritarianism, freedom from worldly behavior, freedom from oath-bound societies, freedom of the Spirit (*see* HOLY
SPIRIT) in worship, and freedom from sin in the experience of entire
sanctification.

Recently, the Free Methodist Church has identified itself closely
with late-20th-century evangelicalism and, consequently, belongs to
the National Association of Evangelicals. Attempts over the past few
decades to merge the Free Methodist Church with the **Wesleyan
Methodist (now Wesleyan) Church**, a denomination with a similar
history and ethos, have not met with success. The Free Methodists
maintain several liberal arts colleges, including Roberts Wesleyan
College in New York, Spring Arbor College in Michigan, Greenville
College in Illinois, and Seattle Pacific University. From its headquarters in Indianapolis, the denomination coordinates an extensive program of foreign **missions**. Worldwide membership in 2000 was approximately 400,000. Membership in the USA stood at 74,000. *See
also* HOLINESS MOVEMENT.

Douglas M. Strong

FREE WILL. The conundrum of divine sovereignty versus human
freedom has perplexed the church since its beginning. The pendulum
has swung between a stress on God's absolute sovereignty and an
emphasis on human autonomy. Central to the debate was the nature
and effect of **original sin**. Some viewed humans as totally corrupt;
others held that they were only corrupt from the neck down.

For his part, **John Wesley** took seriously the dire effects of the
fall. However, while the image of God in human beings was deformed by the fall, it was not destroyed. In particular, Wesley saw
the will as essential to the image of God, as it allowed individuals to
serve God or to rebel. Now, because of sin, the will was under
bondage and people chose to do evil rather than good. **Salvation**
therefore meant restoring the image of God and freeing the will to
do God's will. Wesley believed that such a restoration was completely the work of God since "all men are by nature not only sick,
but 'dead in trespasses and sins.'"

The first move then, must be God's, through the ministration of
prevenient grace. In prevenient grace, God partially restores and up-

holds our sin-corrupted human faculties, so that we might sense our need of salvation. God then makes various overtures via these faculties, as we move into saving relationship, and graciously enables our ability to embrace this offer. But this gracious enablement is resistible. We may ignore or resist God's overtures to the point of silencing them (though the restored potential remains, making possible renewed overtures and **conversion**). By contrast, as we embrace God's wooing we move into deeper experiences of God's forgiving and empowering grace.

Wesley's successors tended to deny or downplay the need for prevenient grace to restore to the will its power of originating action. Prevenient grace was taken somewhat for granted and this made it less central. In addition, individuals such as **John Fletcher**, **Adam Clarke**, and Richard Watson tended to shift the emphasis from restoring grace to creation grace. In America, this trend was strengthened by the widespread adoption of Scottish Common Sense Realism to critique theological expressions of a deterministic affectional moral psychology. This intensified the shift to an intellectualist moral psychology in which the will was no longer identified with the affections, but was viewed as one's free rational ability to choose between (or suppress) various stimuli.

Although the transition was slow and subtle, by the end of the 19th century, free will had largely displaced free grace in American Methodism. In **John Miley**'s systematic theology, for example, the chapter "Freedom of Choice" stands between chapters on the general benefits of the **atonement** and **justification** by faith. Methodologically, as well as doctrinally, he makes freedom of choice decisive. In the 20th century this trend continued in Albert Knudson who understood the power of contrary choice as the essence of metaphysical freedom, making humans "the captain[s] of [their] own soul[s], the determiner[s] of [their] own destiny."

Dale H. Simmons

FREEDMEN'S AID SOCIETY. Following the Civil War, northerners provided education and relief for freed slaves in the South through a federal Freedmen's Bureau and many interdenominational freedmen's commissions. Dissatisfaction soon led several denominations to begin their own efforts, and on August 7–8, 1866, 11 **MEC** leaders met in

Cincinnati to charter a Freedmen's Aid Society. The **General Conference** of 1868 sanctioned the society and encouraged all annual **conferences** to take collections for it. Richard S. Rust became its first corresponding secretary. By the end of the society's first year, it had opened 59 schools, enrolling 5,000 students. As public schools assumed responsibility for primary education, the society gave increasing attention to higher **education**. Beginning with Shaw University (later Rust College) in 1866, by 1882 the society had founded 25 institutions labeled as colleges, universities, seminaries, normal schools, and academies, usually small and understaffed, emphasizing preparation for teaching and ministry. Some southerners resented activities of the society, seeing it as an educational invasion by the North. In 1880, the General Conference directed the society to include work among southern whites as well, and in 1888, its name was changed to the Freedmen's Aid and Southern Education Society to express the broadened mission. Most of the society's work was turned over to the Board of Education for Negroes created by the MEC General Conference in 1920.

Bruce David Forbes

FUNDAMENTALISM arose in late-19th-century America as a response to scientific theories, biblical scholarship, liberal theology, and the erosion of Protestantism's control of American culture. Sciences such as geology and biology challenged traditional Christian views of the age of the earth and the way living things came into existence. Biblical scholars demonstrated that the **Bible** was written by diverse authors and contained factual errors. Liberal theologians emphasized a loving rather than a judging God and a Christ who was more a model of ethical living than a redeemer of lost sinners. Responding to those challenges, Fundamentalists identified five doctrines as being *fundamental* (a word disparaged by **John Wesley**): the verbal inerrancy of the Bible; the divinity of Christ; his virgin birth; the substitutionary theory of the **atonement**; and the bodily Resurrection (sometimes the second coming of Christ). In the 1920s and 1930s, Fundamentalists tried, but failed, to gain control of denominations within the Wesleyan tradition. But following the cultural upheaval of the 1960s, and spearheaded by the "Good News" movement within the **UMC**, Fundamentalists succeeded in making their key concerns the issues debated, often heatedly, within Methodism. These issues include **abortion**, "orthodox" doctrine (the five fundamentals), **homosexuality**, **prayer** in public schools, and **salvation** exclusively through Christ. *See also* MODERNISM/LIBERALISM.

John G. McEllhenney

– G –

GAINES, NANNIE B. (April 23, 1860–April 26, 1932), **MECS** missionary to Japan, was born in Franklin, Kentucky, the daughter of Gustavus C. and Elizabeth (Cromwell) Gaines. She was baptized Ann Elizabeth, but was apparently always called Annie Bett. After her graduation from Franklin Female College, Kentucky, she taught in public schools until she was recruited for mission work in Japan (*see* ASIA). She arrived in Japan on September 23, 1887, and started her missionary work on October 12, 1887, as a teacher in Hiroshima. She taught girls and **women** in Japan from that time until her death. She gave especially significant service as the principal of the Hiroshima Girls School. Under her leadership the school's size and influence grew. Gaines argued for Christian educational work in Japan that was less centered in particular denominations. She discovered the YWCA movement, established in Japan in 1905, to be a means to unify Japanese Christians into a more effective and supportive ecumenical community.

Charles Yrigoyen, Jr.

GAMBIA. *See* AFRICA.

GAMEWELL, MARY Q. PORTER (October 20, 1848–November 27, 1906), fourth missionary sent by the WFMS (**MEC**), opened **women**'s work in North China in 1872 (*see* ASIA). With her partner Maria Brown, she founded a girls' boarding school in Beijing (Peking), the first **mission** school in China to insist that pupils unbind their feet. In 1882 she married Frank Gamewell, thereby transferring from the woman's society to the general mission board. In 1884, the Gamewells went to West China, but antiforeign rioting in 1886 caused the destruction of the mission and they were taken prisoner for 16 days. After their release and a furlough, the Gamewells returned to Beijing, where she trained **Bible** women and tried to improve the lives of Chinese women. In 1900, the antiforeign, anti-Christian Boxer Movement broke out and 70 missionaries plus 700 Chinese Christians crowded into the Methodist mission compound. The group moved into the British legation, where 3,000 foreigners and Chinese Christians underwent siege for nearly two months. After the siege was broken, the Gamewells returned to the USA. Mrs. Gamewell wrote the history of the siege and a booklet, *China: Old and New*.

Dana L. Robert

GARRETT, ELIZA (March 5, 1805–November 23, 1855), philanthropist and churchwoman, was born Eliza Clark on a farm near Newburgh, New York. Of Presbyterian parentage, she may have been an **MEC** probationary member when she married Augustus Garrett in 1825. Heading west in 1829, the Garretts settled in Cincinnati and later in New Orleans. Hardship and sadness stalked these unsuccessful ventures. Their children, Imogene, Charles, and John, died very young. Removal to frontier Chicago in 1834 brought success for Augustus, who prospered in real estate, insurance, and brokerage, becoming Chicago's seventh mayor in 1843. Eliza and Augustus experienced **conversion** at the Clark Street MEC in 1839. Upon Augustus's death in 1848, the childless Eliza managed his fortune judiciously. A pious Methodist, she limited herself to two-fifths of her annual income in order to support benevolent causes. It was with Eliza Garrett's financial backing that the Methodist seminary, named for her despite her reluctance and chartered in 1853, was opened in nearby Evanston, Illinois, the year of her death. Her interest in founding a female college is also well known. Eliza Garrett was a modest, gentle, kindly spirit whose generosity helped assure the permanence of American Methodism's second-oldest theological seminary.

K. James Stein

GARRETTSON, CATHARINE LIVINGSTON (October 14, 1752–1849), early Methodist hostess and spiritual exemplar, was born into one of the wealthiest and most influential families in New York

State. She became a Methodist through a servant's influence and despite her family's opposition. She met **Freeborn Garrettson** in 1788 and they married five years later on June 30, 1793, in the face of her family's disapproval. The Garrettsons built a home in Rhinecliff, New York, that frequently hosted traveling Methodist preachers. **Francis Asbury** affectionately referred to the home as "Traveler's Rest." In addition to their hospitality, the Garrettsons gave freely of their wealth to the church. At her death, Catharine was remembered for her hospitality and her concern for the souls of her friends and family, recorded in her extensive correspondence. She also kept a spiritual diary that provides a window into her inner life. The Garrettsons had one child, Mary Rutherford (1794–1879), who lived with her mother and was also well known for her generosity and hospitality.

Susan E. Warrick

GARRETTSON, FREEBORN (August 15, 1752–September 26, 1827), pioneer American Methodist, was born in Maryland to a wealthy Anglican family. As a young man he was attracted to Methodism by the preaching of **Robert Strawbridge**, **Joseph Pilmore**, and **Francis Asbury**. During the American Revolution he preached diligently in Maryland, Delaware, and Virginia, despite sometimes violent persecution from anti-Methodist mobs. In 1784, he carried the call to the **Christmas Conference** up and down the East Coast. He served the **MEC** as a missionary to Nova Scotia, then as a **presiding elder** and **conference** missionary, mostly in the New York Annual Conference. He traveled extensively and was instrumental in establishing Methodism throughout New York State and into the rapidly opening West. He married Catharine Livingston in 1793 and their home became Methodist headquarters for the region. Garrettson was elected to the first delegated **General Conference** (1812) and to every succeeding General Conference until his death. Always in favor of more democratic administration of the church, he nevertheless remained loyal, refusing to leave the MEC with **James O'Kelly** in 1792. A slave owner until his **conversion**, he became a strong opponent of **slavery**, promoted **missions**, and was an effective administrator. Garrettson stands second only to Francis Asbury as a leader of the early MEC.

Susan E. Warrick

GATCH, PHILIP (March 2, 1751–December 28, 1834), an influential early American traveling preacher, was born in Baltimore and converted under Nathan Perrigo's preaching in May 1772. Gatch Church in Baltimore began on the family farm. After an experience of **sanctification**, and counsel from **Francis Asbury**, Gatch preached in nearby Maryland. Sent to New Jersey by **Thomas Rankin** in 1773, he brought 52 into society membership (*see* SOCIETIES, CLASSES, AND BANDS). Quickly promoted to assistant, he was tarred by a mob near Bladensburg, Maryland, labored in Pennsylvania, and extended the great **revival** in Southside, Virginia, 1776–1777. Although ill health and marriage in January 1778 to Elizabeth Smith ended his travels, Gatch remained on a superintending committee when Wesley's missionaries departed. In 1779, he and other Virginia preachers formed a presbytery and ordained each other (*see* ORDINATION), almost rupturing Methodism until a 1780 compromise suspended their administering **sacraments** pending instructions from Wesley. Abhorring **slavery**, in 1798 the Gatch and Smith families relocated and joined the first Methodist society in Ohio, near Cincinnati. Gatch served in the Ohio Constitutional Convention and for 20 years as a judge, farmed, welcomed **circuit** riders, and preached regularly, always a highly regarded citizen.

Edwin Schell

GENERAL CONFERENCE. The General Conference became the highest legislative body in early American Methodism and retains principal legislative power in some American Methodist churches such as the **UMC**. Since the inception of the General Conference in 1792 in the **MEC** it has met every four years to review the work of the denomination, to set policy, and to revise the *Discipline*. Since 1808, when the MEC formally adopted its Constitution, the General Conference has been a delegated body, its voting members being elected by regional annual conferences. After considerable debate about whether to give laity, and especially lay **women**, a voice and vote in the General Conference, all of the Methodist churches that employ it in their polity finally included both laity and clergy as full voting members by the earlier decades of the 20th century.

Charles Yrigoyen, Jr.

GENERAL RULES. The General Rules, drawn up by **John** and **Charles Wesley** in 1739, were first published in 1743 under the title, "The Nature, Design, and General Rules of Our United Societies." They were adopted in America by the **MEC** at the **Christmas Conference** in 1784. When they were first printed in the **Discipline** in 1789, they had been revised by John Wesley, **Francis Asbury**, and **Thomas Coke**. The 1789 edition included the prohibition of **slavery** in the Methodist societies. The Restrictive Rules of the **General Conference** of 1808 forbade their revocation or change. The General Rules explain both the institutional structure and ethical practices of historic Methodism. They define a society as a company of people "having the form and seeking the power of godliness," who unite to support one another in working out their own **salvation**. They describe the nature and work of the Methodist classes. While the prerequisite for admission was clearly "a desire to flee the wrath to come and be saved from their sins," all who continued in their salvation were expected to manifest it by "doing no harm," "by doing good," and "by attending upon all the ordinances of God." *See also* SOCIETIES, CLASSES, AND BANDS.

K. James Stein

GEORGE, ENOCH (ca. 1767–August 23, 1828), the fifth **MEC** bishop, was born in Lancaster County, Virginia. Devereux Jarratt, an Anglican clergyman with evangelical sympathies, provided George's early Christian nurture. He experienced **conversion** during a **revival** sparked by the preaching of John Easter, a Methodist itinerant who traveled in Virginia in the late 1780s. George soon demonstrated his own abilities as an evangelist, preaching with feeling and so often with tears that he became known as "the weeping prophet." **Francis Asbury** dispatched him to assist in forming a **circuit** on North Carolina's Broad and Catawba rivers. The **conference** admitted him on trial in 1790. Asbury ordained him **deacon** and **elder**. George rode MEC circuits in North and South Carolina and Tennessee and served as **presiding elder** in the Holston and Baltimore areas. In 1816, two months after Asbury's death, George, a widower, was elected bishop (*see* EPISCOPACY) to join **William McKendree**, another John

Easter convert, and Robert Roberts in supervising the MEC's ministries. George participated in the first meeting of the MEC's Council of Bishops in Philadelphia on April 13, 1826. Two years later, while on the road to preside at the Holston Conference, he died in Staunton, Virginia, and was buried in Baltimore.

John G. McEllhenney

GERMANY. *See* EUROPE.

GHANA. *See* AFRICA.

GIBRALTER. *See* EUROPE.

GRACE. John Wesley was a writer, editor, and publisher as well as a preacher in nearly perpetual motion. His hundreds of volumes of original and edited works remain the primary sources of theology in the Methodist tradition. The Wesleyan evangel, the Wesleyan way of explaining Christian doctrine, is distinctive among Christian theologies. The briefest and most apt generic title for Wesleyan doctrine is Paul's fine phrase "the gospel of grace" (Acts 20:24).

"God's unexplained loving kindness" is the best way to translate the word grace. God's unexplained loving kindness works in the universe, among human communities, and within persons. While remembering that grace is one, it helps to speak about various operations of grace. We discern not different graces, but different workings of the same grace.

God's unexplained loving kindness is expressed first in the creation of the world and of humankind. By God's creating grace we were made in the image of God, in true righteousness and holiness (Genesis 1:27; Ephesians 4:24).

God's unexplained loving kindness is not withdrawn from arrogant, disobedient, and thus alienated humanity. Creating grace puts eternity in the deepest part of humanness (soul, mind, heart; Ecclesiastes 3:11). Prevenient (coming before) grace makes us long for God in the deepest part of our humanness (Psalms 42:1–2; 139), disturbing us in our alienation and giving us points of light in our darkened wilderness wandering. **Prevenient grace** is how God our Loving

Parent upholds and calls us, no matter how far we go or how low we sink. Those who respond to prevenient grace come to themselves (repent) and seek reconciliation (Luke 15:17–18).

God's unexplained loving kindness accepts and pardons us—justifies us. **Justification** is what God the Son does for us (John 3:16; Ephesians 2:8–10). Justifying grace restores us to true righteousness and holiness (Ephesians 4:24) in the sight of God, reconciling us to God, to one another, and to our own best selves (II Corinthians 5:17–21). Through creating grace God gave us our being. Through justifying grace God gives us a **new birth** (John 3:3–8; I Peter 1:3, 23).

God's unexplained loving kindness nurtures our growth in true righteousness and holiness. This **sanctification** is what God the **Holy Spirit** does in us (Ephesians 2:10; II Corinthians 5:17, I Peter 1:15–16; 2:5,9; I John 3–5). Sanctification is both a present reality and an ongoing process. Grace at work in us changes our nature. We are not what we were. We do not boast because we know this is God's doing (Ephesians 2:8). We know also that no matter how far we have come in our life in the Spirit there is always more of love.

The core of Methodist spirituality is the life of holiness. Methodism is the disciplined practice of the love of God. And it is here that the concept of **Christian perfection** appears in Wesleyan teaching. Wesley used the term only because it is found in the New Testament (Matthew 5:48; 19:21; Romans 12:2; II Corinthians 7:1; Ephesians 4:13; Philippians 3:12; Hebrews 7:11; 10:1,10; 11:40; James 1:14; 3:2; 4:18).

Christian perfection is not absolute perfection. It is scriptural holiness and the scripture does not apply perfection in the absolute sense to humans. Humans, always subject to ignorance, mistake, infirmity, and temptation, will inevitably "trespass against" one another, and have a "bent to sinning." For Wesley, scriptural Christian perfection was best translated as perfect love. This means having every thought, word, and deed motivated by love. Even perfect love is never at an ending point in us. There is always more of love. Thus if we were as pure as Christ is pure, we would still have need to grow in holiness (Wesley's comment on Luke 2:52).

So important to Wesley was this possibility of life in the Spirit that he believed the reason for "the work of God called Methodism" was to call the whole church to lay claim to scriptural holiness. He believed the grace of God is so powerful that sinful humans are re-created and made truly righteous and holy. Like Paul, he believed we can live "in Christ" (Galatians 2:20). Because disciples receive the Holy Spirit (John 20:22; Acts 2:1–4; 8:17; 19:6) they can experience the life of God in the deepest part of their humanness.

The Wesleyan evangel, then, is a distinctive way of declaring the gospel of grace. Out of unexplained loving kindness God created us. Owing to this unexplained loving kindness God our Loving Parent remains faithful to us even when we are arrogant and alienated. Through unexplained loving kindness God the Son reconciles us and restores us to the image of God. In unexplained loving kindness God the Holy Spirit lives in our souls to keep us close to God moment by moment, and to enable us to walk in love (Ephesians 2:8–10; 5:2). *See also* DOCTRINAL STANDARDS.

Charles W. Brockwell, Jr.

GREECE. *See* EUROPE.

GREEN, ANSON (September 27, 1801–February 19, 1879), Canadian Methodist leader, was born in Middleburgh, New York, and converted at a Methodist meeting in 1819. Four years later, he immigrated to Upper **Canada** and taught near Kingston. Green received his preaching license at the first session of the Canada **Conference (MEC)**, August 1824. He was received on trial in 1825, ordained **deacon** in 1827, and **elder** in 1830. In 1828, when the conference formally became independent, he cast his lot with the Canadians, despite pleas from American clergy. He was chairman of the Augusta District (1832–1835), the Bay of Quinte District (1836–1839), and the Toronto and Hamilton districts (1840–1844). In 1846, he and **John Ryerson** successfully negotiated the reunion of the Canadian and British Wesleyan Methodist churches, and he promoted the union of several Canadian Methodist denominations. Green was conference book steward, 1844–1855, years during which he was a leading church administrator. His first retirement was in 1855, but he was re-elected book steward, 1859–1862 and 1864, and in 1863 was the first Canadian to be appointed president of the Canadian conference.

Green married Rachel Hopkins in 1828. They had one son, Columbus, and a daughter, Eliza.

Susan E. Warrick

GREEN, FREDERICK PRATT (September 2, 1903–October 22, 2000), described by Erik Routley as the first and most obvious successor to **Charles Wesley**, was educated at Rydal School, England, and trained for the ministry at Didsbury College. He was chairman of the York and Hull District (1957–1964). The kindling of his latent skills as an author in the 1940s led to three volumes of poetry and plays including *Farley Goes Out* (1928). Toward the end of his active ministry his talent as a hymn writer led him to serve on the working group established to produce *Hymns and Songs* (1969), a supplement to the 1933 *Methodist Hymn Book*. His prolific retirement bore fruit in two collections of *Hymns and Ballads* (1982 and 1989). He was co-editor of the 1979 *Partners in Praise* and a number of his hymns are included in *Hymns and Psalms*, *The United Methodist Hymnal* (1989), and other works. He has been honored by the Hymn Societies of Great Britain and Ireland and of America and was awarded an honorary doctorate by Emory University, Atlanta. The Pratt Green Trust gives assistance to projects in church music and hymnody. Its major project to date has been the computerized "Hymn Quest" containing the text of thousands of hymn texts and tunes with details of hymnbooks, authors, and composers. *See also* MUSIC.

Philip L. Carter

GRIMSHAW, WILLIAM (September 3, 1708–April 7, 1763), evangelical incumbent of Haworth, Yorkshire, England, described by **Frank Baker** as "the commander-in-chief of **revival** in the north." Born near Preston, he graduated from Christ's College, Cambridge, in 1730. After curacies at Littleborough and Todmorden, he moved to Haworth in 1742. He was hostile to Methodist **preaching** until he came under the influence of William Darney, provoking the gibe, "Mad Grimshaw is turned Scotch Will's clerk." He received first **Charles** and then **John Wesley** at Haworth, forging a firm friendship with them. They entrusted him with the superintendency of an extensive preaching **circuit**

known as the Great Haworth Round, encompassing parts of North and West Yorkshire, Lancashire, and Cumbria.

Grimshaw reported to the archbishop of York in 1749 that, during his incumbency, summer communicants at Haworth had increased from a mere dozen to some 1,200. By then John Wesley was ready to name him as successor to himself and his brother, but Grimshaw died in 1763 from a fever caught while visiting a sick parishioner. His behavior and "language of the market place" were certainly robust, but as John Wesley wrote: "a few such as him would make a nation tremble . . . he carries fire wherever he goes." His favorite text, "To us to live is Christ, to die is gain" was inscribed on the chapel he built for the Haworth Methodists in 1758.

John A. Hargreaves

GUATEMALA. *See* LATIN AMERICA AND THE CARIBBEAN.

– H –

HALE, JOSEPH RICE (March 25, 1935–), evangelist, administrator, and ecumenical leader (*see* ECUMENISM), was born in Texarkana, Texas, to Alfred Clay Hale and Bess Akin Hale. A graduate of Asbury College, Wilmore, Kentucky (B.A.) and Perkins School of Theology, Southern Methodist University, Dallas, Texas (B.D.), he was ordained an **elder** in **MC** in 1960. Following his service as the student pastor of a local church, Hale was appointed to the staff of the denomination's General Board of Evangelism from 1960 to 1975. The first national missioner of the board's newly formed Department of **Evangelism**, he conducted hundreds of New Life **missions** in **Africa, Asia, Europe**, and the USA. In 1975, Hale was chosen general secretary of the **World Methodist Council** with offices at Lake Junaluska, North Carolina, a position he held until his retirement in 2001. In that position he was widely recognized as one of the world's foremost ecumenical leaders. Under his leadership the council expanded its membership and influence. Hale was honored for his ministry with honorary doctorates from Asbury Theological Seminary and Florida Southern College. For his ecumenical service, he was awarded the Great Cross of Merit of the Equestrian Order of the Holy

Sepulchre in Jerusalem (1992) and the World Methodist Peace Award (2001). Hale married Mary Ida Richey on June 2, 1964.

Charles Yrigoyen, Jr.

HAMLINE, LEONIDAS LENT (May 10, 1797–March 23, 1865), **MEC** leader and bishop, was born at Burlington, Vermont, to Mark and Roxanna (Moses) Hamline, staunch New England Congregationalists. Hamline taught school and, for a time, practiced law in Ohio. In 1828 he came under the influence of Methodists while on a trip to New York and was converted. After his return to Ohio he became active in the **camp meeting** movement and other religious meetings. He was licensed to preach in 1829 and was ordained **elder** in the MEC in 1836. In 1837 Hamline was appointed assistant editor of the *Western Christian Advocate*. He was a delegate to the **General Conference**s of 1840 and 1844. At the former he was instrumental in the founding of the *Ladies' Repository*, a popular periodical for MEC **women**, and served as its editor until 1844. Despite warnings from his physicians that his health was too fragile to attend the 1844 General Conference, which dealt with the **slavery** issue, he attended and gave an important address on constitutional authority in the denomination. He was elected to the **episcopacy** at the 1844 General Conference and served eight years, resigning for reasons of health in 1852. His generous $25,000 gift helped to establish Hamline University, St. Paul, Minnesota. Hamline married Eliza Price in 1824. After Eliza's death in 1835, he married Melinda Truesdell in 1836. He is buried in Rose Hill Cemetery, Chicago.

Charles Yrigoyen, Jr.

HANBY, WILLIAM (April 8, 1808–May 17, 1880), **UB** bishop, was born in Washington County, Pennsylvania. In 1830, having moved to Ohio, Hanby experienced an evangelical **conversion**. In that year he also met and married his wife, Ann Miller. Soon afterward he entered the UB ministry. Hanby ministered on several **circuits** in Ohio before being elected publishing agent in 1837. Two years later he was elected editor of the *Religious Telescope*. While at the publishing house, Hanby compiled and published two hymnals, and was co-author of the first official UB history. In 1845 the **General Conference** elected

Hanby to a four-year term as bishop. Four years later he again became editor of the *Religious Telescope*. After 1853, Hanby returned to pastoral ministry in the area of his Westerville, Ohio, home. Hanby was instrumental in founding Otterbein College as well as being a leader in Ohio's abolitionist movement. His home was even used as a "station" on the Underground Railroad. Hanby's son, Benjamin, followed his father into the UB ministry, but is more well known as a composer, especially for his **antislavery** ballad, "My Darling Nellie Gray."

Daryl M. Elliott

HANNAH, JOHN (November 3, 1792–1867), British Methodist leader, was born in Lincoln, England. He became a Wesleyan minister in 1814, moving from rural circuits to Nottingham, Leeds, Manchester, and Huddersfield. Gaining the attention of **Jabez Bunting**, he was chosen to represent **British Methodism** at the **General Conference** of the **MEC** in 1824, to which he returned in 1856. As a renowned preacher and pastor (chairman of the Manchester and Bolton District 1842–1867), with a keen interest in missions (serving as secretary of the missionary society for much of the same period), he occupied a key place in the church. He served as secretary of **Conference** on nine occasions and as its president twice (in 1842 and 1851). His main contribution was in the establishment of theological colleges. He survived initial opposition to the creation of the Theological Institution at Hoxton, London, in 1834, and moved as tutor from there to the Northern Institution at Didsbury, Manchester, opened in 1842, where he remained until his death in 1867. He trained over 400 men as ministers for whom he wrote *A Letter to a Junior Methodist Preacher* in 1836 as the basis for his scheme of **education**.

Tim Macquiban

HARDIE, ROBERT ALEXANDER (June 11, 1865–June 30, 1949), missionary to Korea, was born in Caledonia, Ontario, and graduated from the University of Toronto's medical school in 1890 (*see* CANADA). He spent the next eight years in Wonsan, Korea, as a medical missionary, supported by the Canadian College Mission Board (*see* ASIA). In 1898, the mission was transferred to the **MECS**, and Hardie joined that denomination. He was ordained in

1900, and was appointed preacher in charge of the Wonsan **circuit**, 1900–1908, and **presiding elder**, 1908–1909. He led large-scale **revivals** during this period in Wonsan, Seoul, Songdo, and Pyengyang. In 1909 the Hardies moved to Seoul, where he taught Old Testament at the Union Methodist Theological Seminary until his retirement in 1935. He served as seminary president, 1913–1922, and edited its publication, *Theological World*. From 1923 to 1935, he represented the MECS mission on the editorial staff of the Christian Literature Society of Korea and edited *Christian Messenger*. During these years of multiple obligations he also continued to practice medicine. After retirement on January 1, 1936, the Hardies settled in Lansing, Michigan. Hardie married Margaret Kelly (1862–1946) in 1886. They had four daughters.

Susan E. Warrick

HARKNESS, GEORGIA ELMA (April 21, 1891–August 21, 1974), theologian and ethicist, was born in Harkness, New York, into a Methodist home. She earned a B.D. degree at Cornell University, New York and her Ph.D. degree at Boston University. After brief labors at Elmira and Cornell colleges, Harkness taught at Mt. Holyoke, Massachusetts (1937–1939), Garrett Biblical Institute, Illinois (1939–1950), and Pacific School of Religion, California (1950–1961). Harkness published 37 books. Whether addressing philosophical, ethical, or theological themes, she wrote with intelligent laypersons in mind, as two of her best-known theological works, *Understanding the Christian Faith* (1947) and *Foundations of Christian Knowledge* (1955), indicate. An evangelical liberal influenced by the **social gospel**, Harkness's ethical concerns were evidenced in her denunciation of the Versailles Treaty, racism, unbridled capitalism, war, and the internment of Japanese Americans in 1941. She defended **women's** rights and was an outstanding promoter of women's **ordination** in the **MC**. She was an active ecumenist (*see* ECUMENISM). Combined with her intellectual concerns was a deep devotional piety, augmented, in part, in reaction to a nervous breakdown in 1939. Her poetic side is best manifested by her popular hymn, "Hope of the World," written for the Second Assembly of the **WCC** in 1954. *See also* FEMINISM.

K. James Stein

HARRIS, HOWEL(L) (January 23, 1714–July 21, 1773), founder of **Welsh Calvinistic Methodism**, was born at Trevecka, Wales. Initially intended for holy orders, his father's death in 1731 interrupted his education and he began his career as a schoolmaster. Converted in 1735, he was soon involved in an itinerant ministry and in setting up societies (see SOCIETIES, CLASSES, AND BANDS). He made several applications for **ordination**, but was turned down, and therefore remained an Anglican layman throughout his life.

Harris met **George Whitefield** and the Wesleys in 1739. A long period of cooperation followed despite doctrinal differences with **John Wesley**. He often travelled to London to assist at Whitefield's Tabernacle, but during the latter half of the 1740s he was suspected of heresy. This, coupled with his autocratic manner and the presence of "Madam" Sidney Griffith as his travelling companion, led to tension that resulted in his separation from Rowland and the majority of Welsh Methodists in June 1750. Following the death of "Madam" Griffith in 1752, he retired to Trevecka and established a Christian community that became known as the "Trevecka Family." Fearful of a Catholic invasion in the late 1750s, he joined the militia. When his regiment was disbanded in 1762, he was reconciled with his former co-revivalists and resumed itinerating (see ITINERACY). By then, a new **revival** had broken out in Wales that centered on Llangeitho, and Harris was marginalized by a new generation of Methodists. Following the death of his wife in 1770, Harris's own health began to deteriorate. He is buried at Talgarth.

Geraint Tudur

HARTZELL, JOSEPH CRANE (June 1, 1842–September 6, 1928), **MEC** pastor and missionary bishop, grew up near Moline, Illinois. In 1868 he graduated from Illinois Wesleyan College and Garrett Biblical Institute (now Garrett-Evangelical Theological Seminary) and was admitted to membership in the Central Illinois **Conference**. The following year he married Jennie Culver. After serving several Illinois churches, he was appointed to Ames Chapel, New Orleans, and later served as **presiding elder** for a total of 26 years. He worked with blacks in building schools and hospitals and served on the city's Board of Education. He was also a member of the Freedmen's Aid Society, being elected corresponding secretary in 1888. He was a

General Conference delegate for 20 years, 1876–1896. At the 1896 General Conference a new Congo Mission Conference was authorized (*see* AFRICA). He was elected missionary bishop and assigned to organize it. Hartzell retired in 1916. On his 86th birthday he was assaulted and robbed near his home in Blue Ash, Ohio, and died as a result of his injuries.

Barbara E. Campbell

HASTINGS, SELINA. *See* HUNTINGDON, COUNTESS OF.

HAVEN, GILBERT (September 19, 1821–January 3, 1880), **MEC** bishop and social reformer, was born at Malden, Massachusetts. Member of the New England Annual **Conference** (MEC), he served as a chaplain during the Civil War. After the war he served congregations in New Jersey and New York. He became editor of *Zion's Herald* (1867), and, in 1872, he was elected bishop and assigned to serve at Atlanta, Georgia, in the midst of the postwar Reconstruction era. Haven became exceedingly unpopular with southern Methodists due to his abolitionist views and egalitarian attitudes toward African Americans. He was an ardent supporter of social and legal equality among the races, and he even advocated racial amalgamation. He also became a pioneer advocate of **women**'s suffrage and equality, prohibition, and lay representation at all levels of church conferences (*see* FEMINISM; LAITY RIGHTS; TEMPERANCE). Perhaps the most controversial aspect of Haven's work was his willingness to advocate such views from the standpoint of his southern episcopal assignment. His numerous publications included a volume of prophetic sermons.

J. Steven O'Malley

HAYGOOD, ATTICUS GREENE (November 19, 1839–January 18, 1896), **MECS** bishop, was born in Watkinsville, Georgia. He was home schooled, largely by his mother, a professional teacher. He entered Emory College at Oxford, Georgia, as a sophomore, graduating in 1859. That same year Haygood and Mary (Mollie) Fletcher Yarbrough married and he was admitted on trial to the Georgia **Conference**. Their marriage produced four children. Haygood was a pastor until 1870, including two brief chaplaincies with Confederate forces (1861, 1863–1864). Then for 26 years he was a denominational administrator (Sunday schools and the Board of Missions), editor (general church and annual conference levels), college president (Emory), national agent for an African-American college fund (Slater Fund), and bishop (from 1890). He was elected to the **episcopacy** twice, but declined his 1882 selection. The 1880s were Haygood's most productive and positive years. He earned a national reputation as a southerner who worked for north-south amity and for industrialization of the South, and as a white who promoted African-American advancement. He was also influential in establishing mandatory public education in Georgia. His 1880 Thanksgiving sermon, "The New South," and his 1881 book *Our Brother in Black* are monuments of progressive southern Christian social thought in the years between Reconstruction and the rise of populism. His sister was **Laura Askew Haygood**.

Charles W. Brockwell, Jr.

HAYGOOD, LAURA ASKEW (October 14, 1845–April 29, 1900), **MECS** missionary to China, was born in Watkinsville, Georgia. She was home schooled, largely by her mother, a professional teacher. She graduated from Wesleyan Female College, Macon, Georgia, at 19 after two years of study. Haygood was a teacher from 1862 until 1877 when she became principal of Girls' High School, Atlanta. In 1884 she was sent to Shanghai, China, by the Woman's Board of Missions (MECS) to help administer their work there, succeeding to the leadership office in 1889 (*see* ASIA). Under Haygood, the Clopton School for girls became a teacher training school for Chinese **women**. Her greatest legacy was the McTyeire Home and School, a residence and language school for new missionaries. McTyeire School also educated Chinese women in both Chinese and Western cultural traditions. Haygood had to go home on medical furlough (1894–1896), but returned to China to head all the Woman's Board work in that country. She died and is buried in Shanghai. A home and school was established in Soochow to memorialize her name. One of her brothers, **Atticus G. Haywood**, was an MECS bishop.

Charles W. Brockwell, Jr.

HECK, BARBARA RUCKLE (1734–August 17, 1804), Irish Methodist who was involved with the establishment of Methodism in what would become both the USA and **Canada**. She was born in **Ireland** in 1734 in a community settled by refugees from the German Palatinate. She was raised in a Methodist environment and married Paul Heck in 1760. Sometime afterward the Hecks, along with others from the community, immigrated to New York. The new immigrants no doubt found themselves in a distracting environment in colonial New York, in the 1760s. It was because of Barbara Heck's prodding that the group of Irish Methodist immigrants began to revitalize their faith. She encouraged **Philip Embury** to form a Methodist class meeting around 1766 (*see* SOCIETIES, CLASSES, AND BANDS). This led to the building of the **John Street** meetinghouse in New York in 1768. The Hecks left the American colonies during the Revolutionary War and settled in Canada in 1778. They first lived in Montreal and later in Augusta township, near Brockville, Ontario. In both places she was involved in establishing Methodist class meetings. In 1799, she moved one last time to a new home on the St. Lawrence River.

L. Dale Patterson

HEDDING, ELIJAH (June 7, 1780–April 9, 1852), **MEC** bishop, was born at White Plains, New York. In 1798, at the age of 18, he became an exhorter in the MEC and traveled a **circuit** around the New England area. In 1801 he was admitted on trial in the New York **Conference**. He was ordained a **deacon** by Bishop **Richard Whatcoat** and an **elder** by Bishop **Francis Asbury**. In 1805, because of a boundary change, he became a member of the New England Conference. He served in this conference until he was elected bishop (*see* EPISCOPACY). Hedding attended, either as a delegate or as a bishop, every **General Conference** from 1808 until his death. He favored the delegated General Conference proposal in 1808. He was, initially, in favor of the proposal to make the **presiding elder** an elective position. While opposed to what he considered extreme abolitionists, he helped to start the independent Methodist newspaper *Zion's Herald* in 1823. He was elected bishop in 1824 and traveled through most of the USA. He was considered an authority on the **Discipline**.He died in Poughkeepsie, New York.

L. Dale Patterson

HEDSTROM, OLAF GUSTAV (1803–May 5, 1877), pioneer Swedish-American Methodist preacher, was born in Kronberg Lans, Sweden, and traveled as a sailor to America, where he entered the clothing business in Pennsylvania. He was introduced to Methodism through his American–born wife, Caroline Pinckney. Responding to a call to preach, he was received on trial by the New York **Conference** in 1835. An American, David Terry, and a Swede, Peter Berger, who were the first to undertake mission work among Scandinavian sailors, purchased an old condemned brig in New York harbor. Hedstrom became the first pastor of their rechristened *Bethel Ship* in early 1845. Soon a **Sunday school**, a tract mission, a **Bible** mission, and a program of **evangelism** to incoming boats were commenced. This "North River Mission" became the mother of Scandinavian Methodism in America, as thousands of immigrants and sailors visited the Bethelship in the following years. Among Hedstrom's sailor converts aboard Bethelship were men who subsequently took Methodism to Norway, Sweden, and Finland.

J. Steven O'Malley

HERNÁNDEZ, ALEJO (July 17, 1842–September 27, 1875), was the first Mexican ordained by any Methodist body. Hernández was a seminarian in Aguas Calientes, Mexico, during the French invasion of 1862. He joined the liberal army of Benito Juárez, was captured by the French, and at the end of the war was on the Texas–Mexican frontier. There, his interest in the **Bible**, provoked by an anti-Catholic propaganda pamphlet left behind by a soldier of the U.S. Army that invaded Mexico in 1846, led him across the border into the USA. He became a Protestant and returned to Mexico, where his efforts to share his faith were unwelcome. In 1870, Hernández appeared in the **MECS** in Corpus Christi, Texas, where he became a member and was licensed to preach. In 1871, at the West Texas Annual **Conference** in Leesburg, he was admitted on trial and ordained a **deacon** "for missionary work among the Mexicans." He was appointed to Laredo, Texas. In 1872, Hernández was appointed to Corpus Christi, but after only a few weeks of service Bishop John C. Keener sent him to Mexico City, where he was instrumental in beginning missionary activity for the MECS. In 1874, Hernández became ill and returned to Corpus Christi, Texas, where he died.

Edwin E. Sylvest, Jr.

HINES, GUSTAVUS (September 16, 1809–December 9, 1873), early **MEC** missionary to Oregon and author, was born in Herkimer County, New York, and itinerated in the Genesee **Conference** from 1832 to 1839. Appointed to Oregon, he arrived there by sea in 1840, part of the "Great Reinforcement" of the original 1834 mission. Though he soon thereafter wrote the Mission Board in New York a letter critical of the management of the mission, Hines remained a good friend of its superintendent **Jason Lee**. Apart from a return to New York in 1845–1853, Hines spent the rest of his ministry in Oregon, preaching and serving as first principal of the short-lived Indian Manual Labor School, a founding trustee of the Oregon Institute (later Willamette University), **presiding elder**, and delegate to the **General Conference** of 1868. His books, *Life on the Plains of the Pacific* (1851) and *Oregon and Its Institutions* (1868), provided a national audience with substantial sketches of religious, secular, and natural Oregon. The first book's title in later editions gives a sense of the myth-making potential of Hines' narrative: *Wild Life in Oregon: Being a Stirring Recital of Actual Scenes of Daring and Peril among the Gigantic Forests and Terrific Rapids of the Columbia River . . . giving Lifelike Pictures of Terrific Encounters with Savages as Fierce and Relentless as its Mighty Tides. . . .*

Charles Wallace, Jr.

HOLINESS MOVEMENT. A revival movement rising mainly within American Methodism in the late 1830s. It was dedicated to the promotion of the Wesleyan doctrine of **Christian perfection** understood as a call to Christian believers to experience entire **sanctification** as a second instantaneous work of **grace** subsequent to that of **justification** and regeneration. This crisis of purification and spiritual empowerment was perceived to be the beginning rather than the end of true progress toward Christian maturity.

The weekly "Tuesday Meetings for the Promotion of Christian Holiness," held in the New York City home of Methodist laypersons Walter and **Phoebe Palmer**, and Phoebe's sister, **Sarah Lankford**, constituted the focal point of the early revival. Timothy Merritt's *Guide to Christian Perfection*, begun in 1839, supported the new movement. A parallel holiness initiative was begun at the same time by "New School" Calvinist revivalists Charles G. Finney, Asa Mahan, and other leaders of the Oberlin holiness revival. The formation of the National Campmeeting Association for the Promotion of Holiness by **John Inskip** and other **MEC** pastors in 1867 marked a new phase of holiness **evangelism**. The **EA** and the **UB** supported the revival. The Methodist revival "Wesleyanized" much of post–Civil War **Quakerism** and sectors of the Anabaptist churches. By the end of the Civil War, the revival had spread to **Europe** and the Continent. It reached its peak there in the 1873–1875 holiness meetings of lay holiness evangelists Robert Pearsall Smith and his wife Hannah Whitall Smith. The organization of the Keswick Convention and the higher-Christian life movement that it supported were a direct result of their revivalism. Their work also influenced the German *Gemeinschaftsbewegung*, pietistic deeper-life groups within the Lutheran and Reformed churches of Europe, and the developing Methodist church in Germany. Numerous other smaller Wesleyan holiness and **pentecostal** bodies were organized in England and on the Continent as a result of the revival.

Heated debates over the "holiness question," the movement's aggressive evangelism, and its resistance to the acculturation of what it believed to be basic Wesleyan values and experience to the society around it, created increasing tensions between church and movement. By the early 1880s, the newly organized **Salvation Army** and Church of God (Anderson, Indiana), among others, took their place as holiness churches beside the **Wesleyan Methodist** (1843) and **Free Methodist** (1860) churches, which had already associated with the movement. By the turn of the 20th century, the ongoing controversy produced a spate of new holiness churches and agencies such as the Church of the Nazarene, the Pilgrim Holiness Church, and the Oriental Missionary Society. The movement's adherents who stayed within Methodism also rallied to new holiness institutions such as Taylor University (Indiana), Asbury College (Kentucky), and Asbury Seminary (Kentucky).

The Wesleyan/holiness churches affiliated with the Christian Holiness Association, contemporary successor to the National Campmeeting Association for the Promotion of Holiness, constitute the core of churches most commonly identified as "holiness churches." Several churches which formed out of the holiness revival such as the

Pentecostal Holiness Church, The Church of God (Cleveland, Tennessee), and the Church of Christ are more commonly identified with the pentecostal movement.

Melvin E. Dieter

HOLY SPIRIT. The understanding of the doctrine of the Holy Spirit, the third person of the **Trinity**, begins with the Old Testament progression of God's self-disclosure of his Spirit to his people. The basic term for "spirit" in the Old Testament is *ruach* meaning "breath" or "wind." *Ruach* is an agent of God in the creation of the world (Genesis 1:2); every living thing derives its life from the *ruach* of God (Psalm 104:30); God's "breath" brings skills and wisdom to persons who are called to special tasks (Exodus 35:31–32, Deuteronomy 34:9). It is *ruach* that moved the prophets and the judges (I Samuel 19:18ff; Hosea 9:7; Judges 3:10, 6:34). Ezekiel claims it as the source of his prophetic inspiration (Ezekiel 2:2, 3:24, 11:5). The "Servant of Yahweh" is uniquely endowed with the Spirit (Isaiah 11:2, 42:1). The prophets' promised indwelling presence of the Spirit in the hearts of the people of God (Ezekiel 37:9, Isaiah 48:16, and Joel 2:28) anticipates New Testament understanding of the person and work of the Spirit.

The New Testament continues to associate the Spirit with "wind" and "power" (Greek *pneuma* in John 3:8), but the frequent use of the term "Holy Spirit" indicates a decidedly ethical bent to the developing understanding of the church. Every book of the New Testament refers to the Holy Spirit except Philemon, II John, and III John. The Messiah is uniquely endowed with the Spirit (Luke 1:35, 3:22). Every part of his ministry is associated with the Spirit. At the close of his ministry, Christ promises to his disciples "another" Paraclete, who will baptize them, dwell in them, and empower them to carry out his redemptive ministry in the world (John 14:26, 15:26, 16:7). The Pentecost event marked the fulfillment of Christ's promise and the establishment of his church (Acts 2). The apostolic church lived in the presence and power of the Holy Spirit (I Corinthians 12–14). Through the Spirit believers are sanctified (I Corinthians 6:11), are one with Christ (II Corinthians 1:22), and with one another (I Corinthians 12:4ff). Paul associates Christ and the Spirit so intimately that his discourse about the Christian's life in Christ and life in the Spirit flows almost indistinguishably from one image to the other.

For almost three centuries after the close of the apostolic era the simple, "I believe in the Holy Spirit," of the Apostle's Creed remained the main creedal confession of the church's teaching about the Holy Spirit. It was not until the Council of Constantinople in AD 381 that the Holy Spirit was confessed as "the Giver of life, who proceedeth from the Father, and with the Father and the Son is to be adored and glorified, who spake by the holy prophets." Subsequent controversy concerning the procession of the Spirit from both the Father and the Son as held by the Western church (Council of Toledo in 589) and procession from the Father alone as retained by the Eastern church was one of the primary factors which produced the division of catholic Christianity which persists to this day. Subsequent developments in the **Roman Catholic Church**'s teaching on the Holy Spirit dealt largely with the Spirit's work in the inspiration of scripture, and the authentication of the traditions of the church.

A more personal and experiential emphasis upon the witness and leadership of the Holy Spirit had its roots in a renewed accent on the work of the Holy Spirit among the reformers of the 16th century (*see* WITNESS OF THE SPIRIT). Luther spoke of the Spirit as the creator of new life in Christ. The Spirit was God present in Christ's saving work. However, the Christocentric and forensic focus of Lutheran teaching on **justification** tended to mute any distinct emphasis on the Holy Spirit and **sanctification**. Calvin emphasized more strongly the inner witness of the Spirit and his work in the sanctification of believers, but historically traditional Calvinism also tended to restrict the activity of the Holy Spirit to the word and through the word. The desire for a more personal and intimate relationship with God and Christ through the Holy Spirit was one of the primary impulses that led to the birth of the Pietist movement within the Lutheran and Reformed traditions. The direct influence of the Holy Spirit in the prevenience of **grace** by which God led men and women to himself, the personal inspiration and guidance of the Spirit in life and vocation, and the fellowship of the Holy Spirit were advanced as "true Christianity" against what was regarded to be merely intellectualized and institutionalized expressions of the faith. A call for personal holiness of life and the recognition of the Spirit as the source of life in Christ led to a renewed emphasis on the doctrine of sanctification. **Quakers**, Anabaptists, and Methodists joined with the Pietists in emphasizing a more universal operation of the Holy Spirit in accepting and proclaiming their own variations of these themes. The presence and work of the Holy Spirit in the world was central to **John Wesley**'s understanding of God's plan of personal and cosmic redemption. Wesleyan commitments to the centrality of **prevenient grace**, personal **assurance** of **salvation**, and the optimism of grace constituted a major source of the renewal of interest in the Holy Spirit in the 19th-century Christian church. The first, Wesley's insistence on the universality of the Spirit's redemptive work, provided a biblical alternative to the more restrictive understanding of particular election to salvation; the second, his belief in the reality of the Spirit's personal assurance of acceptance with God, opened up new insights into the possibilities of experiential Christianity; the third, his insistence that the Spirit's presence and power offered the possibility for the restoration of the image of God in the souls of believers, undergirded all his calls to **Christian perfection** in wholehearted love for God and neighbor.

Today the **UMC doctrinal standards** and all smaller related Methodist bodies retain statements concerning the Holy Spirit in harmony with the historical commitments of the Christian church. However, Wesley's, and especially **John Fletcher**'s, broader understanding of the centrality of the work of the Holy Spirit to Christian life and mission opened up the possibility for the rise of the 19th-century Methodist/holiness revival (*see* HOLINESS MOVEMENT. With other like-minded movements it gave birth to a renewed interest in the Holy Spirit unparalleled in post-apostolic Christianity. The revival's emphasis upon the Pentecost event and the continuing presence and power of the Holy Spirit in the world gave birth to both the holiness and the **pentecostal** movements and the centrality of pneumatology to their understanding of ecclesiology, **Christian experience**, and mission.

Melvin E. Dieter

HOMOSEXUALITY refers to sexual attraction for persons of one's own sex, which may or may not include sexual activity. The attraction may be interpreted as innate or learned, the sexual activity as always sinful or affirmable in a covenant relationship. Traditionally, Christians have rejected homosexuality on the basis of the **Bible** and natural law. Because a few biblical texts condemn male homosexuality (Lev 18:22 and 20:13, 1 Cor 6:9, 1 Tim 1:10) and one condemns both male and female homosexuality (Rom 1:26–27), and because nature has tied human procreation to male-female sexual intercourse, the traditional position is that homosexual sex is a sin. Recently, the biblical texts have been seen as culturally conditioned. And it has been reasoned that because homosexuality has appeared, and sometimes been celebrated, in most societies throughout history, it is a natural variant of human sexuality. Research suggests that about 5 to 10 percent of human beings are homosexually oriented, and homosexual behavior appears among more than 450 species in every major geographical region and in every major animal group.

Since the sexual revolution of the 1960s, homosexuality has been a contentious issue in the **UMC**, with the church's official position, adopted in 1972, being that homosexual practice is "incompatible with Christian teaching." The 1984 **General Conference** prohibited the **ordination** and appointment of "self-avowed practicing homosexuals." The 1996 Conference declared: "homosexual unions shall not be conducted by our ministers and shall not be conducted in our churches."

The debate on homosexuality intensified, both inside the church and out, when, in 2000, the state of Vermont, responding to a 1999 decision of the state's Supreme Court that same-sex couples are entitled to marriage-like benefits, approved a bill authorizing "civil unions" for same-sex couples. Four years later, in 2004, the Supreme Judicial Court of Massachusetts declared that "civil unions" treated homosexuals as second-class citizens, and ordered the state legislature to grant homosexuals full access to civil marriage. Meanwhile, in 2003, the U. S. Supreme Court invalidated state laws banning anal and oral sex in private between consenting adults. Responding to those court cases and a large number of same-sex marriages authorized by the mayor of San Francisco in February 2004, President George W. Bush announced his support for an amendment to the U.S. Constitution that would bar same-sex marriage and invalidate any state or municipal law conferring marriage or its corresponding benefits on gay couples. In March 2004, a UMC trial court found the

Rev. Karen Dammann not guilty, even though she told her bishop she was living in a covenanted relationship with another woman and, just before the trial, had married her. However, the 2004 UMC General Conference did not alter its policies regarding homosexual clergy.

John G. McEllhenney

HONDURAS. *See* LATIN AMERICA AND THE CARIBBEAN.

HOOVER, THERESSA (September 7, 1925–), United Methodist Women general agency staff, was born in Fayetteville, Arkansas. After graduation from Philander Smith College (1946), she spent two years on the staff of the Little Rock Methodist Council, then became a field worker of the **MC** Woman's Division of Christian Service (1948). In 1962 she received her M.A. from New York University. She held three additional positions, including 22 years (1968–1990) as head of the division staff. When elected in 1968, she held the highest staff position ever occupied by a black woman in a Methodist agency. She wrote the *Response* magazine monthly feature "Responsively Yours" for 22 years, and was widely known throughout the **UMC** as a teacher, lecturer, and speaker. In 1972, she gave oversight to the creation of United Methodist Women (UMC). She wrote *With Unveiled Face* (1983), a chapter in *Methodism's Destiny in an Ecumenical Age* (1969), and many articles. Hoover was a delegate to the 1976 UMC **General Conference**. She retired in 1990, and the annual Theressa Hoover Community Service and Global Citizen Award (given by the Women's Division, General Board of Global Ministries, UMC) honors her work.

Barbara E. Campbell

HOPKEY, SOPHIA (ca. 1718–?) was niece and ward of Thomas Causton, chief magistrate of Savannah, Georgia, when John and **Charles Wesley** arrived there in 1736. Sophia met **John Wesley** at her uncle's home. She was probably 18 years of age, and Wesley described her as a modest girl, quick to learn, attentive to the needs of others, and possessing a happy, kindly disposition. Wesley became her tutor, fell in love with her, and considered marrying her. Wesley, however, could not make up his mind concerning marriage, and

Sophia, after tolerating his vacillation for some time, married a Mr. Williamson who was living at her uncle's home. Wesley was deeply hurt, and in the ensuing weeks was highly critical of Sophia for what he considered her failure to continue her spiritual exercises. Later, because of an infraction of church law on her part, he refused to serve her communion. Her uncle and her husband were both enraged, charging Wesley with slandering Sophia's character, among other actions. Wesley was never brought to trial and returned to England in 1737. Sophia had a miscarriage that her friends blamed upon Wesley's attitude and conduct toward her. Eventually the Williamsons returned to England. Little or nothing is known of their subsequent life.

Frederick E. Maser

HORNER, RALPH CECIL (December 22, 1854–September 12, 1921), Methodist preacher, holiness evangelist, and church founder, was born near Shawville, Quebec. In 1872, he was first converted, then sanctified (*see* SANCTIFICATION). Soon he began to conduct services. After studying at Victoria College in Cobourg and at a school of oratory in Philadelphia, he was ordained in May 1887. Horner felt called to **evangelism** and spent his next years in evangelistic work. In 1894, however, he was assigned to a **circuit**. He refused to go and was suspended. The following year he was deposed from the Methodist ministry. Although the action resulted from Horner's breach of church **discipline**, many Methodists were concerned by Horner's holiness **revivalism** at which physical "manifestations" were frequently present (*see* HOLINESS MOVEMENT). Horner organized his followers into a new church and obtained **ordination** through the Wesleyan Methodist Connection (*see* WESLEYAN CHURCH) in New York. In 1902, his group was incorporated as the Holiness Movement Church in **Canada**. Its distinctive belief was in a third gift, the **baptism** of the Holy Ghost. A split occurred in 1918 with Horner and some of his followers organizing the Standard Church of America. Both the Holiness Movement Church and the Standard Church were active in mission work, particularly in Egypt.

Marilyn Färdig Whiteley

HOSIER, HARRY (ca. 1750–ca. 1806), known as "Black Harry," perhaps a plantation slave, became, after his **conversion**, a groom to **Francis Asbury**. At the **Christmas Conference**, December 24, 1784, Hosier and **Richard Allen** were the two black (nonvoting) representatives. In addition to the menial labors performed for Asbury, Hosier accompanied him and other itinerant preachers on their rounds, proving himself a self-taught master of homiletics and forensics. The physician, chemist, and Declaration of Independence signer Benjamin Rush (1746–1813) thought him the greatest orator in America. **Thomas Coke** identified Hosier as one of the best preachers in the world. Occasionally, Asbury assigned Hosier to Coke, who directed him to preach at late afternoon or early evening services, reasoning that blacks attended then and whites would remain for sermons. In 1790, Hosier accompanied **Freeborn Garrettson** on an evangelistic tour, traveling to Boston and preaching regularly. Despite his small stature, he could capture the attention of crowds. On more than one occasion he substituted for Asbury, who asserted that he would rather hear "Black Harry" preach than listen to himself. According to Asbury, the first reference to Methodism in the news sheets of New York came from reporting the sermons of Harry Hosier.

Samuel J. Rogal

HOWARD, WILBERT FRANCIS (December 30, 1880–July 10, 1952) was born in Gloucester, England. After taking a degree at Manchester University, he trained for the Wesleyan ministry at Didsbury College. He became New Testament Tutor at Handsworth College in 1919, where he remained until his retirement in 1951, becoming principal when the college reopened after World War II. He was president of the **Conference** in 1944 and was joint chairman of the **World Methodist Conference**s of 1947 and 1951. An internationally renowned scholar, he was awarded honorary degrees at St. Andrews and Manchester. His main scholarly work was in New Testament Greek and St. John's Gospel. He was editor and joint author of Volume II of J. H. Moulton's *Grammar of NT Greek* and was working on Volume III at the time of his death. As well as *The Fourth Gospel in Recent Criticism and Interpretation* (1931) and *Christianity according to St John* (1943), he wrote the more popular *The Romance of NT*

Scholarship (1949), based on his Drew Lectures of 1947, and also contributed I & II Corinthians to the *Abingdon Commentary*.

Cyril S. Rodd

HUGHES, HUGH PRICE (February 8, 1847–November 17, 1902), preacher and reformer, was born at Carmarthen, South Wales. He trained for the Wesleyan Methodist ministry at Richmond College and served in circuits on the south coast and London before moving to Oxford as **superintendent** (1881–1884). His early interest in social and political matters and his editorship of the *Methodist Times* (1885) led him to be chosen as the first superintendent of the West London Mission in 1887, Methodism's response to the needs of the capital. As part of the Forward Movement, he campaigned for a more active social involvement of the church in **education**, in **temperance**, and in gambling questions. His stand on public morality led him to oppose Parnell, the Irish nationalist leader, for which he and others became known as the "Nonconformist Conscience" of the nation. He was instrumental in the creation of the Free Church Council in the 1890s, of which he was first president. Nevertheless his interest in liturgy and **ecumenism** led to conversations with the Church of England at Grindelwald. He represented a strong tradition in Methodism toward supporting the Liberal Party and involvement in local and national politics. He was elected president of the Wesleyan Methodist **Conference** in 1898. He died in the active ministry.

Tim Macquiban

HUMAN RIGHTS are claims or protections to which all persons are entitled simply because they are human, without regard to other status that may give them special rights. Human rights thus are independent of the authority of government, although government power may be important to their enforcement. Governments may give or withhold special rights, for example, the right to drive an automobile or to participate in a social security system, but all governments must respect human rights. Increasingly, international law has developed the principle that those who are responsible for serious violations of human rights may be held accountable by the international community, regardless of the legality of their actions under local law at the time the violations occurred.

Legal scholars divide human rights into two broad categories. First, there are civil and political rights, sometimes called *negative* rights, which protect persons against harm that others might do to them. Various forms of freedom are negative rights, such as the freedom to practice religion. So, too, are most property rights, which do not ensure that everyone will have property, but which protect persons in their enjoyment and preservation of the property that they do have. Modern thinking about human rights originated with the development of ideas about these civil and political rights leading up to the USA Declaration of Independence (1776) and Bill of Rights (1789), and to the French Declaration of the Rights of Man (1789).

In addition to these negative rights, philosophers, jurists, and legislators in the 20th century became increasingly concerned about economic and social rights, sometimes called *positive* rights, which give persons claims to a share of the resources that a society has to offer, as well as protection from external threats. Such positive rights might include a right to essential health care, to a basic minimum standard of living, or to employment at a wage adequate to support oneself and one's family. Both political and civil rights and economic and social rights are found in the Universal Declaration of Human Rights (1948), as well as other 20th-century documents that have attempted to enumerate basic human rights.

Although the origin of the modern language of human rights is largely in secular revolutionary movements, the idea that all persons have value in God's sight guided the work of many Christian leaders during the 18th and 19th centuries. Insistence on care for the poor, opposition to **slavery,** and a rejection of habits that degrade those who practice them united many Methodists in upholding basic human dignity and insisting on protection of the weak and vulnerable in society. Because these missional activities were directed to needs, as well as to protection from harm, the **UMC** Social Principles (see SOCIAL CREED) freely mix both positive and negative rights, holding that both are essential to the life of human beings created in the image of God.

Robin W. Lovin

HUNGARY. *See* EUROPE.

HUNTINGDON, SELINA, COUNTESS OF (August 24, 1707–June 17, 1791), Calvinistic Methodist leader, was daughter to Earl Ferrars and married in 1728 the Ninth Earl of Huntingdon, of Donnington Park, Leicestershire. Affected by the gospel preaching of Benjamin Ingham, who was married to her sister-in-law, she was converted ca. 1738. A friend of the **Wesleys** and **George Whitefield**, she joined the Fetter Lane society in London and introduced many in high society to evangelical preachers. She acted as their patron and protector, offering her living room as a meeting place when open-air preaching was dangerous, and building chapels in Brighton, Bath, Tunbridge Wells, and Spa Fields in London. The opening of the latter resulted in a lawsuit that caused her to break with the Established Church in 1781, forming her own Connection of independent chapels. To train ministers, she opened a college at Trevecka in 1768, near the home of **Howell Harris**. Despite early Methodist endorsement, Joseph Benson, its second headmaster, and **John Fletcher**, its president, resigned in 1771 over the Arminian-Calvinist dispute that divided the Evangelical Revival (*see* ARMINIUS, JACOBUS). The Countess' Connection remained small but independent after her death in 1791.

Tim Macquiban

– I –

INDIA. *See* ASIA.

INDONESIA. *See* ASIA.

INSKIP, JOHN SWANEL (April 10, 1816–March 7, 1884) and **MARTHA FOSTER INSKIP** (August 11, 1819–December 26, 1890), **MEC** leaders in the **holiness** revival following the Civil War, were married in 1836. John Inskip was born in Huntingdon, England. His family came to the USA in 1821, settling in Chester County, Pennsylvania. Converted at the age of 16, he quickly prepared for ministerial appointment. He was ordained an **elder** in the MEC Philadelphia **Conference** (1840). He was instrumental in changing rules that had prevented families from sitting together in worship services and was a committed abolitionist. During the Civil War, John served as chaplain in the 14th Regiment, New York Militia. Martha joined him in the field and their common service to the wounded after the first battle at Bull Run constituted an indicator of how closely intertwined their ministries were to be. After the war, the two became well known for their holiness **evangelism** and leadership of the National Camp Meeting Association for the Promotion of Holiness. Inskip was instrumental in its organization in 1867, served as its president until his death, and developed the periodicals and publications that supported its **revivalism**. At the 48 national camp meetings at which John presided, Martha led devotional services and was one of the first to hold children's services as a regular part of the holiness camp meeting's daily agenda. After John's death, Martha continued her ministry, speaking at camp meetings and in children's and youth meetings, and raising funds for **missions** and new churches. After her husband's death, Martha married Ashley L. S. Bateman in the fall of 1890.

Melvin E. Dieter

IRELAND. George Whitefield visited Ireland as early as 1738; but it was **John Wesley**'s 21 visits between 1747 and 1789 that played a vital part in the development of Irish Methodism. He presided over the **Conference** as often as possible, alternating with **Thomas Coke** in later years. His Irish tours were generally based in Dublin, where he established the Irish Methodist headquarters. By 1789, membership exceeded 14,000.

The leaders of the insurrection of United Irishmen in 1798 included Catholics, Anglicans, and Presbyterians. Methodists generally supported the government. Coke, believing that evangelical **conversion** was a preventative, urged the Irish Conference to act, and in 1799 it established the General Mission under Irish-speaking preachers. It played a major part in the 19th-century growth of Irish Methodism.

The main division within Irish Methodism—between Wesleyans and **Primitive Wesleyans**—took place in 1816, when limited authority was given to the Irish preachers to administer the **sacraments**. Those opposed to this development established a separate Primitive Wesleyan Conference in 1818. The two bodies were united in 1878 to form the Methodist Church in Ireland, which remains united despite the political division of the country in 1922.

Through five city **missions** and in other ways, the gospel is related to the whole of life. The Methodist Church's contribution to **education** is highlighted by Wesley College (Dublin), Methodist College (Belfast), and Gurteen agricultural college in Tipperary.

The failure of the potato crop in 1846–1847 caused a major famine and out of a population of eight million about one million died and another million emigrated. Membership fell from a peak of 44,000 in 1844 to 26,000 in 1855. In 2002 membership stood at 15,924, with a total Methodist community of over 55,000. From the outset Irish Methodism had its greatest influence among people from the Established Church and migrant European minorities (e.g., **Moravians**, Palatines, and Huguenots). Less impact was made on Roman Catholics and Presbyterians. These factors help to account for its uneven distribution.

The founders of Methodism in New York (**Barbara Heck** and **Philip Embury**) and in Maryland (**Robert Strawbridge**) were all born in Ireland. Another important influence in America was that of Irish dissidents, including **James O'Kelly**, **William Hammett**, and **Alexander McCaine**. More than 200 Irish-born ministers served in Canadian Methodism before 1900. Through involvement in the mission agencies of Methodism in Britain and elsewhere, the Irish played an important role in the world church.

Dudley A. L. Cooney and Norman W. Taggart

ITALY. *See* EUROPE.

ITINERACY is the distinctive system employed in Methodism by which pastors are appointed to serve their churches. Not all Methodist denominations have bishops, but churches that have an episcopal form of government use bishops to do the appointing (*see* EPISCOPACY). Other Methodist bodies have alternative means of assigning pastors to their churches. Pastors are obligated to serve the churches to which they are appointed and local congregations are expected to receive the persons appointed as their pastors. Appointments are usually made on an annual basis and are fixed at the annual

conferences of the church. The appointment of a pastor to a local church may be renewed for the following year unless the denomination has a tenure rule that limits the number of consecutive years a pastor may serve in one location. Methodist pastors are said to "itinerate" in this system. When an itinerant pastor no longer wishes to itinerate, or is deemed unable to do so, the person may request or be forced to "locate," that is, to cease being a member of the itinerating ministry. The Methodist itineracy is considerably different from another type of ecclesiastical polity, whereby a congregation has the right and responsibility to "call," or invite, a person to be its pastor.

The itineracy began with **John Wesley** who carried on an itinerant ministry as a priest in the Church of England when he decided to pursue an evangelical **preaching** and pastoral ministry, which involved traveling throughout England, Scotland, Wales, and **Ireland** rather than settling as a parish priest in one location. This itineration enabled Wesley to preach and organize in any community he visited. As the Methodist movement grew, Wesley enlisted the support of **lay preachers**, or assistants, who supervised the work of the Methodist societies and preached in various locations. The expansion of the movement caused Wesley to be more specific in assigning his preachers to distinct and separate circuits of preaching places. By 1791, the year of Wesley's death, there were 72 of these circuits in England, 28 in Ireland, seven in Scotland, and three in Wales. The larger circuits were served by several preachers who visited the various locations on their circuits regularly. Preachers not only itinerated on their own circuits, but also itinerated from circuit to circuit as circumstances required and as their own living arrangements made possible. When distances made regular visits by the itinerants difficult, "local" preachers who were not full-time preachers supplied the pulpits in a community between the itinerant's visits.

Wesley's missionary preachers to America adhered to an itinerant ministry, serving short periods in one location, then exchanging places with another itinerant. **Francis Asbury**, who more than anyone else shaped the life of early American Methodism, was devoted to the itinerant system developed by Wesley. He was determined that Wesley's people in America would follow a similar scheme of preachers being assigned to their churches. Asbury set the example for his preachers by being in constant motion, moving through the nation's cities, towns, and countryside. Asbury's episcopal authority to assign the itinerant traveling preachers to their churches was a powerful instrument of supervision.

Controversies arose in early American Methodism regarding the nature of itineracy and the appointive power of bishops. One of these involved **James O'Kelly** who questioned the authority of bishops to make appointments. Another included a later group of Methodist reformers who challenged the powerful role of bishops in the itinerant system and eventually formed the **MP**.

Methodist churches around the world generally use some form of itineracy, although there are many who believe the system to be outdated and call for it to be reexamined, if not replaced with another form of polity.

Charles Yrigoyen, Jr.

IVORY COAST. *See* AFRICA.

– J –

JACKSON, THOMAS (December 12, 1783–March 10, 1873), Wesleyan minister and historian, son of a farm laborer at Sancton, Yorkshire, England. With little formal education he became a distinguished scholar, serving as connexional editor (1824–1837 and 1839–1841) and tutor at Richmond College (1842–1861). He was President of the **Conference** in 1838 and 1849. He was an able apologist for Methodism against the High Anglican attacks of E. B. Pusey and others. His most significant publications were *The Centenary of Wesleyan Methodism* (1839), a life of **Charles Wesley** (1841), and editions of **John Wesley's** *Works* (1829–1831), Charles Wesley's *Journal* (1849) and the *Lives of the Early Methodist Preachers* (1837–1838; 3rd edition, enlarged, 1865–1866). He also wrote lives of R. Watson and R. Newton. His *Recollections of My Own Life and Times* (1873) is a rich quarry for students of 19th-century Methodism.

John A. Newton

JOHN STREET CHURCH, located at 44 John Street, New York City, is a **UMC** Heritage Landmark. **Philip Embury** organized a Methodist society in his house at 10 Augustus Street, New York City, in September 1766 (*see* SOCIETIES, CLASSES, AND BANDS). Soon he found larger quarters on Barracks Street. In 1767, the Methodists moved to a rigging loft at 120 William Street. A year later, in March 1768, Embury and others purchased two lots on John Street. Embury designed and supervised the construction of a building that was dedicated as Wesley Chapel on October 30, 1768. Meanwhile, on April 11, 1768, Thomas Taylor had written to **John Wesley** on behalf of New York's Methodists and asked for a preacher, "a man of wisdom, of sound faith, and a good disciplinarian." Wesley responded by appointing the first Methodist preachers for America, **Richard Boardman** and **Joseph Pilmore**. They arrived in 1769, and under their leadership American Methodism continued to grow in New York and elsewhere. Although the John Street Methodists experienced disruptions during the Revolutionary War, they hosted **Thomas Coke** when he reached America in November 1784. A new structure replaced the original John Street MEC in 1818. It gave way in 1841, when the city widened John Street, to the present building, which the 1968 UMC **General Conference** designated a Heritage Landmark.

John G. McEllhenney

JONES, ELI STANLEY (January 3, 1884–January 25, 1973), pastor and missionary, began evangelistic work while a student at Asbury College. Jones entered the mission field in 1907. Serving as a pastor and district superintendent, Jones joined this work to an ever-expanding evangelistic mission throughout India (*see* ASIA). He quickly emerged as a much sought after speaker among India's elite. Elected bishop in 1928, he chose to continue his evangelistic mission which by then had expanded beyond the Indian subcontinent through much of the world. His first book, *The Christ of the Indian Road*, urged Christian missionaries to allow indigenous leaders to interpret Christ "though their own genius and life . . . then [it] will be first-hand and vital." Friend of Mahatma Gandhi and other Indian leaders, he actively advocated Indian independence. His service in many fields brought him the Gandhi Peace Prize in 1961. Embracing a native Indian spiritual retreat pattern, Jones established a Christian Ashram that in other mission fields and in America became a symbol of Jones's ministry. His enduring concern for India brought him back to that base six months of each year throughout his ministry. Author of some 26 books ranging from devotional works to an interpretation of Gandhi's contributions, Stanley Jones had become by the close of his life one of Methodism's most respected and influential pastor/evangelists.

Robert C. Monk

JONES, PETER also known as **KAHKEWAQUONABY**, "sacred feathers" (January 1, 1802–June 29, 1856), Canadian Methodist preacher, was the son of Augustus Jones and Tuhbenahneequay (Sarah Henry), the daughter of a Mississauga chief. He was born in Burlington Heights, Upper **Canada**. In 1823, Jones experienced **conversion** at a Methodist **camp meeting**. He was ordained into the Methodist ministry in 1833, the first Indian born in Canada to attain that status. His ministry was devoted to work among Indians. He kept an extensive journal of his life and work, which provides extraordinary insights into the religious, social, economic, and political life of the Indians of Upper Canada. He traveled in England, Scotland, and France raising money for Indian mission endeavors. He married Elizabeth Field of New York City on September 8, 1833. They had five sons, four of whom survived infancy. Failing health caused Jones to retire early from the ministry and his death occurred after six years of intense suffering. He was buried in Greenwood Cemetery, Brantford, Upper Canada.

Charles Yrigoyen, Jr.

JUSTIFICATION is understood in Wesleyan theology as God's act of forgiveness and deliverance from the guilt and penalty of sin. Justification is necessary because human beings are in a state of fallenness, or separation from God. From this lost condition, humans have no power to deliver themselves. As a result of original and personal sin, all human faculties are distorted or depraved. But God has acted in the atoning life, death, and resurrection of Jesus Christ to make **salvation** possible. Divine **grace**, offered freely and universally, is the only ground for justification. Through the working of **prevenient grace**, persons are enabled to recognize their sinful dilemma, to despair of their own capacity for salvation, and to acknowledge their complete dependence upon God. Wesley contended that such conviction of sin was usually the result of preaching the demands of the law of God. Divine grace makes individuals aware of their plight and empowers them to **repentance**. In response to God's action, persons repent of their sin and begin to try to amend their lives. This stage Wesley called "the faith of a servant." Persons have now become responsible agents because grace has made it possible for them to respond to God if they so choose.

Some of the distinctions of Wesley's position are apparent at this point in his understanding of the process of salvation. He differed from Calvinism by viewing all human beings as divinely empowered with ability to respond to grace. He avoided **antinomianism** by his insistence on the doing of "works meet for repentance" when there is opportunity. He denied Pelagianism by his affirmation that all human action for good is enabled solely by divine gift. He diverged from **Roman Catholicism** by making clear that no amount or degree of good works ever allows anyone to merit salvation.

Wesley, in contrast to John Calvin and Martin Luther, understood conviction and repentance as only preliminary to justification. The experience of justification is dependent upon the human response of **faith**. Persons exercise justifying faith when they come to accept their dependence upon Christ for salvation and place their trust and reliance in Christ alone. They are forgiven by God of their sin and pardoned from sin's guilt and punishment. Justification is a change in the relation between persons and God. This change is objective and forensic in nature. The separation and enmity caused by sin are overcome and justified sinners are restored to divine favor and placed in right relationship with God. Although such persons may not experience complete **assurance**, they can know themselves forgiven and adopted as children of God. This relationship retains, however, a moment-by-moment quality for it can be lost if persons cease to depend upon Christ with justifying faith. Final justification is attained only at death.

Another significant characteristic of Wesleyan theology is the distinction between justification and regeneration. These two movements in the process of salvation are simultaneous but not synonymous. Wesley described justification as a "relative" change in which God does something "for us through his Son," while regeneration is "a real change" which God "works in us by his Spirit" (see his sermons, "Justification by Faith" and "The Scripture Way of Salvation"). Wesley differed from the Reformed concept of the imputation of the righteousness of Christ to the sinner. He asserted that justification does not make one righteous in either actual fact or in the judgment of God. In justification the sinner is simply forgiven. It is regeneration that begins the process of **sanctification** through which one will actually be made righteous.

Wesley's doctrine of justification underwent some modifications in the thought of American Methodist theologians. The basic point of difference was the estimation of human moral ability. American Methodists moved quickly and decisively away from Wesley's strong emphasis on **original sin** and guilt, depravity and helplessness. A more optimistic assessment of innate spiritual capacity led to an enlarged role for natural reason and volition in the process of salvation. American theologians placed much more emphasis upon human free will, arguing that without ability to choose, there could be no responsibility for wrong choices. The capability of moral response that Wesley had stressed as a divine gift to be exercised in humility and gratitude was increasingly taken for granted as an inherent human quality. Focus shifted from the objective work of God to the subjective role of the individual. Faith came to be understood as human work, rather than as divine gift.

Throughout the 19th century, there was vigorous and protracted controversy within Methodism over issues related to justification. The moral nature of humankind, especially of infants and children, was discussed in relation to **baptism, conversion**, and nurture. The meaning of justification and, particularly, the precise point in one's life when it occurred, was widely debated. But at least by the latter decades of the century, a consensus position had emerged in which Methodism identified with the liberalism regnant in American religion. With an attenuated awareness of sin, there was a diminished sense of need for human transformation. These tendencies were manifested most clearly, and extremely influentially, in the writings of scholars known as the Boston personalists. Justification was viewed as a subject of limited significance in both theology and experience.

In the middle and late decades of the 20th century, the prevailing religious liberalism began to be challenged by thinkers who sought to recover for Methodism the reality of human sinfulness and need for salvation by divine grace. This tendency was greatly strengthened by the emergence of a neo-Wesleyan movement. With the revitalization of serious study of Wesley's theology came reapprehension of the classical understanding of the process of salvation. Although neo-Wesleyan theology is only one of a variety of streams of thought in contemporary Methodism, it may be an avenue for renewed appreciation of justification as both theological concept and transforming experience. *See also* DOCTRINAL STANDARDS; MODERNISM/LIBERALISM.

Gayle Carlton Felton

– K –

KAZAKHSTAN. *See* EUROPE.

KENYA. *See* AFRICA.

KIDDER, DANIEL PARISH (October 18, 1815–July 29, 1891), **MEC** missionary, editor, and educator, was appointed to the Rio de Janeiro mission in August 1837 (*see* LATIN AMERICA AND THE CARIBBEAN). He arrived on January 10, 1838, and spent much of the next two years traveling through Brazil. After his wife, Cynthia Harriet Russell, died on April 16, 1840, leaving two small children, Kidder returned to the pastorate in New Jersey. On April 6, 1842, he married Harriet Smith, principal of the Worthington (Ohio) Female Seminary. They had two daughters and a son. The 1844 **General Conference** elected Kidder to the new office of editor of Sunday School Publications and Tracts. In this position, he edited the *Sunday School Advocate*. He also was secretary of the MEC Sunday School Union and established **Sunday school** institutes and conventions. From 1856 to 1871 he taught practical theology at newly established Garrett Biblical Institute (Evanston, Illinois), then took a similar position at Drew Seminary (Madison, New Jersey). In November 1880 he became secretary of the MEC Board of Education. Upon his resignation in July 1887, the Kidders moved back to Evanston, where he died. Kidder wrote several books and numerous newspaper and journal articles.

Susan E. Warrick

KIM, HELEN (KIM, KIDECK) (February 22, 1899–February 11, 1970), educator, was born in Inchon, Korea. She graduated from **Ewha Woman's College**, Seoul, 1918, received her B.A. from Ohio Wesleyan University (1924), M.A. (Phi Beta Kappa) from Boston University (1925), and Ph.D. from Columbia University (1931). She served as dean of Ewha Womans College, 1929–1930, its president, 1939–1945, and as president of Ewha University, 1945–1961. Her speech, "The Women of the World," to the WFMS (**MEC**) in 1923 gave impetus to the founding of the World Federation of Methodist Women in 1939. She was vice president of the International Missionary Council, a member of the Korean Methodist Church General Board and the National Council of Korean Women, helped organize the Korean YWCA, and founded the *Korean Times*. She was a delegate to the United Nations, 1956–1959, member of UNESCO, and vice president of the Korean Red Cross. In 1963 she received the order of Cultural Merit (Korea) , the Ramon Magsaysay Award for Public Service, and the Upper Room Citation. At her death she was awarded the order of Diplomatic Merit, First Class, and given a state public funeral. *See also* ASIA.

Barbara E. Campbell

KIRGHIZIA. *See* EUROPE.

KOREA. *See* ASIA.

– L –

LAITY RIGHTS, drawing on what has been called the "republican language" of early American Methodism, bedeviled Wesley's autocratic clericalism ("We are no republicans, and never intend to be") from the outset. Not only was the movement scarcely imaginable apart for the initiative of such unordained, unauthorized laity as

Robert Strawbridge, Philip Embury, and others, but the explicit democratic ideology of the new nation and the implicit sense of equality on the frontier quickly tested the episcopal polity of American Methodism (*see* EPISCOPACY). Often linked with the right of itinerant preachers to have some say over their destinies and the right of local preachers to have any voice at all, lay representation was an issue in several small secessions (**James O'Kelly**'s "Republican Methodists," 1792; the congregationally oriented and New England–based "Reformed Methodist Church," 1814; the New York "Stillwellites," 1820).

Most notable, however, was the **MP** schism, the result of thwarted reforming impulses in the MEC **General Conference**s of 1820–1828. Official publications having been closed to such debate, reformers founded their own. In one, **Ezekiel Cooper**, under a pseudonym, published an influential article on a "Proposed Plan for a Lay-delegation." Another journal's position was clear from its title: *The Mutual Rights of Ministers and Members of the MEC*. A pamphlet war, expulsions (both lay and clergy) from the **MEC**, and further defeat of the reform agenda at the 1828 General Conference galvanized reformers to found a new church. In 1830, delegates, both lay and ministerial, met and named themselves the MP in implicit denial of ecclesiastical hierarchy. Their constitution secured lay representation in the same number as clergy both in annual and General Conferences. However, annual conferences could make their own rules on the admission of "colored" members (thus allowing for regional differences on **slavery** and related racial issues), and lay delegates to the General Conference were required to be white and male.

Laity rights were also major features of the next two separations, the **Wesleyan Methodists** in 1843 and the **Free Methodists** in 1860. Even the **AME** and **AMEZ** evolved to some form of lay representation by 1844 and 1864, respectively. Indeed, the **MECS** adopted a plan for lay representation in 1866 and implemented it in 1870. Within the MEC itself, the issue did not gain credibility until **Matthew Simpson** and other bishops argued for it in General Conferences just prior to the Civil War. Approval for lay representatives to the General Conference came in 1872 and to annual conferences in 1900. Five **women** were elected, but not seated, in the General Conference of 1888, and women finally gained equal laity rights in 1900. Their sisters in the MECS acquired the same rights in 1922.

The 1939 union of the MEC, MECS, and MP affirmed equal representation of ministers and laity in General, annual, and the new jurisdictional conferences, though clergy alone could vote on ministerial qualifications and relations. Laity rights had long since been secured in the parallel **EUB** tradition (1889 for the **UB** and by the 1922 union of the **EC**), and the trend toward increasingly large roles for laity continued after the 1968 union that formed the **UMC**.

Charles Wallace, Jr.

LAMBUTH, WALTER RUSSELL (November 10, 1854–September 26, 1921), **MECS** missionary, medical doctor, and bishop, was born in Shanghai, China, to missionaries James William and Mary Isabella McClellan Lambuth. Lambuth lived on five continents: 1859, in Tennessee and Mississippi; 1864, China; 1869, at Emory and Henry College (two diplomas, 1875) then Vanderbilt University (MD degree and theological study); 1877, China as an ordained **elder** (Tennessee **Conference**); 1881, MD degree from Bellevue Hospital Medical College in New York City: 1882, postgraduate study in Edinburgh and London, then back to China; 1885, with his father opened MECS **missions** in Japan (founded Kwansei Gakuin College in 1889); 1891, in the USA to edit *Methodist Review of Missions*; 1894, general secretary of the MECS Board of Missions; 1910, elected bishop and appointed to Brazil; 1911, mission to Zaire (Belgian Congo) with African-American scholar John Wesley Gilbert; World War I, in Europe with USA troops; 1920, established MECS work in Belgium, Poland, and Czechoslovakia; 1921, founded a short-lived mission in Siberia. Lambuth died at Yokohama, Japan, was cremated, and his ashes buried next to his mother in Shanghai. Lambuth married Daisy Kelley in 1877. Lambuth wrote *Side Lights on the Orient* (1915), *Winning the World for Christ* (1915), and *Medical Missions* (1920). *See also* AFRICA; ASIA; EUROPE.

Charles W. Brockwell, Jr.

LANE, ISAAC (March 3, 1834–December 5, 1937) was a **CME** bishop and a founder of Lane College. Son of his slave owner, he married Frances Ann Boyce and had 11 children. Denied **ordination** on account of race, he was licensed as a **MECS** exhorter in 1856. When the MECS agreed to segregate by forming the CME church, it licensed Lane to preach in 1866. The founding 1866 CME annual **conference** held in Jackson, Tennessee, ordained Lane **deacon** and **elder** on consecutive days and appointed him **presiding elder**, the first and only African American then in that position. Lane stood with CMEs in pride and strength as a freedman rather than submitting to inferior rank in churches (**AME, AMEZ**) founded by northern freedmen. He chose autonomy over being in a church with former slave owners (MECS). A delegate to the 1870 organizing **General Conference**, Lane was elected fifth CME bishop in 1873. Inadequately paid by economically stressed parishioners, Lane split and sold firewood and farmed with his family. He helped the church follow northern and westward migrations of former slaves. One of a few literate leaders among over 300 ex-slave preachers and more than 40,000 ex-slave CME members, Lane inspired commitment and cultivated leaders. Lane helped found Lane College (1887) in Jackson, Tennessee.

Alice G. Knotts

LANKFORD, SARAH WORRALL. *See* PALMER, SARAH WORRALL LANKFORD.

LASKEY, VIRGINIA MARIE DAVIS (January 12, 1900–September 7, 1991), **MC** lay church worker, was born in Lumber, Arkansas. After graduation from Sophia Newcomb College (1921) and Southern Methodist University, Dallas (1922), she taught science in Ruston, Louisiana High School until her marriage to Glenn E. Laskey in 1925. She held membership and offices in many civic and cultural groups, and the MC Woman's Society of Christian Service. She was a delegate to the MC **General Conference** in 1948 and 1952. She served three terms on the MC Board of Missions, including four years as president of the Woman's Division (1964–1968). The division honored her presidency with the $50,000 Fund for Theological Education for Women. Scarritt College (now Scarritt-Bennett Center), Nashville, Tennessee, named its library for her. Other general church responsibilities included membership on the **NCC**, the **WCC**, the

American Section of **WMC**, and the UMC Structure Study Commission (1968–1972). She held membership on several college boards, and on the boards of institutions in the Louisiana **Conference**. In 1981 she was inducted into the United Methodist Hall of Philanthropy.

Barbara E. Campbell

LATIN AMERICA AND THE CARIBBEAN. It has often been thought that Methodism came to Latin America and the Caribbean through organized missionary efforts. Although this may be true in some countries, Methodism was carried throughout the Americas in the heart of faithful lay people. The earliest example occurred when Nathaniel Gilbert, a speaker of the Antigua House of Assembly, and two slave girls were converted by the **preaching** of **John Wesley** in England. They returned to Antigua in 1760 and took Methodism with them. It was the first Methodist work in the Americas. In 1786, **Thomas Coke** was shipwrecked in Antigua and ran into fellow Englishman John Baxter, who was continuing the Methodist services started by Nathaniel Gilbert. That night Coke "preached to a thousand negroes" and later returned to England to plead the cause for a West Indian mission.

In 1820, James Thomson preached the first Protestant sermon in South America, not to be confused with the Methodist John Francis Thomson who preached the first Spanish-language Protestant sermon on May 25, 1867, both in Buenos Aires. In 1868, John Thomson preached the first Spanish-language Protestant sermon in Uruguay and in Paraguay in 1881. Methodist work in South America began earlier, but was confined to English-speaking immigrants due to legal restrictions. The first recorded Methodist effort began in 1832 when a Methodist layperson, whose name is lost to history, organized English-language work in Argentina. He wrote to the **MEC** Missionary Society in New York stating that he had successfully formed a small class, and requested a missionary.

The missionary initiative began when Bishop **James O. Andrew** of the Tennessee **Conference** sent Fountain E. Pitts in June 1835 to survey the opportunities for Methodist work in Brazil, Uruguay, and Argentina. He arrived in Rio de Janeiro on August 19, 1835, and organized a Methodist society (*see* SOCIETIES, CLASSES, AND

BANDS) among English-speaking persons. Returning to the USA in 1836, the same year the **General Conference** approved sending missionaries to South America and Mexico, Pitts dispatched Justin Spaulding to Rio de Janeiro, where he organized a congregation of 40, and, a few months later, a **Sunday school** of 30, including some Brazilians. More permanent work was established in 1875 under the leadership of John James Ranson. The Brazilian Methodist Church petitioned the General Conferences in 1922 and 1926 for resident episcopal leadership to provide direction for the ministry. The failure of the General Conference to act led Brazil to become an autonomous Methodist Church in 1930. By 2003, the Methodist Church of Brazil had grown into eight annual conferences with a total membership of over 150,000. It has a strong network of educational institutions and a prolific printing operation.

Likewise, F. E. Pitts responded to the opportunity in Argentina by sending Dr. John Dempster, who was received by dictator Juan Manuel de Rosas and promptly instructed to "confine his labors to the foreign population." Dempster obliged and asked the mission board to assign a teacher for an English-language school. Visiting Montevideo, Dempster requested a missionary for Uruguay and was sent William H. Norris in 1839. Norris later succeeded Dempster in Buenos Aires in 1842 and, on January 3, 1843, inaugurated a Methodist church building, the first Protestant church in South America. The work became known as the South American Mission and included Uruguay and Paraguay with headquarters in Argentina. In 2003, the Methodist Church continued in Uruguay with 21 congregations and in Argentina with 100.

Under the General Conference mandate of 1836, Mexico was in the plans of the Missionary Society. However the separation of the **MECS** in 1844, the annexation of Texas the same year, and the ensuing Mexican–American war of 1846–1848, which culminated in the Guadalupe Hidalgo treaty, all delayed the mission. Mexican-born priest Benigno Cárdenas, troubled by the role and power of the Roman Catholic Church, visited the Missionary Society of the MEC in New York. Already planning to send Enoch C. Nicholson to New Mexico, the Missionary Society invited Cárdenas to join the **mission**. In front of the governor's palace, Cárdenas preached the first Protestant sermon in Spanish in the newly acquired Southwest on November 20, 1853.

Alejo Hernández, another Mexican-born candidate for the Catholic priesthood, left the seminary in Aguas Calientes, Mexico, to join Benito Juárez's resistance army against the French invasion in 1862. President Juárez's support for the liberals and the new constitution of 1857 guaranteed freedom of religion and the separation of church and state, thus opening the door to Protestantism. While in Juárez's army, Hernández read an anti-Catholic treatise left by North American soldiers during the Mexico-American war entitled "Nights with the Romanists." His curiosity aroused, Hernández went to Brownsville, Texas, to find a Protestant **Bible** and had a profound religious experience. Hernández served as a Methodist pastor from 1871 to 1875.

Farther north, Bishop **Matthew Simpson** (MEC) selected **William Butler** in 1872 to be **superintendent** of the work in Mexico. Bishop **Gilbert Haven** preceded him and arrived in Veracruz in December 1872. On Christmas Day, he was a passenger on the first train of the recently constructed railroad to Mexico City. William Butler arrived in Mexico City on February 23, 1873, and bought a church building, which was originally the first Franciscan monastery in the Americas, located at No. 5 Gante Street. The building was consecrated a Methodist Church and held its first public **worship** service on Christmas Day 1873 with Alejo Hernández as pastor. This church, "Santisima Trinidad," remains an active congregation.

In 1873, the Louisiana Conference (MECS) met in New Orleans under Bishop George F. Pierce and invited Bishop John C. Keener to speak about the Mexico mission. He thrilled hearers with a description of Alejo Hernández's **conversion** and a voice called out, "If there were sufficient money, could you go to Mexico?" An offering raised support and Bishop Keener was off to Mexico on the steamer *Tabasco* for Veracruz. By 1875, he purchased San Andres Chapel, which had been part of a Capuchin monastery. Today it is called "El Mesias" and is an active Methodist congregation on Balderas Street in Mexico City.

The division between northern and southern Methodism was healed in Mexico before it was in the USA. With a shortage of funding from the United States during the Great Depression and a heightened sense of independence, the Mexican church followed Brazil's example and unified both strands of Methodism in 1930 under one autonomous body, La Iglesia Metodista de Mexico. By 2003, the church had six annual conferences with 400 congregations and 40,000 members.

With Methodism established in Mexico and east of the Andes, **William Taylor** introduced a plan to the Missionary Society to establish self-supporting missions on the west coast of South America. Visiting Peru, Bolivia, and Chile, Taylor solicited subscriptions from seamen aboard foreign ships, English-speaking businessmen, and mine operators to establish schools. Returning to New York early in 1878, Taylor, who later became an MEC bishop, arranged to send six preachers and three teachers to Peru and Chile. Among the first wave, Ira Haynes LaFetra became one of the principal founders of Methodism in Chile. J. W. Collier and his sister Edith began work at Iquique, then in Peru, but the War of the Pacific caused them to move to Valparaiso. After the war, James P. Gilliland reinitiated the work in Iquique (now part of Chile) and established a school which exists today. The Methodist work in Chile split in 1909 when the congregation in Valparaiso experienced a "baptism of the **Holy Spirit**" and was expelled from the Iglesia Metodista de Chile. Led by Willis C. Hoover, the congregation started the Iglesia Metodista Pentecostal de Chile (*see* PENTECOSTALISM). This new church spread quickly and today is much larger than its mother church.

From 1886 to 1890, Francisco G. Penzotti, agent of the American Bible Society and Methodist preacher, made several visits from Argentina to Peru. In July 1890 he was arrested for **preaching** in Callao and was imprisoned for eight months before international attention forced his release. Methodist leader in Argentina and Uruguay, Thomas B. Wood, arrived in Lima as superintendent of the newly projected Western District of the South American Conference in 1891. Assisted by his daughter Elsie, several schools were organized including Callao High School (Colegio América), Lima High School (Colegio Maria Alvarado), Victoria School (Escuela América de la Victoria), and Colegio Andino at Huancayo. This Methodist social work continued into the 20th century with the establishment of the Panamericana Normal School in Lima and the La Florida Social Center founded by Martha Vanderberg in a squatters' settlement in Lima. In 2003 the Iglesia Metodista del Peru had 4,400 members in 119 congregations.

Francisco Penzotti with Andrew M. Milne entered Bolivia in 1883 and worked in Tupiza, Potosí, Sucre, Oruro, and La Paz, in addition to other small towns. The following year Penzotti came back to Bolivia with two Bible peddlers, held public services, and established a Sunday school. John F. Thomson arrived from Argentina in 1890 and discovered a Bible Society agent selling Bibles and holding services in La Paz. The permanent founding of the Methodist work in Bolivia is recorded as August 1906 when Francis M. Harrington rode a donkey across the mountains from Chile and organized the first Methodist work in La Paz. In 1907, he launched the American Institute (now called the Colegio Evangélico Metodista), before succumbing to tuberculosis in 1908. In 1912, a second American Institute was founded in Cochabamba by government invitation and later medical work was added. Bolivia became a mission conference in 1916 and an autonomous church in 1969. In 2003, the Iglesia Evangélica Metodista de Bolivia had a strong social presence with 8,600 members and diverse ethnicity (70 percent Aymaras, 15 percent Quechuas, and 15 percent mestizo).

In addition to his work in the Andes, William Taylor also went to Panama and Costa Rica, where he met a number of Afro-Caribbeans who had migrated from Jamaica and were members of the British Wesleyan Methodist Church, yet had no pastor. Taylor appointed Charles W. Birdsall to Panama, but he succumbed to malaria after four months. E. L. Latham followed him and organized a Methodist Society and built a combined chapel, school, and parsonage in Panama City. In 1881 Richard Copp went to Colón and developed the work in both cities for about 10 years. Two Panamanians were called to the Methodist ministry during this period: Edward A. Pitt, who became the first Methodist worker in Costa Rica and Clifford M. Surgeon, who worked in Panama after 1913. In 2003, the Methodist Church of Panama had 14 congregations with 583 members, as well as educational and health care ministries.

E. A. Pitt worked in Costa Rica for several years building churches along the railroad in Limón, Pacuaribo, and Siquirres on the eastern seaboard. Inland, William Taylor began work and was followed by Francisco G. Penzotti, who preached in San José around the turn of the 20th century. In 1920, the MEC established the Panama Mission with George A. Miller as superintendent. Eduardo Zapata of Mexico was appointed pastor-in-charge at San José and C. W. Ports and his wife later came as the first Methodist missionaries. In 2003, Methodism was strongest inland under La Iglesia Evangélica Metodista de Costa Rica, which had 70 churches and 11,500 members. Prior to 1900, American missionary efforts led to the creation of six annual conferences in Latin America: Eastern South American Conference (Argentina and Uruguay), the Bolivia Mission Conference, the Chile Conference, the North Andes Mission Conference (Peru), the Central American Mission Conference (Panama and Costa Rica), and the Mexico Conference. In addition, the newly autonomous West Indian Conference was in the English-speaking Caribbean and related to **British Methodism**.

Mission work began in the Spanish-speaking Caribbean when Robert Fulwood called the Cubans in Key West "a field white for harvest." He named José Vanduzer, who worked among the Cuban immigrants before contracting yellow fever. Vanduzer's last words before his death were, "Don't abandon the Cuban mission." In 1883, the Florida Annual Conference (MECS) assigned Enrique Someillan and Andres Silveira to Cuba. They established a chapel in the Hotel Saratoga on Galiano Street in Havana. Following the defeat of Spain in the Spanish-American War, the Board of Foreign Missions of the Presbyterian Church organized a meeting in New York between the mainline mission boards on June 13, 1898. Together they reached agreements on mission work in Cuba, Puerto Rico, and the Philippines. Bishop **Warren Candler** (MECS) of Florida led a group of missionaries to Cuba on November 23, 1898 (Thanksgiving Day), to preach on the topic, "Why are we in Cuba." From that moment the well-organized Cuban mission grew across the island through strategic cities such as Matanzas, where the first Methodist church was built, Cienfuegos, and Santiago de Cuba. After the Socialist revolution in 1959, the missionaries were recalled and all but eight Cuban pastors remained in Cuba. In 1961, the schools and clinics were nationalized by the government, but the ecumenical seminary in Matanzas remained open. Through heroic sacrifices by the laity, Methodism survived and became autonomous in 1967 when the General Conference elected its first Cuban bishop. The USA embargo of Cuba prohibited North American bishops from traveling; therefore in 1968 Mexican bishop Alejandro Ruiz traveled to Cuba to consecrate Rev.

Armando Rodriguez as bishop. Since 1990, several economic and social factors have contributed to dramatic church growth raising the Methodist Church's membership to 45,000 in 435 churches and missions.

Charles W. Drees, who had been a missionary in Argentina, was named superintendent of the mission in Puerto Rico, arriving on March 25, 1900, and holding the first Methodist service on March 30. Two days later, he organized the First San Juan MEC on April 1, 1900, an English-speaking congregation that later would be called Union Church. Drees founded the first Spanish-speaking church on April 8, 1900, with a group of 30 Puerto Ricans under the name "Iglesia Metodista de la Santisima Trinidad." The Methodist Church of Puerto Rico gained its autonomy from **UMC** in 1992 and had 24,000 members in 72 churches in 2003. The **EUB** also had historical mission work in Puerto Rico, but at the time of the unification with **MC** in 1968, the EUB independent mission churches in Puerto Rico, just as in Brazil and Ecuador, decided to retain their autonomy.

Methodism in Latin America and the Caribbean has been ecumenical (*see* ECUMENISM). Following the 1910 International Missionary Conference in Edinburgh, a Committee on Cooperation for Latin America (CCLA) was formed to organize a 1916 meeting in Panama consisting of the mainline Protestant mission boards. The outcome was the Comity Agreement, which realigned mission work in Latin America to decrease denominational competition. There was similar cooperation within countries, such as the 1914 Plan of Cincinnati, which distributed denominational work specifically in Mexico, although Mexicans believed they were unrepresented. The 1920 MEC General Conference placed all Methodist work related to North America under the Central Conference of Latin America.

The **UB** initiated work in 1899 and a cooperative mission in the Dominican Republic on January 1, 1922. Ten years later this mission joined the **Wesleyan Methodists**, who had been working in the Dominican Republic for a century, and, in 1960, joined with the **Moravians**. By 2003 the Iglesia Evangélica Dominicana had 10,000 members and 55 congregations in addition to educational and health care facilities.

The Primitive Evangelical Methodist Church of Guatemala began in 1922 under the leadership of Truman Furman of the The **Primitive**

Methodist Church (Pennsylvania). Left freestanding from 1938 to 1988, the autonomous body petitioned **CIEMAL** and the UMC General Board of Global Ministries (GBGM) for recognition and became affiliated with UMC at the 1992 **General Conference.**

In recent years Methodist faith communities have emerged in other Latin American countries, where UMC has traditionally worked ecumenically under the Comity Agreement. Under his own initiative, Cuban Methodist bishop Armando Rodriguez attempted unsuccessfully to plant Methodist work in Colombia in the late 1960s. A new Methodist group emerged in 1987 and later affiliated with the GBGM and CIEMAL. In 2003, this group had a total attendance of 1,000 people in 18 faith communities. Besides British Methodism's work on the Bay Islands (Roatan) in Honduras, which has been closely related to work in Belize, the GBGM supported ecumenical efforts in Spanish-speaking Honduras. In 1996, however, the GBGM initiated a new mission in Tegucigalpa with the assignment of Bishop Armando Rodriguez and his wife Alida. Assisted by missionaries from Cuba and Puerto Rico, this UMC mission started 12 congregations with attendance around 1,250. In the early 1990s a small community in Maracaibo, Venezuela, led by Francisco Mendoza, petitioned the GBGM for support. In 1993, the "Methodist Christian Community of Venezuela" was recognized by CIEMAL with three faith communities. Similarly in Nicaragua, a small group became the Asociación de Iglesia Evangélica Metodista de Nicaragua and the GBGM assigned an advisor in the early 1990s to supervise the work. By 2003, there were eight faith communities which focus their ministry on young people. Fleeing the war in El Salvador, refugee Francisco Mayorga became a Methodist in Staten Island, New York, before returning to his native country in 1994 to establish what would become the Iglesia Evangélica Metodista de El Salvador.

Over the years, Methodism throughout the Caribbean and Latin America has gone through a gradual transition from missionary initiative to indigenous leadership. The self-determination movements of the 1960s led many churches, in dialogue with the Methodist Mission Board in New York, to request autonomy in order to adapt to changing political situations, including anti–North American sentiments. The churches historically related to British Methodism were already autonomous and, in 1967, formed The Methodist Church of the Caribbean and the Americas (MCCA), which has eight districts. Those relating to North American Methodism were subject to the General Conference Commission on Structure of Methodism Overseas (COSMOS), which petitioned the 1968 General Conference to enable autonomy if a church desired it. The Methodist Church in Cuba had already voted for autonomy the previous year, and, in 1969, Chile, Argentina, Uruguay, Peru, and Bolivia did the same with Costa Rica and Panama following in 1973. After obtaining autonomy none of the Methodist Churches in Latin America and the Caribbean were "United Methodist." Only recent additions in Bermuda and Honduras are United Methodist. All the other churches are autonomous affiliated (which means that they send nonvoting delegates to UMC General Conference) with the exception of Mexico and the MCCA, which have concordat relationships (reciprocal voting members to General Conference). These autonomous Methodist Churches in Latin America met in Santiago, Chile, in 1973 to form the Concilio Iglesias Evangélicas Metodistas de América Latina (**CIEMAL**). This body has signed an agreement with the GBGM to supervise any new Methodist church plants in Latin America and the Caribbean.

Philip Wingeier-Rayo

LATVIA. *See* EUROPE.

LAY PREACHERS perform some of the duties of ordained clergy while remaining laity (*see* ORDINATION). Lay preachers became an essential feature of Methodism very early in the movement. The Wesleyan Revival's rapid growth soon outstripped even the dedicated labors of **John Wesley** and his small cadre of ordained Anglican priests.

Wesley realized that certain lay members of his societies could, with proper guidance, provide effective leadership. Wesley began allowing lay men and, occasionally, **women**, to exhort and preach in the societies. He sent them out on **circuits** and met with them on a regular basis to counsel, advise, and establish basic procedures. They were authorized to preach, accept new members into the society, and monitor the development of the classes and bands (*see* SOCIETIES, CLASSES, AND BANDS). Since they were not ordained, they were not permitted to administer the sacraments, and they were required to make regular reports to Wesley. Whenever possible, Wesley visited the societies to appraise the work of his lay preachers and the development of faithful discipleship. As the societies became churches and denominations in the 19th century, the lay preacher continued to play a vital role in the life of the church. The lay preacher continued to fill the pulpit and provided other basic pastoral services when the regular ordained traveling preacher was unavailable. Lay preachers continue to minister effectively in most Methodist denominations around the world. *See also* PREACHING.

L. Dale Patterson

LEE, JARENA (February 11, 1783–?), considered the first female **AME** preacher, was born in Cape May, New Jersey, to free parents. In 1804, she experienced **conversion** and joined the Bethel AME in Philadelphia. Plagued with doubts about her **salvation**, she eventually achieved the spiritual goal of **sanctification**. Around 1811, Lee began to feel a call to preach. She approached **Richard Allen**, pastor at Bethel, but did not receive his support. In 1811, she married Joseph Lee, pastor at Snow Hill, six miles from Philadelphia. Within a few years she was a widow with two small children. She returned to Philadelphia in 1818 and received permission from Allen to hold prayer meetings in her home. The following year, during worship at Bethel, she interrupted a sermon to exhort extemporaneously from the text. This time, Allen endorsed her call. She soon began a career as an itinerant preacher, traveling extensively in the Northeast and as far west as Dayton, Ohio. She was widely acclaimed by both white and black audiences, despite some opposition from clergy. Lee's autobiography (1849) is a remarkable document, filled with theological commentary and details about her spiritual struggles and personal encounters. Unfortunately, her activities after 1849 are not known.

Susan E. Warrick

LEE, JASON (June 28,1803–March 12,1845), as superintendent of the **MEC**'s Oregon Mission from 1833 to 1844, successfully planted numerous institutions in the Northwest (the Methodist presence there, Willamette University, and, arguably, even the Oregon Territory), though he was administratively inept and not particularly effective with the Indians. Born in Stanstead, Quebec, he converted to Methodism in 1826, completed a brief course at Willamette Academy in Massachusetts, and returned home as a teacher and local preacher. In 1833, he was ordained as missionary to the Flathead Indians. Lee's overland expedition arrived in Oregon in September 1834, and located along the Willamette River, about 60 miles upstream from the Columbia. Work later spread to Puget Sound, the mouth of the Columbia, The Dalles, and what are now Oregon City and Salem. In 1838–1840, a first trip east to meet personally with the Mission Board resulted in an infusion of new personnel. During a second trip, begun in 1843, his superintendency was under fire and he never returned. On both occasions the publicity he brought helped promote the idea of a USA interest in the Northwest. Stripped of his position (though exonerated by the Board), Lee returned to his hometown, where he died soon after. Final vindication came in 1906 when his remains were brought across the continent and ceremoniously reburied in Salem's Lee Mission Cemetery.

Charles Wallace, Jr.

LEE, JESSE (March 12, 1758–September 12, 1816), influential early preacher, the **MEC**'s "Apostle to New England," its first historian, and the first Congressional chaplain, was born in Prince George's County, Virginia, converted at age 15, and served as class leader (*see* SOCIETIES, CLASSES, AND BANDS) and exhorter before becoming an itinerant in 1783. One of **Francis Asbury**'s first traveling companions (though occasionally at odds with him), Lee later preached and organized in Connecticut in 1789, and following that, in all the New England states and contiguous parts of New York and **Canada**. His *A Short History of the Methodists* (1810) was an unauthorized chronicle of events in which Lee himself was often a participant, including the episcopal election of 1800, which he lost by four votes to **Richard Whatcoat**. Though he scrupulously quotes from membership statistics and **conference** minutes, he also frequently writes in the first person, as in recounting "the beginning of Methodism in Boston" in 1790, when he "went out on the common" and preached from a table. Lee's wit and bluntness (his published description of Asbury is not entirely flattering) probably cost him the **episcopacy**, but make him one of the more colorful early preachers.

He died while serving in Annapolis, Maryland, and was buried, ironically, in the Bishops' Lot in Mt. Olivet Cemetery, Baltimore.

Charles Wallace, Jr.

LEE, LUTHER (November 30, 1800–December 13, 1889), abolitionist and early leader of the **Wesleyan Methodist Church**, was born in Schoharie, New York. His mother was a devout Methodist who died when he was 13. Lee joined the **MEC** in 1820 and began to preach the next year, eventually itinerating in many sections of New York state. In 1837, Lee became convinced of the evils of **slavery** and joined forces with other noted Methodist abolitionists such as **Orange Scott** and **Lucius C. Matlack**. These **antislavery** advocates seceded from the MEC and established an explicitly abolitionist denomination, the Wesleyan Methodist Connection (later called "Church"). Self-educated, Lee was noted for his highly structured argumentation in defense of controversial issues, such as the legitimacy of direct church involvement in antislavery political action and the right of **women** to preach. "Logical Lee," as he came to be known, wrote a well-respected *Systematic Theology*, taught theology at two colleges in Michigan, and received an honorary doctorate from Middlebury College in Vermont. He also served as the editor of the Wesleyan Methodist newspaper from 1844 to 1852. For 20 years, between the death of Orange Scott in 1847 and Lee's return to the MEC in 1867, Lee was the most visible leader of the Connection.

Douglas M. Strong

LEIGH, SAMUEL (September 1, 1785—May 2, 1852), born in Milton, Staffordshire, England, the first missionary sent to **Australia** by the Methodist Missionary Society in England. Ordained in October 1814, he volunteered for service overseas and, in response to an appeal from Wesleyans in the penal settlement in New South Wales, he was appointed to that colony. Leigh arrived at Sydney in August 1815. He organized a **circuit** whose boundaries extended for 150 miles and had some 14 **preaching** places. In 1817, he established the first Australian Wesleyan chapel at Castlereagh.

Leigh's work with soldiers, convicts, and free-settlers took a heavy toll and he appealed to the society for additional missionaries. With support from the principal Anglican chaplain, Samuel Marsden, Leigh attempted to recuperate on a voyage to **New Zealand**. In 1820, chiefly for health reasons, he sailed to England. During the return voyage in 1821, he founded the Hobart mission. In 1822, with the society's blessing, he returned to New Zealand, having decided upon Whangaroa as the site for a Wesleyan mission to the Maori. Numerous setbacks caused him to despair and Marsden persuaded him to return to Sydney in 1823. Leigh continued his work in that **circuit** and subsequently at Parramatta. His wife died in 1831. Grieving and ill, he returned to **circuit** life in England. He died there on May 2, 1852. Leigh is remembered for his courage, devotion, and faithful service in inhospitable lands. His memory is perpetuated in the Leigh Memorial Church in Parramatta and the Leigh Theological College at Enfield, New South Wales.

Lawrence D. McIntosh

LIBERALISM. *See* MODERNISM/LIBERALISM.

LIBERATION THEOLOGY is an approach to Christian theology that emphasizes God's love for those who suffer and who are oppressed by political and economic conditions. Liberation theology appeared first in Roman Catholicism as theologians, inspired by the Second Vatican Council (1962–1965) to relate their theology more closely to specific local conditions, began to reflect on the conditions that affected indigenous people and poor city dwellers in **Latin America**. Christian faith, they insisted, cannot be neutral between the poor and their oppressors, nor can it simply accept human suffering as a necessary part of life. Christians must become active in understanding the causes of suffering and take sides with the poor in their struggle against it. Liberation theology has become associated with the struggle of popular movements to find hope for social recognition and equal rights in many places. Liberation theology is controversial, in part because of the use by some theologians of Marxist analysis to understand and explain social conflict, but emphasis on the proclamation of good news to the poor and on the presence of God in the experience of ordinary people links liberation theology to the early days of Methodism and attracts the involvement of many Methodist theologians.

Robin W. Lovin

LIBERIA. *See* AFRICA.

LIDGETT, JOHN SCOTT, (August 10, 1854–June 16, 1953), Wesleyan minister, born in Lewisham, England. While serving in the Cambridge **Circuit** he became acutely aware of the gulf between rich and poor and the evils of poverty, bad housing, and unemployment. Encouraged and supported by W. F. Moulton, he established the Bermondsey Settlement, where he was warden from 1892 to 1949. His numerous church and civic offices included serving as president of the Wesleyan **Conference** (1908), superintendent of the South London Mission (1909–1918, 1942–1943), first president of the Methodist Conference after the 1932 Union, leader of the Progressive Party on the London County Council, vice chancellor of London University, and chairman of the executive committee of the Central Council for Nursing. Sometimes described as "the greatest Methodist since Wesley," he was made a Companion of Honour in recognition of his work in Bermondsey and toward Methodist Union. He was editor of the *Methodist Times* (1907–1918). Notable among his theological works were his Fernley Lecture on *The Spiritual Principle of the Atonement* (1897) and *The Fatherhood of God* (1902). His two autobiographical works were *Reminiscences* (1928) and *My Guided Life* (1936).

John D. Beasley

LITHUANIA. *See* EUROPE.

LORD'S SUPPER. *See* EUCHARIST.

LOSEE, WILLIAM (1757–October 16, 1832), pioneer preacher in **Canada**, was a British loyalist. In June 1783, he left New York for Nova Scotia, where he was awarded 250 acres of farmland by the British government as a reward for his loyalty. He was converted by the Methodist branch of the Nova Scotia Awakening sometime before 1787. Bishop Francis Asbury ordained him a **deacon** in 1789. After an exploratory trip through the United Empire Loyalist settlements in 1789–1790, where he found a strong lay movement, he received permission to organize the first official **circuit** in what is now Ontario in February 1791. In 1792 Losee was moved east to the

Prescott-Cornwall area, where Paul and **Barbara Heck** had settled. After a disastrous love affair with Elizabeth Detlor (who married Darius Dunham, Losee's successor in Upper Canada), Losee returned to the USA, some say because he became mentally unbalanced by this disappointment and hence was unfit for full-time ministry. He became a farmer and a fishmonger and preached on occasion. Sometime after 1817 Losee married Mary Rushmore. His full-time ministry lasted a mere four years but he had a lasting impact on Upper Canadian loyalist Methodism.

Joanne Carlson Brown

LOVE FEAST. The Methodist love feast was a deliberate revival by **John Wesley** of the meal of Christian fellowship or *agape*, which was practiced with varying success in the early Christian church and revived by the German **Moravians**. Wesley first met it in Savannah, Georgia, on August 8, 1737, and also among Moravians in Germany and London in 1738. When he returned that September to the Fetter Lane Religious Society that he had jointly formed with **Peter Böhler** on May 1, 1738, one of the new monthly rules was to hold a "general love-feast from seven till ten in the evening." When Wesley's followers broke away from Fetter Lane in 1740 they retained the Moravian bands (inner circles which Wesley described as "little companies, so that old English word signifies"). It was primarily for these, whom Wesley termed his Select Society, that he organized his love feasts once a quarter. In London in November 1746, he listed 22 bands for married men, six for single, 43 for married women, 26 for single. In his *Plain Account of the People called Methodist* (1749) he gave an idealized picture of it. Both men and women met, "that we might together 'eat bread' (as the ancient Christians did) 'with gladness and singleness of heart.' At these *love-feasts* . . . our food is only a little plain cake and water. But we seldom return from them without being fed, not only with 'the meat which perisheth,' but with 'that which endureth to everlasting life.'" Methodist emigrants took this practice with them throughout the world, though its relevance tended to shrivel except as a nostalgic "old-time love feast" or as a frail ecumenical substitute intercommunion. *See also* SOCIETIES, CLASSES, AND BANDS.

Frank Baker

LOVELY LANE MEETINGHOUSE was the site of the 1784 **MEC Christmas Conference** in downtown Baltimore. Wesley's missionary, **Joseph Pilmore**, organized the Baltimore Society on June 22, 1772. **Francis Asbury** began a fund, convert Philip Rogers secured a lot, and Captain **Thomas Webb** opened the simple Lovely Lane brick building, where overcrowding later twice collapsed the floor. Hospitable Baltimoreans installed seat backs and heat in December 1784 although annual **conferences** met previously without conveniences. Soon after **Thomas Coke** dispatched the preachers to "reform the nation and spread scriptural holiness," he urged relocation nearby on Light Street and a school superseded the church. After establishing many other congregations, the "mother church" moved in 1885 to a sanctuary designed by Stanford White at 2200 Saint Paul Street. There Lovely Lane Museum displays Conference Historical Society treasures including Asbury's ordination certificate. Buried at Mount Olivet Cemetery, 2930 Frederick Avenue, are Bishops Asbury, **John Emory**, **Enoch George**, and **Beverly Waugh**, also **E. Stanley Jones**, **Robert Strawbridge**, **Jesse Lee**, and the 1966 Bicentennial capsule to be disinterred in 2066. The 1970 UMC **General Conference** designated the original Lovely Lane location at 206 East Redwood Street a Heritage Landmark.

Edwin Schell

LUCCOCK, HALFORD EDWARD (March 11, 1885–November 5, 1960), renowned lecturer, author, and professor of homiletics, was cherished for his incisive yet humorous preaching and writing. Son of Bishop Naphtali Luccock, Halford followed his father in both the pastoral ministry and teaching. Serving several pastorates in New York and Connecticut, he taught part time at the Hartford School of Missions. Appointed to the faculty at Drew Theological Seminary in 1918, he then joined the Board of Foreign Missions (**MEC**) as editorial secretary and became a contributing editor of the *Christian Advocate*. In 1928 he took the position of professor of homiletics at Yale Divinity School, where he served until his retirement in 1953. Holding earned degrees from Northwestern University, Union Seminary, and Columbia University, he received honorary degrees from Syracuse, Wesleyan, Vermont, Yale, and Northwestern Universities.

Luccock published 26 books, including *Communicating the Gospel* (The Lyman Beecher Lectures), *In the Minister's Workshop*, several volumes of *Preaching Values*, and, with Paul Hutchinson, he wrote the broadly used *Story of Methodism*. Luccock's "Daily Meditations" column in *The Christian Herald* enjoyed wide popularity, while his demands for genuine faith and social justice in the "Simeon Stylites" articles in *The Christian Century* were perhaps more widely acclaimed and influential.

Robert C. Monk

– M –

MACEDONIA. *See* EUROPE.

MACLAY, ROBERT SAMUEL (February 7, 1824–1907), **MEC** missionary to China, Japan, and Korea, was born in Concord, Pennsylvania, the son of Robert and Arbella (Erwin) Maclay. Following graduation from Dickinson College, Carlisle, Pennsylvania, he was ordained in the Baltimore **Conference**. In 1847, he was appointed to mission work in China and arrived in Foochow in April 1848 (*see* ASIA). Maclay's outstanding administrative talents led to his being named superintendent and treasurer of the China Mission in March 1852, a position he held for 20 years. The mission work expanded into western China under his leadership. In 1861, he published *Life among the Chinese* and a decade later collaborated on a dictionary of the Chinese language in the dialect of Foochow. From June 1873 until April 1885, Maclay served as a missionary in Japan. He was also responsible for establishing Korean mission work in 1884. In 1888, Maclay resigned from missionary work and was named dean of the Maclay College of Theology in Fernando, California, where he was employed until his retirement in 1893. He was married to Henrietta Caroline Sperry in 1850 and, after her death, to Sarah Ann Barr in 1882.

Charles Yrigoyen, Jr.

MALAYSIA. *See* ASIA.

MARRIAGE is both an ecclesiastical and civil ceremony in which ministers act with dual authority. **Elders** and **deacons** (and unordained local pastors within their appointed charge) have authority to perform marriages. In Methodism, the sacred service celebrates a covenant grounded in the will of God and sustained by divine **grace**. Chief among the purposes of Christian marriage is provision of companionate relationships of mutual dependence within which persons grow in holiness of life. **John Wesley** revised the marriage ritual of Anglicanism for use by American Methodists. He eliminated the giving away of the bride and the use of rings, but these practices were restored in later years. Traditional language about obedience and service on the part of the wife was eliminated in the late 19th and early 20th centuries. In the earliest decades of Methodism, the marriage of ministers was perceived as an impediment to service. Marriage of Methodists to nonbelievers and the marriage of divorced persons were either prohibited or firmly discouraged for much longer. Contemporary Methodism encourages the solemnization of marriages within the context of congregational **worship** and eucharistic celebration (*see* EUCHARIST). Ministers are responsible for appropriate premarital counseling to help persons prepare for lifelong relationships of equality and fidelity. *See also* DIVORCE.

Gayle Carlton Felton

MATLACK, LUCIUS C. (April 28, 1816–June 24, 1883), an abolitionist and early leader of the **Wesleyan Methodist Church**, was born in Baltimore. Because of his **antislavery** views, Matlack was rejected for **ordination** by the Philadelphia **Conference** of the **MEC**. Later, in 1840, he gained the approval of the New England Conference and became a pastor in Providence, Rhode Island. Matlack was increasingly frustrated by the accommodating position taken by the MEC toward slaveholding within its ranks. Along with a number of other abolitionists, Matlack seceded from the MEC in 1842. The next year, these seceders established the Wesleyan Methodist Connection (later called "Church"), a denomination explicitly opposed to "**slavery** and **episcopacy**." Matlack served Wesleyan Methodist congregations in Pennsylvania and Illinois. He also held several leadership positions in the young church: connectional book agent, president of the **General Conference**, and editor of the denominational newspaper,

The Wesleyan, from 1852 to 1856. Matlack faithfully represented the Wesleyan Methodist cause by writing in the paper, by producing a filiopietistic biography of **Orange Scott**, the church's founder, and by creating an apologetic history of the denomination entitled *The Antislavery Struggle and Triumph in the MEC*. Matlack and many other Wesleyan Methodist leaders returned to the MEC in 1867, following the constitutional abolition of slavery.

Douglas M. Strong

MATTHEWS, MARJORIE (July 11, 1916–June 30, 1986), first female bishop (see WOMEN) in any mainline denomination, was born in Onawa, Michigan. Divorced after World War II, she worked as an executive secretary for an auto parts manufacturer from 1946 to 1963. She was ordained an **elder** in the **MC** in 1965 at the age of 49, and served several churches in Michigan, New York, and Florida while pursuing her education. In 1967, she earned a college degree from Central Michigan, followed by a bachelor of divinity degree from Colgate Rochester Divinity School (1970). She then earned her master's degree (in Religion) and a Ph.D. (in humanities from Florida State University (1976).

Matthews became the second woman in the **UMC** to serve as a district **superintendent** (in the West Michigan Annual Conference) and was elected its first woman bishop on July 17, 1980. She served the Wisconsin area for four years, retiring in 1984. She died of cancer in 1986 and was survived by her son and three grandchildren. *See also* EPISCOPACY.

Susan E. Warrick

McCAINE, ALEXANDER (1768–June 1, 1856), one of the founders of the **MP**, was born in Dublin, **Ireland**. In his early 20s, he immigrated to Charleston, South Carolina, ca. 1788. He joined the Methodists while in Charleston and began to preach in the city. For a time he was a traveling companion to Bishop **Francis Asbury** and, in 1797, he joined the **conference** and served **circuits** in the Carolinas and in Virginia. Although he located in 1806 to educate his children, he reentered the itinerant ministry in 1815. In the 1820s, he supported the cause of lay representation, election of **presiding elders**, and curtailment of episcopal power along with other reformers (*see* EPISCOPACY). McCaine wrote several books and articles between 1827 and 1830 defending the reformers' positions and challenging the status quo of the denomination. McCaine was a member of the 1828 and 1830 **General Conference**s that led to the formation of the MP. He was also a member of the committee that prepared the new denomination's constitution and its **Discipline**. He supported the southern cause as the country's sectional crisis escalated. He died in Augusta, Georgia.

L. Dale Patterson

McCLINTOCK, JOHN, Jr. (October 27, 1814–March 4, 1870), **MEC** clergyman, educator, and editor, was born in Philadelphia. He became a bookkeeper in the Methodist Book Concern, New York City, where he was converted. In 1832, he entered the University of Pennsylvania, completing the course in three years with honors. In 1835, he was admitted on trial to the Philadelphia **Conference**, but because of ill health gave up the pastorate. He became a professor of mathematics at Dickinson College, later transferring in 1840 to the chair of classical languages. The same year he was ordained an **elder** in the MEC, and in 1848, was elected editor of *The Methodist Quarterly Review*. In 1853, together with James Strong, he began his *Cyclopaedia of Biblical, Theological and Ecclesiastical Literature*, a work in 12 volumes. In 1856, he was a delegate to two important conferences in Europe, and later served St. Paul's MEC in New York and the American Chapel, Paris, France (1860). He was twice married and had one son, Emory. From 1864 to 1868 he was chairman of the **General Conference** Centenary Committee. He became closely associated with Daniel Drew, who persuaded him to become the first president of Drew Theological Seminary, Madison, New Jersey, which Drew founded in 1867. He is buried in Madison.

Frederick E. Maser

McCOLL, DUNCAN (August 22, 1754–December 17, 1830), pioneer Methodist preacher, was born in Scotland and enlisted in the British army in 1777. In 1778, he sailed to **Canada** with his regiment; later, he was sent to New York. Upon his discharge in 1783, he boarded a ship for Halifax. Bad weather drove the ship off course and the passengers wintered in Bermuda. A fellow passenger was Elizabeth Channal (d. 1819), who introduced McColl to Methodism. In 1784, they set sail again for Halifax, where they married. They first settled in the new town of St. Andrews, New Brunswick, but soon moved to St. Stephen, 20 miles away. Dismayed by their unruly fellow citizens and the absence of social restraints, the McColls began holding prayer meetings in their home in November 1785. A **revival** broke out, and McColl soon gave up his business to become a full-time preacher. He formed a Methodist society in St. Stephen, the first in New Brunswick, and began evangelizing in outlying areas (*see* SOCIETIES, CLASSES, AND BANDS). His calling was formalized in 1792 when he became an itinerant preacher under **William Black**'s direction. **Francis Asbury** ordained him in 1795. St. Stephen remained his base for the rest of his life, although he made many missionary preaching trips. The McColls had no children.

Susan E. Warrick

McCONNELL, FRANCIS JOHN (August 18, 1871–August 18, 1953) was a pastor, university administrator, bishop, theologian, and social activist. He served churches in Massachusetts and New York, became president of DePauw University (Indiana) in 1909, and was elected bishop of the **MEC** in 1912. McConnell's theology and philosophy are examples of Boston personalism. Having graduated from Ohio Wesleyan, he received his S.T.B. and Ph.D. degrees from Boston University. McConnell's first book, *The Diviner Immanence* (1906), was heavily influenced by Borden Parker Bowne, his dissertation adviser. *Is God Limited?* and *The Christlike God* are examples of McConnell's other works. In 1929 he published a biography of Bowne, which was in part a defense of his teacher's views. McConnell was a highly visible proponent of the **social gospel**. He chaired the commission that the Interchurch World Movement appointed to investigate the steel strike of 1919–1920. He was president of the Methodist Federation for Social Service and of the American Association for Social Security, and a sponsor of the National Religion and Labor Foundation. Other positions occupied by McConnell illustrate the range of his interests. He was active in the American Civil Liberties Union, served as president of the Federal

Council of Churches (1928–1932), and held endowed lectureships at Vanderbilt and Yale.

John C. English

McDOUGALL, GEORGE MILLWARD (1820–January 24, 1876), missionary in western **Canada**, was born in Kingston, Ontario. He was converted at the age of 19. In 1842, he married Elizabeth Chantler, who became a distinguished worker in her own right. He engaged in business for several years during which he preached as a layman to the tribes with whom he carried on trade. He and his wife eventually saved enough money for a term at Victoria University (Toronto). In 1850, he was received on trial for missionary work and spent a year working with **William Case** at Alderville. He worked at Lake Huron, Rama and was appointed to Norway House in 1860, with superintendency over all the Indian missions of the Methodist Church in western Canada. Early in 1863, he moved to Victoria on the North Saskatchewan River in Manitoba. This was to serve as his base for wide-ranging missionary work. In 1871, he moved to Edmonton and, in 1872, to Bow River. He worked diligently to calm relations between the Canadian government and native peoples and recruited many workers for the west in his travels through Manitoba with his missionary son, John.

Joanne Carlson Brown

McKENDREE, WILLIAM (July 6, 1757–March 5, 1835) was the fourth bishop of the **MEC** and the first born in America (King William County, Virginia). He served as a volunteer in the American Revolution. The chronology of his Methodist ministry is **conversion** in a **revival** in 1787; becoming a traveling preacher (1788); admitted to full connection and ordained **deacon** (1790); ordained **elder** (1791); briefly joined the **James O'Kelly** schism (1792); **presiding elder** of the Western **Conference** from 1795; and bishop from 1808. McKendree brought the presiding elders into the appointment making process, began the tradition of episcopal reports to the quadrennial **General Conference**s, and won reversal of the 1820 General Conference decision to make the presiding eldership an elective office. His **episcopacy** saw the number of Methodist-related colleges grow from none to six; membership increase by 429 percent and his church the largest religious community in the USA; expansion from six annual conferences to 23; **missions** to **Latin America** and **Africa** and plans for a mission to China (*see* ASIA); establishment of churchwide educational standards for preachers; and foundation of a theological journal still in publication. McKendree seems to have become more accepting of **slavery** over time. When he died this was the most divisive issue in his church. Bishop McKendree remained celibate. He was the last person truly to be bishop of all the members of his communion.

Charles W. Brockwell, Jr.

MEANS OF GRACE are those outward signs, words, or actions that provide the ordinary channels by which God might convey to human beings **prevenient**, justifying, or sanctifying **grace** by the **Holy Spirit**. The term, found in a prayer of General Thanksgiving in the Book of Common Prayer (BCP), is traditionally applied to the **sacraments**, as seen in Article XXV and the Catechism of the BCP.

John Wesley, however, understood the means of grace to fall into two broader categories, "instituted" and "prudential." The instituted means of grace include not only the Lord's Supper (*see* EUCHARIST), but also prayer (private, family, and public), searching the scripture (by reading, meditating, and hearing), **fasting**, and Christian conference (or religious conversation). He understood these "outward ordinances" to be specific means by which not only "the inward grace of God is ordinarily conveyed to man" but also means by which "the **faith** that brings **salvation** is conveyed to them who before had it not." For these reasons, Wesley argued strongly against the **Moravians** who felt that persons who were searching for faith should abstain from exercising the means of grace until they had "true faith," in order to avoid the impression of trying to earn their salvation through these activities. According to Wesley, however, the Lord's Supper itself could be a "converting ordinance," that is, an opportunity through which God's grace could pardon the faithful penitent. And for him, the use of these means by one who was searching for a meaningful faith would prevent what he saw as a great danger: the "indolent inactivity" of **antinomianism**.

For Wesley, the second category, prudential means of grace, includes (for members) doing good, avoiding evil, and attending religious services, a scheme reminiscent of the three **General Rules** by which Methodists evidenced their desire for salvation. For the preachers, the prudential means of grace also include leading services, meeting with the congregation, visiting the members (sick and well), instructing and regulating the society (*see* SOCIETIES, CLASSES, AND BANDS). Wesley recognized that these activities might not produce apparent fruit, which was not the case with yet four other means of grace: watching, denying oneself, taking up one's cross, and exercising the presence of God.

The United Methodist **Articles of Religion** (XVI) refer to the sacraments of the Lord's Supper and **Baptism** as "certain signs of grace, and God's good will toward us, by which he doth work invisibly in us, and doth not only quicken, but also strengthen and confirm, our faith in him." The Confession of Faith (VI) refers to the sacraments specifically as "means of grace." *See also* SACRAMENTS.

Richard P. Heitzenrater

METHODIST CHURCH (MC) was formed by a union of the **MP**, the **MEC**, and the **MECS** at a uniting conference in Kansas City, Missouri, on April 26, 1939.

The MP had been organized in 1830 as a result of dissatisfaction with the **episcopacy** and with the lack of lay representation in the **General Conference** of the MEC. In 1844, the MEC bisected into the MEC and the MECS due to a constitutional difference at the heart of which lay the issue of **slavery**.

Early in the 20th century, an attempt at union of the three churches was prompted by the MP, but union proved to be a lengthy process with discouraging failures along the way. The MECS had no African-American members, whereas the MEC had a large number of African-American members and **conferences**. Union was effected through the creation of the jurisdictional conferences. Whereas the General Conference, meeting every four years, was to continue as the highest legislative body of the church, the jurisdictional conferences were created to elect the bishops, provide members for the general boards, and assist in implementing the programs of the general church. There were six jurisdictions. Five were geographical areas and one racial, named the Central Jurisdiction. It was to include all the African-American churches and conferences. Many African Americans opposed the union because of this element of segregation. Others supported it because it assured the African Americans of a certain number of bishops and representation on every one of the general boards. It was consummated against all opposition.

In two ensuing decades, the church noticeably increased its membership. In addition, a new program was introduced every quadrennium and benevolence giving was greatly increased by a system of "Advance Specials," which in time amounted to over half of the receipts of the Division of World Missions. The general boards were given great power and, in 1952, the idea of a quadrennial emphasis became the law of the church.

During World War II, the General Conference of 1944 reaffirmed its pacifist position of 1939, and, in the same year, the General Conference began a "Crusade for a New World Order" initiated by Bishop **G. Bromley Oxnam**.

Greater emphasis was placed upon lay participation in the planning of the work of the church as well as upon architecture, ecumenicity (*see* ECUMENISM), and liturgy with a revision of the hymnal adopted in 1964. In 1956 the General Conference voted to ordain **women**.

Many considered the Central Jurisdiction discriminatory, and, in 1964, the General Conference devised a two-step plan for its elimination. September 1967 was set as the deadline to transfer all of the Central Jurisdiction's conferences into their appropriate regional jurisdictions. Although this deadline was postponed, by 1968, the Central Jurisdiction had all but disappeared and the MC had become one united body.

Frederick E. Maser

METHODIST EPISCOPAL CHURCH (MEC). The Methodist societies first became a church in America. In 1784, at the **Christmas Conference** in Baltimore, Maryland, 60 preachers received **Thomas Coke**, whom **John Wesley** had ordained, and accepted Wesley's plan for the organization of what was called the MEC. The **Discipline**, the 24 articles that Wesley had adapted from the Thirty-Nine Articles of the Church of England, together with an article acknowledging loyalty to the USA and the order for the **Sunday Service** became the basis of the new church (*see* ARTICLES OF RELIGION). Thomas Coke and **Francis Asbury** were elected general superintendents and assumed the title of bishop (*see* EPISCOPACY). Through experimentation, further structure evolved, which included a **conference** system organized around the quarterly conference, the annual conference, and the **General Conference**. The latter, meeting every four years, became the highest legislative body of the church. Authority and leadership rested almost solely in the hands of the bishops and the preachers.

Although the Methodists shared a common heritage and basic Christian affirmations with most other denominations, theologically the MEC adhered to John Wesley's commitment to the Bible and his teaching that **faith** is guided by scripture, tradition, **experience**, and reason. Distinctive Wesleyan emphases included **prevenient grace**, faith and good works, mission and service, and finally the serving ministry of **worship** in the church. The Wesley tradition insisted that faith experienced in the worshiping community nurtures personal growth and then issues in service to the world.

The MEC, true to its founder John Wesley, was an inclusive body and committed to concern for the outcast, the sick, the aging, the oppressed, and the imprisoned.

The Methodists' deep sense of commitment to mission fit the needs of a new immigrant nation. In 1819, the founding of the Missionary Society gave structure for outreach that eventually included work by the WFMS and WHMS. White settlers on the frontiers in Texas, New Mexico, Arizona, together with blacks and Native Americans, were the first to be reached on this continent. And then **Africa**, South America, **Asia**, India, Scandinavia, Germany, and Russia became fields for Methodist evangelism (*see* EUROPE; LATIN AMERICA AND THE CARIBBEAN; MISSIONS).

Just as the MEC was a dynamic and divergent body, so did this lead to differences and divisions. Several groups broke away. Between 1813 and 1817, large black groups formed independent churches. But the major divisions occurred when the **MP** body seceded in 1830, as did the **MECS** in 1844. These bodies reunited in 1939 in Kansas City, Missouri. Adopting a new constitution, they also adopted a new name. In that historic moment, the MEC with its colleagues in Christ became the **MC**.

Robert Drew Simpson

METHODIST EPISCOPAL CHURCH, SOUTH (MECS) emerged from the growing sectional alienation leading up to the USA Civil War. U. S. senators John C. Calhoun, Henry Clay, and Daniel Webster all viewed the schism in what was the country's largest religious body as a forerunner of national breakup.

The root cause of this division was the issue of how the church should live and minister in the slave states. From its foundational (1784) prohibition of any Methodist owning another person, the **MEC Discipline** by 1844 accommodated conditions under which Methodists, including ministers, might be slave owners.

In 1843, a general convention at Utica, New York, founded the abolitionist Wesleyan Methodist Connection (*see* WESLEYAN CHURCH). Thus northern delegates went to the 1844 MEC **General Conference** in New York City determined to act on the case of Bishop **James O. Andrew** of Georgia who had inherited two slaves from his wife. Southern delegates were equally determined to vindicate Bishop Andrew's behavior and to preserve the principle that a bishop had the right to serve anywhere in the connection.

Georgia law precluded manumission in that state. One slave, a young woman, declined removal to Liberia or another state. Andrew planned to move the other, a boy, to a free state when he grew old enough. The sale of persons was forbidden by the Discipline.

The bishop's offer to resign was unacceptable to the southern delegates. North and South felt that resolution of the Andrew case on their terms was essential to the continued acceptance of their Church in their parts of the USA. New England, northern, and middle Atlantic delegates united in an invincible majority, which ended by requesting Andrew not to exercise his episcopal ministry so long as he owned slaves.

The General Conference next adopted a plan of separation should any southern **Conference** decide to leave the connection. In May 1845, delegates from 15 conferences gathered in Fourth Street MEC in Louisville, Kentucky, and organized the MECS.

Northern offers of reunion just after the Civil War were rebuffed. At Cape May, New Jersey, in 1876, a joint commission declared both churches legitimate and coequal Methodist connections. By the new century, reunion interest was broadly favored in the MECS, but not by the required majority. A 1935 plan, incorporating the **MP** as well, succeeded, resulting in the **MC**.

From the 1840s, the MECS planted churches overseas, eventually having **missions** in China, Japan (*see* ASIA), **Africa**, and **Latin America**. Four major universities, Vanderbilt, Emory, Southern Methodist, and Duke, were MECS foundations. Emory, Southern Methodist, and Duke still retain their church relationship.

Charles W. Brockwell, Jr.

METHODIST NEW CONNEXION was inaugurated on August 9, 1797, at Ebenezer Chapel, Leeds, England, by Alexander Kilham, William Thom, two other former Wesleyan itinerants, and 13 laymen. This followed Kilham's expulsion in 1796 and the refusal of the Wesleyan **Conference** in 1797 to allow lay representation. The 5,000 or so Wesleyan members (about 5 percent) who joined the new body were those who felt that the Plan of Pacification and the further slight concessions of 1797 did not go far enough. They came chiefly from the industrializing towns of northern England and formed about 66 societies (*see* SOCIETIES, CLASSES, AND BANDS), all north of a line from Stoke to Nottingham. A minority held radical political views. The Conference of 1798 adopted the constitution proposed by Kilham and Thom, in which preachers and people had separate "rights." Each **circuit** elected one preacher and one layman to Conference, in contrast to the all-ministerial Wesleyan conference. The Connexion was given a legal basis by a Deed Poll of 1846, which appointed 12 preachers and 12 laymen as guardian representatives.

Kilham's early death in 1798 left Thom the leading figure. His cultured and orderly approach left a permanent mark. The Connexion grew very slowly, taking 25 years to reach 10,000 members. It benefited from troubles within Wesleyanism in 1834 and 1849–1853, but lost 21 percent of its own members when Joseph Barker was expelled in 1841. Ministerial status rose in the 1840s and **ordination** was by imposition of hands by at least 1855. Ranmoor College opened in

1864. The Methodist New Connexion was the most urban of all Methodist bodies, but it was weak in the large cities. Its natural habitat was the medium-sized northern manufacturing towns. From 1798 there was an Irish mission. Membership reached 40,000 by the time it became part of the United Methodist Church in 1907.

E. Alan Rose

METHODIST PROTESTANT CHURCH (MP) was a major division of American Methodism occasioned by rebuffed efforts at reforming episcopal Methodism (*see* EPISCOPACY). It was formed in 1830 after a decade of controversy and united with the **MEC** and **MECS** in 1939.

Agitation for limiting the power of bishops and **presiding elders** (now district superintendents) began at the 1820 **General Conference** of the MEC when a resolution passed, which was subsequently suspended and rescinded, requiring presiding elders to be elected by annual **conferences**. To press the reform agenda, that is, election of presiding elders, full clergy rights for local preachers, and, most important, lay representation at all conferences, William S. Stockton started publication of *The Wesleyan Repository* in Trenton, New Jersey, in 1820, which later became *The Mutual Rights and Methodist Protestant*.

On November 12, 1828, the reformers, led by **Nicholas Snethen**, William Stockton, **Asa Shinn**, and others organized the Associated Methodist Churches at St. John's Church, Baltimore, Maryland. Two years later, on November 2, 1830, they organized and took the name MP with Francis Waters presiding, and W. C. Lipscomb, secretary. The church numbered about 80 ministers and 5,000 members. The new church had no bishops or presiding elders but, instead, had conference presidents elected by annual conferences and stationing committees to make pastoral assignments. Every station and **circuit** was represented at annual conference by laypersons and General Conference had equal lay and clergy representation. The first General Conference was held in Georgetown, District of Columbia, on May 6, 1834.

The MP avoided taking stands on moral and political questions. When it came to the issue of **slavery** this position led to division. The General Conference of 1858 refused to adopt an **antislavery** resolution that had been put forth by Northern and Western Conferences. In

1858, these conferences refused to meet with any conference that tolerated slaveholding and later took the name The Methodist Church. Once slavery was not an issue, desire for reunion increased, and on May 11, 1877, was consummated in Baltimore, Maryland. The MP played a significant role in reopening union conversations between the MEC and MECS. Following the failure of the 1924 plan to unite episcopal Methodism, the MP gave the movement fresh impetus in encouraging the three churches to unite and was the first to approve the Plan of Union in 1936. The uniting conference was in Kansas City in 1939 with James Henry Straughn and John Calvin Broomfield being elected MP bishops to be numbered among the bishops of the newly formed **MC**. Those refusing to enter into union included some churches in Mississippi, Alabama, Missouri, and Louisiana, keeping the name MP and some in the North, especially New Jersey, taking the name Bible Protestant Church. By 1939 the MP reported a membership of 191,863 members.

The church supported missionary work, especially in Japan, China, and India (*see* ASIA). Educational institutions included Adrian College in Michigan, High Point College in North Carolina, Western Maryland College in Maryland, Westminster College in Texas, and Westminster Theological Seminary in Maryland, now Wesley Seminary in Washington, D.C. Publications included *The Methodist Protestant* and *The Methodist Recorder*.

Robert J. Williams

MEXICO. *See* LATIN AMERICA AND THE CARIBBEAN.

MEYER, LUCY JANE RIDER (September 9, 1849–March 17, 1922) founded the **Chicago Training School** for City, Home, and Foreign Missions (**MEC**). Driven by the belief that **women** needed formal education to prepare for lives of Christian service, Rider Meyer sought to revive and modernize the female diaconate. By fall 1887, three women living together in a Chicago flat, wearing distinctive garb, and calling themselves deaconesses, were at work (*see* DEACONESS MOVEMENT). Rider Meyer believed that Methodism desperately needed the maternal element that deaconesses would provide to blunt the dehumanizing conditions she saw in modern, urban, industrial society. The MEC formally recognized the deaconess office at **General Conference** in 1888. Born in New Haven, Vermont, Lucy Jane Rider was the first child of Richard Dunning Rider and his second wife Jane Child. She was educated at Oberlin College (Ohio), the Woman's Medical College (Philadelphia), and the Massachusetts Institute of Technology. She taught at the Chicago Training School for two decades, and was also a prolific writer. Described by one friend as "more than a mild modernist," Lucy Rider Meyer embraced the liberal beliefs of higher criticism, a view that by 1914 placed her in conflict with Fundamentalists, including her own husband, Josiah Shelly Meyer.

Mary Agnes Dougherty

MICHALSON, CARL (June 29, 1915–November 8, 1965), Methodist clergyman and theologian, was born in Waverly, Minnesota. He received his B.A. degree from John Fletcher College, B.D. and M.A. degrees from Drew University, and his Ph.D. degree from Yale University. Two children were born of his marriage to Janet Merrill in 1944. Following brief pastoral labors, he joined the faculty of Drew University, teaching systematic theology there until his tragic death in a plane crash near Cincinnati, Ohio. A prolific author, Michalson's existentialist orientation in theology appears in the titles of some of his major works: *Christianity and the Existentialists* (1956), *Faith for Personal Crises* (1958), *The Hinge of History* (1959), and *Witness of Kierkegaard* (1960), which he edited. *Rationality of Faith* (1964) represented his mature theological thought, while *Worldly Faith* (1967) is a series of lectures published posthumously. Michalson's unique gifts were his capacity for relating Christian theology to the practical questions of human existence, his appreciation for the centrality of the Christ-event, and his concern that Christian **preaching** be a vital proclamation of the church's faith in Jesus Christ. He was a master teacher, delivering his scintillating lectures and powerful sermons without notes.

K. James Stein

MILES, WILLIAM H. (December 26, 1828–November 14, 1892), first bishop of the **CME**, was born in Springfield, Kentucky. Although he was born into **slavery**, Miles was freed in his owner's will.

In 1855 he joined the **MECS**. He was licensed to preach in 1857. When the CME was formed in 1870, he was the first to be elected bishop (*see* EPISCOPACY). He was consecrated by Bishops McTyeire and Pine of the MECS. Bishop Miles served for 22 years as a bishop in the CME. He died in Louisville, Kentucky.

L. Dale Patterson

MILEY, JOHN (December 25, 1813–December 13, 1895), **MEC** minister and theologian, was born near Hamilton, Ohio, in 1813, graduated from Methodist-related Augusta College in Kentucky, earning his B.A. 1834 and M.A. 1837, and in 1838 entered the church's ministry through the Ohio **Conference**. Miley served several churches in his native Ohio until 1852 when he transferred to the New York East Conference. For the next 20 years, he served churches in New York and Connecticut until 1873 when he was called to the professorship of systematic theology at Drew Theological Seminary in Madison, New Jersey. In his lectures to students at Drew and in a steady stream of articles and books, Miley took on the task of developing a Methodist theology for his day. Two of his books made him chief theological tutor to Methodists in the Victorian era. *The Atonement in Christ* (1879) explained the dominant theories of the **atonement** and defended the "Governmental Theory," which aimed to preserve the justice of God's demands. His two-volume *Systematic Theology* (1892–1894) presented a "Methodist Arminianism" (*see* ARMINIUS, JACOBUS) which differentiated Methodism from Calvinism and **Roman Catholicism** and which acknowledged the insights and limitations of the scientific method of his time. Miley served his church as a clergy delegate to five **General Conferences** (1864, 1872, 1876, 1888, and 1892), was a fraternal delegate to the MECS in 1886, and gave the keynote address at the Methodist Centennial Conference in Baltimore in 1884.

Kenneth E. Rowe

MILLER, GEORGE (February 16, 1774–April 5, 1816), successor to leadership of the **EA** after the death of **Jacob Albright**, was born in Pottstown, Pennsylvania, of German immigrant parents. A trained millwright, he opened his own mill in 1798. That year he first heard

Albright preach and was impressed. Two years later he married Magdalena Brobst. In 1802, he was surprised when Albright stopped at his home to ask for lodging. Their conversations stimulated his heartfelt interest in religion, and he joined the evangelist's movement, became a class leader (*see* SOCIETIES, CLASSES, AND BANDS), and, in 1805, sold his mill property to become an itinerant preacher. Largely through Miller's inspired preaching, people responded, new classes formed, more **circuits** were added, and the Albright movement doubled its membership. By 1807 he was elected **elder**, and assumed primary leadership when Albright died the following year. Miller assumed the founder's responsibilities for writing the society's **Articles of Religion** and first **Discipline**, which he published in 1809. By that year, serious health problems restricted his own ministry to writing and preaching as strength permitted. From 1809 to 1813, he continued to preside at annual **conferences**, to assign preachers to circuits, and to write.

Donald K. Gorrell

MISSIONS. Methodism from its beginnings was a missionary movement among the working classes of Britain and then on the American frontier, where it achieved its greatest success in the early 19th century. The system of preaching **circuits** and class meetings was a highly effective mission strategy (*see* SOCIETIES, CLASSES, AND BANDS). Only as Methodism became firmly established was a distinction made in America between ministerial and missionary appointments, missionaries being those sent to places where the church was not yet self-sufficient—either at home or abroad. **John** and **Charles Wesley** had launched an abortive attempt at cross-cultural missions when they went to Georgia in 1735 to evangelize the American Indians. **Thomas Coke**, one of Wesley's superintendents for America, was the greatest proponent of missions in early Methodism and almost single-handedly organized the spread of Methodism to the West Indies and Sierra Leone.

Prior to the organization of British (1818) and American (1819) denominational missionary societies, individual Methodists engaged in cross-cultural missions. John Stewart, an African American, was the first known Methodist missionary to the American Indians, beginning work among the Wyandotts of Ohio in 1816. His example and that of others led to the formation of the Methodist Missionary Society (MMS) in New York, founded to facilitate the efforts of annual **conferences** in mission work. The first missionary sent under the MMS was **Melville Cox**, who went to Liberia in 1833. Local groups of mission enthusiasts continued to support individual missionaries through the early 19th century, most notably **Ann Wilkins**, missionary to Liberia from 1837 to 1856.

The great era of worldwide Methodist expansion occurred from the 1840s to World War I. Among other locations, the **MEC** entered China and Argentina (1847), Germany (1849), India (1856), Japan and Mexico (1873), Korea, Angola, and Singapore (1885), Southern Rhodesia (1898), the Philippines (1899), and Congo (1911). The **MECS** entered China (1848), Brazil (1867), Mexico (1871), Japan (1886), Korea (1895), Cuba (1899), and Congo (1914). The **MP** entered Japan (1880), India (1906), and China (1909). The **EA** opened work in Germany (1850), Japan (1875), and China (1904). The **UB** sent missionaries to Sierra Leone (1853), China (1889), Japan (1895), Puerto Rico (1899), and the Philippines (1901). Methodist missions were characterized by evangelistic zeal, commitment to higher **education** and the improvement of the status of **women** around the world, and provision of indigenous leadership for church and society.

The creation of the **MC** in 1939 consolidated MEC, MECS, and MP mission work under the Board of Missions and Church Extension. Three divisions of the Board of Missions reflected the major emphases of the church on women's mission work, mission within the USA, and foreign mission. During the life of the MC, missions increasingly came under indigenous control. The number of missionaries leveled off and then began to drop in the late 1960s. During the first 20 years of the **UMC**, social concern rather than **evangelism** defined mission for many Methodists. In the 1990s, however, Methodist renewal in the former Soviet bloc gave a new impetus to holistic definitions of mission. *See also* AFRICA; ASIA; EUROPE; LATIN AMERICA AND THE CARIBBEAN.

Dana L. Robert

MIYAMA, KANICHI (dates uncertain), an early Japanese convert to Methodism in America, immigrated to the San Francisco area in

1876. Arriving in the USA, he met Otis Gibson, who was then district superintendent of the Chinese mission work in the San Francisco area. Miyama had been given a letter of introduction to Gibson by a mutual friend. Gibson had been a missionary to China (*see* ASIA). It was through Gibson that Miyama not only learned English but also about the gospel. Miyama was baptized in 1877 and became a leader in Japanese work in the San Francisco area. In 1886, he was ordained a **deacon** in the California **Conference (MEC)**. In 1888, Miyama transferred to Hawaii, where he began work among the Japanese immigrants. In 1890, he returned to Japan and became a member of the Japan Conference (MEC). He was ordained an **elder** that year. Miyama was active in the Japan Conference when it merged with other conferences from the MEC and **MECS** to form the independent Methodist Church in Japan in 1907.

L. Dale Patterson

MODERNISM/LIBERALISM. Liberalism and conservatism, modernism and **fundamentalism** are, respectively, the left and right poles of a theological continuum. To the right of an ever-shifting center are persons who hold that Christian truths are timelessly encapsulated in the words of scripture, taken more or less literally, and in the classic doctrines of Christianity. Theologians on the left believe they have the responsibility of restating Christian truths for the age in which they live. They explain that every expression of Christianity, whether biblical, doctrinal, or theological, is colored by the social, economic, philosophical, and political conditions of its time. More specifically, liberals see the **Bible** as a collection of ancient documents, some more legendary or poetic than historical, some ethically dubious, in which the word of God is to be uncovered. Liberals search for the Jesus of history, rather than settling for the Christ of the creeds. Out of their research comes, among other propositions, the assertion that the substitutionary doctrine of the **atonement** is a bloodthirsty myth: No good God would sentence one of his sons to death, so as to be free to forgive his other children. Instead of emphasizing the sacrifice of Jesus, liberals present him as "the man for others"—the one who lived and died and continues to live to reveal God's saving love for individuals and God's demand for justice in society. Hence, liberalism is the principal theology of the **Social Gospel**.

A forthright Methodist critic of liberalism during the first half of the 20th century was Harold Paul Sloan (1881–1961). One of the liberals he denounced was **Harris Franklin Rall**. Early in the 1970s, the Forum for Scriptural Christianity ("Good News") took up the cudgels against liberalism in the **UMC**, condemning what was read as an affirmation of theological "pluralism" in the 1972 *Book of Discipline* (*see* DISCIPLINE). Other groups such as the Confessing Movement and UMAction joined the antiliberal crusade, whose principal theological spokesman is Drew Theological School professor **Thomas C. Oden** (1931–). One target is UMC bishop C. Joseph Sprague (elected in 1996), whose liberal manifesto *Affirmations of a Dissenter* (2003) elicited demands that he be charged with heresy.

John G. McEllhenney

MOLDOVA. *See* EUROPE.

MORAVIANS. Led by a German, Count Nicholas Ludwig von Zinzendorf (1700–1760), and tracing their origins to the Bohemian Brethren of the 15th century, the Moravians were a group of German pietists (*see* PIETISM) who emphasized personal religious experience based on Bible study, **prayer**, and contemplation. Based on Zinzendorf's Moravia estate, Herrnhut, they were influential in the theological journeys of **John** and **Charles Wesley**. The brothers first met Moravians on board ship on the way to their Georgia mission in 1735. Relationships with the Moravians deepened during the Wesleys' time in America and continued after both brothers returned to England. Moravian views on **salvation** and **conversion** were especially significant for both brothers. After his **Aldersgate experience** in 1738, John Wesley visited Herrnhut and engaged in discussions with Zinzendorf. Later both brothers increasingly disagreed with, and parted from, the Moravians who, in the estimation of the Wesleys, undervalued the role of the **sacraments** and other **means of grace** in one's salvation. Methodism, however, owed much to the Moravians, including the emphasis on **assurance**, the **love feast**, and **watchnights**. *See also* SOCIETIES, CLASSES, AND BANDS.

Charles Yrigoyen, Jr.

MOTT, JOHN RALEIGH (May 25, 1865–January 31, 1955), **MEC** layperson, **mission** advocate, ecumenist (*see* ECUMENISM), and international leader, was born in Livingston Manor, New York, but raised in Postville, Iowa, where he and his mother were active in the local MEC. Mott was educated at Upper Iowa College and Cornell University. While at Cornell in 1888 he had a life shaping **conversion** during an address by J. E. K. Studd who had been influenced by D. L. Moody. Mott helped organize and lead the Student Volunteer Movement and the World Student Christian Federation. At the same time he held various offices in the International YMCA. These duties granted Mott the opportunity to travel extensively around the world forming networks of church leaders for the goal of proclaiming Christ to the whole world. He was offered and refused the presidencies of five colleges as well as the deanship of Yale Divinity School. He declined the offer to be ambassador to China in 1912. Mott is best remembered for leading the ecumenical movements known as Faith and Order as well as Life and Work. He chaired the continuation committee of the Edinburgh World Missionary Conference (1910) and was a key figure at all major ecumenical conferences until mid-century. Under Mott's tutelage, these movements came together as the **WCC** in 1948 with Mott being named an honorary president. In 1946, he received the Nobel Peace Price. He published 15 books. His life spanned the entire developmental period of the worldwide missionary and ecumenical organizations of the 20th century. He died in Evanston, Illinois, and as an honorary Episcopal canon is buried in the National Cathedral, Washington, D.C.

Robert J. Williams

MOZAMBIQUE. *See* AFRICA.

MURRAY, GRACE (1716–1803). Born in Newcastle upon Tyne, England, in 1736 she married Alexander Murray, a seaman who died at sea six years later. She became housekeeper at the Orphan House, where she met both **John Wesley** and John Bennet, one of his preachers. She accompanied Wesley on one of his **preaching** tours in **Ireland**, where they contracted a **marriage** *de praesenti*, a form of betrothal. Bennet also proposed marriage to her. After a long period of hesitation on Wesley's part and increasing bewilderment on hers, she was finally persuaded by **Charles Wesley** to marry Bennet. After his death she continued to lead meetings for **prayer** and fellowship. She settled in Derbyshire, where she was renowned for her saintliness.

Pauline M. Webb

MUSIC. Every 30 years or so Methodists publish an official hymnal for use in public **worship**. The 1989 **UMC** hymnal is the latest in a long line of "official" hymnals dating back to the first in 1784. The **UB** and the **EC,** which united with the **MC** in 1968, also produced a succession of hymnals beginning in 1795 and 1810, respectively.

Not all were popular, especially the first. Although the Methodists adopted **John Wesley**'s *Collection of Psalms and Hymns for the Lord's Day* along with his revised *Book of Common Prayer* as standards for public worship in their new church in 1784, both books quickly fell into disuse. Neither matched the informal style of worship American Methodists favored for their chapels and **camp meetings.** The new church preferred the smaller, already popular "pocket" hymnbooks whose "spiritual songs" mixed Wesleyan doctrine with evangelical fervor. These spiritual songs are the forerunner of **revival** music, **Sunday school** songs, white and black gospel songs, charismatic choruses, and most of what is heard in evangelical churches today. Two years later (1786) Bishops **Francis Asbury** and **Thomas Coke** prepared *A Pocket Hymn Book* of their own, adding hymns for **Baptism** and the Lord's Supper (*see* EUCHARIST) now that they had become a church with ordained ministers. In revised form it was one of the first books to be published by the newly formed MEC publishing house in 1790. Revised again in 1802 and 1808, this Methodist version of the popular pocket hymnbook served the denomination until 1821.

Formal hymns, psalms, and chorales, mostly British in origin, predominated in official hymnbooks after 1821 as Methodists upscaled themselves into America's Protestant mainstream. The influence of the Oxford Movement's rediscovery of the late classical and medieval hymnody of the 16th century to the 18th century was naturally felt first in the Episcopal Church, but it expanded in the 1870s to other denominations, including the Methodists. Musical editors of Victorian-era Methodist hymnals were now university professors.

But camp meetings and revivals required simple choruses that throngs of people could learn quickly. So did the Sunday school. As a result, unofficial Methodist songbooks, which capitalized on the use of informal songs, spirituals, and other American folk hymns, became so popular that they threatened to take over congregational hymn singing. A two-hymnbook tradition evolved—a formal, upstairs hymnal for "church" services and an informal downstairs hymnal for the Sunday school and fellowship meetings. Sunday school hymnals, like the succession of *Cokesbury Hymnals,* published in 1923, 1928, and 1938, and **Homer Rodeheaver**'s *Christian Service Songs,* first published in 1939, are still widely loved because they are different from the official hymnals.

African-American spirituals combined African and American elements and characteristically employed simple verses and refrains sung alternately between soloist and people. They could be sorrowful, like "Nobody Knows the Trouble I've Seen" or jubilant, like "Didn't My Lord Deliver Daniel?" They expressed not only the faith and hope Christians have always sung about, but were also coded protests against white oppression (*see* SLAVERY AND AMERICAN METHODISM).

The music of the Methodists did not escape the turbulence of the 1960s and 1970s. Traditions came unglued. Guitar music was ground out quickly and without much thought. Organs were turned off in some churches. But in the 1980s Methodists turned their organs on again as their love affair with the guitar waned. A broad range of diverse musical styles, from Renaissance to contemporary compositions, enlivened Methodist worship. To celebrate Methodism's diverse musical traditions, three collections were rushed into print: Asian-American hymns in *Hymns from the Four Winds* (1983), Hispanic-American hymns in *Celebremos II* (1983) and Native American hymns in *Voices* (1992). The 1989 UMC hymnal contained a greater diversity of musical traditions and styles than any previous hymnal. During the 1980s, the UMC recovered singing psalms in public worship, reflected in the antiphons and chants suggested to accompany the new translation of the Psalter in the 1989 hymnal. By the turn of the 21st century, contemporary hymns and praise songs and choruses were sung in many congregations.

In the beginning, Methodist converts were expected to buy their own hymnbooks and bring them to church on Sunday. So pocket-sized hymnbooks were the order of the day. Tiny by today's standards in order to fit into pockets and pocketbooks, latter-day Methodists wonder how Victorian eyes were able to read them in dimly lit sanctuaries and without bifocals. After the Civil War, the publishing house marketing strategies shifted to bulk buying by local church "Official Boards." The 1878 MEC hymnal was the first to find its way into pew racks in large numbers for the convenience of worshippers.

In the beginning tunes were not tied to texts of hymns. Musical settings depended on local use. Congregations sang all of their hymns to a few well-known tunes. Methodists began to publish separate collections of hymn tunes beginning with *The Methodist Harmonist* in 1821. But tunes for congregational singing were not added to an official hymnbook of the MEC until 1857, when the 1849 book was offered with tunes as an option. The 1878 MEC hymnal was the first to be published with tunes, just in time for the growing presence of choirs and organs to help Methodists sing God's praise. The MECS and the UB added tunes to their standard hymnals in 1874. The EA followed suit in 1877. *See also* MUSICAL INSTRUMENTS.

Kenneth E. Rowe

MUSICAL INSTRUMENTS. Use of musical instruments in Methodist public **worship** was slow to gain wide acceptance. Today's use of synthesizers, drums, guitars, and prerecorded music is a far development from the arguments of Methodists in the late 18th century over the use of a "whistle," the pitch pipe's contemptuous name. Proponents of the whistle won. For Methodism's first century pitch pipes outnumbered other musical instruments. After getting the pitch, a "precentor" or "cantor" would line-out the hymn to the congregation. A century later Methodists fought over organs, first reed organs, known popularly as "pump organs," and later pipe organs. The battle was largely won by 1870. Congregations proudly displayed their expensive organ pipes up front behind the preacher. At the same time, every **Sunday school** had a piano and many had full orchestras to accompany their opening and closing "exercises." Electronic organs, introduced in the 1940s, were less expensive alternatives to purchasing new pipe organs or maintaining old ones. In the 1980s rhythm and electronic instruments found a place along with pianos and organs. In many settings prerecorded accompaniments reduced the need for instruments. Musical instruments have become unquestioned and published instrumental music to accompany the church's hymnody is widely available. *See also* MUSIC.

Kenneth E. Rowe

MYANMAR. *See* ASIA.

– N –

NAMIBIA. *See* AFRICA.

NAST, WILHELM (June 15, 1807–May 6, 1889), prominent German-American publisher who became the founder and guiding light of German Methodism, was born in a Lutheran home in Stuttgart, Germany. Buffeted by religious skepticism during his student days, the youthful Nast immigrated to America, where he met Adam Poe, an MEC **presiding elder**, who helped guide him toward a personal experience of regeneration and Christian **assurance**. Nast was received on trial in 1835 by the Ohio **Conference** (**MEC**) and appointed missionary to German immigrants in the vicinity of Cincinnati. The German mission soon broadened its scope, and Nast personally conducted evangelistic trips into several states, establishing German Methodist work in Kentucky, Illinois, Missouri, Wisconsin, and Iowa. His converts numbered in the thousands. His work also led to the founding of a successful MEC mission program in Germany (*see* EUROPE). Nast maintained cordial relations with the German-oriented work of the **EA**, but, unlike the latter, his mission was officially integrated into the connectional structures of Methodism. His most enduring legacy was his work as editor (1839–1889) of *Der Christliche Apologete*, the official organ of German Methodism. He married Margaret McDowell, and the couple had five children.

J. Steven O'Malley

NATIONAL COUNCIL OF THE CHURCHES OF CHRIST IN THE USA (**NCC**) is a cooperative ecumenical agency with representatives from 36 Protestant, Anglican, and Orthodox denominations with a combined membership of about 45 million Christians (*see* ECUMENISM). It is, according to the NCC constitution "a community of Christian communions, which, in response to the gospel as revealed in the scriptures, confesses Jesus Christ, the incarnate Word of God, as Savior and Lord, relying upon the transforming power of the **Holy Spirit**, [and] brings these communions into common mission, serving in all creation to the glory of God." It provides a forum for discussion and for coordination among denominations and its leadership. The NCC was founded in Cleveland, Ohio, November 28–December 1, 1950, growing out of interchurch efforts of the Evangelical Alliance (1867) and especially the Federal Council of Churches of Christ in America (1908). It continued the mission, witness, and service of 12 interdenominational organizations. Its work has included advocating racial justice and liberation, especially during the civil rights movement in the 1960s, **education**, stewardship resources, **missions**, **evangelism**, faith and order, support of regional ecumenism, and relief work in cooperation with Church World Service. The Revised Standard Version and New Revised Standard Version of the **Bible** were published by the NCC. Methodist churches in the NCC are the **AME**, **AMEZ**, **CME**, and **UMC**, and formerly the **MC** and **EUB**.

Robert J. Williams

NELLES, SAMUEL SOBIESKI (October 17, 1823–October 17, 1887), Methodist minister and educator, was born at Mount Pleasant, near Brantford, Upper **Canada**. He attended two academies and then Genesee Wesleyan Seminary in New York State and Victoria College at Cobourg, and graduated from Wesleyan University, Middletown, Connecticut, in 1846. In 1850, he was ordained a minister of the Wesleyan Methodist Church in Canada, and appointed professor and acting principal of Victoria College. The following year he became principal, and, in 1854, he was appointed president. When the institution became Victoria University in 1884, Nelles became its president and chancellor, holding that position until his death three years later. Upper Canada Academy opened in 1836 and reorganized five years later to become Victoria College. Its future was uncertain when Nelles became acting principal and over the next 37 years his leadership strengthened it both financially and educationally to become one of the nation's leading centers of learning. He participated in the plan for federation that would move Victoria University to Toronto as part of one provincial university three years after his death.

Marilyn Färdig Whiteley

NEW BIRTH. This concept is rooted in the New Testament, especially Jesus' conversation with Nicodemus recorded in John 3:1–10. **John Wesley** spoke of experiencing God's accepting, justifying **grace**. He believed that **justification** by **faith** and new birth are inseparable from each other, although they could be distinguished for analysis and discussion. He taught that justification is the redemptive work God does for us, while the new birth is the work God does in us. Wesley's sermon, "The New Birth," is the clearest statement of his views on the new birth. The purpose of the new birth experience is to lead people to a life of holiness in which they are more sensitive to the presence and will of God, the circumstances of others, and their own need to think, speak, and act as disciples of Christ. In another of his sermons, "The Marks of the New Birth," Wesley spoke of three characteristics that distinguish one who has experienced the new birth: faith, hope, and love. Many hymns of **Charles Wesley** speak of the new birth, including the section, "For Mourners brought to the Birth," in the early popular Methodist hymn book, A *Collection of Hymns for the Use of The People Called Methodists* (1780). Methodists have emphasized new birth throughout their history, especially in those places where **revivalism** and the **camp meeting** have been prominent. *See also* CONVERSION; EXPERIENCE, CHRISTIAN.

Charles Yrigoyen, Jr.

NEW ZEALAND. New Zealand Methodism had its beginnings in 1822 through the Pacific expansion of the British Methodist Missionary Society. Much of its ethos has therefore been Wesleyan though other streams of Methodism have contributed to its history.

The initial focus was on work among Maori, first at Kaeo in the northern part of the North Island, and then, after the sacking of that station, at Mangungu in 1828. The missionaries concentrated on learning the Maori language and on **education** as well as **worship** and **evangelism**.

Two factors shifted the initial focus. From 1840 onward, an increasing number of pakeha (white-skinned, usually English) arrived and began to establish larger towns. Then the New Zealand wars of the 1860s, mainly over the large areas of land being given over to pakeha settlement, had a disastrous affect on Maori attitudes to Christian faith.

Early Methodist missionaries, ministers and lay people, undertook considerable pioneering work in new settlements, outback rural areas, and goldfields. They usually brought over the structures of **British Methodism** and established **circuit**s, districts, **preaching** plans, quarterly meetings, **Sunday schools**, and other features.

Bible Christians were in New Zealand from 1841, **Primitive Methodists** from 1844, and the **United Methodist Free Church** from the 1850s. The two smallest Methodist churches—the Bible Christians and the United Methodist Free Church—joined with the largest group, the Wesleyans, in 1897, and the Primitives united with them in the Methodist Union of 1913. At the time of union, New Zealand Methodism had 442 churches, 487 other preaching places, 22,226 members, and 30,191 Sunday school scholars.

Australasian Methodists (**Australia** and New Zealand) became independent of the British Conference in 1855. Linked with Australia for the next 58 years, New Zealand had its own conferences from 1874 and became completely autonomous at the time of Methodist Union.

While the Methodist Church in New Zealand provided theological **education** from the 1840s in various settings, the earliest emphasis was on Maori pastors. Most early ministers were British-trained but this changed toward the end of the 19th century.

By then Methodism had spread to most towns and settlements within the country, and while never much more than 10 percent of the population, it made its influence felt through a high profile within the **temperance** movement of the 1880s and the eventual establishment of city missions. The focus on social concerns and justice grew during the early 20th century, and the adoption of a **Social Creed** in the 1920s, partly as a result of changed attitudes during World War I, was an indicator of a move toward a more socially conscious movement (*see* SOCIAL GOSPEL). While the tensions between Wesleyans and Primitives remained, the basic source of disagreement was between the "evangelical" and "liberal" Methodists (*see* MODERNISM/LIBERALISM). Liberal thinking tended to dominate 20th-century Methodism, but theological conflict became intense toward the end of the century especially around the issues of sexuality and the admission of homosexual persons to ordained ministry (*see* HOMOSEXUALITY). As a result there have been minor splits by conservative groups.

The latter half of the 20th century was also dominated by other important shifts. The immigration of people since the 1960s from large Methodist churches in **Tonga, Fiji, and Samoa** dramatically changed the cultural mix of the church with each of these groups now having independent synods while still working closely with the pakeha-dominated section. These groups have formed large congregations of their own as part of New Zealand Methodism. This stands in contrast to *palangi* (Pacific for "white European") congregations, which have generally been in decline during the past 50 years.

A significant movement toward organic union in the 1960s and 1970s failed to eventuate in a uniting church, including New Zealand Anglicans. However, the movement did spawn a large number of local union and cooperating parishes from the late 1940s onward so that by the beginning of the new millennium approximately two-thirds of Methodist parishes and members belong to them, mainly with members of the Presbyterian Church.

In the early 1980s, a strong movement toward biculturalism between Maori and pakeha began both within church and society. It has aimed at self-determination for Maori people and groups in things Maori, and shared consensus decision making in matters affecting both partners. By moving away from the Westminster system it has given the smaller Maori group an equal say along with the remaining and much larger tauiwi group. This has dramatically affected connexional structures, power-sharing, finances, resource distribution, and decision making. In the light of these moves New Zealand Methodism has changed dramatically and the church here is probably unique among Methodists in some of its features and nomenclature.

Frank Hanson

NEWCOMER, CHRISTIAN (February 1, 1749–March 12, 1830), third bishop of the **UB** church, was born in Lancaster County, Pennsylvania. Although Newcomer was descended from Swiss Mennonite immigrants, he felt stifled by Mennonite spirituality and experienced an evangelical **conversion** in 1771. In 1775, Newcomer moved to Maryland, where he struggled with a call to preach to others about his new faith. He finally began preaching in 1777 and soon became associated with the revival movement among the Germans headed by **Philip William Otterbein** and **Martin Boehm**. Newcomer gradually moved into the leadership of this developing UB movement. He participated in all the early conferences that helped formally organize the movement into a church. With the deteriorating health of Otterbein and Boehm, Newcomer assumed more of the leadership responsibilities. After the founders' deaths, Newcomer was chosen to succeed them as bishop. As bishop, he was instrumental in holding the church's first **General Conference** in 1815, which adopted a confession of faith and formal church **Discipline**. Because of his extensive travels during more than 50 years of itinerant ministry, Newcomer became known as the "St. Paul" of the UB church.

Daryl M. Elliott

NICARAGUA. *See* LATIN AMERICA AND THE CARIBBEAN.

NICHOLSON, EVELYN RILEY (June 30, 1873–February 15, 1967), missionary leader and peace advocate, was born in a parsonage in Jackson, Minnesota. She graduated from DePauw University, Indiana (Phi Beta Kappa). After graduate study she taught at Crandon International Institute, Rome (1903–1904), and spent a year at the American School for Classical Studies, where she also edited *Roman World*. From 1906 to 1917 she was teacher and Head of the Latin Department, Cornell College, Mt. Vernon, Iowa. In 1917, she married Bishop Thomas Nicholson. She was president of the WFMS (**MEC**), 1921–1939, and a founder and first president of the World Federation of Methodist Women, 1940–1945. She was a delegate to three International Missionary Council meetings, and addressed the Oxford Council (1923) on "The Place of Women in the Church on the Mission Field." In 1924 she wrote *The Way to a Warless World*, the first MEC publication on peace published after World War I (*see* WAR

AND PEACE). She helped draft the 1924 MEC **General Conference** peace resolution, and was a delegate to three later General Conferences.

Barbara E. Campbell

NIGERIA. *See* AFRICA.

NISWONGER, ELLA (April 5, 1865–August 2, 1944), the first woman ordained by the **UB**, was born in Montgomery County, Ohio, one of 10 children. She attended Union Biblical Seminary, Dayton, Ohio (later Bonebrake Theological Seminary; today United Theological Seminary), and on May 4, 1887, became the first woman to graduate from the school's regular seminary course. On September 13, 1889, she was ordained by the Central Illinois **Conference**, following the **General Conference** decision in May approving the **ordination of women**. In 1901, Niswonger became the first woman ministerial delegate (from the Central Illinois Conference) to a UB General Conference. She served for 43 years in pastorates in Kansas and Illinois, retiring in 1930 to care for her sister Catherine, also a UB pastor (ordained in 1892). Their brother Winfield was a UB pastor as well (ordained in 1887). Ella Niswonger died in Springfield, Illinois, and was buried in Dayton, Ohio.

Susan E. Warrick

NORTH, FRANK MASON (December 3, 1850–December 17, 1935), **MEC** minister, **social gospel** leader, ecumenical leader (*see* ECUMENISM), and hymn writer, received his doctorate from Wesleyan University, Connecticut (1894), married twice, and had three sons. He served six congregations in the MEC New York **Conference** (1873–1887). North was corresponding secretary of the New York City Church Extension and Missionary Society (1887–1912), developing churches as community centers for clubs, continuing **education** in life skills, child care, and social activism. He supervised inner-city parishes, multiracial centers, and congregations serving immigrants. From 1912 to 1924 he led the MEC Board of Foreign Missions. A founder of the Methodist Federation for Social Service (1907), he helped organize the Federal Council of Churches in America (FCC) in 1908 and revised the MEC **Social Creed** for adoption by the FCC as the Social Creed of the Churches. He chaired the FCC's executive committee (1912–1916) and served as president (1916–1920). For representing USA churches in wartime relief, North was honored by Greece and France. North's hymn writing expressed his passion and conviction about God's saving **grace** known through Jesus and God's message of hope to the poor and those ravaged by war. Best known of his 10 hymns is, "Where Cross the Crowded Ways of Life."

Alice G. Knotts

NORWAY. *See* EUROPE.

– O –

O'BRYAN, WILLIAM (February 6, 1778–January 8,1868), founder of the **Bible Christians**, was born at Luxulyan, Cornwall, England, the son of William O'Bryan, farmer and tinner. A studious and deeply religious boy, it seemed likely that he would "take the gown" and receive Anglican **ordination**, but under the influence of **Adam Clarke** he became a local preacher in 1800 and developed into an itinerant freelance evangelist. Rejected for the ministry because of his family responsibilities, he engaged in independent evangelizing in parts of Cornwall and Devon largely uninfluenced by Wesleyan Methodism. His relationship with the **circuit superintendent**s became more and more strained because of his disregard of Methodist rules and his apparent self-sufficiency, and he was twice expelled from membership. At Stratton near the Devon border, although no longer a Wesleyan, he, with the circuit steward, made a proposal to the circuit that would have given him some recognition within the circuit and at the same time allowed him to pursue his independent **mission** work. This was not acceptable and, on October 1, 1815, O'Bryan wrote: "I entered on my circuit at Mary-Week and Hex." Within a week 22 members had been enrolled at Lake Farm, Shebbear, among them the teenager James Thorne, who would eventually lead the denomination. The following decade saw the rapid spread of the Bible Christian movement, but also witnessed a deteriorating relationship between O'Bryan and his followers, which led to a final break in 1829. Following this he immigrated to North America, living there in self-imposed exile, the denomination continuing without him. All his life O'Bryan was a tireless, indeed a compulsive, traveller. His evangelistic tours in Devon, Cornwall, London, and Kent were succeeded by long journeys from New York to Ohio and across the Canadian border. He published a journal of his American travels. He died in New York in 1868 and was buried in Greenwood cemetery, Brooklyn. *See also* BRITISH METHODISM.

Thomas Shaw

ODEN, THOMAS CLARK (October 21, 1931–), **UMC** clergyperson and theologian, was born in Altus, Oklahoma. He received his B.A. degree from the University of Oklahoma, B.D. from Southern Methodist University's Perkins School of Theology, and M.A. and Ph.D. degrees from Yale University. Three children were born of his marriage in 1952 to Edrita Pokorny. Before joining the Drew University Theological School faculty in 1970, Oden taught at Perkins School of Theology and Phillips University. Oden's scholarly breadth is evidenced by more than 50 volumes he has published or edited, and by the wide range of topics he has addressed, including psychotherapy, counseling, scripture, and ethics, in addition to systematic theology. His magnum opus is the three-volume work in systematic theology: *The Living God* (1987), *The Word of Life* (1989), and *Life in the Spirit* (1992). In 1979, in *Agenda for Theology*, Oden announced his dissatisfaction with current Christian theology's accommodation to modernity. Modernity is best described by its unrestricted human freedom, which has resulted in contemporary society's boredom and emptiness. Theology cannot continue wandering after the latest cultural fads and movements. Oden's solution, as his theological works richly demonstrate, is to reappropriate the power and beauty of the classical orthodoxy of the first Christian millennium.

K. James Stein

O'KELLY, JAMES (1757–October 16, 1826) was an American Methodist preacher and leader of the O'Kelly Schism in 1792. Little is known of his early life other than his birth in **Ireland** and emigration to America in 1778. He became a Methodist itinerant and in 1784 was voted an **elder** at the organizing **conference** of the **MEC**. He was a highly independent personality, and at the first **General Conference** of the MEC in 1792 he proposed that the preachers be permitted to object to their appointment by **Francis Asbury** and, if sustained by the conference, be given another appointment. The motion was defeated, and O'Kelly walked away with other followers, including **William McKendree**, to form the Republican Methodist Church. McKendree later rejoined the MEC. Although O'Kelly was disappointed that more Methodists did not join his ranks, he took with him a large number of members, especially in Virginia, where he was well known and where almost 4,000 MEC members joined his new church. His denomination, however, failed to grow. In 1801, he changed its name to the Christian Church, and, after a number of subdivisions, his remaining churches joined with the Congregationalists in the Congregational Christian Church. He died in North Carolina.

Frederick E. Maser

OLIVER, ANNA (1840–November 20, 1892), first woman to graduate from an American theological seminary and pioneer **MEC** pastor, was born near New Brunswick, New Jersey. Baptized Vivianna Olivia Snowden, she changed her name in the early 1870s so as not to embarrass her family when she decided to enter the ministry. Educated in Brooklyn public schools and Rutgers Female College in New York City (A.B. 1859, M.A. 1860), Oliver began her career as a public school teacher in Connecticut. In addition to teaching, she took an active role in **women**'s suffrage and **temperance** movements. In 1868, Oliver volunteered to teach black children in Georgia under the auspices of the American Missionary Association (AMA). She resigned a year later after learning that the AMA paid female teachers less than men who did the same work. In 1870, she relocated to Cincinnati, Ohio. Oliver's temperance talks in Ohio's town halls and churches encouraged her to think about becoming an ordained minister. In 1873, she enrolled in Boston University School of Theology. Armed with a B.D. degree (1876) and a license to preach, Oliver served First MEC in Passaic, New Jersey (1876–1877), and Willoughby Avenue MEC, Brooklyn (1879–1883). In 1880, Oliver and **Anna Howard Shaw** led an unsuccessful campaign for **ordination** at the MEC **General Conference**.

She continued to preach her message of personal holiness and social responsibility until her death in Greensboro, Maryland. *See also* FEMINISM.

Kenneth E. Rowe

ORDINATION is the liturgical act occurring in a service of worship conferring to certain persons ministerial orders by the laying on of hands and the invocation of the **Holy Spirit**. This rite recognizes that God calls persons to service as ordained ministers and that the Holy Spirit empowers them for service with the necessary gifts and **grace**. Ordination grants the authority to preach and teach the scriptures, administer the **sacraments** of baptism and communion (*see* EUCHARIST), and order the life of the church, usually referred to as the ministry of word, sacrament, and order.

Before someone can be ordained, it is customary that certain qualifications be met, including educational requirements, adherence to the **doctrinal standards** of the church, and demonstration of appropriate gifts. In all branches of Methodism, men and **women** may be candidates for ordination.

In American Methodism the threefold patterning of ministry prevails with ordination for those who are to be **deacon**s and **elder**s but consecration for those elected as bishops. Bishops are not a third order of ministry but an office within the order of elder. Bishops ordain deacons; bishops assisted by other elders ordain elders; bishops consecrate bishops. In British Methodism there is a single ordination for ministry that is enacted by the president of the **Conference** and other designated ministers. There are no bishops.

In the 18th century within Methodism in England, **John Wesley** permitted the use of preachers who were not ordained. However, only those ordained by the Church of England could administer the sacraments. As Methodism grew in the American colonies, the inability of unordained preachers to serve the sacraments was keenly felt. In 1779, several preachers met in Virginia to grant to themselves sacramental authority. Francis Asbury thwarted this effort. American independence made Wesley realize he had to provide for the sacraments in Methodism. On September 1, 1784, he ordained **Richard Whatcoat** and **Thomas Vasey** for service in America and the next day he ordained **Thomas Coke** as superintendent. Wesley justified his irregular actions by claiming that presbyters (elders) and bishops were of the same order and that presbyters could ordain under extraordinary circumstances (*see* EPISCOPACY). He felt these conditions were met by his leadership of the Methodists and the need of the Methodists in America. Before his death, Wesley also ordained others for service in Scotland and England. British Methodists ceased the practice of laying on of hands for ordination following Wesley's death and did not regularize the form of ordination until 1836.

The variations for the ordering of ministry are illustrated in the **EUB** and its predecessors. The **EA** practiced the dual ordination for deacons and elders while the **UB** had a single ordination. Upon the **EC** and UB union in 1946, the EUB took over the single ordination but, upon its merger with the **MC** in 1968, the dual ordination prevailed again. Within American Methodism, ordination is closely linked with clergy membership in the annual conference. In 1996, **UMC** created an order of permanent deacon for persons ordained to word and service. The order of elder is reserved for persons ordained to word, sacrament, and order. Thus ended the Methodist two-step process in which persons seeking elder's ordination were first ordained deacon. Since 1996 both deacons and elders are eligible for full clergy membership in an annual conference in the UMC.

Important ecumenical agreements (*see* ECUMENISM) on ordination and the relationship of the ordained with the whole people of God are *Baptism, Eucharist, and Ministry* (WCC) and *The COCU Consensus* (The Consultation on Church Union).

Robert J. Williams

ORIGINAL SIN. Responding to an age of Deism and rational religion, and in particular to a work by John Taylor, in 1756 **John Wesley** produced his theological treatise, *The Doctrine of Original Sin According to Scripture, Reason, and Experience.* In this work Wesley appealed to empirical evidence to demonstrate that "universal misery is a consequence of universal corruption." In addition, he maintained that original sin, closely associated with the fall of Adam and Eve, affects the image of God (*imago dei*) in which humanity was created in three ways. First, the *moral image*, which constitutes righteousness and true holiness, was utterly destroyed by the fall. Humanity now had a contrary principle within. Atheism, pride, self-will, and love of the world comprised the very essence of this depravity. Second, the *natural image* of God, that is, the powers of understanding, liberty, and will, were greatly corrupted, though not destroyed. Third, the *political image*, humanity's place of authority within a created order, was disrupted by the fall though it too was not utterly effaced.

Though Wesley did not insist on the language that Adam was a "federal head," since such language is not found in scripture, he nevertheless referred on occasion to Adam as "the representative of all mankind," and thereby indicated that the guilt of original sin is communicated to all humanity, infants included: "We suffer death in consequence of their transgression. Therefore we are, in some sense, guilty of their sin." Moreover, in a way similar to Augustine, Wesley affirmed that "natural generation is the means of conveying the sinful nature (depravity) from our first parents to their posterity," though he clearly indicated that natural generation is not itself sinful.

Beyond this, Wesley's conception of **prevenient grace** helped him to avoid the deterministic implications of his largely Augustinian doctrine of original sin in several ways. First, the utter corruption of the moral image, noted above, is the state of humanity *apart from the grace of God*. But since there is no one who is lacking in prevenient grace, no one is so utterly corrupted. Second, appealing to the **atonement** of Jesus Christ, and highlighting the element of responsibility, Wesley denied that anyone is liable to eternal punishment due to Adam's sin alone. Third, though humanity is inclined and predisposed to evil, through the original corruption which remains, this inclination may be conquered through grace or one may choose to follow it and thereby commit actual sin.

Original sin, then, is the "foundation of the **new birth**," that which makes it necessary, and **salvation** is continued in the process of **sanctification** until the heart is cleansed from this root sin, a state of grace which Wesley called **Christian perfection**.

Viewing Adam as a "representative of humanity," Richard Watson, an early British Methodist theologian, attested that depravity is communicated universally and constitutes not a positive evil, but a depravation of the Spirit (*see* HOLY SPIRIT). Nevertheless, Watson, in a departure from Wesley's teaching, denied the transfer of original guilt to the rest of humanity due in no small measure to Watson's emphasis on human responsibility.

In America during the late 18th and early 19th centuries, both **Thomas Coke** and **Francis Asbury** instructed the itinerant preachers under their care to be ever mindful of the extent of original sin. Indeed, early American Methodism not only rejected the moralism of the Unitarians and Deists, with their overly optimistic anthropology, but, through the writings of **Nathan Bangs**, also took issue with Hopkinsianism, a teaching which maintained that "Adam conveyed neither sin, nor guilt, nor moral depravity to his descendants." Facing a different theological direction, Bangs repudiated the term Arminian (*see* ARMINIUS, JACOBUS), for he believed that the revivalistic culture of 19th-century America had placed too much emphasis on human ability, **free will** in particular, and not enough on the grace of God.

Toward the middle of the century, Daniel Whedon, responding to the work of the British theologian **William Burt Pope**, maintained that the guilt of Adam is not imputed until "man makes the depravity of his nature the object of his own choice." Thus, in a way similar to the emphasis of **Wilbur Fisk** before him, Whedon, on the one hand, denied hereditary guilt, but, on the other hand, he affirmed a "hereditary nature personally made guilty." For his part, and in a way very similar to Wesley, Pope underscored both hereditary depravity *and* hereditary guilt.

In 1892, in his treatise "The Arminian Treatment of Original Sin," which was appended to his *Systematic Theology,* **John Miley**, like some of the American Methodist theologians before him, inextricably linked guilt with free personal agency and thereby denied the intrinsic guilt of inherited depravity. Moreover, in a way reminiscent of the work of British theologian Richard Watson, Miley considered inherited depravity not as a positive evil but as "the withdrawal of God's Spirit." Beyond this, Miley postulated that it was by natural generation that this depravity was communicated to all humanity.

With the dominance of evangelical liberalism (*see* MODERNISM/LIBERALISM) in American Methodism during the early 20th century, both doctrines of inherited guilt *and* inherited depravity were quietly put aside in the wake of a higher critical reading of the Genesis narratives and the more optimistic view of humanity which was typical of the era. For example, Albert Knudson, professor at Boston University, maintained that it was the free activity of the will that gave rise to sin and on this basis denied both inherited guilt and inherited depravity. In fact, in emphasizing the "metaphysical freedom" of the individual, Knudson went so far as to deny the doctrine of original sin itself as an "extrabiblical" construction.

Despite these trends, the latter part of the 20th century witnessed a renewed interest in the doctrine of original sin due in no small measure to the horrific violence of the century and to the influence of the Christian realism of the American theologian Reinhold Niebuhr. Indeed, the American Methodist theologian Colin Williams took pains to restate the essence of Wesley's teaching on original sin in a way which would speak to the modern age in terms of its new biblical understanding and also in terms of its broader ecumenical context (*see* ECUMENISM). *See also* DOCTRINAL STANDARDS.

Kenneth J. Collins

ORWIG, WILLIAM W. (September 25, 1810–May 29, 1889), **EA** bishop, editor, and historian, was born in Orwigsburg, Pennsylvania. In 1828 Orwig became a minister with the EA and began his career as an itinerant preacher in eastern Pennsylvania. He was elected **presiding elder** in 1833. In 1836 Orwig began a seven-year tenure as editor of *Der Christliche Botschafter*, the denomination's German newspaper. Orwig again served in this capacity from 1849 to 1854 and from 1863 to 1867. Due to the growth of the church, the **General Conference** of 1859 increased the number of bishops to three. Orwig was elected to fill the new position. As bishop, Orwig advocated the position that only the entirely sanctified were saved and would go to heaven. This aroused intense opposition from various quarters of the church, which resulted in his defeat for reelection in 1863. Orwig was one of the denomination's first historians with his history of the EA in 1858. For two years he served as president of Union Seminary in New Berlin, Pennsylvania. He also wrote a catechism for the church, edited several hymnals, and in later years wrote several books on theology.

Daryl M. Elliott

OSBORN, GEORGE (March 29, 1808–April 18, 1891), Wesleyan minister who served as a secretary of the Wesleyan Methodist Missionary

Society (1851–1868) and as theological tutor at Richmond College (1868–1885). An able scholar, he wrote a preface to **John Wesley**'s *Collection of Psalms and Hymns*, edited the *Poetical Works of John and Charles Wesley* in 13 volumes (1868–1872), and compiled a *Wesleyan Bibliography* (1869). He gave the first Fernley Lecture in 1870 on *The Holy Spirit, His Work and Mission*. Twice president of the Conference (1863 and 1881), he was a powerful conference speaker. Steeped in and jealous of the traditions of Wesleyanism, his ministry was in the mold of **Jabez Bunting**, conservative and authoritarian. He had an acute legal mind and took a leading role in cases involving Methodism. He espoused the cause of popular **education** and supported Wesleyan day schools. He was a founder of the Evangelical Alliance (1845). *See also* BRITISH METHODISM.

William D. Horton

OTTERBEIN, PHILIP WILLIAM (June 3, 1726–November 17, 1813), German Reformed pastor and co-bishop with **Martin Boehm** at the founding of the **UB**, was born into the family of a Reformed minister and teacher at Dillenberg, Nassau, Germany. Educated at the Herborn Academy, the intellectual and pietistic center of the German Reformed Church, William absorbed the moderate Calvinism of the Heidelberg Confession and its heartwarming spiritual devotion. Ordained June 13, 1749, he briefly ministered and taught in Germany, but in 1752 he responded to an appeal for missionaries to German settlers in Pennsylvania.

For 22 years Otterbein served as pastor in Lancaster, Tulpehocken, and York, Pennsylvania, and Frederick, Maryland. In 1762, he married Susan LeRoy, who died six years later. He never remarried or had descendants. While at Lancaster (1752–1758) a personal religious experience kindled an evangelical zeal to share his faith with others. In his congregations he sought to promote vital and personal religion and experimented with small group devotions. In addition, he preached in rural areas and shared in evangelistic gatherings. At a large meeting in Isaac Long's barn (ca. 1767) Otterbein was so impressed by the preaching on personal **salvation** by Mennonite bishop Martin Boehm that afterward he embraced the speaker and exclaimed "*Wir sind brüder* (We are brothers)." This occasion initiated a fellowship of evangelical preachers from Mennonite, Reformed, Amish,

Moravian (*see* MORAVIANS), and Lutheran traditions that eventually led to the formation of the UB.

In 1774 Otterbein accepted a call to an independent German Reformed congregation in Baltimore, Maryland, where he was pastor until his death. One person who urged him to take the pastorate was Methodist **Francis Asbury**, who became a longtime friend. At the founding **conference** of American Methodism, Otterbein was one of the **elder**s who shared in Asbury's ordination (December 27, 1784). The independence of the Baltimore congregation enabled Otterbein to continue clergy relations with the German Reformed Church, although he and Boehm were elected bishops of the newly organized UB movement (September 25, 1800). He was active in both until he suffered serious illness in 1805 and confined activities to Baltimore thereafter. Religious leaders continued to seek his counsel, but **Christian Newcomer** assumed leadership as the nascent UB took shape.

Following Boehm's death in 1812, UB clergy in Pennsylvania elected Newcomer as bishop for one year (May 6, 1813), although technically he was not yet ordained, which disturbed fellow preachers in Ohio. They wrote to Father Otterbein asking him to ordain one or more preachers by the laying on of hands so they could perform the same for others. Six weeks before his death, Otterbein, assisted by Methodist Elder William Ryland, ordained Newcomer, Joseph Hoffman, and Frederick Shaffer (October 2, 1813), thus regularizing the reception and **ordination** of preachers in the new denomination.

At Otterbein's funeral service Lutheran, Methodist, and Episcopalian clergy officiated, and at a memorial service four months later Bishop Asbury paid tribute to his esteemed friend. He is buried in the courtyard of his Baltimore church, which still stands.

Donald K. Gorrell

OUTLER, ALBERT COOK (November 17, 1908–September 1, 1989), professor, theologian, ecumenist, was born in Thomasville, Georgia. He graduated A.B. from Wofford College (1928), B.D. from Emory University (1933), and Ph.D. from Yale University (1938). He married Carlotta Grace Smith on December 18, 1931. He was on the faculty of the schools of theology at Duke University (1938–1945), Yale University (1945–1951), and Southern Methodist University (1951–1979). Several institutions, including the University of Notre

Dame, recognized him with an honorary degree. Professor Outler, intentionally a Methodist theologian while actively an ecumenist (*see* ECUMENISM), became the leading Methodist statesman of his day. He was a member of every **General Conference** from 1960 to 1984, and from 1968 to 1972 chaired the new **UMC**'s Doctrinal Study Committee, whose report set the framework and tone for subsequent theological discussions in the denomination. His academic fields included systematic theology, patristic studies, pastoral care, church history, and Wesley studies. His early work in historical theology focused on Augustine, his later work on the sermons of **John Wesley**. In addition, he was active in the administrative work of the university, from designing curricular programs to establishing long-range master plans. Outler's scholarly work was used not only in his service to the university and the denomination but also in his ecumenical endeavors, which included leadership in the Faith and Order Commission of the **WCC** (1953–1963). He was a Methodist delegate-observer to the Second Vatican Council (1962–1965) and subsequently participated in many bilateral dialogues. He was especially interested in encouraging ministry that emphasized the pastoral office.

Richard P. Heitzenrater

OXNAM, G. (GARFIELD) BROMLEY (August 14, 1891–March 12, 1963) **MEC** bishop, author, and ecumenical leader (*see* ECUMENISM), graduated from the University of Southern California (A.B. 1913) and Boston University (S.T.B. 1915). He married Ruth Fisher in 1914 and had three children. He served the Church of All Nations in Los Angeles (1917–1926) and became identified with the labor movement, taught at Boston University School of Theology (1927), and was president of DePauw University, Indiana (1928). Elected bishop in 1936, he served the Omaha, Boston, New York, and Washington episcopal areas (*see* EPISCOPACY). He wrote more than 20 books. As secretary of the Council of Bishops (1939–1956) he inspired an **MEC** Crusade for World Order and launched the custom of episcopal visits to other continents. Oxnam chaired the General Board of Education (1939–1944) and the Division of Foreign Missions of the General Board of Missions (1944–1952). He engineered the relocation and transformation of Westminster Seminary in Maryland to Washington, D.C., as Wesley Seminary. Oxnam presided at the Federal Council of Churches (1944–1946) and the formation of the **NCC** in 1950. He served as president of the **WCC** from 1948 to 1954 and later belonged to its Central Committee. Called to testify before the House Un-American Activities Committee, his testimony helped end an era in USA history of anticommunist defamation of character.

Alice G. Knotts

– P –

PAKISTAN. *See* ASIA.

PALMER, PHOEBE WORRALL (December 18, 1807–November 2, 1874), Methodist layperson, revivalist, feminist (*see* FEMINISM), humanitarian, and editor, was born in New York City. Palmer became the most significant catalyst in the movement to promote Christian holiness or the "higher Christian life" in the 19th century (*see* HOLINESS MOVEMENT). She eventually took over the leadership of the Tuesday Meetings for the Promotion of Holiness, where for some 35 years representatives from nearly all major Protestant denominations in America came to receive the experience of entire **sanctification**. Following **John Fletcher**, Hester Rogers, and William Carvosso, Palmer developed her own version of the Wesleyan doctrine of entire sanctification, known as "altar theology." Palmer's "shorter way" to sanctification was promoted through her 10 books and the widely circulated *Guide to Holiness*, a journal that she edited from 1864 to 1874. In addition, Palmer spread her message as a featured speaker at more than 300 **camp meetings** and **revival** campaigns across the USA, **Canada**, and the British Isles. Believing that perfect love issued in service to humanity, Palmer was active in social reform, the most notable of these efforts being the mission built in New York's **Five Points** district in 1850. While the merits of her altar theology were questioned, Palmer's influence on Methodist clergy and laity was profound and lasting. *See also* PALMER, SARAH WORRALL LANKFORD.

Dale H. Simmons

PALMER, SARAH WORRALL LANKFORD (April 23, 1806–1896) was a Methodist layperson and sister of **Phoebe Palmer**. A vigorous proponent of the doctrine of entire **sanctification**, Sarah established the Tuesday Meetings for the Promotion of Holiness in her home in 1836 (*see* HOLINESS MOVEMENT). Here leaders from various denominations, as well as about 200 laypeople, came together for Bible reading, **prayer**, and personal **testimony**. These meetings became the prototype for 238 similar meetings held around the world. For years Sarah earnestly sought entire sanctification but was unable to *feel* the operations of divine **grace**. Then, in 1835, she read in *The Life of Hester Ann Rogers*, "Reckon yourself dead, indeed, unto sin and thou art akin to God from this hour. 0, begin, begin, to reckon now: fear not, believe, believe, and continue to believe." Sarah now had a "breakthrough" and forever jettisoned the troublesome Wesleyan belief that one must have a palpable "inward impression on the soul," or "**witness of the Spirit.**" Henceforth, the ground for her assurance was *belief* in the naked scriptural promise *independent* of any supporting "sensible evidence." This "discovery" became the foundation upon which her sister, Phoebe, built her distinctive "altar theology." Two years after Phoebe's death, Sarah married her brother-in-law, Walter Palmer, and assumed her sister's place as editor of the *Guide to Holiness*.

Dale H. Simmons

PAPUA NEW GUINEA. *See* TONGA, FIJI, AND SAMOA.

PARAGUAY. *See* LATIN AMERICA AND THE CARIBBEAN.

PAYNE, DANIEL ALEXANDER (February 24, 1811–November 2, 1893), **AME** bishop and first president of Ohio's Wilberforce University, was born in Charleston, South Carolina. He settled in New York City in 1835, then attended Gettysburg Theological Seminary in Pennsylvania until 1837. Although he had intended to pursue pedagogy, Payne, already a Methodist, became a preacher, eventually joining the AME in Philadelphia. After his AME ordination in 1843, he rose quickly in the denomination. Pastorates in Washington, D.C., and Baltimore preceded his election in 1848 as the first AME historiographer. In 1852, he was elected to the **episcopacy**. His tireless crusade for an educated AME ministry motivated his purchase of Wilberforce University in 1863 from the MEC. As an AME bishop he presided in New England, the Middle Atlantic states, the Midwest, and **Canada**. After the start of the Civil War, Payne brought a clerical contingent to Charleston to spread the denomination to South Carolina, North Carolina, Georgia, Alabama, and Florida. He attended the First Ecumenical Conference on Methodism in London (1881) and the World's Parliament of Religions in Chicago (1893). He wrote several books, including an autobiography, *Recollections of Seventy Years*, and *History of the AME*. Payne married his first wife, Julia A. Ferris, in 1847. She died in childbirth. In 1854, he married Eliza J. Clark and became a parent to her three children.

Dennis C. Dickerson

PEACE. *See* WAR AND PEACE.

PEAKE, ARTHUR SAMUEL (November 24, 1865–August 19, 1929), the son and nephew of English **Primitive Methodist** ministers, was born in Leek, England, and went to St. John's College, Oxford, in 1883. In 1890, he accepted a lectureship at Mansfield College, Oxford, and was elected to a Theological Fellowship at Merton College. In 1892, William Hartley recruited him to the staff of Hartley College, Manchester, where he remained for the rest of his life. In 1904, he was appointed professor of biblical exegesis at the University and dean of the faculty of theology, and in 1925, became pro-vice-chancellor. He was elected president of the Society for Old Testament Study in 1924 and edited the society's first volume of essays, *The People and the Book* (1925). He received honorary degrees from Manchester (1906), Aberdeen (1907), and Oxford (1920) universities. Best known for the one-volume *Commentary,* which he edited (1919), his most important biblical studies are *The Problem of Suffering in the Old Testament* (1904), *A Critical Introduction to the New Testament* (1909), *The Bible: Its Origin, Its Significance and Its Abiding Worth* (1913), and commentaries on Hebrews (1902), Colossians (1903), Job (1905), Jeremiah and Lamentations (1910, 1912), and Revelation (1919). Peake remained a layman, but he played a vital part in enabling Primitive Methodist ministers and others to accept critical biblical scholarship without losing their faith. He was also prominent in the endeavor for church unity, being one of the Primitive Methodist representatives on the Methodist Union Committee from 1918, one of six representatives of the Free Churches at meetings with the Anglicans at Lambeth Palace from 1922 to 1925, and attending the Lausanne meeting of Faith and Order in 1927. *See also* BRITISH METHODISM.

Cyril S. Rodd

PENTECOSTALISM is the name given to a group of churches that trace their origins to the **holiness movement** that developed among the Methodists in the 19th century, although other influences also contributed to its rise. The name is taken from the biblical event known as the Day of Pentecost described in Acts 2. Pentecostalism emphasizes the presence and work of the **Holy Spirit** in the lives of individuals and congregations as well as the gifts which accompany the Spirit's presence, especially *glossolalia* (speaking in tongues) and the other *charismata* (gifts of the Spirit) mentioned in Romans 12 and I Corinthians 12. Among the better-known pentecostal churches are the Assemblies of God, Church of God in Christ, and Church of God (Cleveland, Tennessee).

Charles Yrigoyen, Jr.

PERFECTION, CHRISTIAN. *See* CHRISTIAN PERFECTION.

PERRONET, VINCENT (baptized December 12, 1693–May 7/8, 1785), son of a Swiss father from Château d'Oex who came to England ca.1680. A scholarly child, he was educated at a school in the north of England and at Queen's College, Oxford. He was curate of Sundridge and, from 1728, vicar of Shoreham (Kent), where he encountered opposition for much of his incumbency. In 1746 he invited **John Wesley** and **Charles Wesley** into his parish. Charles Wesley on his first visit, described the riotous reaction as that of "wild beasts." Resistance to the Methodists continued, but grew less extreme. Both brothers relied heavily on Perronet's advice and support. He attended the 1747 **Conference** and John Wesley addressed his *Plain Account of the People Called Methodists* to him. He became known as the

"Archbishop of the Methodists" and on at least one occasion mediated between the brothers. Only after the death of his wife Charity (*née* Goodhew) in 1763 was a Methodist society in Shoreham formally established (*see* SOCIETIES, CLASSES, AND BANDS). Previously, meetings had been held in the vicarage. Known both for great holiness of life and for his scholarship, he published pamphlets defending John Locke's *Essay on the Human Understanding*. His sons Edward (1721–1792) and Charles (1723–1776) were both Methodist preachers for a time. Edward, remembered as the author of the hymn "All hail the power of Jesu's name," published a poem *The Mitre* (1757) critical of the Church of England and became pastor of the **Countess of Huntingdon**'s chapel and then of an Independent congregation in Canterbury. Charles helped to form a Methodist society in Dublin. They were estranged from the Wesleys through their advocacy of separation from the Established Church.

Peter S. Forsaith

PHILIPPINES. *See* ASIA.

PIETISM was a reform movement in European Lutheran and Calvinist churches in the last quarter of the 17th and the first half of the 18th centuries. Reflecting the "heart religion" traversing Europe (such as English **Puritanism**, French **Roman Catholic** Jansenism, and the Hasidic movement in eastern European Judaism), Pietism reacted against a Protestantism perceived as excessively creedal and formal, and lacking in concern for its adherents' personal **faith** and life. Pietism stressed church reform (partially through lay conventicles), devotional reading of the scriptures, the **new birth**, a **sanctification** ethic, and an optimism based on eschatological hope (*see* ESCHATOLOGY). Classical Pietism advocated little theological change and remained within the church. While Johann Arndt (1555–1621) is frequently called the father of Lutheran Pietism, Philipp Jakob Spener (1635–1705) led the movement through the publication in 1675 of his *Pia Desideria*, and other activities. August Hermann Francke (1663–1727) energetically directed the social, educational, and missional reform movements that emanated from the institutions connected with Halle University. Leading Calvinist Pietists were Gisbert Voet (1588–1676) of the Netherlands,

Theodore Untereyck (1635–1693) in the lower Rhineland, and Jean de Labadie (1610–1674).

K. James Stein

PILMORE, JOSEPH (October 31, 1739–July 24, 1825), first of Wesley's missionaries to America, was born in Tadmouth, Yorkshire, England, of Anglican parents. As a young Wesley convert, he attended Kingswood School. He was a traveling preacher from 1765 in East Cornwall and Wales. He and **Richard Boardman** volunteered for America and, in October 1769, were warmly welcomed to Philadelphia. There Saint George's Church was soon acquired, but missionary outreach lagged until **Francis Asbury** arrived in 1771. Pilmore organized societies in Baltimore in June 1772 and began Methodism in Norfolk en route to Charleston, South Carolina, and **George Whitefield**'s orphan house at Savannah, Georgia. Left without appointment when **Thomas Rankin** arrived in 1773, he sailed home. Refused ordination by the bishop of London, Pilmore resumed his Methodist ministry in 1776 in England and Scotland and as assistant in Dublin. Omitted from the **conference** "Legal Hundred" by Wesley, Pilmore withdrew. Ordained an Episcopal priest in Connecticut in 1785, he served in founding Episcopal conventions and preached faithfully until 1821, even during epidemics, lastly at Saint Paul's, Philadelphia. Always of evangelical spirit, Pilmore began a large **Sunday school**, held prayer meetings, and left a legacy to Moravian missions (*see* MORAVIANS). Pilmore's wife, Mary Benezet Wood, and daughter preceded him in death.

Edwin Schell

POLAND. *See* EUROPE.

POPE, WILLIAM BURT (February 19, 1822–July 5, 1903) was the outstanding English Wesleyan theologian of the 19th century, whose three-volume *Compendium of Christian Theology* (1880) remained a standard text for over a generation. In his own view, however, the shorter *Higher Catechism of Theology* (1883) was a more balanced and felicitous statement of his position. He taught at Didsbury College (1867–1886), was president of the **Conference** in 1877, and served as chairman of the Manchester District (1877–1885). He gave the Fernley Lecture in 1871 on *The Person of Christ*. Stressing the Methodist contribution to theology, he wrote an important essay (1873) on its particular ethos and contributed a classic chapter to the *Wesley Memorial Volume* (1881). In his own theological work, however, he drew widely from patristic, Reformed, and Eastern traditions. He laid particular emphasis on the inner Trinitarian dynamics of **salvation**, on the eternal sonship, and on what he called "the great obedience" of the incarnate Son. He stressed the inner **witness of the Spirit** and the doctrine of perfect love (*see* CHRISTIAN PERFECTION). A meticulous textual scholar, he was, like many of his generation in the Wesleyan ministry, suspicious of the "higher criticism" of the **Bible** and of the notion of evolution. His work thus marks the end of an era, though his encouragement of **J. S. Lidgett** undoubtedly contributed to new and important developments in Methodist theology. *See also* BRITISH METHODISM.

David J. Carter

PORTUGAL. *See* EUROPE.

POTTER, PHILIP A. (b. 1921), a leading figure and renowned preacher in the world ecumenical movement. Born on the island of Dominica, he trained for the Methodist ministry at Caenwood, Jamaica, and Richmond College, England. As secretary of the British Student Christian Movement he led the youth delegation to the first Assembly of the **WCC** in 1948. After service in Haiti he was appointed to the WCC's Youth Department in 1954. In 1960 he was elected president of the World Student Christian Federation and became the first overseas minister to be a secretary of the Methodist Missionary Society. He was appointed director of World Mission and Evangelism in the World Council of Churches in 1967 and was elected its general secretary, 1972–1984. *See also* ECUMENISM.

Pauline M. Webb

PRAYER. It can be said that Methodism was born of prayer, for some scholars claim the small group prayer meeting which **John Wesley** led on Thursday evenings at Oxford, called the Holy Club, was the beginning of the Methodist movement. It is interesting that the first book Wesley ever published was *A Collection of Forms of Prayers for Every Day of the Week*, issued in 1733. He continued to publish those prayers as late as 1772 because he still firmly believed in the value of devotional order and method in the Christian life. In some ways John Wesley still belonged to the Holy Club. One of his most famous prayers has been included in the 1989 UMC hymnal as "A Covenant Prayer in the Wesleyan Tradition," which reads:

> I am no longer my own, but thine.
> Put me to what thou wilt, rank me with whom thou wilt.
> Put me to doing, put me to suffering.
> Let me be employed by thee or laid aside for thee,
> exalted for thee or brought low by thee.
> Let me be full, let me be empty.
> Let me have all things, let me have nothing.
> Freely and heartily I yield all things
> to thy pleasure and disposal.
> And now, O glorious and blessed God,
> Father, Son, and Holy Spirit,
> thou art mine, and I am thine. So be it.
> And the covenant which I have made on earth,
> let it be ratified in heaven. Amen.

Taking its cue from the Holy Club, Methodism, especially in America, pioneered a prayer ministry of midweek services that became a vital part of church life. In these meetings, young Christians learned to exercise spiritual gifts, and other denominations quickly adopted this informal **worship** service. By the end of the 19th century it became a standard feature of evangelical churches. Prayer services in the **camp meetings** of that era were sometimes spiritually explosive. **John Inskip** called the congregation to prayer during an evening service of the 1869 National Camp Meeting in Manheim, Pennsylvania. The presence of God seemed so awesome that moans and shouts simultaneously burst from the people, causing one eyewitness to exclaim, "The people were face to face with God."

Methodism of that era developed another prayer ministry called Praying Bands, an informal organization of laity that promoted **revivals** in the local churches. The Troy Praying Band in New York, founded in 1858 by Joseph Hillman, claimed to hold more than 200 revivals in a 20-year span. During these meetings more than 20,000 persons were converted, reclaimed, or received the experience of entire **sanctification**, and this ministry contributed to the founding of the Round Lake Camp Meeting Association in 1867.

By the mid-20th century, as society changed, so did these emphases on prayer, and many churches discontinued the midweek service. The ministry of prayer in many local churches now seems to center in private devotion, small groups, and in personal, pastoral, and corporate prayer as vital acts of public worship.

Kenneth O. Brown

PREACHING. Radical preaching, that is, preaching the gospel to the common people in an uncommon way, helped produce Methodism. **John Wesley** witnessed such preaching when **George Whitefield** spoke in the open air on April 1, 1739. Although shocked, the next day Wesley "submitted to be more vile," and preached in the open air himself. This event dramatically changed his ministry, and outdoor preaching became the scandal that made him famous. Methodism in America traces its history to the preaching of **Robert Strawbridge** and others. From their work came the **circuit** riders, canvassing the frontier, preaching in homes, log meeting houses, outdoor stands, and **camp meetings**, helping the church achieve phenomenal growth. Preaching not only helped produce Methodism, it enabled the church to reach out to the needs of society, including minorities. When the American **holiness movement** arose, its preachers included blacks and unordained **women**, as well as the premier preacher of the day, **Matthew Simpson**. They supported prominent reforms, and such preaching helped bring a new social conscience to Methodism, one that combined dynamic spiritual transformation with the **social gospel**. This dual emphasis continues to empower the preaching of the church, much as it did in the days of John Wesley. *See also* FIELD PREACHING.

Kenneth O. Brown

PRESIDING ELDERS. The office of presiding elder, now called district **superintendent** in the UMC, was developed in the **MEC** as an extension of the superintending function of bishops (*see* EPISCO-

PACY). The role of presiding elder was to assist the bishop in the supervision of the pastors in the area in which the presiding elder was stationed. The office was clearly defined for the first time at the MEC 1792 **General Conference**, although the title did not appear regularly in the MEC Minutes until 1797. In the earlier years of the MEC there was considerable debate about whether the presiding elder should be appointed by the bishop or elected by clergy colleagues in the annual **conference**. The MEC and **MECS** followed the episcopal appointment of their presiding elders/district superintendents. The **EUB** favored their election. In the UMC district superintendents are appointed by the bishop and serve as key leaders in the connection between local churches and the annual conferences to which they belong. *See also* ELDER; SUPERINTENDENT.

Charles Yrigoyen, Jr.

PREVENIENT GRACE. One of the distinctive theological emphases of Wesleyan theology, the term literally means, "the **grace** that comes before," the grace that leads one to the fullest expression of God's saving and pardoning love. **John** and **Charles Wesley** did not employ the term "prevenient grace." They used the term "preventing grace" which for them did not mean that which hinders relationship with God, but divine grace that facilitates a response to God's offer of forgiveness and new life. John Wesley spoke of preventing grace in several places in his writings, including his sermon, "Free Grace," where he described it as grace which is "free in all and free for all," universally present in everyone. Prevenient grace illuminates the destructive nature of sin, discloses the way of **salvation**, frees the human will to accept or reject God's offer of reconciliation, and leads us to **repentance**. The Wesleyan understanding of freedom of the human will, made possible by prevenient grace, is a concept which differentiates the Wesleyan tradition from Lutheran and Reformed theological viewpoints, which hold that the human will is not free because of sin.

Charles Yrigoyen, Jr.

PRIMITIVE METHODISTS (BRITISH). One of several British Methodist secessionist movements in the generation following the

Wesleys, Primitive Methodism attempted to restore the tradition's original fervor and had particular success among the rural working classes before reuniting as part of the Methodist Church in 1932. Initial inspiration came from the eccentric American evangelist **Lorenzo Dow,** who advocated **camp meetings** while on a preaching tour of England. In 1807, two of his hearers, **Hugh Bourne** and **William Clowes,** organized a series of such meetings, the most famous of which took place on Mow Cop, a rugged hill on the Cheshire–Staffordshire border. Methodist authorities, threatened by the unauthorized and effervescent, expelled both. Small groups of like-minded people coalesced around each, and, in 1811, Bourne's "Camp Meeting Methodists" and the "Clowesites" united as Primitive Methodists with 34 preaching places and 23 preachers. The first Primitive Methodist Conference was held in Hull in 1820. Over time, "connexional" organization developed, and the movement expanded throughout England and Wales. The strength of Primitive Methodism lay chiefly in northern England—Yorkshire and Durham—but it also flourished in the agricultural areas of East Anglia and in southern England, chiefly among the lower classes, and as time passed with a sprinkling of successful manufacturers and businessmen. In 1829, the denomination was given legal status and an American mission was authorized, followed by various colonial missions.

A book room was established at Bemersley in 1820 that eventually moved to Holborn Hall, London. A connexional magazine and other monthly publications became part of its output. There were a series of hymnbooks, the Hartley Lecture, a weekly newspaper, and books by prominent writers in the connexion. A theological institute opened in Sunderland in 1868, to be succeeded by Hartley College in 1881. Elmfield College, York, and Bourne College, Quinton, Birmingham, were educational establishments. Orphanages were opened at Harrogate and Alresford.

To the 1932 union of **British Methodism** the Primitives contributed over 222,000 members, 1,100 ministers, 13,000 local preachers, and a key figure in the protracted negotiations, the biblical scholar **Arthur S. Peake.** Socially, Primitives were quite active in trade unionism, and a recent study has documented the importance of female preachers in the denomination's early successes.

Charles Wallace, Jr. and William Leary

PRIMITIVE METHODISTS (USA) arose from the efforts of **Hugh Bourne** and **William Clowes**, two British Methodist ministers who had been influenced by **Lorenzo Dow**. Dow, originally from Connecticut and known as "Mad Lorenzo," went with his wife to England to introduce frontier style **camp meetings**, which failed to appeal to Wesleyan Methodists, with the exception of Bourne and Clowes. Expelled from the mainline connection, they formed the Primitive Methodist Church in 1811. In 1829 four of their missionaries went to the USA: William Summersides, Thomas Morris, Ruth Watkins, and Thomas Knowles. The four confined their activities to Connecticut, New Jersey, New York, and Pennsylvania. By 1840, the group had determined to separate from the British church and to focus its activities in the coalfields of western Pennsylvania. Two years later, a Primitive Methodist church was organized at Galena, Illinois, and a Midwest **Conference** was formed. In 1889, East and Midwest united into a **General Conference**, and, by 1894, six distinct districts had emerged: Eastern, Wyoming, Schuylkill, Pittsburgh, Western, and Florida. One should not confuse the present Primitive Methodists with another short-lived group of the same name. In 1792, at Charleston, South Carolina, William Hammett formed a Primitive Methodist Church as a protest against Bishop **Francis Asbury** and the centralized authority of the **MEC**.

Samuel J. Rogal

PRIMITIVE WESLEYAN METHODISTS (IRELAND). Early Irish Methodists had more support from landed and entrepreneurial classes than the English, which prolonged their link with the Established Church. It was not until 1814 that the Irish **Conference** was strongly urged to allow the administration of the **sacraments**. After two years of considerable agitation, the Conference gave conditional approval in 1816. Opponents convened a conference at Clones in October and stationed 19 local preachers as itinerants. In January 1818, a committee formulated their constitution, which was adopted in July, with the name Primitive Wesleyan Methodist Society. They took approximately one-third of the Wesleyan membership. Primitive Wesleyan Methodists continued to receive the sacraments in the Church of Ireland. A. Averell was elected president for life. In time the society's ministers adopted clerical style and dress. From the

1850s, they suffered a steady decline in numbers. The Disestablishment of the Irish Church in 1870 raised the question of the Primitive Wesleyan Methodist future. Several of its preachers were ordained to fill vacant Church of Ireland parishes, leaving Methodist interests to prevail. The Wesleyan and Primitive Wesleyan Conferences reunited in 1878 as the Methodist Church in Ireland.

The connexion was effectively confined to **Ireland**. A number of Primitive Wesleyan emigrants from Lisbellaw in Ulster settled on Lake Huron, **Canada**, where they built a chapel and worshipped for some years without reference to the parent body. Only in 1862 did they inform the Primitive Wesleyan Conference of their existence. A preacher was sent, but he returned after three years, perhaps because of failing health. The congregation then affiliated with the Methodist Episcopal Church.

Dudley A. L. Cooney

PUNSHON, WILLIAM MORLEY (May 29, 1824–April 14, 1881), Wesleyan minister, was born in Doncaster, England, to a Methodist family with trading connections in Hull and Sunderland, where he became a local preacher. His uncle, Benjamin Clough, encouraged him to enter the ministry and he trained at Richmond College. He was appointed to Hinde Street, London, in 1858 on the strength of his growing reputation as a preacher and public lecturer. His lectures on John Bunyan, William Wilberforce, and the Huguenots were highly popular and raised much money for the Watering Places Fund and the Metropolitan Chapel Building Fund. His wife's death and overwork ruined his health, which he tried to restore by a grand tour of Europe. He went to **Canada** as British representative to its **Conference** and served as its president (1868–1873). He was instrumental in the building of the prestigious Metropolitan Church, Toronto (1872), colloquially known as "Mr. Punshon's Church." Returning to Britain he was elected president in 1874 and was secretary of the Wesleyan Methodist Missionary Society from 1875 until his early death. Proceeds from his published lectures went to the Thanksgiving Fund and his *Sabbath Chimes* was a well-loved devotional on the Christian year. He was a founder and director of the *Methodist Recorder* and its first editor.

Timothy S. A. Macquiban

PURITANISM AND METHODISM. Central to 16th- and 17th-century English Puritanism, and undergirding its political, ethical, and religious impulses, was a passionate concern for personal experiential **faith**. Such faith when combined with fervent evangelicalism brought many modifications to English Christianity. **John Wesley**'s own family heritage ran deep in this Puritan community with four of his grandfathers being ejected from the Church of England in 1662. It was at Oxford and during his early Methodist ministry that he "rediscovered" Puritan teachings and writings. Puritan instruction in "practical divinity" prompted him to comment, "They lead us by the hand in the paths of righteousness, and shew us how we may most surely and swiftly grow in grace." In his *Christian Library*, abstracted from English authors to instruct Methodists in practical divinity, Puritan authors predominate and one-third of all his abridgements are from Puritan sources. To mention a few examples of his direct dependence on such sources: Wesley's sermon on conscience is that of his grandfather Samuel Annesley; Joseph Alleine's covenant service is incorporated in Methodism's **watch night** service; arguments by Richard Baxter and John Goodwin against **antinomianism** are consciously embraced by Wesley; and Baxter's instructions for pastoral visitation are appropriated into Wesley's *Minutes*. Other affinities and similarities are numerous. Puritan sources continued to be used by later Methodist leaders.

Robert C. Monk

– Q –

QUADRILATERAL. Although **John Wesley** never utilized this term, it is commonly used to denote the four sources from which he drew his understanding and practice of the Christian **faith**: scripture, tradition, reason, and **experience**. The four are not listed together in any place in his published works. However, each of them appears frequently in his writings and occasionally they appear in close proximity. **Albert C. Outler** is usually credited with identifying and describing these four as Wesley's basic sources. Scripture, tradition, and reason figured prominently in Anglican theological methodology in Wesley's day, while experience generally assumed a lesser role. For the Wesleys, tradition, reason, and experience were always subservient to scripture and were employed in the interpretation and application of scriptural truth.

Scripture includes the 66 books of the Old and New Testament in the **Bible**. Tradition encompasses such items as traditional creeds, for example the Apostles' Creed, and the historic writings of faithful men and women who have reflected on and practiced their Christian faith over the centuries. Reason, as God's gift, is required to do careful theological work and to relate faith to the secular world in which we live. Experience is the personal and corporate appropriation of God's **grace** enabling Christians to claim faith and witness as their own (*see* EXPERIENCE, CHRISTIAN). The **UMC** publishes a document titled "Our Theological Task" in its *Book of Discipline*, which urges its members to consider the quadrilateral in formulating their views on the faith and its relationship to life.

Charles Yrigoyen, Jr.

QUAKERS. The name commonly given to the Religious Society of Friends grew out of the ministry of George Fox in mid-17th-century England. The nickname Quaker was given to the group because of their early propensity to tremble when they were moved by the **Holy Spirit**. Fox believed that the "Inner Light," the immediate presence of Christ within a person's soul, constituted the ultimate religious authority. Personal obedience to the "Inner Light" was essential to true Christianity. Plain dress, refusal to take oaths, pacifism, and social activism, especially against **slavery**, all testified to their belief that pride was the chief obstacle to becoming a true Christian. Robert Barclay's *Apology for the True Christian Divinity* (1676) is the most extensive systematic exposition of Quaker beliefs. Nineteenth-century Quakerism was torn by numerous divisions (Hicksite, Guernyite, and Wilburite). Presently the movement numbers only a little more than 100,000 members in the USA. Approximately 40 percent of these constitute the Friends United Meeting, corresponding to mainline Protestantism; 25 percent are members of the Evangelical Friends Alliance, strongly influenced by and affiliated with the Methodist/**holiness movement**; 20 percent make up the Friends General Conference, known for its social activism. Scattered, mostly more conservative, meetings and groups make up the remainder.

Melvin E. Dieter

– R –

RALL, HARRIS FRANKLIN (February 23, 1870–October 13, 1964) was born in Council Bluffs, Iowa, to a parsonage family of the former **EA**. He received his B.A. degree from the University of Iowa, A.M. and B.D. degrees from Yale University, and the Ph.D. degree from Halle-Wittenberg University in Germany. Two daughters were born to his marriage in 1897 to Rose St. John. After her death in 1921, he married Maud St. John. Following pastoral service in Connecticut and Maryland, Rall was called in 1910 to become president of the Iliff School of Theology. In 1915, he became professor of systematic theology at Garrett Biblical Institute in Evanston, Illinois, retiring in 1945. Rall wrote or edited 23 books. Most important among these were: *A Faith for Today* (1936), *Christianity: An Inquiry Into Its Nature and Truth* (1940), *The Christian Faith and Way* (1947), and *Religion as Salvation* (1953). The influence of Albrecht Ritschl's practical kingdom of God theology upon him explains Rall's strong leadership in the Methodist Federation for Social Service. A devout man, Rall insisted that theology must emphasize God's saving purpose for persons revealed in Jesus Christ. Through his life, teaching, and publications he exerted a vast influence on American Methodism.

K. James Stein

RANKIN, LOCHIE (1851–September 13, 1929), **MECS** missionary to China, was born in Milan, Tennessee. In 1877 she volunteered for mission work in China and was commissioned by Bishop Holland N. McTyeire in April 1878 (*see* ASIA). She was the first unmarried female missionary sent under the sponsorship of the **women** of the MECS. Rankin arrived in China in 1878 and undertook her first assignment as an assistant at the Clopton Boarding School in Shanghai. She mastered the Chinese language sufficiently to open a new school in 1879 in Nanziang, a city about 15 miles from Shanghai. In that year she was joined by her sister Dora, who worked with her until Dora's death in 1885. Following her sister's death, Rankin opened another school in nearby Kading. When the Woman's Board of Foreign Missions of the MECS decided to close the Nanziang and Kading schools in 1909, Rankin assumed a new assignment to open a boys' school in Huchow. During her 49 years of missionary service in China, Rankin witnessed major changes in Chinese life, including the Boxer Rebellion in 1900 and the birth of the Chinese Republic in 1912. She was buried in Woodlawn Cemetery, Nashville.

Charles Yrigoyen, Jr.

RANKIN, THOMAS (1738–May 17, 1810), Scottish-born preacher and confidant of **John Wesley**, he convened the first **conference** of Methodist preachers in Philadelphia, July 1773. His pious upbringing, boyhood impressions in Dunbar, Scotland, of a ministerial calling, and association with religious soldiers culminated in a long-sought **conversion** experience. Meanwhile, denied college, Rankin traded in Charleston, South Carolina, then tutored himself in Methodist doctrine before joining Wesley in Sussex in 1761. As assistant for Cornwall and Newcastle, his **revivals** and fearlessness impressed Wesley, who often traveled with him. Sent to America in 1773 with **George Shadford**, Rankin rigidly disciplined preachers on **circuits** that were expanding despite the widening American Revolution. Rankin, a staunch loyalist, returned to England in 1778, leaving his antagonist, **Francis Asbury**, the de facto American leader supervising 15 appointments, 37 traveling preachers, and almost 7,000 members—an increase from 1,160 members and 10 preachers in 1773. Stationed in London, he married Sarah Bradshaw, a widow, in 1779. Named to Wesley's "Legal Hundred" conference corporation in 1784, he was ordained for England in 1789 and appointed to the Publishing Committee in Wesley's will. Rankin frequently dined with Wesley and was present at his death. He preached regularly in London until very old. *See also* BRITISH METHODISM.

Edwin Schell

RANSOM, REVERDY CASSIUS (January 4, 1861–April 22, 1959), **AME** bishop, was born in Flushing, Ohio. He was educated at Oberlin College and Wilberforce University from which he was graduated in 1886. He was pastor of several AME congregations in Pennsylvania, Ohio, Illinois, Massachusetts, and New York. At the Institutional Church and Social Settlement (Chicago) and at the Church of Simon of Cyrene (New York City) he pursued **social gospel** ministries. The **General Conference** of 1912 elected Ransom editor of the *AME*

Church Review. In 1924 the denomination elevated him to the **epis-copacy**. He presided at different times in Kentucky, Tennessee, Louisiana, South Carolina, Ohio, West Virginia, and western Pennsylvania until 1948. He wrote numerous works, including *Preface to the History of the AME Church* (1940) and an autobiography, *The Pilgrimage of Harriet Ransom's Son*. When the Republican Party in 1918 refused to nominate an African American for New York's 21st congressional district, Ransom launched an unsuccessful independent candidacy. In 1933 he called for representatives of black denominations to meet in Washington, D.C., to establish the Fraternal Council of Negro Churches. He served as president from 1934 through 1937. Ransom was married three times: first to Leanna Watkins, then to Emma S. Conner from 1886 until her death in 1941, and finally to Georgia Myrtle Teal, who survived him.

Dennis C. Dickerson

REPENTANCE. Fundamental to the Judeo-Christian tradition is the belief concerning repentance. In the Old Testament, two elements are basic: turning to God, and regretting sorrowfully a wrong done or a good omitted. The New Testament, while not neglecting Old Testament meanings, strongly emphasizes the turning from sin to God, forsaking the alienation which sin causes. Christian repentance turns on an acceptance of Christ as the source for righteous living. **John Wesley**'s view of repentance is heavily involved with his understanding of **justification** or pardon and the work of **sanctification**. In his explanatory *Notes* on Matthew 3:8 Wesley observed, "repentance is of two sorts: that which is termed legal and that which is styled evangelical repentance. The former is a thorough conviction of sin. The latter is a change of heart (and consequently of life) from all sin to all holiness." Hence, repentance in Wesley's view is of two kinds. There is repentance before justification and that consequent to it. The second is crucial for it requires us to confront the daily sin that remains in our hearts.

Robert Drew Simpson

REVIVALS AND REVIVALISM. Revivals are commonly understood to be special periods of religious renewal in which God, through the **Holy Spirit** and the agency of persons inspired and directed by the Holy Spirit, calls men and women to spiritual rebirth and Christian discipleship. Some who are committed to predestinarian theologies may reserve to God alone any agency in the rise of the phenomenon. Most contemporary revival movements, however, believe revivals are the result of a synergism of divine providence and the actions of men and women who seek to create a spiritual milieu conducive to the individual's response to God's word and Spirit. The latter understanding led to the rise of revivalism, or the commitment to utilize special public efforts in designated special periods for direct gospel appeal to the emotional and affectional as well as the intellectual and rational natures of the hearers. There is an expectation of an immediate and direct response to the appeal of the evangelist.

Although revivalism as a movement has surfaced throughout Christian history in both Catholic and Protestant traditions, it became especially dominant in the American religious and even national experience. Persistent revivalism in **camp meetings**, tent meetings, Bible conferences, and churches spurred the rapid growth of revivalistic traditions such as the Methodist and the Baptist throughout the 18th and 19th centuries. It still plays an important role in the expansion of these and many other traditions. In such churches, the term "revival" now designates the extended renewal services (once called protracted meetings) as frequently as it does the spiritual phenomenon itself.

Methodism has played as formative a role as any other entity in the development of revivalism. The 18th-century Wesleyan revival is commonly regarded as a primary feeder root, shaping and sustaining the expansive evangelical growth and revivalism of the 19th century. The rapidly expanding Methodist movement in the USA, in turn, played a very significant, if not dominant, role as its evangelical Arminian (*see* ARMINIUS, JACOBUS) revivalism drastically altered the revivalistic theology of much of Calvinism. **Francis Asbury,** father of American Methodism, and **Phoebe Palmer,** mother of the American **holiness movement**, are now recognized as pivotal figures in revival history.

The history of revivals and revivalism in America includes a series of awakenings paralleling national development, from the pre-revolutionary period to the revivals of the post–World War II period identified with the ministry of Billy Graham and the widespread charismatic renewal. Historian William McLoughlin contends that each of these periods of spiritual renewal formed an integral part of successive periods of dramatic cultural and political change by which the nation adapted its religious values and democratic institutions to constantly developing challenges.

The importance which revivalism attaches to a personal relationship with God established on crisis experiences of **grace** often leads its critics to charge that the movement tends to ignore the importance of Christian nurture and growth in grace. Revivalism's emphasis on personal **experience** and piety has also raised charges that its theology mutes concern for social activism. Historian Timothy L. Smith's work on revivalism and social reform indicates that such charges fail to take into account the movement's crucial role in the abolitionist, **temperance**, and women's rights movements of the 19th century (*see* FEMINISM).

Melvin E. Dieter

RICE, SAMUEL DWIGHT (September 11, 1815–December 15, 1884), minister and educator, was born in Houlton, Maine. In 1815, he moved with his family to Woodstock, New Brunswick, **Canada**. He studied at Bowdoin College, Massachusetts, then returned to New Brunswick and began a career in business. In 1834, he was converted, and this eventually led him to enter the Wesleyan ministry. He was received on trial in 1837, ordained four years later, and served pastorates in New Brunswick. In 1843, he married Fanny Lavinia Starr of Halifax, Nova Scotia. Rice moved to Upper Canada in 1847, where he worked both in the pastorate and in education. He spent one year at the Muncey Industrial School at Mount Elgin, and four at Victoria College, Cobourg. In 1861, he was active in the establishment of the Hamilton Wesleyan Female College, subsequently serving as its governor and as its principal. He was elected president of the **General Conference** of the Methodist Church of Canada in 1882, and, in September of 1883, he was chosen to be general superintendent of the Methodist Church, effective the following July when the four Methodist bodies in Canada were officially united under this name.

Samuel Rice died in Toronto after holding this office for only five months.

Marilyn Färdig Whiteley

RICHARDSON, HARRY VAN BUREN (June 27, 1901–December 13, 1990), **MC** theological educator devoted to improving race relations, was born and grew up in Jacksonville, Florida. He graduated from Western Reserve University (A.B. 1924), Harvard University (BSTh 1932), and Drew University (Ph.D. 1945 in sociology of religion) and was ordained. In 1927, he married Selma T. White. He served as chaplain of Tuskegee Institute from 1932 to 1948. As president of Gammon Theological Seminary (1948–1958), he turned the school from postwar disarray toward stability by cooperating with Morehouse School of Religion (Baptist), Turner Theological Seminary (**AME**), and Phillips School of Theology (**CME**), to develop the Interdenominational Theological Center (ITC), acclaimed in the 1960s as the world's foremost concentration of accredited theological education specializing in black religious studies. During his presidency of ITC, 1958–1968, three other schools joined the consortium. Richardson coordinated a program to train rural black pastors. He provided leadership for the **NCC**'s General Board (1950), the Southern Regional Council, Atlanta Urban League, Urban Renewal, Negro Division of Community Services, the United Negro College Fund, the Georgia Council of Churches, and the National Council of Christians and Jews. He was a member of the Council of Evangelism (**MEC**) and the Methodist Rural Life Fellowship (1959). Richardson published three books, including *Dark Salvation*.

Alice G. Knotts

RICHEY, MATTHEW (May 25, 1803–October 30, 1883), minister and educator, was born at Ramelton in northern **Ireland**. Although his parents were Presbyterians, he attended Methodist prayer meetings and was converted at the age of 14. In 1819, he immigrated to Saint John, New Brunswick, **Canada**. He became a Methodist probationer in 1821, and he was admitted to full connection in 1825. In the same year he married Louisa Matilda Nichols. Richey served on **circuits** in the Maritimes until 1835, when he was transferred to

Montreal. From 1836 to 1840, he held the position of principal of Upper Canada Academy in Cobourg. In 1840, following the dissolution of the union of the Canadian **conference** with the British Wesleyans, Richey and Joseph Stinson organized a new Canada Western District under supervision of the Wesleyan Methodist Missionary Society. When the British conference moved toward reconciliation, however, Richey worked for that reunion, which took place in 1847. He became president of the Canada Methodist Conference in 1849. Following an accident that year, Richey returned to Nova Scotia. After the new Conference of Eastern British North America was formed in 1855, he served as president (1856–1861 and 1867–1868). Retiring in 1870, he died 13 years later in Halifax.

Marilyn Färdig Whiteley

RIGG, JAMES HARRISON (January 16, 1821–April 17, 1909), a leading English Wesleyan educator, theologian, church leader, and ecclesiastical statesman, was principal of Westminster College from 1868 until his retirement in 1903. He vigorously defended Wesleyanism against both Anglican and Congregationalist detractors. Deeply loyal to the **Conference** during the 1849–1851 disruption, he nevertheless advocated reform and a greater participation of the laity in church government. He was president of the Conference in 1878 and 1892. He published a substantial volume, *Essays for the Times* (1866), and wrote major studies of European elementary **education** (1873) and of comparative ecclesiology, *Principles of Church Organization* (1887). He strongly defended the retention of Wesleyan elementary schools against those who wanted them placed under the new School Boards. In this and other matters he was increasingly seen as old-fashioned in the more liberal atmosphere at the turn of the 20th century.

David J. Carter

RIPLEY, DOROTHY (1769–December 23, 1831), was the daughter of William Ripley, Methodist preacher and stonemason, of Whitby, Yorkshire, England, companion of Wesley on his Yorkshire journeys. She determined to become an itinerant **revivalist** preacher, but the Wesleyans forbade such **women** preachers after 1803. Influenced by the **Quakers** and their concern for the welfare of black slaves, she went to the USA in 1801, returning to Britain in 1803. She subsequently crossed the Atlantic at least eight times. A correspondent of the Quaker Gurney family of York and Hurford family of Bristol, she received support from a variety of denominations. Her account of travels in 1805–1806 in *The Band of Faith* (1822) indicates an interest in work among prisoners in jails in New York and Baltimore, among the poor in the almshouse at Philadelphia, and among the Indians of Oneida County, New York. She preached before Congress in Washington, D.C., in 1805, before setting off for Georgia and South Carolina to preach the gospel of pity to slave owners. Describing herself as "a citizen of the world," she returned to England in 1818, accompanying the American evangelist **Lorenzo Dow**. She died in Virginia.

Tim Macquiban

ROBERTS, BENJAMIN TITUS (July 25, 1823–February 27, 1893), founder of the **Free Methodist Church**, was born in Gowanda, New York. Roberts graduated from Wesleyan University (1848) and entered the **MEC** ministry in the Genesee **Conference**. Appalled by the declining spirituality of the church, Roberts soon became involved in a reform movement to call Methodism back to its early virtues. Matters came to a head in 1857 when Roberts wrote a stinging newspaper article titled "New School Methodism." His clerical colleagues charged him with "insubordination and contumacy" and expelled him from the conference in 1858. Ironically, while the trial was in progress, the conference voted unanimously to have Roberts officiate at the funeral of William Kendall and to preside at the anniversary of the American Bible Society. An appeal to the **General Conference** of 1860 was refused. Rejected by his denomination, Roberts and several others formed the Free Methodist Church in 1860. Roberts stressed free pews, entire **sanctification**, abolitionism (*see* ANTISLAVERY), women's rights (*see* FEMINISM), rejection of secret societies, and **temperance**. In addition to serving as the denomination's first superintendent, Roberts edited the church's monthly magazine *The Earnest Christian* and founded Chili Seminary, now Roberts Wesleyan College. At the Genesee Conference centennial celebration in

1910, the delegates rescinded the decision of 1858 and posthumously restored Roberts's credentials.

Dale H. Simmons

ROBERTS, GRANVILLE ORAL (January 24, 1918–), evangelist, college president, and television minister, was born in Pontotoc County, Oklahoma. Roberts is the son of Ellis Roberts, a minister in the Pentecostal Holiness Church (*see* PENTECOSTALISM). In 1935, Roberts experienced **conversion** and was subsequently healed of tuberculosis. Over the next 12 years, Roberts built a successful career as an evangelist and pastor in the Pentecostal Holiness Church. In 1947 Roberts launched an independent healing ministry. A moderate in the divine healing movement, Roberts stressed that God healed through prayer and medicine. A pioneer in mass mailing, Roberts also mastered the use of radio and television to reach ever wider audiences. In 1965 he opened a university that has grown into a $250 million ultramodern campus with four graduate schools. Ecumenically oriented (*see* ECUMENISM), Roberts assisted in the formation of the Full Gospel Business Men's Fellowship in 1951, participated in Billy Graham's Berlin Congress on World Evangelism in 1966, and transferred his religious affiliation to the **UMC** in 1968. Recently, costly projects combined with increased competition led Roberts to resort to controversial fundraising techniques. Moreover, Roberts has increasingly associated himself with the radical leaders of the independent charismatic movement known as the "Faith Movement." Both developments have further alienated Roberts from the broad support base he enjoyed in the 1970s.

Dale H. Simmons

ROBERTS, HAROLD (September 20, 1896–October 4, 1982), Methodist statesman, was born at Ashley, Cheshire, England, and raised in Welsh Methodism in Manchester. He was educated at University College of North Wales, Bangor, and Wesley House, Cambridge. A friend of **Donald O. Soper, Leslie D. Weatherhead,** and **William E. Sangster,** all of whom consulted him, he was considered a better preacher than any of them, but a less effective writer. As minister at Wesley Memorial Church, Oxford (1929–1934), the

"LD" (Learned Doctor) had an immense influence on a mixed group of undergraduates and leading British Methodists, including Harold Loukes, A. Raymond George, and Rupert E. and Margaret Davies. He became tutor in theology, first at Headingley College (1934–1940), then at Richmond College (1940–1968), with a wartime interlude in the Ipswich **Circuit**), where he was principal from 1955. Through his report on *The Mission and Message of Methodism* (1946) he had much influence on the postwar church. As Methodist chairman of the Anglican-Methodist Conversations, he was responsible both for the scheme devised and for commending it to Methodism. He was president of the 1957 **Conference** and president of the **World Methodist Council** (1951–1956), helping to set up a new mechanism for linking World Methodism more closely and ensuring greater Third World participation. He was chairman of the governors of both Westminster and Southlands Colleges during the postwar period of growth and change. He encouraged **women** and the younger generation to speak in Conference. *See also* BRITISH METHODISM.

John H. Lenton

ROBINSON, JANE MARIE BANCROFT (December 24, 1847–May 29, 1932), leader in the **MEC deaconess movement**, was born in West Stockbridge, Massachusetts. Her education included degrees from New York Normal School in Albany and Syracuse University. She also studied in Switzerland and France. In 1888, the WHMS (MEC) chose her to supervise its deaconess work. She supervised the society's Deaconess Bureau from 1889 to 1904. Convinced that the society needed its own training school, she invested her considerable administrative skills in organizing it. The Lucy Webb Hayes Deaconess Home Training School in Washington, D.C. was dedicated on October 17, 1891, and named in honor of Lucy Webb Hayes, former first lady and first president of the WHMS. Jane Bancroft married George Orville Robinson on May 7, 1891. Supervision of the WHMS Deaconess Bureau passed to her half-sister, Henrietta Ash Bancroft, in 1904. Robinson went on to serve in a number of offices in the WHMS, as lay delegate to the MEC **General Conference** in 1908 and 1920, and as a delegate to Ecumenical Methodist Conferences in

Toronto (1911) and London (1921) (*see* WORLD METHODIST CONFERENCES). *See also* FEMINISM; WOMEN.

Mary Agnes Dougherty

RODEHEAVER, HOMER ALVAN (October 4, 1880–December 18, 1955), musical director and evangelist, was born at Union Furnace, Ohio. After studying music at Ohio Wesleyan University, he became director of sacred music at Bob Jones College (Tennessee). He established himself as a musical evangelist when, in 1909, he began a 22-year association with Billy Sunday. Rodeheaver viewed the evangelical musical service as informal, congenial, and enjoyable, with emphasis upon vocal and horn solos. Although he recognized the popularity of musical arrangements by such contemporaries as **Ira D. Sankey**, he realized the appeal of lighter, more theologically optimistic, and less traditional sacred **music**. Thus, ragtime syncopation and bass arpeggios became the order of his evangelistic day. Rodeheaver's principal (and most profitable) contribution to sacred music began in 1910, when he founded the Rodeheaver Hall-Mack Company, a publisher of gospel music at Winona Lake, Indiana. Then followed the establishment of Rainbow Records and his recording, in 1913, of the highly popular gospel piece, George Barnard's "The Old Rugged Cross." Rodeheaver published and recorded the three most significant gospel hymnodists of his day: Bentley Deforrest Ackley (1872–1958), Alfred Henry Ackley (1887–1960), and Charles Hutchison Gabriel (1856–1932). In 1936, Rodeheaver toured **Africa** and later produced gospel music programs for the CBS and NBC radio networks. His remains lie in Oakwood Cemetery, Warsaw, Indiana.

Samuel J. Rogal

ROMAN CATHOLICISM AND JOHN WESLEY. Few will argue with **Albert Outler**'s assertion as to Wesley's "stoutly anti-Papist" views, particularly that he "never changed his childhood conviction that Roman Catholics were still committed, on principle, to intolerance and to the subversion of English liberties." Nonetheless, there stood principles of Catholic Christianity that helped to form the basis of his own theology. Wesley's agreement with Catholic Christianity (as separate from the Roman Catholic Church) begins with his attention to the doctrine of holiness, which he believed had been too long neglected by Protestants. The Calvinists (among them John Newton and James Hervey) objected, declaring Wesley part Papist for his teaching of evangelical perfection (*see* CHRISTIAN PERFECTION). Wesley countered that he did not teach papal doctrine, but instead defended the Catholic piety and scriptural philosophies of Thomas à Kempis, the Marquis De Renty, and Gregory Lopez. During his fellowship at Lincoln College, Oxford, Wesley shaped the heart of his connection with Catholic Christianity. From the early church fathers he learned about complete and uncompromising Christianity. Their idea of the Christian life focused on the spiritual quest for holiness of heart and life and the doctrine of evangelical perfection. In the end, Wesley's own understanding of the gospel became his bridge between the early Protestant doctrine of **justification** of faith and the Catholic appreciation of the idea of holiness.

Samuel J. Rogal

ROMANIA. *See* EUROPE.

RUSSIA. *See* EUROPE.

RUTER, MARTIN (April 3, 1785–May 16, 1838), **MEC** pastor and educator, was born in Charlton, Massachusetts. Licensed to preach at 15, **elder** at 18, Ruter understood his ministry to be itinerant even though he held numerous education and **conference** administration posts. Delegate to seven **General Conference**s, Ruter helped to write the 1816 plan for the ministerial courses of study and supported the 1820 General Conference decision that each annual conference establish a Methodist college. Western book agent for the Methodist Book Concern from 1820 to 1828, he helped itinerants disseminate Methodist literature through the west. Though self-taught, Ruter served as principal of Wesleyan Academy (New Market, New Hampshire) and president of Augusta College (Augusta, Kentucky). While president of Allegheny College (Meadville, Pennsylvania), Ruter volunteered to serve as a missionary to the recently established Republic of Texas (1836). Superintendent of the mission, Ruter was assisted by Littleton Fowler and Robert Alexander. Traveling just over six months in Texas he was able to report the establishment of 20 societies, 12 local pastors, several churches constructed, and the charter for a Methodist college (now Southwestern University) for which a substantial endowment had been committed. Ruter's exemplary Texas ministry was cut short by his untimely death.

Robert C. Monk

RWANDA. *See* AFRICA.

RYAN, HENRY (April 22, 1775–September 2, 1833) was appointed **presiding elder** of the Bay of Quinte **circuit** (Upper **Canada**) in 1805 by the New York **Conference** (**MEC**), with **William Case** his assistant. The two men introduced the **camp meeting** to Upper Canada at Hay Bay in 1805. From 1810 to 1824, Ryan served terms as presiding elder of the Genesee Conference's Canadian districts. The years were marred by conflict with the British Wesleyan Methodists, and Ryan did not readily accept the 1820 agreement that allowed the British to focus on Lower Canada and the MEC on Upper Canada. Ryan soon began campaigning for the complete independence of the Canada Conference, and he violently disagreed with the 1824 decision for gradual separation of the Canadian body from the MEC. After his 1825 retirement, he spent all his time agitating for immediate independence. He grew increasingly strident and irrational, and, in 1827, he was charged with circulating incendiary literature and disturbing the church's unity. Undeterred, he founded his own church, the Canadian Wesleyan Methodist Church. The denomination, always small, merged with the New Connexion after Ryan's death (1841). Ryan married Huldah Laird in 1794. They had at least three children. Among his grandchildren were **Jennie Fowler Willing** and **Charles Henry Fowler**.

Susan E. Warrick

RYERSON, ADOLPHUS EGERTON (March 24, 1803–February 19, 1882), Canadian pastor and educator, was born near Vittoria in Ontario's Niagara Peninsula. After a **conversion** experience around 1820 he joined the Methodists over his family's objections. He was early involved in **camp meetings** and served as a missionary to the

Credit River Nation for two years. Ryerson was a chief opponent of the establishment of the Church of England in **Canada**. He was the first editor of *The Christian Guardian*, the Canadian Methodist newspaper, first issued in 1829. He worked for unification of Canadian Methodism and, after much struggle, he was instrumental in the formation of the Canadian MEC in 1847. Ryerson held many positions within the church, including president of the **General Conference**. He served pastorates between his national church duties. It was from a pulpit in Toronto that Ryerson was chosen the first president of Victoria College (1841–1847). From 1844 to 1876, he was the superintendent of education in Canada West (Ontario); during his tenure public education was established in Canada. Ryerson wrote three major works: *The Loyalists of America and Their Times*, *Canadian Methodism: Its Epochs and Characteristics*, and an autobiography, *The Story of My Life*.

Joanne Carlson Brown

RYERSON, JOHN (June 12, 1800–October 8, 1878), Canadian Methodist leader, was born at Long Point, Upper **Canada**. Five of the six sons born to this Anglican family became Methodist preachers, despite their father's objections. Ryerson began itinerating on the Long Point Circuit in 1820. From 1825, the year of his ordination as **elder**, until 1843, he served as **presiding elder**, chairman, or superintendent of almost every **circuit** and district in Upper Canada. He led the opposition to **Henry Ryan**, and helped negotiate the friendly separation of the Canadian church from the MEC in 1828. He advocated union with the British church in 1832. Following the union's collapse in 1840, he and **Anson Green** helped achieve reunion in 1846. In 1843, Ryerson was elected president of the Wesleyan Methodist Church in Canada. From 1849 to 1857, he was elected codelegate or vice president of the **conference** each year, the highest office to which his fellow Canadians could elect him in the united church. The Ryerson brothers were instrumental in organizing Upper Canada Academy (Cobourg), later Victoria College. Ryerson retired in 1860 and died near Simcoe, Ontario. He married Mary Lewis in 1828. They had a son and a daughter.

Susan E. Warrick

– S –

SACRAMENTS. A religious ceremony considered especially sacred because of God's acting through the sacrament or because it is a sign or symbol of a significant reality. The **UMC** understanding of the sacraments is informed by the 16th **Article of Religion** (1784), which John Wesley slightly abridged from Article 25 of the Thirty-Nine Articles of the Church of England (1562). It states: "Sacraments ordained of Christ are not only badges or tokens of Christian's men's profession, but rather they are certain signs of grace, and God's good will toward us, by which he doth work invisibly in us, and doth not only quicken, but also strengthen and confirm, our faith in him." The UMC recognizes only two sacraments, **baptism** and the Lord's Supper (*see* EUCHARIST).

Revivalist piety by no means entailed a disdain for the sacraments. The Methodists broke from the Anglican Church in 1784 partly because it would not permit unordained American Methodist preachers to administer baptism or the Lord's Supper. Early American Methodists paired sacraments with fervent **preaching** in their quarterly meetings and revivals (*see* REVIVALISM). But by the middle of the 19th century, Methodists made more of adult **conversion** than baptism, and they continued to celebrate the Lord's Supper quarterly even though many local churches had resident pastors.

In the mid-20th century, some Methodists viewed recovery of the sacraments as a means of renewal. This growing interest in the sacraments found expression in *The Book of Worship for Church and Home* (MC, 1944) and the formation of The Order of Saint Luke in 1946. Reformed liturgies for the Lord's Supper and baptism found their way into general use beginning in 1972. By the early 21st century, an increasing number of local churches encouraged the full and active participation of the laity in frequent sacramental services that embodied ancient Christian traditions. *See also* MEANS OF GRACE; WORSHIP.

Kenneth E. Rowe

SALVATION can be defined as the restoration of sinful human beings to communion with God. According to **John Wesley**, salvation is a process that includes gradual and instantaneous elements. He described this process, the "order of salvation," in various ways. Here is a representative list of the stages which comprise it: the calling of sinners to repent and believe, **repentance** accompanied by efforts to obey the moral law, the act of **faith**, **justification** or the forgiveness of sin, adoption as a child of God, regeneration, **sanctification**, **Christian perfection**, and final blessedness.

Certain emphases characterize Wesley's doctrine of salvation. Wesley insists upon the primacy of **grace**. Apart from grace, human beings can do nothing. However, Wesley finds a place in his theology for freedom of the will. God reshapes the deformed will and enables men and women to respond to Him. Justification, a relative change, is essential. It is subordinated, however, to sanctification, a real change. Sanctification involves two dimensions, ethical and spiritual. The regenerated person leads a disciplined life and performs good works as he or she grows in the knowledge and love of God. Holiness is both social and individual. Social holiness includes supporting fellow Christians as they grow in faith and love, fulfilling the responsibilities appropriate to one's station in society, serving people in distress, and contributing to the renewal of public life.

During the 19th century, certain aspects of the Wesleyan heritage were transformed while others were carried in new directions. These developments were due in part to nontheological factors. American culture, activist, imbued with optimism, individualistic, convinced of American exceptionalism, shaped the life of the churches. As Methodists moved up in the social hierarchy, a shift in their expectations and self-understanding occurred. The rate of social change accelerated over time, stimulated by industrialization, immigration, and the growth of cities. In one way or another, the churches responded to these changing circumstances. Methodist theology was influenced by German philosophy, especially romanticist conceptions of **experience** and the idealists' analysis of God's immanence, and by new developments in psychology and the social sciences.

Here are examples of these developments in Methodism. First, salvation by character, or conformity to standards of behavior acceptable to Methodists. The roles of grace and free will have now been recast. Human beings are pictured as autonomous moral agents who ask God for the grace needed to fulfill their aspirations. Second, appreciation of the ways the social environment influences human personality. This can be observed in the growing reliance upon the **Sun-**

day school, the creation of program-centered churches, offering a wide variety of activities, and the emergence of the **social gospel**, a phrase which may refer to ministries in urban and industrial settings, correcting particular abuses by means of negotiation or political action, or an attack upon systemic evil through the restructuring of economic and social institutions. Third, an emphasis upon the work of the **Holy Spirit** in the individual soul, which the renewed concern for Christian perfection, dating from mid-century, the eventual formation of holiness denominations (*see* HOLINESS MOVEMENT), and the Methodist contribution to the **pentecostal** movement illustrate. *See also* DOCTRINAL STANDARDS.

John C. English

SALVATION ARMY. An international organization as well known for its extensive social services as it is as a Wesleyan/holiness denomination. The church grew out of evangelistic crusades led by **William** and **Catherine Booth** in London's East Side slums in 1865. The Booths started their own ministries there after the **Methodist New Connexion** had denied their request to enter full-time **evangelism** under the church's sponsorship. In 1878, the Booths' Christian Mission took on its present military format and began its rapid expansion around the world into **Canada**, France, Germany, India, Sweden, the USA, and other countries. Commissioner George S. Railton and seven women Salvationists arrived in New York in March 1880 and other missionaries arrived in Canada in July 1882. By the end of the decade, the army with its aggressive street evangelism and growing social services was already active in 43 states in the USA. Early opposition to the movement was widespread. The streets of the cities were the Salvationists' preaching and promotion centers. Their songs, sung lustily with single-minded zeal and accompanied by brass bands and the beat of bass drums, often seemed closer to the **music** of the saloons which their missionaries entered to secure converts and funds than that of the churches. They were easily caricatured and ridiculed, often by the establishment in the church as well as in the surrounding society. The army's ability, however, to maintain a vigorous evangelism along with an urgent concern for the physical as well as the spiritual well-being of society's underclasses largely overcame early negative images. Its ever-present soup kitchens, city missions, group homes, day care centers, homes for the physically challenged, family counseling centers, hospitals, free clinics, support centers for armed personnel, and disaster relief services have made it one of the most respected charitable agencies in the world. Advocacy for homeless and needy persons has become such a public hallmark of its ministries that the organization is now often known more readily as a social agency than as a church, especially in the USA.

Officers (clergy) and soldiers (laypersons) who sign the army's "Articles of War" constitute its activist core. Officer couples always hold equal rank. The "Articles" require ready and obedient response to the directions of those officers under whom they serve and subscription to 11 doctrinal statements, including the Wesleyan doctrine of entire **sanctification**. The remainder of the articles outline the Salvationists' understanding of the evangelical concerns common to most of the free churches of the 19th century. The exception is their nonobservance of the **sacraments** of **baptism** and the Lord's Supper (*see* EUCHARIST).

Before the founding of the Christian Mission, American Methodist holiness evangelists James Caughey and **Phoebe Palmer** had already greatly influenced the Booths' adoption and adaptation of the theology and ethos of the Wesleyan/holiness revival. The church constitutes the largest single entity within the family of Wesleyan/holiness churches and is an active member of the Christian Holiness Association. In 2003, the army operated in more than 100 countries and territories, with a North American constituency of approximately 475,000 and an international constituency of about 1,600,000.

Melvin E. Dieter

SAMOA. *See* TONGA, FIJI, AND SAMOA.

SANCTIFICATION is the transformation of the human will by the **Holy Spirit**, so that evil or self-centered motives are displaced and the will conforms to the love of God. The actions and life of the person reflect this transformation, so that others see love expressed in action. **John Wesley** believed that this transformation could be so complete that the faithful Christian who experiences this transforming power could know his or her actions to be free of conscious sin. This doctrine of "entire sanctification" or **"Christian perfection"** Wesley regarded as the distinctive teaching that God had given the Methodists to proclaim.

Like most theologians influenced by the Protestant Reformation, Wesley and his 18th-century contemporaries in the Church of England agreed that **salvation** is by **grace** alone. This Protestant watchword meant for him that when God forgives a person's sin, it is solely the result of God's gracious choice and action. Nothing human beings can do can earn this gift or entitle them to God's forgiveness. Even when a person responds to the message of **faith** and turns to God seeking forgiveness, Wesley believed this to be the result of God's **prevenient grace**, preparing the way and providing the opportunity for **repentance**. When God accepts or justifies a person, setting aside past sins and providing entry into new life, this is entirely God's action. Nothing about a person's life or action merits God's acceptance, and all spiritual anxiety over whether one is ready for or worthy of it is simply misplaced. The point is not to do something for God, but to trust God's action on our behalf, an action already complete in Christ's sacrifice for us.

On this doctrine of **justification** by faith, Wesley and most Protestant theologians of his time would have agreed. To be sure, Wesley emphasized the experience of justification, more than just the idea of it. His own **conversion** experience at **Aldersgate** in 1738 had to do with knowing the truth that his own sins were forgiven, and his **preaching** thereafter was intended to bring others to that experience. His critics might reject his **revivalistic** methods, but they did not doubt his theology of justification by faith.

The differences arose over what happens after justification. Precisely because forgiveness of sins is God's action, Protestants were rarely optimistic about the effect of faith on subsequent conduct. Knowing oneself forgiven by God might lead to a turning away from certain obvious evil conduct, especially if one had been trying, unsuccessfully, to change one's life by one's own power. For the most part, however, a realistic expectation would include continued faults and failures, even by those who had been justified by faith.

For Wesley, by contrast, the experience of justification by faith should be followed by a continuing **experience** of the presence of

God in one's life. Regeneration, the restoration of those parts of life which had been destroyed by the effects of sin, and sanctification, the development of motives shaped by love, should be evident in the experience of believers and in the conduct observed by their neighbors. This is not because Christians suddenly acquire the power to do for themselves what they could not do before, but precisely because grace, which gave them the acceptance that they could not earn, continues to work in their lives, transforming them in ways they could not accomplish on their own.

It is key to Wesley's understanding of sanctification that we must not place limits on this power of God working in us to transform our lives and conform our wills to God's own law of love. Thus, the possibility of "entire sanctification" or "Christian perfection" became the hope and expectation that he held out to every Christian in his preaching. The transformation that begins in the experience of justification has no stopping point short of the complete conformity of our life and actions to the will of God.

Wesley's doctrine of sanctification was not easily accepted by those who were more impressed with the evident persistence of human sinfulness, even among those who claimed an experience of grace. The idea of Christian perfection lent itself in some ways to caricature, as though the Methodists claimed that they were all completely free of sin, or as though Wesley's followers, who were often plain people of limited education, believed that they could not err or be mistaken. Wesley, however, continued to preach Christian perfection, and to demand that the preachers in his connection proclaim it as well. UMC **elders** are still asked prior to their **ordination** historic questions that Wesley formulated, including "Are you going on to perfection?" and "Do you expect to be made perfect in love in this life?" An affirmative answer is expected.

Wesley not only preached his doctrine of sanctification. He also defended it to a skeptical public. His short treatise, *A Plain Account of Christian Perfection* (1767), has become a classic of Methodist theology, answering objections, correcting misimpressions, and clearly stating key ideas. Sanctification is a moral, rather than an intellectual transformation, Wesley explained. Sanctification does not protect one from errors of fact or accidental misconduct. What sanctification does is to keep us from consciously choosing to do what is morally wrong; and it can do this so completely that we may know ourselves motivated by nothing but the love of God that works in us. Later Methodists have not consistently followed Wesley's emphasis on Christian perfection. His case for sanctification as a further working of grace that can be expected to follow the initial experience of justification has, however, been central to the idea of the "second blessing" in holiness churches of Wesleyan origin (*see* HOLINESS MOVEMENT). Similarly, the firm belief that we cannot set limits on God's power to transform existing conditions has been extended from individuals to the whole society by Methodists concerned with social transformation. The "social holiness" which connected Methodism to the wider movement of the **social gospel** is also a legacy of John Wesley's doctrine of sanctification. *See also* DOCTRINAL STANDARDS.

Robin W. Lovin

SANGSTER, WILLIAM EDWIN (June 5, 1900–May 24, 1960) was born in London. He had no family connection with Methodism, but attended Radnor Street **Sunday School** and mainly through its influence entered the Wesleyan ministry. He trained at Handsworth and Richmond Colleges. His outstanding gifts as a preacher drew large congregations, especially at Scarborough (1932–1936) and Brunswick, Leeds (1936–1939). His appointment to Westminster Central Hall, London, coincided with the opening of World War II and for 16 years he exercised a powerful ministry there. During the war he lived in a small flat on the premises, so that contact could be maintained with people who sheltered each night in the crypt. His postwar Sunday evening congregations were the largest in London. He was alive to contemporary thought and his sermons were relevant to the human situation. He was elected president of the **Conference** in 1950 and five years later became general secretary of the Home Mission Department. Sangster was a prolific author. Among his most widely influential titles were *Methodism Can Be Born Again* (1938; rev. ed., 1941) and *Methodism's Unfinished Task* (1947), together with his books on preaching, reprinted as *The Art of the Sermon* (1954). His doctoral thesis was published as *The Path to Perfection* (1943). He gave the Sam P. Jones Lectures at Emory University (*Let Me Commend*, 1948) and the Cato Lecture (*The Pure in Heart*, 1954). Muscular dystrophy forced him to retire in 1959, but during two years of illness he continued to write and to promote **prayer** cells.

John D. Beasley

SANKEY, IRA DAVID (August 28, 1840–August 13, 1908), singer, evangelist, and associate of Dwight L. Moody, was born in Edinburgh, Pennsylvania. Sankey joined the **MEC** at the age of 15 and quickly rose to prominence as choir leader, **Sunday school** superintendent, and director of the YMCA. While serving in the Union army (1861–1863), he formed a **music** club, the "Singing Boys in Blue." After the war, Sankey married and worked in his father's bank as a tax collector and assistant. In 1870, he met Dwight L. Moody at the International YMCA meeting in Indianapolis. At Moody's urging, Sankey moved to Chicago to assist in the northside mission and around the city. The two were inseparable from then until Moody's death in 1899. Accompanying himself on a small reed organ, Sankey could fill a large hall with his clear baritone voice. More a musician than a lyricist, Sankey's talent lay in taking poems with evangelistic themes and setting them to tunes borrowed from popular dance and march rhythms. Sankey was also gifted at developing songs that supplemented Moody's sermons, establishing the "gospel hymn" as a crucial part of modern **revivalism**. His immensely popular hymnals, compiled in association with several other authors, broke circulation records for their genre.

Dale H. Simmons

SCOTT, ORANGE (February 13, 1800–July 31, 1847), abolitionist and founder of the **Wesleyan Methodist Church**, was born in Brookfield, Orange County, Vermont. Scott came from a very poor family and attended only 13 months of formal elementary education. At a **camp meeting** held near Barre, Vermont, in September 1820, Scott was converted to Christ and joined the **MEC**. Almost immediately, he became a class leader (*see* SOCIETIES, CLASSES, AND BANDS) and was licensed as an exhorter. Thus began Scott's rapid rise as a leader in New England Methodism. In 1821, he started itinerating as a Methodist preacher. The next year he was received into the New England **Conference** on trial. Only three years later, Scott was appointed pastor of a prominent church in Charlestown, Massachusetts. Soon thereafter he was made a **presiding elder**, supervising the pastors of the Springfield District.

During his tenure on the district, Scott became convinced of the evils of **slavery** and the need to work actively for its abolition. He wrote and spoke frequently on the topic. He also took the bold step of sending William Lloyd Garrison's **antislavery** newspaper, the *Liberator*, to 100 New England Conference preachers. His efforts resulted in a majority of the Conference members becoming abolitionists and also led to his election as the head of the New England delegation to the 1836 **General Conference** in Cincinnati. Scott's vocal support of antislavery at that Cincinnati meeting thrust him into the national Methodist spotlight.

Due to his public defense of abolitionism, Scott was removed from his position of leadership of the district. Scott used the situation as an opportunity to accept employment as a traveling "agent" (lecturer and fund raiser) for the American Anti-Slavery Society. During this time, Scott urged abolitionists to become active in partisan politics through the auspices of the Liberty Party, a stance that directly challenged the nonpolitical views of Garrison, the antislavery movement's de facto leader. Meanwhile, in the ecclesiastical arena, Scott witnessed the increasing implacability of the Methodist hierarchy regarding the cause of abolition. By the early 1840s, he gave up on the possibility of any significant reform within the **MEC**.

Scott and several other leading abolitionists, including **Luther Lee** and **Lucius C. Matlack**, seceded from the MEC in 1842. They formally organized the Wesleyan Methodist Connection (later called "Church") in 1843. For the next four years, until his death, Scott worked indefatigably for the success of the new Connection. Scott's particular concern was the development of a viable newspaper and book concern, so that the message of the Wesleyans could be diffused broadly. The importance of his role as the leading advocate and spokesperson for the denomination was evident by the popularity of a derisive name regularly hurled at the Wesleyan Methodists: the "Scottites." Scott's unexpected death from tuberculosis was a severe loss to the young denomination.

Douglas M. Strong

SCRIPTURE. *See* BIBLE.

SERBIA. *See* EUROPE.

SEYBERT, JOHN (July 7, 1791–January 4, 1860), itinerant preacher and second bishop of the **EA**, was born near Manheim, Pennsylvania, to German immigrant parents. Converted in 1810 by followers of **Jacob Albright**, Seybert became a class leader (*see* SOCIETIES, CLASSES, AND BANDS) and then **circuit** rider in the movement. Zealous to reach unconverted Germans, he led **revivals** in Pennsylvania, Ohio, and New York. With his commitment and success, the EA elected him **presiding elder** and placed him in other leadership roles. At the EA **General Conference** in 1839 the denomination was restructured so that its primary mission was to Germans from Ohio to the Great Plains as well as in the East. To lead the church into this new era of growth they elected John Seybert as their first bishop since Jacob Albright's death. A lifelong bachelor dedicated to evangelical ministry, he willingly traveled from Pennsylvania to the Rocky Mountains, in **Canada** and the USA. By horseback and wagon he traveled an estimated 175,000 miles during his ministry. Finding a scarcity of German reading material in the West, he and his preachers distributed **Bibles** and other literature. Worn out by recurring malaria and increasing feebleness, he died and was buried near Bellevue, Ohio.

Donald K. Gorrell

SHADFORD, GEORGE (December 19, 1739–March 11, 1816), was born in Lincolnshire, England, and became a Methodist in 1762. At the invitation of **John Wesley** he became an itinerant minister in 1768. Responding to the appeal of Captain **Thomas Webb** at the 1772 **Conference** in Leeds, he volunteered to serve in America. With **Thomas Rankin** he was appointed in 1773 and participated in the first conference of American Methodism that year in Philadelphia. Shadford served in New York and Philadelphia. Appointed with Edward Dromgoole as his assistant to the Brunswick **Circuit** in Virginia in 1775, Shadford played a significant role in the great **revival** that began in late 1775 and continued into 1776. The revival affected Methodists and Anglicans in Virginia. The Anglican missionary priest, Devereux Jarratt, was also important in its leadership. The increase in membership of the Methodist societies made Virginia the focus of Methodism's numerical strength in the colonies. In 1776, Shadford, loyal to the Crown, along with other Methodists, signed a petition protesting the proposal to disestablish the Anglican Church in Virginia. He returned to Britain in 1778 and was appointed to Epworth. George Shadford was among the preachers named in John Wesley's Deed of Declaration.

Edwin Sylvest

SHAW, ANNA HOWARD (February 15, 1847–July 2, 1919), suffragist, grew up on the Michigan frontier and at an early age decided she wanted to be a minister. Through great hardship, including the opposition of her family, she worked her way through Albion College, Michigan, and Boston University School of Theology, graduating in 1876. After serving churches as a local **deacon**, she and **Anna Oliver** applied for full **ordination** in the **MEC** in 1880. Both **women** were denied, and Shaw then turned to the **MP**, which ordained her the same year. In response to the sickness she saw in the slums of Boston she earned a degree in medicine from Boston University. Still feeling the need for large-scale social change she was a tireless worker for **temperance** and then devoted her life to working for the vote for women (*see* FEMINISM). To that end she was president of National American Woman Suffrage Association from 1904 to 1915. She was a witty, well-respected orator and as such was much in demand. She was drafted by President Woodrow Wilson as the chair of the Woman's Committee of the National Council of Defense when the USA entered World War I and died of pneumonia while on a speaking tour promoting the League of Nations.

Joanne Carlson Brown

SHINN, ASA (May 3, 1781–February 11, 1853), Methodist minister and a principal founder of the **MP**, was born of **Quaker** parents in New Jersey. In 1789, the family moved to western Virginia, where young Shinn received an irregular education. His religious **conversion** came about in 1798 through the preaching of Robert Manly, a Methodist **circuit** rider. Shinn joined the Baltimore **Conference** of the MEC in 1801, became a preacher, and traveled the

Redstone circuit in southwestern Pennsylvania. Shinn remained in Pennsylvania during 1803–1807, before returning to Baltimore to marry Phebe Barnes and to serve circuits in Maryland and the District of Columbia (1807–1816). In 1816, he experienced the first of four periods of mental disorder (the others in 1820, 1828, and 1843), supposedly caused by a skull fracture in his youth. Nonetheless, throughout his years of stability, he performed effectively in the Baltimore and Pittsburgh conferences. Beginning in 1824, Shinn assumed an active interest in the reform movement within the **MEC**. He advocated lay representation, the election of **presiding elder**s, and lessening the authority of bishops. On November 2, 1830, he joined a convention of reformers at Baltimore to form the MP. Shinn published two significant theological tracts: *An Essay on the Plan of Salvation* (1812) and *On the Benevolence and Rectitude of the Supreme Being* (1840). He died in a mental hospital at Brattleboro, Vermont.

Samuel J. Rogal

SIERRA LEONE. *See* AFRICA.

SIMPSON, MATTHEW (June 21, 1811–June 18, 1884), **MEC** bishop, was born in Cadiz, Ohio, of devout MEC parents. He learned to read by the time he was three, later becoming proficient in several languages. He studied medicine, opening an office in May 1833. In 1834, he closed his office and became a traveling preacher in the Pittsburgh **Conference**. In 1835, he married Ellen Verner. After filling several appointments, he became vice president of Allegheny College, Pennsylvania, and, in 1839, president of Indiana Asbury University in Greencastle. He was a delegate to the **General Conferences** of 1844, 1848, and 1852, was elected editor of *The Western Christian Advocate* in 1848, and in 1852 became a bishop. He became widely known for his oratorical ability, and, in 1857, preached at the World's Conference of the Evangelical Alliance in Berlin, where he was presented to the king of Prussia. He became a close friend and advisor to Abraham Lincoln, preaching his funeral oration in Springfield, Ohio, on May 4, 1865. In 1863 Simpson settled permanently in Philadelphia. In 1881 he delivered the opening address at the first Ecumenical Methodist Conference in London (*see* WORLD METHODIST CONFER-

ENCES). He died in Philadelphia. Among his best-known literary works is the *Cyclopaedia of Methodism* (1878).

Frederick E. Maser

SIN. *See* ORIGINAL SIN.

SINGAPORE. *See* ASIA.

SLAVERY AND AMERICAN METHODISM. Slavery was already a part of the social life of America when the **MEC** was formed in 1784. The Methodists, however, were for the most part opposed to slavery, a position they had inherited from **John Wesley**, who wrote a very effective pamphlet against slavery in addition to giving great encouragement to those seeking to stamp out slavery in the British Empire. The organizing **conference** of the MEC wrote a strong statement against slavery and passed legislation by which the Methodists were to have a year to begin emancipating their slaves and five years to complete the task. Failure to fulfill these requirements would result in withdrawal or expulsion.

However, the rule met with great opposition not only from the general public but also from many Methodists themselves. Gradually the rule of 1784 was weakened and by 1816 it was admitted by the **General Conference** that "little can be done to abolish a practice so contrary to the principles of moral justice." Eventually, the matter was left in the hands of the individual conferences.

Although some of the **MECS** ministers sought to show the scriptural basis for slavery and pointed to the benefits derived by the African Americans from slavery, no major work defending slavery in principle was ever written by a Methodist. However, numerous traveling preachers and local preachers were slaveholders. On the other hand, led by **Thomas Coke** and **Francis Asbury**, Methodists had always sought to evangelize African Americans.

In the interest of unity, the northern church opposed the abolitionists, although certain pastors, such as **Orange Scott,** stood strongly against slavery. In 1843 Scott was instrumental in forming the **Wesleyan Methodist Church**, which opposed slavery and the authority of the **episcopacy**. A year later the MEC divided into the MEC and the MECS, partly over a constitutional question intertwined with the problem of slavery. Ironically, the northern church did not take a strong stand against slavery until 1864 when the holding of slaves became an impediment to church membership. This was only after the civil authorities had emancipated the slaves.

The Civil War, however, did not bring an end to slavery, except in name. African Americans, especially in the South, were not only segregated but also given little opportunity for education or advancement. The MEC through its **Freedmen's Aid Society** proved a powerful force in educating African Americans. Among the many schools and colleges established were: Rust College at Holly Springs, Mississippi (1866), Clark College in Atlanta, Georgia (1869), Claflin College in Orangeburg, South Carolina (1869), and Meharry Medical College in Nashville, Tennessee (1876).

The **UMC** General Conference has been particularly intent on securing racial justice by passing numerous resolutions seeking to eliminate racism in the church, the nation, and the world. Its aim is summarized in its Social Principles (*see* SOCIAL CREED). The church looks forward to the day when no form of racism will be tolerated and freedom in its fullest meaning will be a reality. *See also* ANTISLAVERY.

Frederick E. Maser

SMITH, AMANDA BERRY (January 23, 1837–February 24, 1915), **AME** holiness evangelist, was bought out of **slavery** by her father. She was married at 17 to Calvin M. Devine, who disappeared in 1862. She later married James Smith, an ordained **deacon** in the Old Bethel AME Church, Philadelphia. She had five children; a son, Will, and a daughter, Mazie, survived. The Smiths moved to New York City, where she worked as a domestic servant and washerwoman. Smith regularly attended **Phoebe Palmer**'s Tuesday meetings and experienced entire **sanctification** in September 1868. After her husband and son died in 1869, Smith began preaching in black churches in New York and New Jersey. In 1870, at a holiness **camp meeting** (*see* HOLINESS MOVEMENT), she first spoke before a white audience. She became a full-time evangelist and camp meeting speaker in northern and southern states, often breaking the color barrier. In 1878–1879, she traveled to England and India, then was a missionary in **Africa**, 1881–1889. In 1899, she opened a home for black orphans in Harvey, a Chicago suburb. The Amanda Smith Industrial School for Girls was destroyed by fire in 1918. She died in Sebring, Florida, and was buried in Homewood, Illinois.

Susan E. Warrick

SNETHEN, NICHOLAS (November 15, 1769–May 10, 1845), leading associate of **Francis Asbury** in the early years of American Methodism, was born on Long Island, New York. Snethen began his distinguished service as an itinerant in the **MEC** in 1794. His early assignments were to **circuits** in New England and Charleston, South Carolina. He was assigned in 1800 and 1801 as the traveling associate of Bishop Francis Asbury, a post that earned him the affectionate title of "Francis Asbury's Silver Trumpet." Later appointments were in Baltimore, Philadelphia, Georgetown, Alexandria, and Frederick. He also served as chaplain of the USA House of Representatives (1811). Snethen is perhaps best remembered for his involvement in the reform movement in Methodism that included opposition to the **episcopacy** and the office of **presiding elder.** He presided at the organizational **conference** of the **MP.** After affiliating with the new body in 1830, he contributed to the *Methodist Repository* and its successor, *Mutual Rights.* In 1830, Snethen became a member of the Ohio Conference and he served congregations in that state and in Louisville, Kentucky, until his retirement to Indiana. In 1834, he became an editor of the *Methodist Protestant,* the official organ of the new denomination. He married Susannah Hood Worthington in 1803.

J. Steven O'Malley

SOCIAL CREED (1907), written by **Harry F. Ward** for the Methodist Federation for Social Service, was adopted by the 1908 **MEC General Conference.** Revised by **Frank Mason North** and adopted in 1908 by the Federal Council of Churches, it spawned social pronouncements by many denominations. Informed by inner-city ministries of deaconesses (*see* DEACONESS MOVEMENT) and pastors with immigrants, industrial laborers, and the unemployed, and sobered by the failure of charity to end major social ills, the first Social Creed opposed **human rights** violations of the capitalist system.

It affirmed the worth and equality of all persons, the principle that **salvation** applies to human social institutions, and the role of Christians in making institutions more Christ-like. The MEC Social Creed invited Christians to create a new social and economic order based on justice, cooperation, and profit sharing. It stood for labor conditions characterized by equal rights, abolition of child labor, fair wages, and health and safety regulations. UMC social pronouncements fall into three groups. The Social Creed is designed for use in **worship**. Guidelines established by the Social Principles speak for the church and identify areas of outreach and concern. *The Book of Resolutions* provides public statements that assist the church in its work.

Alice G. Knotts

SOCIAL GOSPEL. The social gospel targeted social Darwinism, learned from socialism, and adopted liberal theology. An Englishman, Herbert Spencer (1820–1903), and his American disciple, William Graham Sumner (1840–1910), applied Charles Darwin's (1809–1882) theory of "the survival of the fittest" to society, creating social Darwinism. They maintained that if society is to progress, government must do nothing to restrain "fit" individuals and nothing to sustain "unfit" individuals — allow the poor to die off and society will evolve naturally, producing better human beings.

Socialists, employing the economic analysis of Karl Marx (1818–1883), argued that the organization of economies determines the ideologies, such as social Darwinism, used to justify them. Replace capitalism with socialism and people will take it for granted that no person should be allowed to drop through society's cracks.

Liberal theology, accepting 19th-century German biblical scholarship and philosophical assumptions, emphasized the *immanence* rather than the transcendence of God, maintained the *organic* rather than the individualistic nature of human society, highlighted the *teachings* rather than the **atonement** of Jesus, and stressed the human potential for *good* rather than its proclivity for evil.

Among the social gospel theologians who adopted liberal theology was Walter Rauschenbusch (1861–1918), a Baptist, who, announcing that the competitive spirit of capitalism was anti-Christian, went on to articulate the social gospel's theology: Christ's death reveals humanity's corrupt social vision; **faith** is seeing God at work in the world and claiming a share in the divine task of building a better world for human beings on earth, instead of offering heaven as a reward for enduring a cut-throat world.

Targeting social Darwinism, social gospel leaders lobbied for government programs to curb the ruthless "fit" and protect the suffering "unfit." Methodism, ever specific and practical, enumerated those programs in its **Social Creed**. Methodist **Frank Mason North** expressed his confidence that socialism could be Christianized.

John G. McEllhenney

SOCIAL PRINCIPLES. *See* SOCIAL CREED.

SOCIETIES, CLASSES, AND BANDS. At the beginning of **John Wesley**'s ministry he reasoned that if people were to be successful in living the Christian life, they must be brought together for mutual support, education, and pastoral oversight. Borrowing from the success of various English religious societies, Wesley created Methodist societies for his followers. "Society" came to mean a local or regional group of Methodists which met weekly. Since Wesley intended the society to supplement, not replace, the church, societies did not meet when the local Anglican parish church held worship. As the number of societies grew, Wesley continued to refine their operation and developed a series of **General Rules** to guide them. Methodists were expected to attend society meetings regularly for worship, **preaching**, and fellowship.

The class meeting was originally created by Captain Foy in Bristol in 1742 to finance the Methodist chapel called the New Room. Wesley quickly realized that the class meeting offered an additional means for cultivating discipleship. Whereas the society could be any size and allowed both Methodists and visitors, the weekly class meeting was designed to be small and attendance by non-Methodists was restricted. Each class, supervised by a carefully chosen leader, was designed to be a place of support, confession, **prayer**, and stewardship. It was here that the **lay preacher** was particularly active. Classes were subsets of the societies and every Methodist was expected to be present for class meeting.

Bands were modeled on a structure effectively employed by the **Moravians**. Wesley instituted bands in 1738, several years before the first Methodist class meeting. Bands, smaller than classes, were for Methodists only, and segregated by gender and marital status. Bands provided an intimate setting for spiritual self-examination. Each week, members reviewed a series of seaching questions compiled by Wesley. Bands, classes, and societies were meant to support and enable the individual's growth in faithful discipleship. As the Methodist movement evolved into denominations in the 19th century, many functions of these groups were redistributed among other church ministries, including the **Sunday school** class and the mid-week prayer service. *See also* GENERAL RULES.

L. Dale Patterson

SOCKMAN, RALPH WASHINGTON (October 1, 1889–August 29, 1970), one of American Methodism's premier 20th-century preachers, was born in Mount Vernon, Ohio. After one year as associate pastor, he became pastor of the Madison Avenue **MEC**, New York City, . degree from Columbia University. For the next 44 years, he guided the same congregation, leading it as it changed its name to Christ Church and erected new facilities on Park Avenue. Sockman's 36 years on the National Radio Pulpit made him one of the best-known Methodist preachers in the United States. His books, such as *The Higher Happiness, How to Believe,* and *The Whole Armor of God,* gained him a reading congregation. A mid-century *Christian Century* poll named him one of the six foremost clergymen of all denominations in the nation. Sockman lectured at New York's Union Theological Seminary and Yale University, headed the Carnegie Foundation's Church Peace Union and the Methodist Board of World Peace (*see* WAR AND PEACE), and served on the Central Committee of the **WCC**. He married Zellah Widmer Endly on June 15, 1916. They had a daughter, Elizabeth. Sockman retired in 1961 and died in New York City.

John G. McEllhenney

SOPER, DONALD OLIVER (January 31, 1903–December 22, 1998) was born in London and educated at St. Catherine's College and Wesley House, Cambridge. He became superintendent of the West London Mission in 1936, supervising its extensive social work and serving as chaplain at Holloway and Pentonville prisons. At Kingsway Hall he preached to large crowds and became famous as an open–air orator on Tower Hill and in Hyde Park, London, a ministry he sustained for over 60 years. He early established a reputation as a superb broadcaster. He was president of the **Conference** in 1950 and was president of the Methodist Sacramental Fellowship, of the Methodist Peace Fellowship, and of the Fellowship of Reconciliation. His pacifism (*see* WAR AND PEACE) and support of the Labour Party sprang directly from his understanding of the gospel. In 1965 Soper entered the House of Lords. He travelled throughout the world to preach and speak and, in retirement, maintained a heavy program of work, battling courageously into his nineties against loss of mobility. He was the author of many books, especially on Christian apologetics and social concerns. *See also* BRITISH METHODISM.

Kenneth G. Greet

SOULE, JOSHUA (August 1, 1781–March 6, 1867), seventh bishop of the **MEC**, was born in Bristol, Maine, the lineal descendant of *Mayflower* immigrant George Soule. Soule was licensed to preach at 17, admitted to the New England **Conference** on trial at 18 (1799), and appointed **presiding elder** of the Maine District at 23 (1804). When he was 26 (1808) his plan for a delegated **General Conference** became effectively the first constitution of the MEC. During his quadrennium as book agent (1816–1820), Soule established *The Methodist Magazine* (1818), which has had various names but continuous successors down to the current *Quarterly Review* of the UMC. Soule was dedicated to a powerful **episcopacy**. He was elected bishop in 1820 but refused consecration because the General Conference had changed the presiding eldership to an elective office. Four years later, this was rescinded and Soule, once more elected bishop, accepted the office. In 1845, he adhered to the new connection, the **MECS**, again largely on the strength of his view of episcopacy. Soule was noted for his intellect, will, energy, and homiletical and administrative abilities. He died in Nashville and is buried on the campus of Vanderbilt University alongside Bishops **William McKendree** and Holland N. McTyeire.

Charles W. Brockwell, Jr.

SOUTH AFRICA. *See* AFRICA.

SOUTH AMERICA. *See* LATIN AMERICA AND THE CARIBBEAN.

SPAIN. *See* EUROPE.

SPRINGER, JOHN MCKENDREE (September 7, 1873–December 2, 1963) and **HELEN EMILY CHAPMAN RASMUSSEN SPRINGER** (April 21, 1868–August 23, 1949) were the founders of MEC **missions** in the Congo. Helen Chapman went to Angola in 1891 as one of Bishop **William Taylor**'s self-supporting missionaries. Marrying fellow missionary William Rasmussen, she served two terms cut short by malaria and then the death of her husband. Her son died several years after her return from Angola, and, in 1901, she went to Southern Rhodesia as the first missionary there of the WFMS (**MEC**). She lived in Shona villages, translated hymns and scriptures, and established Methodist girls' education. She published a Shona grammar in 1905. John Springer went to Southern Rhodesia in 1901 as supervisor of the Old Umtali Industrial Mission. The Springers married in 1905 and began to explore unmapped territory. They traveled from Northern Rhodesia to the Congo, scouting locations for mission stations. Returning to the USA, they pressed for the establishment of the Congo Mission. After they returned to **Africa** and founded mission stations over a two-year period, the Congo Mission was formally approved and John Springer appointed as superintendent. In 1936 he was elected bishop for Africa, serving until retirement in 1944. The Springers were popular speakers and each wrote books presenting the needs and opportunities of Africa. They pioneered Methodist higher education in Africa, having founded the Congo Institute. After Helen's death, John Springer married another Congo missionary, Helen Everett, and remained in Mulungwishi until political unrest forced his return to America in 1963.

Dana L. Robert

SRI LANKA. *See* ASIA.

ST. JOHN, EUGENIA (dates uncertain), **MP** clergywoman, was married to Charles H. St. John (1854–1904), a medical doctor and

MP and **MEC** pastor. Eugenia began her pastoral career by preaching for her husband during his illness, and she preached for 11 years before her 1889 ordination by the Kansas Annual **Conference** (MP). The couple were successful evangelists in Nebraska and Kansas for some years. Eugenia was elected by the Kansas Conference as its ministerial delegate to the 1892 MP **General Conference**, the first at which **women** delegates were seated. She was thus the first woman clergy delegate to any General Conference in the United Methodist tradition. During the debate over seating women at that 1892 Conference, she said, "Dare this conference stand before the omen given by God and frustrate his will for the upbuilding of his church by your prejudices? . . . The great question of the future is whether you will have power to conquer the forces of sin, and I tell you it will need every woman that can be found to stand side by side with the good-minded men in this work if the church is to be triumphant." *See also* FEMINISM.

Susan E. Warrick

STEPHENSON, THOMAS BOWMAN (December 22, 1839–July 16, 1912), Wesleyan minister and architect of a more socially minded Methodism, through the establishment of two major institutions. The son of John Stephenson (1799–1861), Irish itinerant and missionary to Bermuda, he was born at Newcastle upon Tyne, England. A Liberal in politics and musically gifted, his ministry was atypical. He sang in the streets and was the first to hire a theater for use in his mission. In 1869, with the help of two laymen, he founded the National Children's Home, and, in 1873, was set apart as its principal. Always eager to use everyone's talents, including the laity and **women**, he employed a deaconess at Bolton in 1868. A visit to Kaiserswerth deaconess center in Germany in 1871 encouraged him to develop opportunities for women to serve in the church through the "Sisters of the Children" in the National Children's Home and Orphanage and later through the Wesley Deaconess Order, following the publication of his book *Concerning Sisterhoods* (1890) (*see* DEACONESS MOVEMENT). He was the chief mover behind the admission of laymen to the Wesleyan **Conference**, first speaking for it in 1873 and becoming secretary of the Thanksgiving Fund in 1878. An expert money-raiser and publicist, Stephenson began magazines, such as

Highways and Hedges, wrote many hymns, especially for children, and composed a service book for them. He was president of the conference in 1891. Excessive work and money-raising tours affected his health and forced him to relinquish his responsibility for the National Children's Home in 1900 and for the Deaconess Order in 1907.

John H. Lenton

STRAWBRIDGE, ROBERT (ca.1732–1781), the first American **circuit** rider, was born in Drumsna, County Leitrim, **Ireland**. He devoted his life secondarily to farming and primarily to itinerating as a Methodist lay preacher. After he immigrated to America, he took it upon himself to baptize and officiate at the Lord's Supper (*see* BAPTISM; EUCHARIST). Having experienced a Methodist type **conversion**, probably in the early 1750s, Strawbridge preached in northwestern Ireland until he and his wife, Elizabeth Piper, settled on Sam's Creek, Frederick County, Maryland, about 1760. There he evangelized his neighbors, organized a class around 1763, formed a society about 1766, and built a log meeting house (*see* SOCIETIES, CLASSES, AND BANDS). Strawbridge baptized a child about 1762 and soon began serving communion. These actions brought him into conflict with the preachers whom **John Wesley** commissioned to organize Methodism in America. Strawbridge, ignoring their instructions, continued to act like an ordained minister (*see* ORDINATION). His preaching itineraries took him throughout eastern Maryland, into Virginia, and as far north as Philadelphia and Trenton. A persuasive speaker, he won many converts. Several early American Methodist preachers called Strawbridge their spiritual father, including **Freeborn Garrettson** and an African-American slave named Jacob Toogood. Although Strawbridge's name disappeared from the American Methodist Minutes in 1776, he continued to preach until his death.

John G. McEllhenney

SUNDAY SCHOOL has long been, especially for children, the chief agency in Methodism for Christian formation, **education**, and nurture. **John Wesley** supported the work of early leaders such as **Hannah Ball**, offered his encouragement and advice, and wrote curriculum materials. Wesley taught children's classes himself and expected

his preachers to do so. The first American Sunday school was probably the one begun by **Francis Asbury** in Virginia, ca. 1786. The
MEC officially recognized the Sunday school as an institution of the
church in 1790 and encouraged preachers to establish them wherever
worship services were held. These early schools taught both Christian faith and basic literacy. In 1827, the Methodist Sunday School
Union was founded and **Nathan Bangs** was appointed its corresponding secretary.

The Sunday school in Methodism was much more closely related
to the structure of the church than was the case in most other denominations. New schools were formed, both to advance missional outreach and to provide training for those already in the church. Gradually, classes began to be offered for persons of all ages. Vast amounts
of literature, including curriculum and teaching materials, periodicals, tracts, and books were published and widely disseminated. Sunday school libraries were established and became important sources
of religious reading materials. Because most of the leaders were
laypersons, there was a great need for teacher training, which was accomplished through teachers' magazines and numerous Sunday
school institutes and conventions. These activities provided unusual
leadership and development opportunities for **women**, who constituted the majority of the teachers. The primary goals of the Sunday
school were to foster **conversion** and commitment to Christ and to
provide instruction and nurture in Christian growth.

The 1860 through 1910 period was one of both rapid growth and
diligent refinement of the Sunday school movement. The most influential figure was **John H. Vincent,** who became general agent of the
Methodist Sunday School Union in 1866. Vincent emphasized appropriate preparation of teachers and improved curriculum. His work
led to the adoption of uniform lessons.

The phenomenal growth of the Sunday school from 1900 to 1960
has been described by Walter Vernon as "the most remarkable development in the history of American Methodism." Changes in curriculum and teaching methods were guided by contemporary psychological and educational theories. Graded lessons were introduced in 1910.
The MEC modified its structure in 1924 in a way that has impacted
the Sunday school since. The Board of Sunday Schools was merged
into a Board of Education with one of its departments called "Church

Schools." The intention was to make the educational program of the church more diverse and comprehensive. In 1960, enrollment in Methodist Sunday schools was 7,800,000 with average attendance of 4,200,000. Since that time both figures have declined precipitously. The UMC in 1972 created sections on Christian education and church school publications within the General Board of Discipleship. For a variety of institutional, societal, and theological reasons, Sunday school has ceased to be the effective avenue into church membership and Christian discipleship that it was for so many for so long.

Gayle Carlton Felton

SUNDAY SERVICE. When Methodists in North America were formed into an independent church in 1784 (*see* MEC), **John Wesley** provided them with a modest revision of *The Book of Common Prayer* of the Church of England, retitled *The Sunday Service of the Methodists in North America, With Other Occasional Services.* Wesley's preface indicates his conviction that no ancient or modern liturgy "breathes more of a solid, scriptural rational piety." As its name indicates, the book is a service book for use on the Lord's Day for public **worship.** Wesley retained full services of Morning and Evening Prayer and the Lord's Supper with Collects, Epistles, and Gospels for each Sunday in the church year plus Christmas Day, Good Friday, and Ascension. "Occasional Services" include **baptism** of infants, baptism of adults (but not the rite of confirmation), **marriage**, burial, and ordinations. The **Articles of Religion** were retained, though pared back to 24 from 39. A Psalter, censored of 34 psalms and verses from 58 others "highly improper for the mouths of a Christian congregation," is the largest single unit in the book. Wesley updates language, removes service **music** (although abundant congregational song in the form of hymnody is presupposed by *A Collection of Psalms and Hymns for the Lord's Day,* which was bound with it), drops references to the British government or the Church of England, and changes priestly absolutions to prayers for pardon. Throughout "priest" becomes "**elder**" and "bishop" becomes "**superintendent**." Though reprinted in 1786 and 1790, the book hardly survived Wesley as far as American usage was concerned. One year after his death, the 314-page *Sunday Service* was replaced by 37 pages of "ritual" in the 1792 book of *Discipline.*

Kenneth E. Rowe

SUPERINTENDENT. Superintendency has been an important function in the structure of Methodism since **John Wesley** created the office of superintendent for American Methodism in 1784, naming **Thomas Coke** and **Francis Asbury** "general superintendents" of the work. Wesley preferred the title superintendent to bishop and was irate with the Americans when they adopted the episcopal title. Many of the American Methodist churches refer to their chief spiritual and administrative leaders as bishops, for example, **UMC,** **AME, AMEZ,** and **CME.** However, some of the American Methodist denominations, such as the **Wesleyan Church,** prefer to use the term general superintendent for their top leadership. Many Methodist churches, especially in the United States, refer to those who assist bishops and administer groups of churches (districts) in the annual **conference** under the bishop's direction as district superintendents, earlier called **presiding elders.** In **British Methodism** circuit superintendent ministers are the spiritual and administrative leaders of the **circuit**s, which are composed of several churches. Many Methodist churches in other parts of the world whose historical roots are in British and American Methodism are familiar with the task of superintendency and may utilize the title in their structures. *See also* EPISCOPACY.

Charles Yrigoyen, Jr.

SWAIN, CLARA A. (July 18, 1834–December 25, 1910), the first woman medical missionary, sailed for India in 1869 with **Isabella Thoburn** as the first missionaries of the WFMS (**MEC**) (*see* ASIA). Swain had studied medicine for four years prior to her appointment. Arriving in Bareilly, she worked in a girls' orphanage, taught a medical class of young **women,** and opened a medical practice, treating 108 patients in the first six weeks. In 1871, she was given 40 acres of land by the Nawab of Rampore upon which to open a dispensary and build the first hospital for women in India, which opened in 1874. In 1885 the Rajah of Rajputana asked Swain to become palace physician to serve his wife and children. Seeing an opportunity to open Christian work in a province with no missionaries, she resigned from the WFMS. Swain opened a dispensary and attended the Rajah's family for 10 years, doing both evangelistic and medical work. In 1896 she retired from the mission field. She made a final visit to India in 1906 to celebrate the jubilee of Methodist **missions** there. Extracts from her letters were published in 1909 as *A Glimpse of India*.

Dana L. Robert

SWEDEN. *See* EUROPE.

SWEET, WILLIAM WARREN (February 15, 1881–January 3, 1959), noted Methodist historian, gave special attention to the history of Methodism on the American frontier, especially in his *Methodism in American History*. He pioneered gathering and interpreting primary source material. Much of this data was included in his four-volume study, *Religion on the American Frontier*. Sweet's work applied to religious studies the thesis of the American historian Frederick Jackson Turner, which asserted the central role of the frontier, with its indigenous factors, in interpreting the distinctive aspects of American culture. Himself a product of the late frontier, Sweet was born in Baldwin City, Kansas. He was a graduate of Ohio Wesleyan University (1902), Drew Theological Seminary (1906), Crozer Theological Seminary (Th.M., 1907), and the University of Pennsylvania (Ph.D., 1912). In addition to the University of Chicago, (1927–1946), where he held the first chair in American church history, he also taught at Ohio Wesleyan (1911–1913) and DePauw in Indiana (1913–1927). His last posts were at Methodist seminaries, including Garrett (1946–1948) and Perkins (1948–1952). He trained a group of younger historians who influenced the study of American religion in the next generation.

J. Steven O'Malley

SWITZERLAND. *See* EUROPE.

– T –

TAJIKISTAN. *See* EUROPE.

TAYLOR, VINCENT (January 1, 1887–November 28, 1968) was born at Accrington, England, and trained for the ministry at Richmond College. He was appointed New Testament Tutor at Headingley College in 1930, becoming principal in 1936. Despite having had no university training (his first degree was the external London B.D.), he pursued his studies during his years in **circuit** and later published a series of New Testament studies, including trilogies on the **atonement** (*Jesus and His Sacrifice* [1937], *The Atonement in New Testament Teaching* [1940], and *Forgiveness and Reconciliation* [1948]) and on Christology (*The Names of Jesus* [1953], *The Life and Ministry of Jesus* [1955], and *The Person of Christ in New Testament Teaching* [1958]), as well as a major commentary on Mark's Gospel (1952). His account on form criticism in *The Formation of Gospel Tradition* (1945) introduced it to many students in a readily understandable way. Taylor was also noted for his championship of Streeter's Proto-Luke hypothesis (e.g., in *Behind the Third Gospel* [1926]). He was elected president of the Society for New Testament Study and his scholarship was recognized by the Burkitt Medal and by honorary degrees from the universities of Leeds, Dublin, and Glasgow.

Cyril S. Rodd

TAYLOR, WILLIAM (May 2, 1821–May 18, 1902), **MEC** evangelist, missionary, and bishop, was born in Rockbridge County, Virginia. On August 28, 1841, he underwent a **conversion** experience that restored him, to use his own words, to a proper "standing in the Kingdom and family of God." In October 1842, Taylor began an itinerant ministerial career. Less than a year later, he was received on trial in the MEC Baltimore Annual **Conference**. In 1845, he was ordained a **deacon**, received into full membership, and appointed to the Sweet Springs **Circuit**. The following year he married Annie Kimberlin. From the outset of his ministry, William Taylor preached holiness as a biblical doctrine. From 1849 to 1862, he was an evangelist in California, New York, Maryland, New Hampshire, Pennsylvania, Ohio, Indiana, Illinois, Iowa, and **Canada**. For eight years beginning in 1862 he was engaged in an evangelistic ministry that took him to England, **Australia**, South Africa, the West Indies, Ceylon, and India (*see* ASIA). Later he was a missionary to South America (*see* LATIN AMERICA). Taylor attended the MEC **General Conference** in 1884, which consecrated him as bishop for **Africa** with the authority to open **missions** and to develop Methodist churches anywhere in Africa. He retired to Palo Alto, California, in 1896. *See also* HOLINESS MOVEMENT.

Kenneth J. Collins

TEMPERANCE refers to the passionate and powerful crusade against beverage alcohol. Beginning with Wesley, Methodists always recognized the dangers of excessive use of intoxicating liquors. Early American Methodists focused antialcohol efforts on maintaining strict church discipline and trying to reform individuals. The decades immediately after the Civil War witnessed a sharp increase in the liquor traffic. In response, Methodist churches became deeply involved in political action, aiming for local and state options to control alcohol and later devoting themselves to working for national legal prohibition. Methodists provided leadership and support for the National Prohibition Party, Woman's Christian Temperance Union (WCTU), and Anti-Saloon League. Methodist laywoman and WCTU president **Frances Willard** was perhaps the most influential individual in the movement. Recommendations against the use of wine in Holy Communion (*see* EUCHARIST) began as early as 1864 and eventually became mandatory in the **MEC**. Commitment to the cause of temperance became the dominating concern of Methodism. The battle against liquor became so all-consuming that other evils were ignored and prohibition was hyped as a panacea for society. The proponents of prohibition expected utopia with the passage of the 18th Amendment, but these hopes proved unrealistic and the amendment was repealed in 1933.

Gayle Carlton Felton

TESTIMONY is a practice that has its theological roots in **John Wesley**'s doctrine of **assurance**. Wesley believed that those who are in saving relationship with God can receive God's gift of the **witness of the Spirit** and find their **faith** validated by increasing holiness of life. Those who have this assurance are to offer testimony to others, both by the example of their lives and by the public statement of their spiritual **experience**. By so doing, they will become instruments through whom the Holy Spirit will draw others to Christ. In the teaching of some later Methodists, such as **Phoebe Palmer**, the obligation of public testimony became requisite to continued living in holiness. Testimony was most commonly a feature of the class meetings (*see* SOCIETIES, CLASSES, AND BANDS), **love feasts**, and midweek **prayer** services, some of which were called "Testimony Meetings." Persons usually stood and spoke with passion and conviction about the work of God in their lives and especially about particular blessings they had received. Both **women** and men were expected to give testimony. In later years, testimonies tended to become hackneyed and the practice declined. Its revival may be encouraged by use in new services of baptismal reaffirmation and renewal of faith.

Gayle Carlton Felton

THOBURN, ISABELLA (March 29, 1840–September 1, 1901) was the first missionary appointed by the WFMS (**MEC**). Thoburn sailed to India in 1869 with **Clara Swain** (*see* ASIA). An experienced teacher, she was drawn to India because her brother **James Thoburn** was a missionary there. Arriving in Lucknow, Thoburn opened a school for girls and began evangelistic work among secluded **women**. The WFMS purchased property, enabling her in 1871 to open a boarding school. Thoburn taught **Sunday school** among the poor and directed the work of Bible women. On her second furlough she helped to found the **deaconess movement** in the MEC, training deaconesses in Chicago, Cincinnati, and Boston before her return to India in 1890. Despite the opposition of those who believed women in India could never be educated, her boarding school developed into **Asia**'s first college for women, receiving a government charter in 1895. Thoburn became famous as an educational missionary and spoke on the higher education of women at the New York Ecumenical Missionary Conference in 1900. Her pupil and eventual assistant principal at the college, Lilavati Singh, accompanied her and also spoke to great effect. Thoburn returned to India, where she died of cholera. *See also* MISSIONS.

Dana L. Robert

THOBURN, JAMES MILLS (March 7,1836–November 28,1922), MEC missionary to India and missionary bishop, was born in St. Clairsville, Ohio. Educated at Allegheny College, Meadville, Pennsylvania, he joined the Pittsburgh **Conference** of the MEC in 1858 and was appointed a missionary to India in 1859 (*see* ASIA). Except for a three-year furlough (1863–1866) and years of failing health (1908–1922), Thoburn devoted his life to India. He served in Nynee Tal, Gurhawl, Moradabad, Lucknow, Calcutta, and as **presiding elder** of the Calcutta district, South India Conference. He was founding editor of *The Indian Witness* and published more than eight books and other addresses. He was an influential advocate for church growth, **evangelism**, and missionary work, and especially enhanced American church interest in mission work. In 1888, he was elected a missionary bishop for India and Malaysia on the first ballot. This provision of MEC polity at that time enabled the **General Conference** to elect persons to the **episcopacy** and then restrict their authority to designated regions outside the USA. He retired in ill health in 1908 and died in Meadville, Pennsylvania, where he is buried. His sister was missionary **Isabella Thoburn**. *See also* MISSIONS.

Robert J. Williams

TILLY, DOROTHY ROGERS (June 30, 1883–March 16, 1970), Woman's Society leader, antilynching crusader, interracial leader, and stateswoman, was born in Hampton, Georgia. She graduated from Reinhardt Junior College (1899) and Wesleyan College (1901), and married Milton Eben Tilly in 1903. Tilly directed children's work for the North Georgia **Conference**, **MECS** (1916), cultivating interracial projects. Through the Woman's Missionary Society (MECS) and the MC Woman's Society of Christian Service she promoted leadership development for black women and educational facilities for children of sharecroppers. Tilly engineered defeat of Governor Eugene Talmadge to secure support for a home for delinquent black girls. She served on the National Conference on Cause and Cure of War, the U.S. Children's Bureau, the Emergency Committee for Food Production, and the Federal Council of Churches. Through the Association of Southern Women for the Prevention of Lynching (1930–1942) and as director of Women's Work of the Southern Regional Council (1944), Tilly investigated every southern racial lynching, organized **women** to help prevent lynchings, and mobilized women's votes to defeat uncooperative sheriffs and judges. Tilly served on President Harry S. Truman's Committee on Civil Rights (1947–1948), which produced a report that accelerated desegregation. Tilly founded and led the multifaith interracial women's Fellowship of the Concerned (1949–1970) in pursuing courtroom justice and working for integration.

Alice G. Knotts

TINDLEY, CHARLES ALBERT (ca. July 7, 1856–July 26, 1933), African-American **MEC** minister, was born of slave parents in Berlin, Maryland. His father, on receiving his freedom, was too poor to educate his son, who, in his early years, educated himself with the aid of a kindly schoolteacher. He married Daisy Henry and moved to Philadelphia, where he became a hod carrier and then sexton of Bainbridge Street MEC (formerly John Wesley MEC). He was converted, attended night school, and pursued the **conference** course of studies, being admitted on probation in 1885 to the Delaware Conference (MEC). He was ordained **deacon** in 1887 and **elder** in 1889. After a number of appointments, he became pastor of the church where he had been sexton. His preaching, his street services, and his community activities attracted great crowds, necessitating a larger sanctuary. He built Tindley Temple on Broad Street, seating 3,000 persons. He also became a hymn writer. Several of his hymns appear in various hymnals. He was a delegate to seven **General Conference**s and twice considered for the **episcopacy**. After the death of his first wife, he married Jenny Cotton. His funeral was attended by 5,000 persons in Philadelphia.

Frederick E. Maser

TONGA, FIJI, AND SAMOA. It was missionary zeal and a highly disciplined evangelical thrust that caused the members of the British Wesleyan Missionary Society to penetrate the islands of the South Pacific—Tonga (1822), Fiji (1835), and Samoa (1835).

Initial efforts by Walter Lawry (1793–1859) in Tonga were short-lived until John Thomas (1797–1881) and John Hutchinson resumed work in 1826 at Tongatapu. Soon other missionaries arrived and the work spread to Ha'apai and Vava'u. In July 1834, a **revival** brought almost all of Vava'u into Methodism resulting from a service led by a Tongan preacher. Its impact was felt throughout Tonga in a few weeks and many converts offered to accompany missionaries to Fiji and Samoa. That "Pentecost" set a tone of urgency to extend Methodist mission to neighboring Fiji and Samoa.

A unique feature of Pacific missions was the role and function of islanders, particularly chiefs. In 1830, the ruling chief of Ha'apai, Taufa'ahau, afterward to become king of Tonga, was converted under the name George Tupou I. Ratu Seru Cacobau, the most powerful chief in Fiji at the time, shared a similar **conversion** experience in 1854. Through the example of these leaders many people openly embraced Christianity. The first missionary to Samoa was the Samoan chief Saivaaia, converted while visiting relatives in Tonga. He returned home in 1828 and invited relatives and neighbors to embrace the Tongan religion. The new "lotu" religion found favor among the chiefs and they petitioned Tonga for a European missionary.

Methodism's success was mixed with setbacks. Tongan Methodism experienced a series of divisions and splits beginning in 1885. Attempts to restore harmony and unity under royal patronage after 1918 were partly successful. Today three Methodist groups exist outside the main Free Wesleyan Church of Tonga. Fiji was challenged by the influx of Asian Indians as indentured laborers under British rule beginning in 1874. Missionaries were withdrawn from Samoa in 1839 due to an agreement made in London between the Home Mission and the London Missionary Society.

In 1855 responsibility for Pacific **missions** was handed to the newly created Australasian Methodist **Conference** (*see* AUSTRALIA; NEW ZEALAND). Fresh support of missionaries and resources enabled developments in education, publishing, and training of local teachers. Moreover, Australasia decided to reopen work in Samoa and sent Martin Dyson in 1857. As early as the 1870s, Tonga, Fiji, and Samoa sent missionary teachers to Papua New Guinea, the final frontier of mission in the Pacific, under the wise guidance of George Brown.

Autonomous conference status was achieved in all three countries—Tonga (1924), Fiji (1964), Samoa (1964)—yet they remained members of the **General Conference** of Australasian Methodism. Leadership remained under European missionaries until the three Methodist churches elected their own presidents—Tonga elected Sione Amanaki Havea (1971), Samoa chose Kamu Tagaolo (1966), while Fiji selected Setareki Tuilevoni (1964). The final break from Australasia came as that church joined the newly organized Uniting Church of Australia in 1977.

The beginning of the 20th century was marked by progress in ministries at home and the development of overseas connections. Programs in the areas of secular **education**, religious education, health, and family life highlighted the participatory role of the church in society. The church in Tonga is responsible for the secondary education of more than 60 percent of Tongan students.

While some Pacific migrants feel at home with their parent churches in New Zealand, Australia, and the **UMC**, some by consensus opted to establish Tongan, Fijian, and Samoan Methodist congregations with direct affiliation to their home church. These churches have provided environments conducive to island **worship** life as well as exchange of cultural values.

In 1987, Fiji suffered two military coups, which were important turning points in the country's political and religious history, and which left the Methodist Church with an identity crisis. Fiji's experience typifies the issues confronting Pacific churches today. Globalization versus Pacific cultural values, individual rights versus communal interests, and new religious groups versus traditional mainline churches have led to a renewed call for authentic Christian witness.

From its beginnings, Methodism was characterized by the Wesleyan emphasis on heartfelt **testimony** to the saving and sanctifying power of Christ and the **Holy Spirit** (*see* SALVATION; SANCTIFICATION). It pervaded the lives of Pacific islanders. The stress on holiness, derived from the Wesleys' evangelical revival, was manifested in a specifically Pacific way. Methodist fellowship expressed in hymns celebrating saving **grace** was woven into the fabric of Pacific Methodist culture. For them, to be Tongan, Fijian, or Samoan meant being Methodist, and being Methodist was part of being fully Tongan, Fijian, or Samoan. To recapture that spirit in this century is the mission for these Pacific trination Methodists.

Eteuati Tuioti

TRINITY, THE HOLY, the defining doctrine of orthodox Christianity, was a legacy to Methodism, part of **John Wesley**'s Anglican birthright. Its most concise statement may be found in the version of the **Articles of Religion** he authorized for his *Sunday Service of the Methodists in North America* in 1784. There, Article I, "Of Faith in the Holy Trinity," was brought over almost verbatim from the Church of England formulation. The mystery of the Three Persons in One Substance, to echo the ancient formula, has rarely been the focus of doctrinal speculation in Methodism, but the basic orthodoxy it speaks has always been woven into the tradition's more practical concern for the "order of **salvation**." Enshrined in the structure and diction of **Charles Wesley**'s hymns ("Maker, in Whom We Live" is one of the more explicit examples), it also appears in John Wesley's *Notes on the New Testament* (as in his gloss on Hebrew 9:14), and his sermon, "On the Trinity," concludes with words that similarly connect the doctrine to his evangelistic program: "I do not see how it is possible for any to have vital religion who denies that these Three are One."

British Methodists occasionally dealt theologically with the Trinity, during and after Wesley's life. **John Fletcher**, writing against Calvinism, made a Trinitarian dispensationalism part of his scheme: an age of the Father (God's Old Testament revelation to Israel), an age of the Son (inaugurated by the coming of Christ), and an age of the **Holy Spirit** (begun at Pentecost) were also seen as features that might be recapitulated in each believer's relationship to God. When **Adam Clarke**, author of the influential biblical *Commentary*, departed from Wesley on the issue of the eternal Sonship of Christ, other early-19th-century theologians took up their pens in defense of the Trinity as revealed truth, most notably Richard Watson.

American Methodist Trinitarian exposition played little part in the various denominational rivalries Methodism engaged in over the years (with the obvious exception of Deists and Unitarians), nor did it figure in any of the movements that left the **MEC**, usually not over theology, but race, polity, or **slavery**. Even the wrangling over **sanctification** did not question Methodism's basic Trinitarian assumptions.

Two exceptions have occurred at both ends of the 20th century. Early on, Borden Parker Bowne (1847–1910) developed a theology influenced by 19th-century German idealism. His thought extended the theological conversation far enough to draw a heresy charge in 1904, in part for his alleged denial of the Trinity. He was, however, acquitted by his annual **conference** and his "personalism" became the reigning theological approach within American Methodism for a generation or more.

The issue surfaced again following 1984, when the UMC Council of Bishops appointed a Committee on Our Theological Task. Part of its report, adopted at the 1988 **General Conference**, affirmed the traditional language (Father, Son, and Holy Spirit), mandating it for **ordination** services, while also retaining the possibility of the functional titles (Creator, Redeemer, Sustainer) favored by those interested in nonsexist references to God. Reinterpretation of the doctrine remains an option, but its centrality to the Methodist theological tradition seems assured. *See also* DOCTRINAL STANDARDS.

Charles Wallace, Jr.

TRUEMAN, GEORGE JOHNSTONE (January 31, 1872–February 18, 1949), Canadian educator, was born near Sackville, New Brunswick. He began his teaching career at the age of 19, initially at Upper Sackville (1891–1894), then as principal of St. Martin's Superior School (1895–1900). In 1900, he entered Mount Allison University, graduating two years later with a baccalaureate degree, followed by a master's degree in 1904. He returned to academia as principal of Charlotte County Grammar School, 1904–1905, Riverside Consolidated School, 1905–1908, and Stanstead Wesleyan College (Quebec), 1908–1920. Trueman earned a Ph.D. from Columbia University (New York) in 1919. From 1920 to 1922, he worked as an associate secretary of the Board of Education of the Methodist Church of **Canada**. In 1923, he was invited to become president of Mount Allison University, and was associated with the school for the rest of his life. During his tenure, he oversaw the university through union of the Faculty of Theology with the Presbyterian College in Halifax, the Great Depression, three fires, and the incorporation of the Ladies' College into the university. Trueman married Agnes Fawcett of Upper Sackville in 1897.

Susan E. Warrick

TUBMAN, HARRIET (ca. 1820–March 10, 1913), abolitionist leader, was born into **slavery** near Cambridge, Maryland, one of 11 children. Despite her marriage to John Tubman, a black freeman, Harriet escaped to Philadelphia in 1849. Her affiliation with the legendary Underground Railroad enabled Tubman to return 19 times to Maryland to lead about 300 slaves, including her parents, north to freedom. She became such a notorious outlaw to slaveholders that rewards for her capture amounted to $5,000. Tubman also performed notable service as a spy, scout, and nurse in the Union army during the Civil War. She helped to manumit slaves who followed her to federal military installations. Tubman secured from slaves important intelligence about the Confederacy that she reported to Union army authorities. She aided federal troops in various military ventures in South Carolina and Georgia. Later she married Nelson Davis, a black Union soldier. After much maneuvering, she ultimately convinced the federal government in 1890 to grant her a pension because of her husband's military service. Years earlier Tubman purchased land in Auburn, New York, from William Seward, Lincoln's secretary of state. She settled her parents and other family members in the home she had built. Tubman also belonged to the Thompson Memorial AMEZ. In 1903, she donated her home to the **AMEZ**.

Dennis C. Dickerson

TUNISIA. *See* AFRICA.

TURNER, HENRY MCNEAL (February 1, 1834–May 19, 1915), **AME** bishop, was born to free parents, Hardy and Sarah Turner, in Newberry, South Carolina. He joined the **MECS** in 1848 and was licensed to preach in 1853. He traveled as an evangelist until he entered the ministry of the AME in 1858. He was pastor of two congregations in Baltimore prior to a significant appointment to Israel Church in Washington, D.C. In 1863, Turner became a chaplain to black troops in the Union army. He came to Georgia after the Civil War as a Freedmen's Bureau agent, but mainly pursued politics and preaching. In 1868 he was elected to the Georgia House of Representatives, but within a short time he and other black legislators were expelled. He held other political posts in Macon and Savannah. His principal interest lay in the spread of the AME. As Georgia's AME superintendent Turner played a major role in drawing thousands of newly emancipated blacks into the denomination. In 1880 he became a bishop and presided over episcopal districts in the Northeast, the Gulf states, **Canada**, Bermuda, and other areas. In 1891 he established the denomination in Sierra Leone and Liberia (*see* AFRICA). In 1896 he led the denomination into South Africa, where it merged with the Ethiopian Church. Turner founded the *Southern Christian Recorder* (1889) and the *Voice of Missions* (1892). He was married four times, to Eliza Ann Peacher, the mother of his four children, to Martha Elizabeth DeWitt, to Harriet Wayman, and to Laura Pearl Lemon, who survived him.

Dennis C. Dickerson

– U –

UKRAINE. *See* EUROPE.

UNITED BRETHREN IN CHRIST, CHURCH OF THE (UB). The UB church's beginnings are rooted in the late-18th-century revival that occurred among the Germans of Pennsylvania, Maryland, and Virginia. Around 1767, the German Reformed pastor, **Philip William Otterbein**, and the Mennonite preacher, **Martin Boehm**, met at an evangelistic meeting held in a barn near Lancaster, Pennsylvania. Sharing the same evangelical experience, these men of diverse backgrounds embraced each other, with Otterbein exclaiming, "We are brothers." This was the beginning of the UB movement. Originally, neither Otterbein nor Boehm intended to create a new denomination, but only to revive the already-established German churches.

Along with preachers such as George Geeting and **Christian Newcomer**, the new movement gradually became more organized. In 1800 a **conference** was held near Frederick, Maryland, where Otterbein and Boehm were elected bishops and the organization officially given the name, "United Brotherhood in Christ Jesus." After their founders' deaths, the UB adopted an official **Discipline** modeled on the Methodists, and held their first **General Conference** in 1815.

As the Germans moved into the newly opened Midwest territories, UB ministers followed. Gradually, use of the English language became dominant throughout the church. Like most **revivalist** denominations, the UB emphasized zealous preaching leading to heart-felt **conversion** as the normal entrance into the Christian life. Theologically, the young church possessed Otterbein's heritage of German **Pietism**, Boehm's Mennonite tradition of a simple lifestyle, and the Arminian (*see* ARMINIUS, JACOBUS) Wesleyanism of the church's third bishop, Christian Newcomer, who was strongly influenced by Methodism. Throughout the 19th century the Wesleyan doctrine of entire **sanctification** was also popular among UB ministers. Socially, the church opposed **slavery**, the use of alcohol, and the rising popularity of secret societies, such as the Freemasons. Following the Civil War a controversy arose over the church's opposition to secret societies. This issue eventually divided the denomination in 1889 when a constitutional change allowed members of these groups to join the church. Some of those who opposed this change followed Bishop **Milton Wright**, who was a primary organizer of the breakaway Church of the **United Brethren in Christ (Old Constitution)**.

With its headquarters and publishing house located in Dayton, Ohio, the UB church continued to grow throughout the early 20th century. Foreign mission fields were located in Sierra Leone, China, Japan, Puerto Rico, and the Philippines. In 1933, the UB began formal talks with the **EC** regarding union. In 1946, the two denominations finally merged, forming the **EUB**. At the time of the merger the UB church consisted of 450,000 members. In 1968, the EUB merged with the **MC** to create the **UMC**.

Daryl M. Elliott

UNITED BRETHREN IN CHRIST (OLD CONSTITUTION). In 1889, the **UB** church had a schism over the adoption of a new confession of faith, constitution, and dropping the church's prohibition against membership in secret societies. Bishop **Milton Wright** was a primary leader of this schism. The intent of these individuals was to continue as the "true" UB church, remaining loyal to its original constitution, confession, and antisecrecy rule. Out of 200,000 UB members before 1889, only 15,000 to 20,000 sided with this "Old Constitution" movement. During the next decade, protracted legal battles occurred between these two UB churches over the ownership of church property. In most instances, the courts sided with the larger group. The "Old Constitution" United Brethren eventually established a college and a publishing house in Huntington, Indiana. Since most church buildings were lost in the courts, much money and effort was spent on rebuilding. Over the years the Church of the United Brethren in Christ (Old Constitution) faced many struggles and grew slowly. In 2003 the church consisted of about 400 churches in nine countries, with a total membership of 37,000.

Daryl M. Elliott

UNITED EVANGELICAL CHURCH. *See* EVANGELICAL ASSOCIATION/EVANGELICAL CHURCH

UNITED METHODIST CHURCH (UMC). The UMC came into being on April 23, 1968, in Dallas, Texas. It united the **MC**, formed in 1939, and the **EUB**, created in 1946. Defining itself as "a part of the Church Universal, which is one Body in Christ," it welcomes "all persons, without regard to race, color, national origin, or economic condition."

The UMC understands itself as a connection: "Our identity is in our wholeness together in Christ. Each part is vital to the whole. Our mission is more effectively carried out by a connectional life." Connectionalism, both in time and space, characterizes the denomination. MC connections with **John Wesley** and EUB connections with **Jacob Albright, Philip William Otterbein**, and **Martin Boehm** link the UMC to the 18th-century Evangelical Revival. In turn, these 18th-century spiritual leaders tie their spiritual descendants to 17th-century **Pietism** and the mainstream of 16th-century Protestantism. John Wesley, as a theologian committed to what he termed "Primitive Christianity," extended the connections back to the first five centuries, the classic period for the development of Christian **worship** and theology.

The doctrinal position of the UMC reflects these connections in time. The MC **Articles of Religion**, prepared by Wesley for the **MEC** in 1784, and the EUB Confession of Faith of 1962, constitute, along with *Wesley's Sermons, Notes Upon the New Testament,* and *General Rules*, the UMC's **doctrinal standards**. Taken together, these documents affirm the basic Christian beliefs expressed in the Apostles'

Creed and distinctive UMC emphases, such as tightly linking **faith and good works**, the **witness of the Spirit**, and **Christian perfection**. The UMC identifies its dedication to connectionalism in space by defining the annual **conferences** as "the fundamental bodies of the Church." These conferences, composed equally of lay and clergy members, connect the local UMC congregations in a particular geographical area.

Annual conference members select delegates to the jurisdictional conference for their region of the USA. These regions are northeastern, southeastern, north central, south central, and western. Delegates to the quadrennial meetings of the jurisdictional conferences elect bishops, who function as the chief executive officers of one or more annual conferences, appoint the pastors of the local churches, and serve as the denomination's principal connectors. Annual conference members also select delegates to the quadrennial **General Conference**, which has "full legislative power over all matters distinctively connectional." General Conference actions connect all the annual conferences in the United States and the annual, provisional, and missionary conferences of the worldwide UMC.

The Judicial Council connects UMC leaders, conferences, and agencies to the denomination's Constitution by ruling on the constitutionality of their acts and their conformity to General Conference legislation.

A number of general agencies provide connectional support for the ministries of conferences and churches, clergy and laity. They deal with matters such as administration, archives and history, Christian unity and interreligious concerns, colleges and universities, communications, discipleship, finance, **missions** in the USA and around the world, pensions, publishing, race, societal issues, **Sunday schools**, the status and role of **women**, theological education, and **worship**.

John G. McEllhenney

UNITED METHODIST FREE CHURCHES, the largest of the three denominations that came together in Great Britain as the United Methodist Church in 1907. As the name implies, they themselves were the product of a union of the Wesleyan Methodist Association and the Wesleyan Reformers. Negotiations were opened between the two groups in 1851, and attempts were made in 1853 to broaden them to include others. Terms of a union were finally agreed in 1856 and a uniting Assembly met at Baillie Street chapel, Rochdale, in 1857. Though the Wesleyan Methodist Association had a slight majority, the Reformer James Everett was elected president. The United Methodist Free Churches were eager for union with other liberal Methodists. Other Reform **circuits** joined individually over the next 10 to 15 years, so that the total membership grew between 1857 and 1867 from 39,968 to 67,488, with over 6,000 on trial. The distinguishing features of the United Methodist Free Churches were **circuit** autonomy and freedom to be represented in the Assembly by whichever minister or layman they elected, with only four ex officio members. This represented an attempt to unite connexionalism and Congregationalism and worked in practice. In general, the United Methodist Free Churches had all the familiar features of Methodism, such as an annual **Conference** (though called the Assembly), **circuits**, **itineracy**, and class tickets (*see* SOCIETIES, CLASSES, AND BANDS). Everett produced a denominational hymnbook, based on the Wesleyan one, with **John Wesley**'s portrait as its frontispiece. There was a *Magazine*, they published annual *Minutes of Conference*, and they started overseas **missions**. *See also* BRITISH METHODISM.

Oliver A. Beckerlegge

URUGUAY. *See* LATIN AMERICA AND THE CARIBBEAN.

– V –

VAN COTT, MARGARET ANN NEWTON (March 25, 1830–August 29, 1914), **MEC** preacher, grew up in New York City, the eldest child of a wealthy real-estate broker. She married Peter P. Van Cott in 1848 and ably managed his pharmaceutical business after he became chronically ill in 1850. They had two daughters, Rachel (who died as an infant) and Sarah Ellen Conselyea. Raised an Episcopalian, "Maggie" Van Cott had a **conversion** experience in 1857 or 1858. She began attending Methodist prayer meetings and joined the MEC in 1866, the year her husband died. That year she also began leading prayer meetings at the **Five Points Mission** in New York's slums. She was a skilled speaker, and pastors began asking her to hold **revival** meetings at their churches. In September 1868, she received an exhorter's license, and, on March 6, 1869, the quarterly **conference** of the Stone Ridge MEC (New York) granted her a local preacher's license, making her the first woman licensed to preach in the MEC. She was an immensely popular revivalist and traveled extensively throughout the USA until her retirement in 1902. She died at her home in Catskill, New York, and was buried in nearby Cairo. *See also* WOMEN.

Susan E. Warrick

VARICK, JAMES (1750?–July 22, 1827), first **AMEZ** bishop, was born in Newburgh, New York. His father, Richard Varick, was a member of a slaveholding family of Dutch heritage. His slave mother eventually gained her freedom and settled with her son in New York City. Although he became a shoemaker, how and where he gained his formal education is unclear. Either as an adolescent or as a young adult, Varick was converted and joined the **John Street MEC**. The steady increase of black members at John Street during the 1790s caused racial conflict within the congregation. In 1796 Varick joined other blacks who withdrew from the congregation to form a separate African Chapel. Varick, whose license to preach was issued sometime between 1796 and 1800, became a major ministerial spokesman for black Methodists in Manhattan. He was ordained a **deacon** on May 18, 1806, and **elder** on June 17, 1822. Growing clerical power within the MEC, the presence of Varick and other ordained preachers, and the desire of black Wesleyan groups in New York City; Long Island; New Haven, Connecticut; and Philadelphia and Easton, Pennsylvania, to unite precipitated the founding of another Wesleyan denomination, the AMEZ, on June 22, 1821. James Varick was consecrated the first bishop on July 30, 1822. Varick married Aurelia Jones in ca. 1798. They had four children, Daniel, Andrew, Emeline, and Mary.

Dennis C. Dickerson

VASEY, THOMAS (ca.1746–December 27, 1826), itinerant British Methodist preacher, was sent to America in 1784 with **Thomas Coke** and **Richard Whatcoat** to explain John Wesley's plan for American Methodism. As a youth he was the orphan ward and designated heir of a wealthy uncle who disowned him when he became a Methodist.

He began to travel as a Methodist itinerant in 1776 and was ordained by Wesley before he sailed for America with Coke and Whatcoat. He remained in America for several years and is mentioned frequently in **Francis Asbury**'s journal. Before returning to England, where he accepted a curacy with Wesley's consent, he was ordained by Bishop William White of the Protestant Episcopal Church in America. In 1789, he returned to the British Methodist **itineracy** and served in various Methodist **circuit**s for 22 years. Vasey was appointed as reader to City Road Chapel, London, where the trustees objected to the presence of any unordained person within the communion rail or the reading desk. As he aged, his reading became more indistinct, but he was looked upon as a Methodist patriarch and was greatly loved. After receiving a pension from the trustees at City Road, he retired to Leeds.

Frederick E. Maser

VAZEILLE, MARY. *See* WESLEY, MARY VAZEILLE.

VENEZUELA. *See* LATIN AMERICA AND THE CARIBBEAN.

VINCENT, JOHN HEYL (February 23, 1832–May 9, 1920) was an **MEC** pastor in northern New Jersey (1853–1857) and Illinois (1857–1866). Vincent developed "Palestine Classes," a **Sunday school** teacher training program in biblical history. In 1861, he convened the first Sunday School Teacher's Institute in America. In 1866, he became general agent of the MEC Sunday School Union and in 1868 was elected corresponding secretary. As secretary, he edited Sunday school publications and introduced a system of printing lessons as separate pages or leaves. In 1874, with Lewis Miller, he founded the **Chautauqua** (New York) Sunday-School Teachers Assembly, which soon grew into the Chautauqua movement. In 1878, Vincent launched the Chautauqua Literary and Scientific Circle, a home study course. Vincent was elected bishop in 1888. He served in Buffalo (New York), 1888–1892; Topeka (Kansas), 1893–1900; and Zurich, Switzerland (1901–1904), where he oversaw the church's European work. He retired in 1904 to Indianapolis. After the death in 1909 of his wife, Elizabeth Dusenberry, he moved to Chicago, where his son was dean of the University of Chicago. Vincent wrote, preached, and lectured extensively in retirement. He died in Chicago and was buried with his wife in Portville, New York.

Susan E. Warrick

– W –

WALKER, ALAN EDGAR (June 4, 1911–January 29, 2003), evangelist, ecumenist, and social activist, was born in Sydney, **Australia**. Son of Alfred Edgar Walker and Violet Lavis Walker, he was educated at Leigh College and ordained into the Methodist ministry in 1935. In addition to his work as a local church pastor and **circuit superintendent**, he served from 1958 to 1978 as the superintendent of the Sydney Central Methodist Mission, which he built into a significant social welfare and evangelical organization. He was director of World **Evangelism** for the **World Methodist Council** from 1978 to 1987. In 1963, Walker founded Life Line, a telephone counseling service that is now an international organization. In 1981 he was knighted by Queen Elizabeth II and five years later he and his wife, Winifred Channon Walker, received the World Methodist Peace Award from the World Methodist Council. Throughout his life, Walker was committed to evangelistic **preaching** and social action. He opposed the Vietnam War, condemned racism in Australia, challenged colonialism in the Pacific, and was twice expelled from South Africa for his anti-apartheid stance. Known around the world for his powerful preaching and effective Christian witness, Walker influenced countless men, women, and young people. *See also* ECUMENISM.

Charles Yrigoyen, Jr.

WAR AND PEACE. War and peace are social conditions marked by whether or not there is armed conflict between organized military groups. In theological terms, "peace" also refers to the ultimate harmony between God and God's creatures in which human conflict ceases. Christians have usually believed that God's will for peace imposes an obligation to work against all violence, but they have differed on how opposition to violence is to be accomplished. Pacifists hold that Christians must witness for peace by refusing to cooperate with the organized violence of war. This may involve refusing military service, or complete withdrawal from the systems of politics and government that make organized warfare possible. Other Christians believe that in a sinful world, it is sometimes necessary to use force to restrain those who would wage war. Christians who hold this belief allow participation in a "just war" which is fought to resist aggression, fought with restraints on injury to the innocent, and fought with the objective of restoring peace. Still other Christians accept military service as part of their obligation to obey secular authority. Finally, some Christians accept the possibility of legitimate grounds for war in principle, but concentrate their attention on the corrupting influence of military power, which results in many conflicts that are unnecessary and unjustified.

From the beginning of **John Wesley**'s ministry in 1739 until his 70th birthday in 1783, England was at war, mainly with France and then with England's North American colonies. He could hardly avoid pondering a Christian's duty in wartime. Yet he wrote no primer on war and peace. But from time to time, over the course of his long ministry, in sermon and essay, in tract and hymn, in private and public letter, Wesley offered counsel to his converts and advice to his king.

Wesley was ahead of his time in calling Methodists to be peacemakers. In a 1748 sermon, "Sermon on the Mount III," he asserted preservation of peace as the first duty of Christians and Christian governments as is peacemaking in times of conflict. Peacemaking is not limited by the normal boundaries of kinship, friendship, nationality, or like-minded people. Self-love is the enemy of peacemaking, and seeking the common good is essential to its meaning. In a 1757 treatise on **original sin** Wesley dealt with war's causes and condemned armed conflict as destructive to the work of God.

While Wesley wanted to see an end to all wars, he knew that wars will occur, and that, when they do, his government must exercise its responsibility under God to safeguard and defend its people. However, love remains an operative principle in war with its powerful mandate to love the enemy. During the long European wars he was active in ministry to French prisoners of war.

Although Wesley equated peacemaking with Christian vocation and declared war morally wrong, he did not insist on pacifism as the only defensible Methodist attitude toward war. Following the mainstream of western Christian ethics he affirmed some wars may be "just" as he did at the first conference of Methodist preachers in 1744. While Wesley commended soldiers like John Haime, recruited young men to enlist, and preached and prayed with troops wherever he could, he also supported the persecuted pacifist preacher John Nelson. Conscientious objection as well as active soldiering are compatible with Wesleyan teaching.

Wesley's own preference is the just war ethic, though not a martial, nationalistic, crusading spirit. However, his just war position is not morally binding on Methodists. The clear inference is that he placed attitudes toward war in the category of opinions on which Christians may differ sincerely, not in the category of dogmatic truths of the Christian faith.

Wesley certainly believed that the power of government to restrain evil by force is an authority granted by God, but he also criticized political pride, pomp, and waste of wealth by those in authority. Methodists have been prominent in antiwar movements and in humanitarian relief for the victims of war, but Methodists have also served as military chaplains, ordinary soldiers, and military leaders.

The Social Principles of the UMC declare that war is incompatible with the teachings and example of Christ. The Social Principles place a primary moral obligation on nations to resolve their disputes without resort to armed conflict, but no explicit statement is made on how individual Christians are to live out this commitment to peace, or how they are to relate to their governments when efforts toward peace are not forthcoming.

In recent years, much attention has been focused on the problem of nuclear weapons of mass destruction, and on the strategy of deterrence, which attempted to secure peace by threatening any power that initiated a nuclear war with complete devastation of its economic capacity and social structure. With the end of the era of deterrence between the USA and the former Soviet Union, the problem of war has shifted to smaller regional wars, including civil conflicts within nations. These wars pose difficult moral problems because they often result from claims of oppression and violation of rights, and because they are difficult to control and bring to resolution. The need to care for the victims of such wars remains an important humanitarian concern.

Robin W. Lovin and Kenneth E. Rowe

WARD, HARRY F. (October 15, 1873–December 1966), was an **MEC** minister, educator, and **human rights** activist. Born in England, Ward graduated from Northwestern University (B.A. 1987), Harvard (M.A. 1898) and Wisconsin University (LL.D. 1931). He was a pastor to immigrants and laborers in Chicago's slums (1900–1913). Ward co-founded the Methodist Federation for Social Service (MFSS, 1907). He wrote its **Social Creed**, adopted by the MEC and Federal Council of Churches in 1908, which defended rights of workers. Ward taught Christian Ethics at Boston University School of Theology (1913–1917) and Union Theological Seminary (1918–1941) while serving as executive secretary for the MFSS (1911–1944). During and between major USA labor disputes, Ward built labor and religious coalitions that transcended race, class, party, and faith in pursuit of social equality. A prodigious **social gospel** author, Ward founded and chaired the American Civil Liberties Union (1919–1940) to defend civil liberties not as personal rights but as the essential vehicle for social change. Ward organized the American League Against War and Fascism; the New America movement (1933–1938), which anticipated a breakdown of capitalism and sought to replace it peacefully with a planned social economy rooted in economic democracy; and the Religious Freedom Committee. Denied recognition in official denominational circles, Ward was labeled a Communist and pursued by the FBI.

Alice G. Knotts

WARE, THOMAS (December 19, 1758–March 11, 1842), a leader of early American Methodism, was born in Greenwich, New Jersey. His mother adhered firmly to the doctrine that God selects some persons for heaven and damns others to hell. His father, though devout, could not believe in an arbitrary God. Ware himself became convinced that Christ died for all. He served briefly as a soldier in the American Revolution, took a longer time to recuperate from "camp fever," and found spiritual peace when he was 21 through the preaching of Caleb

Pedicord, a Methodist itinerant. **Francis Asbury** validated Ware's readiness to challenge young people to face their lack of spiritual purpose by appointing him in 1783 to the Dover, Delaware, **Circuit.** Between then and his retirement in 1826, he traveled preaching circuits and functioned as a **presiding elder** in Maryland, New Jersey, New York, Massachusetts, Vermont, Tennessee, Virginia, North Carolina, and Pennsylvania. While supervising the Philadelphia District, he married Barbary Miller in 1797. They had four children. Ware attended the 1784 **Christmas Conference** and left an account of it in his *Sketches,* first published in 1839. From 1812 to 1816, he and Daniel Hitt directed the MEC's publishing enterprises.

John G. McEllhenney

WATCH-NIGHT. It was almost certainly late in the evening of Friday, March 12, 1742, at Kingswood on the outskirts of Bristol, England, that **John Wesley** engaged in his first British watch-night. His journal records, "Our Lord was gloriously present with us at the watch-night, so that my voice was lost in the cries of the people. After midnight about an hundred of us walked home together, singing and rejoicing and praising God." When he had arrived in Bristol from Wales the previous weekend he had been informed that several members had "spent the greater part of the night in prayer and praise and thanksgiving," and some thought that he should put an end to it. Thinking it over carefully, and realizing that the vigils held by the ancient Christians on the eve of some festivals had sometimes been mishandled, he publicly announced a watch-night near the full moon, when he himself would preach, and described the occasion in his *Plain Account of the People Called Methodists.* "Abundance of people came. I began preaching between eight and nine, and we continued till a little beyond the noon of night, singing, praying, and praising God." On April 9 he held the first watch-night in London, and it soon became fairly common in most larger cities on the Friday nearest to the full moon from about 8:30 pm till just after midnight. Watch-nights were introduced into America by **Joseph Pilmore** in Philadelphia and New York in 1770, but here, as also in England, New Year's Eve became a favored occasion, sometimes associated with the Covenant Service.

Frank Baker

WAUGH, BEVERLY (ca. October 25, 1789–February 9, 1858), 11th bishop of the **MEC**, was born in Fairfax County, Virginia. Waugh joined the Baltimore **Conference** in 1809 and served as a **circuit** rider and **presiding elder** for 19 years. He was elected assistant book agent for the church in 1828, book agent in 1832, and bishop on the first ballot at the 1836 **General Conference**. From 1852 he was the church's senior bishop. During the **MP** movement Waugh at first favored the election of presiding elders but did not continue in reform sympathy. Though personally opposed to **slavery**, he used his presiding power to squelch abolitionist resolutions in his annual conferences. He tried to avoid MEC schism in 1844 by urging deferral of the case of Bishop **James O. Andrew**. When division came Waugh remained with the MEC. Waugh traveled the whole church, working diligently in the itinerant general superintendency pattern of **Francis Asbury**. Waugh and Catharine B. Bushby married in 1812. Waugh died in Baltimore and is interred in Mount Olivet Cemetery with Bishops **Francis Asbury**, **Enoch George**, and **John Emory**.

Charles W. Brockwell, Jr.

WEALTH. John Wesley provided spiritual **disciplines** that had the unintended effect of making those who practiced them better off financially. Understanding money's tendency to corrupt spirituality, he admonished his Methodist people, after meeting the basic needs of their families and perhaps capitalizing a business, to return to God the remainder of their income through relieving the distress of the poor. No matter how ardently Wesley admonished his followers, he found himself admitting that Methodism's disciplines made people moderately well off, which, in the natural order of things, vitiated Methodism's spiritual dynamic. Wesley's uneasy conscience about money remained a constant of Methodist history. But defying Wesley's injunction to build preaching-houses that were "not more expensive than is absolutely unavoidable," lest "the necessity of raising money will make rich men necessary," Methodists treasured rich members who helped pay for grand edifices. An occasional voice, such as that of **Benjamin T. Roberts**, declared that the poor, Wesley's chief concern, felt unwelcome in buildings where the wealthy adorned the best pews and treated the poor "as objects of charity, rather than equals." Wesley's uneasiness with money resurfaced in the **social gospel** and the **Social Creed**. His misgivings are reflected in the **UMC**'s Social Principles in the 21st century.

John G. McEllhenney

WEATHERHEAD, LESLIE DIXON (October 14, 1893–January 3, 1976), British Methodist preacher and author, was born in London, educated in Leicester, and Cliff and Richmond Colleges, leaving early to become probationer Methodist minister in Surrey. He served as army chaplain in Mesopotamia and India, where he stayed until returning to Britain in 1922. His reputation as a preacher took him to two center city churches, Oxford Road in Manchester (1922–1925) and Brunswick in Leeds (1925–1936), where he exercised a vigorous ministry attracting large crowds. For the rest of his ministry, he served as minister of the City Temple Church, London, outside the Methodist connection. His interest in psychology, in spiritual healing, and in pacifism (*see* WAR AND PEACE) attracted critics as well as admirers, with some accusing him of heresy. At Leeds and London he established clinics pioneering the involvement of the church in counseling and addressing the taboos surrounding sexuality. His London Ph.D. thesis was published in 1951 as *Psychology, Religion, and Healing*. Despite opposition, Weatherhead was elected **Conference** president in 1955. Much in demand as a lecturer, broadcaster, and preacher, for which he was made a Commander, Order of the British Empire in 1959, he remained a controversial figure to the end with the publication of his last book in 1965, *The Christian Agnostic*.

Tim Macquiban

WEBB, THOMAS (1724–December 10, 1796), soldier and Methodist preacher, was born in England and rose to the ranks of quartermaster and then lieutenant in the British army. He fought in the French and Indian War, losing his right eye and suffering a serious arm wound at Quebec in September 1759. Returning to England to retire on captain's pay, Webb came under the influence of **John Wesley**, converted to Methodism, and proved a capable substitute lay preacher. Webb returned to America in 1766 in the employ of the barrackmaster at Albany, New York. He began to appear, in full military uniform and sword, at Methodist meetings in New York City, proclaiming himself a soldier of the cross and a spiritual son of Wesley. For the next 16 years, Webb remained in America, initially assisting **Philip Embury**. His name appeared first on the subscription list for the building (in 1768) of Wesley Chapel, where he preached the dedicatory sermon from a pulpit built by his own hands. Afterward he preached in Burlington, New Jersey; Long Island, New York; Philadelphia; and Baltimore. Webb journeyed to England in 1772–1773. When he returned to America later in 1773, he did so in the company of **Thomas Rankin** and **George Shadford**, two assistants whom Wesley had assigned to preach in the American colonies. At some point during the American Revolution (perhaps 1783), Webb returned to England, residing in Bristol and continuing to work for Methodism. He died suddenly at Bristol, with burial in Portland Street Chapel.

Samuel J. Rogal

WELSH CALVINISTIC METHODISM (or Presbyterian Church of Wales) was established as a result of the **revival** activities of **Howell Harris**, Daniel Rowland, and other Welsh revivalists who during the 18th century gave Welsh Methodism its distinctive Calvinistic inclination. The Calvinists at Watford near Caerphilly held the first joint association meeting in 1743, the year before **John Wesley**'s first **Conference**. Despite pressure from many within the movement, the early leaders resisted calls for secession from the Established Church, and this remained the general policy until the end of the 18th century. Uneasy relations between Harris and Rowland reached a climax in the disruption of 1750. Many of Harris's followers joined the Rowland camp, Harris withdrew to Trevecka, and the movement suffered a setback for some years.

Following the pioneering work of the early itinerant preachers in north Wales, further advances were made in the area through the labors of Thomas Charles of Bala who joined the Methodists in 1784, but, as persecution increased in the 1790s, preachers were forced to seek the protection of the Toleration Act, thus becoming dissenters. Full secession followed in 1811 when **ordination**s were held at Bala in the north and Llandeilo in the south. A Confession of Faith based on the Westminster Confession was drawn up in 1823 and the Constitutional Deed was completed in 1826. In 1840 a missionary society was established to work in India; missionaries were also sent to Brittany early in the 20th century. Colleges for the training of ministers were established at Bala in 1837, Trevecka in 1842, and Aberystwyth in 1906. Theological training is currently conducted at Aberystwyth, while Bala and Trevecka are mainly used for youth and lay activities.

In 1919, a reconstruction Commission was inaugurated to streamline and modernize the constitution. A *Shorter Declaration of Faith* was published in 1921, but the 1823 Confession was retained as an historical document. The Calvinistic Methodist or Presbyterian Church of Wales Act 1933 created a legal identity for the church and gave equal standing to the two titles by which it is commonly known. By 1995, it consisted of 939 churches (of which 219 were English), employed 119 full-time ministers, and had 51,720 members. *See also* BRITISH METHODISM.

Geraint Tudur

WESLEY, CHARLES (December 18, 1707–March 29, 1788), was the youngest son of **Samuel Wesley**, rector of Epworth, Lincolnshire, England, and his wife **Susanna**. He was brother of their oldest son Samuel and of **John**, five years older than Charles. All three, like their father, were ordained clergymen of the Church of England. The two younger brothers, to the distress of the oldest, who died in 1739, collaborated in raising a separate evangelical society within the Church.

The Wesleys' large family included seven girls who grew to maturity. Susanna Wesley gave all her children a sound biblical, moral, and theological training, while the sons went on to Christ Church, Oxford, and graduated M.A. In 1716, Charles entered Westminster School (annexed to Westminster Cathedral), where he became captain, and, under the eye of his oldest brother, Samuel, imbibed a strong churchmanship, a love of Greek and Roman classics, and a skill in translating their verse.

Charles matriculated at Christ Church in 1726 and was elected Student in 1727, his brother John having been elected to a similar position as Fellow of Lincoln College, Oxford. On January 22, 1729, Charles wrote to John: "God has thought fit to deny me at present your company and assistance. 'Tis through your means, I firmly believe, God will establish what He has begun in me, and there is no one person I would so willingly have to be the instrument of Good to me as you." Henceforth Charles constantly kept his finger on his spiritual pulse, maintained a diary, "went to the weekly **Sacrament**, and persuaded two or three young scholars to accompany" him, thus gaining "the harmless nickname of Methodist."

Charles joined John's mission to Georgia on October 14, 1735, to serve Governor James Edward Oglethorpe as "secretary for Indian Affairs," but in order to assist John he also accepted **ordination** as priest by the bishop of London on September 29. His narrow piety satisfied neither him nor Oglethorpe, nor his parishioners, and through lying on the bare ground he contracted dysentery and fever. After less than six months, on July 26 he was happy to escape "such a scene of sorrows" to England (via Charleston and Boston) bearing Oglethorpe's dispatches to the Georgia trustees in London.

Although Charles Wesley was a born preacher and a born hymn writer, neither gift was realized until his **conversion** on May 21, 1738. He borrowed some of John's sermons to preach in Georgia, and did not add anything to his brother's *Collection of Psalms and Hymns* in Charleston, 1737. Like his brother John he had been awestruck by the vivid personal **faith** of the **Moravians** who sailed with them to Georgia, and both he and John (who returned to England on February 1, 1738) became disciples of **Peter Böhler**, a Moravian missionary awaiting passage to Georgia. Böhler warned both Anglican priests that God's **salvation** from sin did not come from right belief or devout **worship**, but from simple faith in God. This Charles found on May 21, 1738, which was for him (as Charles wrote bold script in his diary), "The Day of Pentecost." Two days later he composed his first evangelical hymn. On the following evening his journal proclaimed from his sickroom in Little Britain, London: "Toward ten my brother was brought in triumph by a troop of our friends and declared, 'I believe!' We sang the hymn with great joy, and parted with a prayer."

Charles Wesley's great gifts were at last set free. Frequently in those early days he would preach in the open air to a spellbound crowd gathered by his rich voice singing one of his own hymns. The magnificent blossoming of his evangelical hymns began in 1739, with the joint publication of three editions of *Hymns and Sacred Poems* by the two brothers. By 1746, John and Charles had jointly published some 500 of the "classical hymns" of Methodism, with a slight admixture of writings by others. Unquestionably the vast majority were by Charles, though literary sleuths still enjoy the whodunit, "John or Charles?" These printed books also enriched people's devotions and theology. In fact it is debatable whether the Methodist public were more aroused and informed by their sermons or their hymns. Nor did Charles ever stop. For the next 50 years from 1739 to his death in 1788 he produced about 180 hymns a year.

It was on a preaching mission (to **Ireland**) that Charles Wesley fell deeply in love with a charming Welsh girl, Sarah Gwynne (*see* WESLEY, SARAH GWYNNE). He was 39, she 20. After a toilsome romance, punctuated by love poems later transformed to hymns, they were married by brother John on April 8, 1749. Three of their children survived: Charles (1757–1834), Sarah (1759–1828), and Samuel (1766–1837). Both boys were musical prodigies, feted by royalty. Samuel introduced Johann Sebastian Bach to the British public, and he fathered the great church musician, Samuel Sebastian Wesley (1810–1876).

Charles disagreed strongly with his brother John over many things. He broke up John's legal "spousal" to **Grace Murray**, thus hastening him into the jealous arms of Mary Vazeille (*see* WESLEY, MARY VAZEILLE). He raised successful opposition against the lay itinerant preachers who sought to administer the sacraments, and, in 1784, sarcastically bemoaned John's securing ordination via Dr. **Thomas Coke** for the American preachers (*see* EPISCOPACY). Yet he remained an almost silent partner in the evangelical enterprise of John, whose tribute at his death was, "his least praise was his talent for poetry."

Frank Baker

WESLEY, JOHN (June 17, 1703–March 2, 1791), the founder of the Methodist movement within the Church of England, was born in Epworth, England, the second surviving son of **Susanna** and **Samuel Wesley**, who provided his early training in learning and religion. Charterhouse School in London (1713–1720) prepared him for Christ Church, Oxford, where he received his baccalaureate degree in 1724.

Wesley's vocational interests at the university led him to seek **ordination** as **deacon** in 1725 and as priest in 1728, as well as a fellowship at Lincoln College in 1726. At the same time, he became more serious about religion and learning, and began to preach in many churches in and around Oxford, as well as in his father's parish.

Wesley's developing concern for holy living was soon shared by his brother **Charles** and some of their friends, who began to gather around John to share his vision of the Christian life, best typified as "meditative piety." He began to form small societies at Oxford to promote his view of holy living, a development he later called "the first rise of Methodism."

Going then as a volunteer missionary and priest to the new colony in Georgia at the end of 1735, Wesley hoped to preach to the Indians but spent most of his time serving the needs of parishioners in Savannah and Frederica. The establishment of Methodist societies there he later called "the second rise of Methodism."

Upon his return to England in 1738, he helped form, with the **Moravian**, **Peter Böhler**, a religious society at Fetter Lane, London, which he later called "the third rise of Methodism." Under Böhler's tutelage, Wesley experienced, on May 24, 1738, an **assurance** of faith, which he had been seeking for years as the hallmark of the **Christian experience**.

Wesley's adoption of the Moravians' radical emphasis upon faith caused him to be excluded from many of the pulpits in the land. Wesley therefore followed the suggestion of his friend **George Whitefield** and, in Bristol in April 1739, he began to preach outdoors. This practice of **field preaching** served to invest the Methodist revival with new vitality and allowed Wesley to preach his message of **justification** by faith to vast crowds that included many unchurched people.

His constant concern, however, was to provide opportunities for Christian growth and nurture (**sanctification**) for those who were moved by the **Holy Spirit** during the **preaching**. This emphasis caused him to split from the Moravians and to further refine his theology. Wesley enhanced the combination of **evangelism** and nurture through the widespread formation of Methodist societies, which provided for fellowship and discipline within the movement, especially through small groups called bands and classes (*see* SOCIETIES, CLASSES, AND BANDS). John joined with his brother, Charles, to write and publish many of the poems which, when put to tunes, helped to popularize the use of hymns in religious services, thereby providing a vehicle for spreading Wesleyan ideas among the populace.

He kept in touch with his expanding movement by constantly traveling throughout the British Isles, by maintaining a voluminous correspondence, and by producing a virtual library of literary resources for his people. Indefatigable, Wesley traveled about 250,000 miles by horse, preached nearly 50,000 times, and produced over 400 publications during his 66-year ministry. The sale of his many publications provided substantial support for many of the Methodist charitable programs.

The Wesleyan movement ministered largely to the poor and disenfranchised working classes. To help these people in his societies, he raised money and collected clothing. He started the first free medical dispensary in London. He gave loans to start small businesses and provided subsidized housing for widows and orphans. He visited prisoners and supported **education** in charity schools. Wesley made extensive use of lay persons as leaders within the growing network of societies throughout the land, relying upon **lay preachers**, band and class leaders, visitors of the sick, stewards, trustees, and others, to fulfill the purpose for which he understood God had raised them up: "to spread scriptural holiness throughout the land."

In order to maintain a high degree of doctrinal and procedural uniformity within the movement, Wesley in the 1740s began to gather many of his preachers together yearly for a **conference**, a gathering that eventually was legally established to provide leadership of the movement after his death. In the meantime, Wesley did not hesitate to produce sets of rules and guidelines for his preachers and people.

Among the works that appeared were the collected sermons in his *Sermons on Several Occasions*, which contained what he felt to be the "essential doctrines." His preachers were required to preach no other doctrines than those contained therein and in his Bible commentary, *Explanatory Notes upon the New Testament*.

Although he constantly claimed unity with the Church of England and uniformity with its Thirty-Nine Articles (*see* ARTICLES OF RELIGION), Book of Common Prayer, and Book of Homilies, Wesley emphasized three points as the "grand doctrines" of Methodism (*see* DOCTRINAL STANDARDS): **repentance**, which he called the "porch" of religion; justification by faith, the "door" of religion; and sanctification or holiness, "religion itself." His mature theology, focused on soteriology (the *via salutis*), is the reflection of his lifelong spiritual pilgrimage and is perhaps best exemplified in his sermon, "The Scripture Way of **Salvation**" (1767). Scriptural themes, imagery, and language are the sum and substance of most of his rhetoric. All of his homiletical endeavors were aimed toward the application of the gospel message of faith working through love in the lives of Christians everywhere.

Contemporaries differed in their perspective on Wesley, their view typically determined by whether or not they agreed with his theology. By most accounts, he was not an impressive orator. Nevertheless, Wesley reflected in his person many of the ideals he preached, such that a Swedish visitor who heard Wesley preach in 1769 remarked, "He is the personification of piety, and he seems to me as a living representative of the loving Apostle John."

Wesley died in his 88th year. His obituary in the *Gentleman's Magazine* noted that he was "one of the few characters who outlived enmity and prejudice, and received, in his latter years, every mark of respect from every denomination," and added that "he must be considered as one of the most extraordinary characters this or any age ever produced."

Richard P. Heitzenrater

WESLEY, MARY VAZEILLE (1710–October 1781), as a 41-year-old Methodist widow of a London merchant, nursed **John Wesley** in her home after he slipped on icy London Bridge and injured his foot. The accident occurred less than two years after the forced breakup of his relationship with **Grace Murray**, his best prospect for anything approaching marital happiness. Soon thereafter, on February 17 or 18, 1751, the two were married. The alliance was not a good one. Her unwillingness to itinerate with her husband and his refusal to reduce his travels to accommodate the marriage set the stage. The action was provided by his affectionate correspondence with a number of Methodist women and her consequent jealousy. Quarrels, sometimes violent on her side and always detached on his, led finally to her leaving, beginning in 1757. The laconic Latin response in his journal was

"Non eam reliqui; non dimisi; non revocabo (I have not left her; I have not sent her away; I will not call her back)." She died in October 1781 and was buried in south London before Wesley was informed. Contrary to her many Methodist detractors, her tombstone extols "a woman of exemplary piety, a tender parent and a sincere friend."

Charles Wallace, Jr.

WESLEY, SAMUEL (ca. December 17, 1662–April 25, 1735), Anglican clergyman, poet, biblical scholar, and father of **John** and **Charles Wesley**, was born at Winterbourne Whitchurch, near Blandford, Dorset. In March 1678, after attending the Dorchester Grammar School of Henry Dolling, he proceeded to London, there to be educated for the ministry in an Independent school operated by Theophilus Gale. Having arrived after Gale's death, young Wesley continued his education under Edward Veal (or Veel) at Stepney, followed, in 1680, by further studies at the Newington Green academy of Charles Morton. Daniel Defoe may well have been one of his Dissenter schoolmates.

Wesley's literary career began at Newington Green, where he penned lampoons against the government, the church, and the nearby Presbyterian academy of Thomas Doolittle. On November 18, 1684, Wesley entered Exeter College, Oxford, graduating BA on June 19, 1688. While still an undergraduate, in 1685 he published, anonymously and under the imprint of John Dunton, a volume of poems entitled *Maggots*, dedicated to Dolling. In 1688, to honor the birth of the Pretender (James Francis Edward Stuart), he contributed verses to *Strenae Natalitiae Academiae Oxoniensis*.

During his final year at Oxford, Wesley abandoned the Nonconformist views of his father and embraced the Church of England. On August 7, 1688, Bishop Thomas Sprat ordained him **deacon**, and on February 24, 1690, he received **ordination** as priest. Prior to his marriage in 1689 to the 20-year-old Susanna Annesley (*see* WESLEY, SUSANNA), Wesley served curacies in London and a term as a chaplain aboard a man-of-war. In February 1690, he received the living at South Ormsby, Lincolnshire, a parish of 36 houses and 260 inhabitants. His literary efforts focused upon assisting Dunton with the *Athenian Gazette* and the publication of *The Life of Our Blessed Lord* *and Saviour Jesus Christ* (1693), an heroic poem in 10 books and dedicated to Queen Mary. In 1694, he received the M.A. from Cambridge, followed by his dismissal from South Ormsby for refusing to allow James Saunderson's mistress in his church. Then, in 1695, came an appointment to Epworth, Lincolnshire, that living being combined with neighboring Wroote in 1723. There he would remain, writing and attempting to sustain a wife and 19 children (eight of whom died in infancy).

In addition to his miscellaneous occasional verse and sermons, he wrote a controversial tract on the *Education of Dissenters in Their Private Academies* (1703, published anonymously and without his knowledge) and, in verse, *The History of the Old and New Testament* (1704). However, he devoted most of his time to 53 treatises on the book of Job, published posthumously in 1735 and 1736 as *Dissertationes in Librum Jobi*. The author considered almost every critical question or problem associated with the Old Testament book, collating the original Hebrew text with Greek and Latin versions.

On June 4, 1731, Wesley suffered severe injuries when he was thrown from a wagon, and his last years proved difficult. He died at Epworth, severely in debt, but knowing that his sons had established themselves firmly in the Church he had served for so long. His remains lie in Epworth churchyard.

Samuel J. Rogal

WESLEY, SARAH GWYNNE (October 12, 1726–December 28, 1822), wife of **Charles Wesley**, was born in Garth, Breconshire, Wales, to Marmaduke Gwynne and Sarah Evans Gwynne. The Gwynnes were friendly to early Methodist **preaching**, and especially to Charles Wesley who met and fell in love with their daughter although she was 19 years younger. Before Charles was permitted to marry Sarah, he was required to show her family that he was financially able to support her. Finally satisfied that Charles could provide for their daughter, the family gave their blessing to Sarah and Charles, who were married by **John Wesley** on April 8, 1749. Following their **marriage**, Charles and Sarah moved to Bristol, where they lived happily despite periods of Charles's absence for his itinerant preaching and pastoral duties in the Methodist movement. Eight children were born to their marriage, five of whom died in infancy and three of whom, Charles, Jr. (1757–1834), Sarah (1759–1828), and Samuel (1766–1837), moved with their parents to London in 1771. Charles's wife was a constant support throughout his ministry. Considerable extant manuscript correspondence between Charles and Sarah provides important insights into their relationship and family life. Sarah Wesley died in London and is buried near her husband in the old St. Marylebone churchyard.

Charles Yrigoyen, Jr.

WESLEY, SUSANNA ANNESLEY (January 20, 1669–July 23, 1742), wife of **Samuel Wesley** the elder and mother of **John** and **Charles Wesley** (as well as 17 other children), was born in Spittal Yard, London, the youngest daughter and the 22nd of the 24 children sired by the noted Nonconformist minister Samuel Annesley (ca.1620–1696). Despite her **Puritan** upbringing, she familiarized herself, at an early age, with the controversies between the Church of England and Nonconformity. In 1682, at age 13, in the year her older sister, Elizabeth (d.1697), married the bookseller John Dunton, Susanna determined to cast her theological lot with the Church of England.

Seven years later, in 1689, 20-year-old Susanna Annesley wed Samuel Wesley, seven years her senior and holder of a curacy in London. The couple spent their first 18 months of married life in the capital, where their first son, Samuel, was born on February 10, 1690. That August, Wesley received the living of South Ormsby, Lincolnshire. During the seven years there, Susanna gave birth to six additional children: Susanna (b.1691) and the twins, Annesley and Jedediah (b.1694), who died in infancy; Mary (b.1696), who reached the age of 38, while Emilia (b.1692) and Susanna (b.1695) survived to ages 79 and 68, respectively. After the Wesleys settled into the rectory at Epworth, 12 more children followed: an unidentified child (b.1698), the elder John (b.1699), Benjamin (b.1700), unnamed twins (b.1701), and an unnamed son (accidentally smothered by a nurse) never survived beyond infancy; Mehetabel (1697–1750), John (1703–1791), Martha (1706–1791), and Charles (1707–1788) led full if not always comfortable lives; Anne (b.1702) lived at least until 1742, while Keziah (1709–1741), the last of the brood, died not having married.

Susanna Wesley's most significant contribution to the history of Methodism assumed the form of the education and training of her children, tasks abdicated to her by her husband's continued literary preoccupations and fiscal struggles. During the first three months of each child's life, she set fixed times for dressing, changing of clothes, setting in the cradle, and rocking to sleep. She taught them to respect her wishes, to expect punishment when earned, and to cry softly. The family dinner table provided another view of household regularity; the child came to the table as soon as he or she could wield a knife and fork. Susanna taught her children to ask quietly for anything that they wanted and to eat everything that she provided them. She tolerated no eating or drinking between meals. Evening prayers came at 6:00, followed by supper. She put the youngest child in bed by 7:00 and the eldest by 8:00.

Susanna also conducted her children's religious training, which included proper prayers, blessings, collects, catechism, and scripture. She began to work with each child after he or she had reached the age of five years, teaching numbers and letters within the first two days. She taught them to spell and to read lines and then complete verses from scripture. The Epworth parsonage school day consisted of two sessions: from 9:00 am until noon, then from 2:00 to 5:00. They filled the remaining hours with household chores. Susanna Wesley died in London, with her body laid to rest in Bunhill Fields.

Samuel J. Rogal

WESLEYAN CHURCH, an evangelical denomination in the holiness tradition, was formed by the merger of the Wesleyan Methodist Church and the Pilgrim Holiness Church. The Wesleyan Methodist Church was established as a result of controversy in the **MEC** over two issues: slaveholding and the power wielded by the church's hierarchy. During the 1830s and early 1840s, many Methodist ministers and lay people became strongly committed to the abolition of chattel **slavery**, both within the denomination and within the larger civil society. These abolitionists agitated for **antislavery** reform at various annual **conferences** and at the **General Conferences** of 1836 and 1840, but were stymied by the ecclesiastical authorities in their efforts to effect significant change in church policy. Consequently, several prominent Methodist abolitionists from New England and upstate

New York, particularly **Orange Scott, Luther Lee**, and **Lucius C. Matlack**, seceded from the MEC and organized the Wesleyan Methodist Connection (later called "Church") in Utica, New York, in 1843. The new denomination was opposed to "slavery and **episcopacy**." The popularity of the Wesleyan Methodist secession threatened to disrupt the entire MEC in the North. This threat forced northern Methodist leaders to assume a more definitive antislavery stance, and thus played an important part in the 1844 split between northern and southern Methodists.

In 1867, following the constitutional abolition of slavery, and after a failed attempt to unite the Wesleyan Methodist Church with the **MP**, a large number of Wesleyan Methodists returned to the MEC. The remaining portion of the Wesleyan Methodist denomination coalesced around themes that were prevalent in the emerging **holiness movement**, particularly the promotion of the doctrine of entire **sanctification** and the rejection of worldliness. By worldliness, the Wesleyans referred to certain current trends within the American church such as an increase in formalized **worship**, the use of alcohol or tobacco, the wearing of ornate apparel, attendance at theaters and dance halls, and membership in secret societies (such as the Masons).

It was during this period in the late 19th century that the formative strands of the Pilgrim Holiness Church began to arise. MEC preacher Martin Wells Knapp and **Quaker** preacher Seth C. Rees co-founded the International Holiness and Prayer League in 1897 as an informal evangelistic association. An increasing sense of alienation from mainline Methodism and a growing denominational consciousness encouraged the members of the league to organize an independent church body, which banded together with six other small holiness groups to form the Pilgrim Holiness Church in 1922. The Pilgrims were noted for their emphasis on premillennialism and the doctrine of divine healing as well as entire sanctification.

The Wesleyan Methodist and Pilgrim Holiness churches united in June 1968 as the Wesleyan Church, a denomination that is related to other evangelical groups by its membership in the National Association of Evangelicals. The Wesleyan Church maintains several liberal arts colleges, including Houghton College in New York, Central College in South Carolina, and Indiana Wesleyan University. From their headquarters in Indianapolis, the Wesleyans coordinate an extensive **missions** program. Worldwide membership in 2003 was 300,000, with a constituency of 700,000.

Douglas M. Strong

WHATCOAT, RICHARD (February 23, 1736–July 5, 1806), **MEC** bishop, was born in Gloucestershire, England of Anglican parents. Converted in 1758 under Methodist preaching, he became a class leader (*see* SOCIETIES, CLASSES, AND BANDS) and steward at Wednesbury, where he experienced **sanctification** in 1761. Admitted to the **Conference** in 1769, he served Oxford and Bedford **Circuits** and then was assigned to northern **Ireland**. After a critical illness in Ireland, he was reappointed to easier duties in Wales, Cornwall, and Salisbury. Whatcoat agreed to come to America with **Thomas Coke**, was ordained, and assisted at the **Christmas Conference**. He was a traveling companion to **Francis Asbury**. Wesley instructed Coke to convene a 1787 **General Conference** to appoint Whatcoat a **Superintendent**. Thinking that Wesley might recall Asbury, the Americans retaliated by omitting Wesley's name from their Minutes, but Whatcoat was elected bishop in 1800 in preference to **Jesse Lee**. Thereafter, he and Asbury traveled widely. Incessant labor weakened Whatcoat by 1803, but the infirm bishop resumed an itinerant ministry in 1804. Whatcoat is buried in Dover, Delaware.

Edwin Schell

WHITE, MOSES CLARK (July 24, 1819–October 24, 1900), first **MEC** missionary to China (*see* ASIA), was born in Paris, Oneida County, New York. White was educated at Wesleyan University, Connecticut, and Yale Divinity School. After being received on trial as a member of the New York Annual **Conference**, White was appointed in 1847 to be a missionary to China. In the same year he married Jane Isabel Atwater, who had also dedicated her life to missionary service. The Whites arrived in Foochow in September 1847. White remained in China until 1853 managing a medical dispensary in Foochow and translating the Gospel of St. Matthew into the Chinese dialect of the area. After his return to the USA in 1853 he received a medical degree from Yale University and practiced medicine in New Haven, Connecticut. He also served on the faculties of Yale University and Wesleyan University, Connecticut.

Charles Yrigoyen, Jr.

WHITEFIELD, GEORGE (December 27, 1714–September 30, 1770), transatlantic **revivalist**, was born and raised in a tavern in Gloucester, England. Though descended from a respected ancestral line of gentlemen clergy, Whitefield's immediate family was not socially well placed. His mother had in mind a greater destiny than innkeeping for her youngest child, and she hoped that her high aspirations for him would be fulfilled in a clerical career. Toward that end, Whitefield was encouraged to pursue his primary education at the nearby parish school. In 1732, he was able to gain admittance to Pembroke College, Oxford. Whitefield's attendance at Oxford was financially possible because he agreed to be a "servitor," a poor student who acted as a servant for wealthier students.

While at Oxford, Whitefield made the acquaintance of **Charles Wesley**. At that time, Charles, his brother John, and several other Oxonians were meeting together regularly in a small group for mutual accountability in disciplined holy living. The "Methodists" (as the members of this so-called Holy Club were nicknamed) encouraged rigorous self-examination through daily **prayer** and scripture reading, weekly reception of the **eucharist**, regular **fasting**, almsgiving, and deeds of charity. Whitefield's participation in the ascetic program of the Methodists fanned his religious interests. While back in Gloucester for a visit in the spring of 1735, he experienced the "**new birth**" in Christ, a subjective sense of personal piety expressed in a datable **conversion**. Within weeks, Whitefield was sharing with others about their need for the new birth experience. The **preaching** of this evangelical message soon became the centerpiece of Whitefield's vocation.

After his 1736 graduation from Oxford and his **ordination** as a **deacon** in the Church of England, Whitefield was persuaded by the Wesley brothers to work as a missionary in Georgia. By the time Whitefield arrived in America, however, the disillusioned Wesleys had already gone back to England, never to return to the New World. Whitefield had a more productive visit to Georgia. It was but the first of seven trips he would make to the American continent.

On both sides of the Atlantic, Whitefield became famous as a popular "Grand Itinerant" who expounded the gospel any time and any place that he could obtain an audience. Whitefield often spoke in parishes of the Church of England, the church to which he was ordained a priest in 1739, but when Anglican churches were closed to him, he delivered his sermons in Dissenting chapels. Indeed, Presbyterian and Congregationalist meetinghouses were his most typical preaching sites in America. If no church buildings were available, Whitefield spoke in the open air, a novel device that he appropriated from fellow revivalist **Howell Harris**. Whitefield first preached outdoors in 1739 at Kingswood, a coal-mining settlement near Bristol, England. It was Whitefield who urged the practice of **field preaching** on his friend **John Wesley**. The success of this tactic convinced both Whitefield and Wesley that traditional ecclesiastical strictures could not keep out the proclamation of the gospel, for the whole "world was their parish."

All accounts agree that Whitefield had an unusual gift of expression and remarkable public speaking ability. Prior to his **conversion** he studied acting, and his performance skills transferred over to the ministry. Whitefield's mesmerizing oratory and charismatic personality help to explain his longstanding friendships with persons who had very different religious convictions (Benjamin Franklin) and social status (Lady Selina, the **Countess of Huntingdon**) than his own.

Whitefield's most successful trip to America was from 1739 to 1740. He itinerated from Maine to Georgia and, by providing the catalyst for the "Great Awakening," became America's first intercolonial celebrity. The new-birth experience as preached by Whitefield provided colonists with a common religious identity and vocabulary that predated the political unity of the American Revolution. It also broke down barriers of class, race, and gender. Whitefield's message was popular with people of every station in life: men and women, slaves and slave owners, illiterate farmers and students at Yale. On later trips to America he encountered severe criticism from more traditional clergy, especially from Bostonians such as Charles Chauncy and members of the Harvard faculty, but by then his reputation with the general populace was firmly established.

Whitefield also faced opposition in his home country. For example, though his articulation of Calvinism was well suited to the prevailing theological milieu in America and Scotland, it met with some disapproval in England. Whitefield entered into a long controversy with John Wesley over theological issues such as predestination, **Christian perfection**, and the perseverance of the saints. The result was a split among the Methodists. "Wesleyan Methodists" came to be distinguished from "Calvinistic Methodists," and Whitefield became the symbolic leader of the latter faction. In this role, he was elected Moderator of the first Calvinistic Methodist **Conference** in Wales. He also supervised the evangelistic work of preachers who were under the patronage of Lady Selina, a group known as the "Countess of Huntingdon's Connection," and he offered oversight for those associated with the Tabernacle (his preaching hall in London), a group which came to be referred to as the "Tabernacle Methodists."

Despite Whitefield's attempts to provide a structure for the Calvinistically inclined Methodists, he was always more of an evangelist than an organizer. In comparison, Wesley's tightly knit connection of societies and his close supervision of preachers succeeded in establishing a larger, more enduring institution among the non-Calvinistic Methodists. But Methodists of all stripes owe a great deal to Whitefield for his homiletical innovations and for his popularization of evangelical **experience** within British and American culture. Predictably, Whitefield was preaching right up until the day before his death. He died and was buried in Newburyport, Massachusetts.

Douglas M. Strong

WILKINS, ANN (June 17, 1806–November 13, 1857), **MEC** missionary to Liberia, was born in the Hudson Valley, New York. A schoolteacher, she was married at 17 to Henry F. Wilkins, who later abandoned her. In September 1836, she attended a **camp meeting** in Sing Sing, New York. There she heard an address by John Seys, superintendent of the Liberian mission, and offered herself as a missionary teacher (*see* AFRICA). She arrived in Liberia on July 28, 1837. She taught at the White Plains Manual Labor School and at the Liberia **Conference** Seminary (Monrovia), and organized a school at Caldwell. However, it was her Female Boarding School, founded in 1839 at Millsburg, which was her most enduring contribution. Ann Wilkins served in Liberia for 19 years, a remarkable record in an era when malaria claimed so many missionaries, sometimes just a few weeks after their arrival. She briefly returned to the USA in 1841 for her health, and, in 1853, was so ill that she retired from the mission. However, the next year she accompanied three women teachers back to Liberia. She retired again in 1856 and arrived in New York on April 23, 1857. She died seven months later.

Susan E. Warrick

WILLARD, FRANCES ELIZABETH (September 28, 1839–February 18, 1898), was born in Churchville, New York, the daughter of Josiah F. and Mary T. (Hill) Willard. At age 18 she entered Northwestern Female College, Evanston, Illinois, graduating in 1859. She became a Methodist at 21. In 1860 Willard began her career as a teacher and for 14 years pursued that vocation as well as public lecturing. She assumed the presidency of Evanston College for Ladies in 1871, the first woman to achieve such a post. The school later merged with Northwestern University. At this time Willard forsook education and focused her full attention upon the emerging **temperance** movement. By 1891 she had become president of the Woman's Christian Temperance Union and played an important role in the formation of the Prohibition Party as well as fostering the cause of **women**'s suffrage. Willard's ability as a lecturer, political leader, and prolific author won her national and international fame. At 51 her health and energies were spent. Her crusade has lived on, clearly visible in the contemporary cause of **feminism** and memorialized in the Frances E. Willard statue in the rotunda of the USA capitol.

Robert Drew Simpson

WILLIAMS, PETER (?–February 1823), notable early African-American Methodist layman, was born into **slavery** in New York City, and converted in his youth (ca. 1766–1768) under the preaching of **Philip Embury** and **Thomas Webb**. Eventually, Williams became sexton of the new Wesley Chapel on **John Street** and for a while lived in the preachers' house, which his wife Molly kept and where they hosted **Francis Asbury**, **Thomas Coke**, **Richard Whatcoat**, and other itinerating worthies. He also served as one of the Methodist community's first undertakers. When his master, a tobacconist and a loyalist, left the country after the Revolution, the John Street trustees purchased Williams's freedom for £40, and he paid them back in a little over two years. Although illiterate, he entered the tobacco business and prospered enough to buy his own shop, house, and other property. He was known as a liberal supporter of Methodist causes. Interested in the welfare of African Americans, Williams was instrumental in the founding of Zion Church, mother congregation of the **AMEZ** tradition. He helped secure Asbury's blessing for the venture, raised money for it, and was one of the congregation's original trustees in 1801. Williams's only son, Peter, Jr. (d. 1840), left the **MEC**, obtained a formal education, and became a highly esteemed Episcopalian priest.

Charles Wallace, Jr.

WILLING, JENNIE FOWLER (January 22, 1834–October 6, 1916), reformer and organizer, was born in Ontario, **Canada**, granddaughter of **Henry Ryan**. The family moved to a farm near Newark, Illinois, when she was eight. She had at least two brothers, including **Charles Henry Fowler**. At age 19, she married William C. Willing, **MEC** pastor. The couple had no children. He encouraged her interests and independence, and arranged for her to receive a local preacher's license (1877). She was a popular evangelistic speaker. Jennie Willing was a prolific writer whose work often appeared in MEC women's periodicals. She taught English language and literature at Illinois Wesleyan University (Bloomington), beginning in 1874. A social reformer, she was a leading suffragist in Illinois and a founder of the Woman's Christian **Temperance** Union in 1874. She organized the Northwestern Branch of the WFMS (MEC) in 1870 and served as recording secretary. She became general organizer of the WHMS (MEC) at its founding in 1880. The Willings moved to New York City in 1889, and her concern turned to immigrant girls. After her husband died in 1894, she remained in New York and founded the New York Evangelistic Training School in 1895. She died in New York.

Susan E. Warrick

WITHROW, WILLIAM HENRY (August 6, 1839–November 12, 1908), minister, journalist, and author, was born in Toronto, **Canada**, and attended Victoria College, Cobourg. He entered the ministry of the **Methodist New Connexion** Church in 1861, and then studied at the University of Toronto, receiving a B.A. in 1863 and an M.A. in 1864. Also in 1864, he was ordained and married Sarah Anne Smith. Two years later he transferred to the Wesleyan Methodist Church in Canada, and was received in full connection in 1868. In 1878, he became the assistant to the president of the **conference**, and editor of **Sunday school** publications. Following the union of the Wesleyan Church with other Methodist bodies in 1874, the new church inaugurated a monthly publication, the *Canadian Methodist Magazine*, and Withrow was appointed editor. In addition to writing a host of articles and reviews for the magazine, he published a number of books, including *The Catacombs of Rome* (1874) and a series of didactic novels. In 1884, he was elected a Fellow of the Royal Society of Canada. After the magazine was discontinued in 1906, Withrow continued to edit several Sunday school periodicals until his death in Toronto.

Marilyn Färdig Whiteley

WITNESS OF THE SPIRIT. John Wesley viewed the doctrine of the witness of the Spirit, or Christian **assurance**, as "one grand part of the testimony which God has given" the Methodists "to bear to all." Romans 8:16 provided Wesley's scriptural warrant: God's Spirit (*see* HOLY SPIRIT) bears "witness with our spirit that we are children of God." His own spiritual journey shaped the doctrine.

Sailing through tempests on the Atlantic, Wesley discovered that he feared death and doubted God. His doubts intensified when August Spangenberg asked him shortly after he arrived in Georgia if God's Spirit bore witness with his spirit that he was a child of God. Wesley answered in the affirmative, but suspected he spoke in vain. Back home in England, on May 24, 1738, in a religious event called "**Aldersgate**," God's Spirit released Wesley from the reign of sin. Wesley described how he felt: "I felt I did trust in Christ, Christ alone for **salvation**, and an assurance was given me that he had taken away *my* sins, even *mine,* and saved me from the law of sin and death." Wesley coupled this personal overcoming of fear and doubt with Romans 8:16 and I John 5:10 and formulated his doctrine of the witness of the Spirit. This doctrine, whose benefits Wesley never claimed for himself, holds that God's Spirit testifies to a person's spirit that he or she is a child of God, whose sins have been blotted out. The Spirit impresses itself on the soul, providing assurance of salvation. "The immediate result of this testimony," Wesley emphasized, "is 'the fruit of the Spirit'; namely, love, joy, peace; long-suffering, gentleness, goodness.'" The difference between the assured person's life and that of one who lacks the witness is comparable to the difference "between a smooth and a rough sea."

Wesley's own sea did not remain smooth after Aldersgate, however. So he modified his doctrine of the witness. Four days after Aldersgate, Wesley awoke feeling peace, one of the fruits of the witness, but not joy, another expected fruit. Twenty-eight years later, he wrote to his brother Charles and confessed he felt that he had never loved God. Yet God had favored him to the extent of using him to bring others to an experience of the Witness. How was Wesley to explain the fact that some believers, like himself, seemed to act as if God had said to them, "I love you," while feeling as if the words had not been spoken? Writing to Thomas Rutherforth in 1768, Wesley argued that the Spirit gives a few souls "an assurance from God of [their] everlasting salvation." More souls gain a witness that excludes "all doubt and fear" from their lives. The majority of Christians fear God and do what is right (Acts 10:35), while experiencing a sense of God's favor that is frequently weakened, even interrupted, "by returns of doubt or fear." Finally, some Christians may live in God's favor while never feeling the Spirit's witness. "Therefore," Wesley concluded, "I have not for many years thought a consciousness of acceptance to be essential to justifying faith." *See also* CHRISTIAN EXPERIENCE; DOCTRINAL STANDARDS.

John G. McEllhenney

WITTENMYER, SARAH ANN (ANNIE) TURNER (August 26, 1827–February 2, 1900), president of the Woman's Christian **Temperance** Union (WCTU), 1874–1879, was born near Sandy Springs, Ohio. She married William Wittenmyer in 1847. The couple moved to Keokuk, Iowa, in 1850. All but one of her five children, a son, died in infancy. With the outbreak of the Civil War in 1861, Wittenmyer joined other Keokuk **women** in starting the Soldiers' Aid Society. In fall 1862, the Iowa State Legislature appointed her agent to its own

Sanitary Commission. She designed the Diet Kitchens program, which prepared healthy, balanced meals in safe, clean kitchens, and she eventually supervised 200 women who operated Diet Kitchens in army hospitals. After the war, Wittenmyer promoted the Ladies' and Pastors' Christian Union and edited *The Christian Woman*, a monthly periodical (1872–1883). Sentiment in favor of woman's suffrage grew so strong within the WCTU that Wittenmyer's loss of the presidency to **Frances Willard** in 1879 did not come as a disappointment. Considered conservative by later generations of churchwomen, Wittenmyer nevertheless advanced the idea of the systematic employment of women in the church. In 1872, she and Susanna M. Fry tried to revive the deaconess office (*see* DEACONESS MOVEMENT) in Methodism. Although the effort was unsuccessful, Wittenmyer was convinced that women's church work needed to be professionalized.

Mary Agnes Dougherty

WOMEN. From the earliest days of the Evangelical Revival, women's involvement in Methodism was essential to the movement's success. Certainly influenced by his mother's example (*see* WESLEY, SUSANNA), **John Wesley** respected women as co-laborers, even supporting a woman's right to preach, provided there was "an extraordinary call," as in the case of **Mary Bosanquet**. Since Methodism was largely a lay movement, and since women were (and are) a majority of the laity, growth heavily depended on women's activity and leadership. From faithful attendance in **worship** to service as missionaries, teachers, pastors' wives, preachers, organizers, fund-raisers, and reformers, women's role was one of almost ceaseless activity.

As Methodism spread worldwide in the 19th century, women operated within the constraints of their "sphere." Woman's sphere was the home (and the children in it) and the church (though always in a subordinate position). In reality women were often in the marketplace, but the public world was "properly" the realm of men. The unintended consequence of this segregation was that women often worked together independently, learning skills and gaining experience that otherwise would have been difficult to attain, including financial management, public speaking, planning, and organization. As a result, "sphere" became an increasingly elastic concept, as energetic women's notions of "women's work" reflected their growing confidence. Women accepted the arduous task of raising money for countless charitable causes. They organized and taught **Sunday schools**. Women's benevolent societies fed, clothed, housed, and educated the needy, especially women (including prostitutes) and children. Church work also led to women's involvement in social and political reform, particularly **temperance**, civil rights, and suffrage.

The primary outlet for church women's energies, however, was **missions**. The earliest women's missionary societies raised money for the "parent" (male-led) societies, but soon began to focus on supporting missionary wives and the occasional unmarried woman missionary. By the 1860s, missionary wives, encumbered by family obligations, were begging mission boards for more single women free to bring the gospel to their sheltered Asian sisters (*see* ASIA). The formation in 1869 of the Woman's Foreign Missionary Society of the **MEC** signalled the beginning of a tremendous new effort. Over the next several decades, virtually all other Methodist and Wesleyan denominations joined the MEC in organizing women's home and foreign mission societies. A popular motto was "Women's Work for Women and Children." Women's missions often emphasized **education** and medical care for women and girls. In countries where women were usually not educated, the impact was especially profound. Institutions such as **Ewha Woman's University** in Korea are legacies of the woman's missions movement.

The **deaconess movement**, begun in the 1880s, was church women's response to the growing problem of the urban poor. Though engaged in "women's work," the deaconess was the church analog to the social worker, and signalled a new professionalism for women, as did women's increasing participation in higher education and church administration. Most significantly, the ordained ministry also began to slowly open to women beginning in the 1880s, and eventually the **episcopacy** as well.

As opportunities for women in the church have expanded, more traditional areas of "women's work" have sometimes been devalued. It is still true, however, that at every level of church work, women engage in almost ceaseless activity in the furtherance of the Gospel.

Susan E. Warrick

WOOD, ENOCH (January 31, 1759–August 17, 1840), master potter and gifted sculptor, was born in Burslem, Staffordshire, England, taking over his father's pottery business in 1784. He married Ann Bown, correspondent and friend of Hester Ann Rogers, in 1780. This connection may have introduced him to **John Wesley** who sat for Wood, probably in 1784, in one of his many visits to the potteries. The bust of Wesley was exhibited at the Methodist **Conference** at Leeds that same year and commended by **John Fletcher**. **Adam Clarke** almost fifty years later declared it to be "the most happily executed of all" and "the only proper likeness of this illustrious man." The model of Wesley's head and shoulders was subsequently remodeled by Wood and used by numerous other potters. Large quantities of busts were made up to ca. 1820 in basalt, terra cotta, earthenware, and creamware. Wood also made busts of **George Whitefield** (ca. 1790) and possibly Adam Clarke (ca. 1820).

Tim Macquiban

WOODSWORTH, JAMES SHAVER (July 29, 1874–March 21, 1942), was a controversial and influential Canadian Methodist Church minister (*see* CANADA) as well as a national social and political leader. Woodsworth was educated in Canadian colleges and at Oxford University. He was ordained in 1900. While at Oxford, the impact of horrible social conditions in London and the inability of English Methodism to give constructive leadership led him to question his **ordination**. Twice he attempted to resign his orders, but was challenged rather to employ his convictions in serving the All People's Mission in Winnipeg. Here was set the direction of his life-long career as a political and humanitarian reformer. Woodsworth urged Methodists to give leadership in social reform, but his voice was more readily heard outside the church. After several posts in the church, his social and political convictions finally led him to resign his orders. Now as a concerned citizen, he was freed of church restrictions. In 1919, he was deeply involved in the longshoreman's strike and risked arrest for seditious libel. In 1921, he was elected to the Canadian House of Commons. From this position he fought during the remainder of his career for numerous social reforms, including concern for the underprivileged, and pensions for the aged and the unemployed. With the advent of World War II, he resigned his post in government in opposition to Canadian involvement in the war.

Robert Drew Simpson

WORLD COUNCIL OF CHURCHES (WCC) is a cooperative ecumenical agency with participation by 340 Protestant, Anglican, and Orthodox denominations on every continent and with observer status by the Roman Catholic Church, headquartered in Geneva, Switzerland (*see* ECUMENISM). It was organized in 1948, but steps toward organization were initiated in the 1930s. The modern impetus for such a world organization originated at the Edinburgh Missionary Conference (1910). Later, the Universal Christian Council for Life and Work and the Faith and Order movement merged into a new world body, the WCC. In 1961, the International Missionary Council became a part of the WCC at the New Delhi Assembly. The Constitution of the WCC states that it "is a fellowship of churches which confess the Lord Jesus Christ as God and Savior according to the scriptures and therefore seek to fulfill their common calling to the glory of the one God, Father, Son and Holy Spirit." Participation is by churches or denominational bodies with regional councils of churches and world Christian communions having nonvoting observer status. It seeks theological convergence, assists victims of disasters and injustice, opposes racism, trains ecumenical leaders, and speaks for justice and liberation. The WCC marks its history by gathering representatives from all member churches in an assembly. These have been held in Amsterdam (1948), Evanston (1954), New Delhi (1961), Uppsala (1968), Nairobi (1975), Vancouver (1983), Canberra (1991), and Harare, Zimbabwe (1998).

Robert J. Williams

WORLD METHODIST CONFERENCES. In 1876, the **MEC** proposed a conference of Methodists from around the world. The first Ecumenical Methodist Conference met in 1881 at Wesley's Chapel, City Road, London. Twenty-eight Methodist denominations were represented. Further Conferences were held in Washington, D.C. (1891), City Road, London (1901), Toronto (1911), Westminster Central Hall, London (1921), Atlanta (1931), Springfield, Massachusetts (1947), and Oxford (1951). On the latter occasion the **WMC** was created and the Conference then became known as the World Methodist Conference. It was decided that in the future the Conference would meet every five years. Additional sessions have been held at Lake Junaluska, North Carolina (1956), Oslo (1961), London (1966), Denver (1971), Dublin (1976), Honolulu (1981), Nairobi (1986), Singapore (1991), Rio de Janeiro (1996), Brighton, England (2001), and Seoul, Korea (2006). The scope of the Conferences has grown steadily. Delegates from 70 Methodist bodies attended the Brighton meeting. These assemblies are opportunities for Christian witness, the exchange of ideas, inspiration, and fellowship. They have no legislative authority. Relatively small numbers of delegates attended each of the earlier Conferences. Many of these individuals occupied high office in their respective denominations. The more recent Conferences have attracted thousands of persons, representing a broad range of backgrounds and interests.

John C. English

WORLD METHODIST COUNCIL (WMC). The WMC is an association of autonomous churches standing within the Methodist tradition. The purpose of the Council is to draw together Methodists belonging to different racial, national, and linguistic groups, to encourage the development of theological unity and shared moral standards, to facilitate Methodist participation in the ecumenical movement (*see* ECUMENISM), to support Christian minorities in need, and to promote **evangelism**, youth ministries, and Christian **education**. As of 2003, the Council was composed of approximately 70 churches with a membership of 39,000,000 individuals and a constituency of more than 74,000,000 persons. Council policy is determined by a group of 250 to 500 persons, designated by their respective churches, who meet once every five years. The organization maintains a headquarters at Lake Junaluska, North Carolina, and a European office in Geneva, Switzerland. Its newsletter, *World Parish*, is published six times a year. Among the activities of the Council are conversations with churches belonging to other traditions; sponsoring a world evangelism program and the World Methodist Evangelism Institute, an international exchange of ministers and lay persons; presenting a World Methodist Peace Award; the Oxford Institute of

Methodist Theological Studies; organizing International Christian Youth Conferences; consultations on education, **worship**, and family life; and maintaining Epworth Old Rectory.

John C. English

WORSHIP. The forms of worship used in American Methodism reflected the social and cultural setting of American Methodists. These forms of worship often have had more in common with those of other American denominations than with English precedents.

John Wesley remained a priest of the Church of England throughout his lifetime, highly esteeming the *Book of Common Prayer* (BCP) even while supplementing it with other forms. In 1784 he sent his followers in the newly independent USA a large book, entitled *The Sunday Service of the Methodists in North America, with Other Occasional Services*. It was his revision and abridgement of the 1662 BCP.

Wesley was, it turned out, a poor judge of the American situation. Though the *Sunday Service* was reprinted in 1786 and 1790, it hardly survived Wesley as far as American usage was concerned. One year after Wesley's death, the *Sunday Service* was replaced by 37 pages of "Sacramental Services &c." in the 1792 *Discipline*. Gone were morning and evening **prayer**, the psalms, litany, and collects, epistles, and gospels for the Lord's Supper (*see* EUCHARIST). Abbreviated orders remained for both **sacraments** along with weddings, funerals, and ordinations. These services appeared thenceforth in successive editions of the *Discipline*, designated "The Ritual" after 1848 (**MEC**) and 1870 (**MECS**). Both churches added services for the reception of members, MEC in 1864 and MECS in 1866, called confirmation after 1964, and various dedications.

"The Ritual," however, was only used on those occasions when the sacraments or occasional offices were celebrated. Methodist worship centered on **preaching** services, simple guidelines for which appeared in the *Discipline* beginning in 1792. A full order of worship for Sundays without communion was not adopted until 1896. The new order became standard in the MEC and MECS after its publication facing the title page of the common hymnal of 1905.

In the first half of the 19th century preaching services were informal and mostly lay led, since congregations were linked on large **circuits** and ordained pastors showed up once a month. Sacraments were administered at quarterly meetings on each circuit. Once yearly **camp meetings** were held in which crowds assembled from considerable distances for several days to hear hellfire preaching and hearty hymn singing. At times the services developed highly emotional reactions.

In the latter half of the century, residential pastors became the rule but quarterly communions remained standard. **Sunday schools**, often larger than the church, developed worship services of their own. Camp meetings went upscale at mountaintop and lakeside/seaside sites, where Victorian-era Methodists gathered for preaching for conversion, the sawdust trail, the mourner's bench, and to vacation with the gospel.

Throughout the 19th-century protracted meetings, all part of the revival system, bypassed much of the historic content and forms of Christian worship in favor of a pragmatic spirit that pointed to results calculated in the number of converts.

In the early 20th century, as Methodists became more affluent and educated, emotional displays were discouraged and spontaneity was relegated to the midweek prayer meeting. The **UB** revised its rituals in 1921 and the new hymnal of 1935 contained more elaborate worship resources. The MECS remained the most conservative and made only minor changes in the services derived from Wesley. The MEC was less reluctant to change. Minor changes occurred in 1916, major changes in 1932. A new hymnal, jointly produced by the MEC, MECS, and **MP** in 1935 contained four orders for Sunday worship, including Wesley's order for morning prayer. The trend was heavily in the direction of dignified order, both in liturgy and in **music**. Only the African-American Methodist churches retained the spontaneity, rhythmic music, and high degree of participation characteristic of 19th-century worship patterns.

However, revision of sacramental services among African-American churches has been more conservative. The African Methodist Episcopal Church, African Methodist Episcopal Zion Church, and the Christian Methodist Episcopal Church retained the general services of 1792 of the parent church largely unrevised through the 1980s (*see* AME, AMEZ, CME).

Church architecture and worship habits reflected the times. The trend everywhere was toward more formal structures. By the 1920s, the churches were in the midst of the second Gothic revival. Victorian churches built in auditorium style (semicircular sanctuaries with curved pews on sloping floors with central pulpits and choir loft and organ pipes behind) gave way to Anglican-style Gothic churches, complete with divided chancels and elaborate altars. Choral music came to be a normal part of worship, often at the expense of congregational singing. The Christian year was rediscovered, along with liturgical colors. Candles joined the cross on countless communion tables. Robed chairs processed down center aisles and ministers appeared in pulpit gowns instead of cutaways. In this period standards of preaching also changed, moving away from the free style of the evangelists, who were now frowned upon. Sermons were better structured and full of literary allusions, testimony to standards set by seminary preaching courses.

Two widely different styles dominated church architecture of the 1950s and 1960s: red-bricked, white-pillared, tall-spired colonial or clean-lined, natural finished, A-framed modern. Widely different styles of worship services were held in them. Major revision of worship services occurred in 1959 when the **EUB** revised its *Book of Ritual* and in 1964 when the **MC** revised its *Book of Worship* and hymnal. Sixteenth-century words and phrases dominated because the revisions were essentially a recovery of inherited liturgies. Published on the eve of a two-decade movement to reform worship in all of the churches, neither church was able to take full advantage of the new insights that soon brought forth fresh liturgies for sister churches, Catholic and Protestant alike. Mid-1960s worship leaders, refusing to believe that recovery of past forms was the answer to making worship relevant, preferred to experiment with new forms of worship. So casual communions and chummy prayers, balloons, and guitars predominated.

To bring order out of the chaos the newly united **UMC** in 1970 authorized an Alternate Rituals Project. The resulting 17-volume Supplemental Worship Resources series was by far the most ambitious worship project in Methodist history. The new liturgies and worship resources were not designed to replace the service books of 1959 and 1964, but to give churchgoers more options. The first in the series, a new communion service, was published in 1972. Written in contemporary language, the service was not simply a revision of Wesleyan texts but an attempt to follow classical and universal patterns. Fresh services for **baptism** with confirmation and renewal possibilities followed in 1976, new **marriage** and burial rites in 1979, and a new ordinal in 1980. A major feature of the revised rites has been a concern to make the language of worship fully inclusive. Final versions of each came into wide use with the publication of the UMC hymnal in 1989. Additional resources for worship leaders were made available in the UMC *Book of Worship* in 1992. Along the way United Methodists traded literary preaching of the early decades of the 20th century for lectionary preaching. Freestanding communion tables replaced altars attached to the chancel wall. White albs and colorful stoles replaced the longstanding ministerial black.

By the turn of the 21st century, worship in many local churches was increasingly informal and employed contemporary **music**, readings, dance, and drama. Many resisted this tendency in favor of more traditional forms of worship and music.

Methodists in Great Britain (see BRITISH METHODISM) inherited two traditions from the Wesleys. Chapels in the prayer book tradition used the *Book of Common Prayer* or Wesley's *Sunday Service,* which continued to be printed until 1882 when the Wesleyan Methodists issued their own revision of the 1662 BCP. Town and village churches had morning prayer with hymns and sermon; town churches offered Communion monthly, village churches quarterly. Methodist Chapels in the free church tradition (**Primitive Methodist, Bible Christian**, Free Methodis,t and some Wesleyan Methodist) adapted Wesley's weekday preaching service for Sunday morning and evening worship. Four times a year a much abbreviated Communion service was added at the end of the preaching service.

When the several branches of Methodism united in 1932, a new *Book of Offices* was commissioned. Published in 1936, the new service book contained two orders of service—the first similar to the Anglican 1662 *Book of Common Prayer*; the second an abbreviated form for use at the end of a preaching service containing some of the same material, only rearranged. Collects, epistles, and gospels for the church year were restored. Ecumenical patterns replaced prayer book patterns and contemporary language replaced Elizabethan language in the extensively revised 1975 *Methodist Service Book.*

These services were further revised in the 1999 *Methodist Worship Book*. During the modern period Communion services became more frequent and the full service is more often used.

Kenneth E. Rowe

WRIGHT, MILTON (November 17, 1828–April 3, 1917), **UB** bishop, was born in Rush County, Indiana. Wright was ordained by the UB in 1856 and subsequently moved to Oregon as a missionary. He returned to Indiana in 1859 to marry Susan Koerner. Two of their children, Wilbur and Orville, invented the airplane. After serving as a minister in Indiana, Wright became theological professor of Hartsville College in 1868. Wright's opposition to liberalizing the denomination's stand against secret societies brought him to the attention of like-minded UB leaders. In 1869, they helped elect Wright editor of the denomination's newspaper, the *Religious Telescope*. After two terms as editor, Wright was elected bishop in 1877. After 1885, Wright became embroiled in the controversy over secret societies, as well as efforts to change the UB constitution and confession of faith. Wright fought these changes at the 1889 **General Conference**, but he was ignored. It liberalized the rule against secret societies and adopted a new constitution and confession. Wright and his followers immediately organized a new church around the earlier UB constitution and principles. Wright remained bishop in this "Old Constitution" church and led its legal battles over church property (*see* UNITED BRETHREN IN CHRIST, [OLD CONSTITUTION]). Wright retired in 1905.

Daryl M. Elliott

WRIGHT, RICHARD (dates uncertain) was sent by **John Wesley** with **Francis Asbury** to America in 1771. Wright served on **circuits** in Maryland, Delaware, Virginia, and New York City. He participated in the Philadelphia **conference** of 1773 that defined the course of American Methodism. Asbury and others viewed him as self-aggrandizing, opportunistic, and as one who preferred the lifestyle of the city to that of rural circuits. The conference of 1774 sent him back to England. Appointed to West Cornwall, he served there until 1776. The minutes of the British Conference show that Wright left the ministry in 1777.

Edwin E. Sylvest, Jr.

– Y –

YEAKEL, REUBEN (August 3, 1827–March 5, 1904), editor, bishop, and official historian of the **EA**, was born in Montgomery County, Pennsylvania. He entered the ministry of the EA in 1853. Yeakel was corresponding secretary of his denomination's missionary society (1859–1963) and editor of its **Sunday school** literature between 1863 and 1871. Elected bishop in 1871, he served for two quadrennia, but refused reelection to become principal of Union Biblical Institute in Naperville, Illinois. In conjunction with his labors as assistant editor of *Der Christliche Botschafter* (1883–1887), Yeakel turned increasingly to scholarship. Already in 1877 he had published *Jakob Albrecht und seine Mitarbeitern*, the English version of which was entitled *Jacob Albright and His Co-laborers*. Lacking documentation for this undertaking save for Albright's journal and other brief accounts, Yeakel relied heavily upon conversations with **John Dreisbach**, the only one of Albright's early collaborators to reach old age. Yeakel published his major work, *Geschichte der Evangelischen Gemeinschaft*, in two volumes (1890–1895). The English translation appeared in 1895 under the title, *History of the Evangelical Association*. His 1897 biography of Bishop Joseph Long (1800–1869) was Yeakel's last important publication.

K. James Stein

– Z –

ZAMBIA. *See* AFRICA.

ZIMBABWE. *See* AFRICA.

Bibliography

Research and writing on the history of Methodism and the Wesleys continues at a breathtaking pace. Essays and books open new areas of knowledge and ask fresh questions about Methodism's origins and development not only in Great Britain and North America, but in other parts of the world. Articles in regularly published periodicals such as *Methodist History*, *Proceedings of the Wesley Historical Society*, and *Journal of the Wesleyan Theological Society* probe new areas, challenge traditional hypotheses, and offer refreshing insights into Methodist history and theology. Studies on the role of Methodism in forming culture are among the most notable books to appear recently. One exceptional volume is the work edited by Nathan O. Hatch and John H. Wigger, *Methodism and the Shaping of American Culture* (2001).

The 2003 tercentenary of John Wesley's birth, as expected, resulted in the publication of a number of new biographies and studies of his theology. They include Kenneth J. Collins, *John Wesley: A Theological Journey* (2003) and Roy Hattersley, *A Brand from the Burning: The Life of John Wesley* (2002). While these do not supplant Henry Rack's *Reasonable Enthusiast: John Wesley and the Rise of Methodism* (1989), Richard P. Heitzenrater's *Wesley and the People Called Methodists* (1995), and Randy Maddox, *Responsible Grace: John Wesley's Practical Theology* (1994), they provide readable and insightful interpretations of his life and thought. Work continues on the publication of the new 35-volume collection of *The Works of John Wesley* (Bicentennial Edition, 1978–). The 300th anniversary of Charles Wesley's birth in 2007 will create renewed interest in his life and contribution to Methodism, especially to its hymnody.

We call attention again to a few outstanding resources for the study of Methodist history. The two-volume *Encyclopedia of World Methodism* (1974), no longer in print and somewhat dated, remains a reliable source of information about world Methodism. *The History of American Methodism* (three volumes, 1964) and *A History of Methodism in Great Britain* (four volumes, 1975–1987) are standard sources worthy of study. *A Dictionary of Methodism in Britain and Ireland* (2000), edited by John A Vickers, is a volume packed with brief articles on persons, events, and concepts. Recent historical studies of Methodism beyond North America and Great Britain include Patrick Ph. Streiff's important survey, *Methodism in Europe: 19th and 20th Century* (2003). A very useful collection of American Methodist primary source documents is Russell E. Richey, Kenneth E. Rowe, and Jean Miller Schmidt, editors, *The Methodist Experience in America* (2000).

The bibliography which follows is not intended to be exhaustive. It does, however, give information about some of the most important books on the history and theological heritage of Methodism. Before listing those publications we offer a listing of important libraries and depositories of Methodist materials, especially in Great Britain and North America.

Asbury Theological Seminary, 204 North Lexington Avenue, Wilmore, KY 40390
www.asburyseminary.edu

Center for EUB Studies, United Theological Seminary, 1810 Harvard Blvd., Dayton, OH 45406
www.united.edu

Drew University Library, Drew University, Madison, NJ 07940
www.drew.edu

Duke Divinity School Library, Duke University, Durham, NC 27706
www.lib.duke.edu

Free Methodist World Headquarters, Winona Lake, IN 46590
www.freemethodistchurch.org

General Commission on Archives and History, The United Methodist Church, 36 Madison Avenue, Madison, NJ 07940
www.gcah.com

Methodist Archives, John Rylands University Library of Manchester, 2004 Oxford Road, Manchester M13 9PP England
www.rylibweb.man.ac.uk

Perkins School of Theology, Southern Methodist University, Dallas, TX 75275
www.smu.edu/bridwell

Pitts Theology Library, Candler School of Theology, Emory University, 505 Kilgo Circle, Nashville, TN 30322
www.pitts.emory.edu

Robert W. Woodruff Library, Atlanta University Center, 111 James P. Brawley Drive, SW, Atlanta, GA 30314
www.auctr.edu

W. A. Bell Library, Miles College (CME), 5500 Avenue G, Birmingham, AL 35208
www.miles.edu

Wesley Center for Applied Theology, Northwestern Nazarene University, 623 Holly Street, Nampa, ID 83686
wesley.nnu.edu

Wesley Centre, Westminster Institute of Education, Oxford Brookes University, Oxford, OX3 0BP England
www.brookes.ac.uk/schools/education/wco/msuindex.html

Wesley Theological Seminary, 4500 Massachusetts Avenue, NW, Washington, DC 10016
www.wesleysem.edu

Wesleyan Church Archives and Historical Library, P.O. Box 50434, Indianapolis, IN 46250
www.wesleyan.org/gensec/archives

Wilberforce University (AME), Wilberforce, OH 45384
www.wilberforce.edu

William J. Walls Heritage Center, Hood Theological Seminary (AMEZ), 701 West Monroe Street, Salisbury, NC 28144
www.livingstone.edu

World Methodist Council Library, P.O. Box 518, Lake Junaluska, NC 28745
www.worldmethodistcouncil.org

Titles in the bibliography are organized as follows:

B. History of Doctrine
C. Representative Methodist Theologians
VI. Worship, The Sacraments, and Hymnody
VII. Church Organization
VIII. Periodicals

I. GENERAL REFERENCE WORKS

A. Bibliographies

Batsel, John and Lyda. *Union List of United Methodist Serials 1773–1973.* Evanston, Ill.l.: General Commission on Archives and History, UMC, with the United Methodist Librarians' Fellowship, and Garrett Theological Seminary, 1974.

Calkin, Homer L. *Catalog of Methodist Archival and Mansucript Collections.* [Alexandria, Va.]: World Methodist Historical Society, 1982–. Part 2: Asia, 1982. Part 3: Australia and the South Pacific, 1982. Part 6: Great Britain and Ireland, 1985–1991.

Cornish, George, ed. *Cyclopaedia of Methodism.* 2 vols. Toronto: Methodist Book Room, 1881, 1903.

Gage, Laurie E. *English Methodism: A Bibliographical View.* Westcliff-on-Sea, Essex: Gage Postal Books, 1985.

Gray, C. Jarrett, Jr. *The Racial and Ethnic Presence in American Methodism: A Bibliography.* Madison, N.J.: General Commission on Archives and History, UMC, 1991.

Green, Charles A., comp. *Methodist History Cumulative Index, 1982–1997.* Madison, N.J.: General Commission on Archives and History, UMC, 1998.

John Rylands University Library of Manchester. *Methodist Archives: Catalogues, Handlists, Bibliographies and Some Important Reference Works.* 2nd edition, revised. Manchester: John Rylands University Library, 1991.

Jones, Charles E. *The Charismatic Movement: A Guide to the Study of Neo-Pentecostalism, with Emphasis on Anglo-American Sources.* 2 vols. Metuchen, N.J.: Scarecrow Press, 1992, 1995.

——. *A Guide to the Study of the Holiness Movement.* Metuchen, N.J.: Scarecrow Press, 1974.

—— *Guide to the Study of the Pentecostal Movement.* 2 vols. Metuchen, N.J.: Scarecrow Press, 1992.

Norwood, Frederick A. "Historical Study in Methodism [1988]." *Lutheran Historical Conference* 13 (1990): 173–193.

——. "Methodist Historical Studies 1930–1959." *Church History* 28 (1959): 391–417; 29 (1960): 74–88.

——. "Wesleyan and Methodist Historical Studies 1960–1970: A Bibliographical Article." *Church History* 40 (June 1971): 192–199. Reprinted in *Methodist History* 10 (January 1972): 23–44.

Queen, Louise L., comp. *Methodist History Index, 1962–1982*. Madison, N.J.: General Commission on Archives and History, UMC, 1984.

Rose, E. Alan. *A Checklist of British Methodist Periodicals*. London: World Methodist Historical Society Publications, 1981.

Rowe, Kenneth E., ed. *Methodist Union Catalog, Pre-1976 Imprints*. Metuchen, N.J.: Scarecrow Press. 1975–. 7 volumes (A–I) published to date.

Walls, Francine E. *The Free Methodist Church: A Bibliography*. Winona Lake, Ind.: Free Methodist Historical Center, 1977.

Warrick, Susan E., ed. *Women in the Wesleyan and United Methodist Traditions: A Bibliography*. Revised edition. General Commission on Archives and History: www.gcah.org, 2003.

B. Directories

Directory of World Methodist Publishing. Nashville: United Methodist Publishing House, 1991.

The United Methodist Directory & Index of Resources, 2003. Nashville: Cokesbury, 2003. [published annually]

World Methodist Council Handbook of Information, 2002–2006. Lake Junaluska, N.C.: World Methodist Council, 2003.

C. Encyclopedias

Abbott, Margery Post, Mary Ellen Chijioke, Pink Dandelion, and John W. Oliver, eds., *Historical Dictionary of the Friends (Quakers)*. Lanham, Md.: Scarecrow Press, 2003.

Harmon, Nolan B., ed. *Encyclopedia of World Methodism*, 2 vols. Nashville: United Methodist Publishing House, 1974.

Hill, Samuel S., ed. *Encyclopedia of Religion in the South*. Macon, Ga.: Mercer University Press, 1984.

McClintock, John, and James Strong. *Cyclopedia of Biblical, Theological, and Ecclesiastical Literature*. 12 vols. New York: Arno Press, 1970. Reprint of the 1867–1887 edition.

Reid, Daniel G., Robert D. Linda, Bruce L. Shelley, and Harry S. Stout, eds. *Dictionary of Christianity in America*. Downers Grove, Ill.: InterVarsity Press, 1990.

Simpson, Matthew. *Cyclopedia of Methodism*. New York: Gordon Press, 1977. Reprint of 1878 edition.

They Went Out Not Knowing: An Encyclopedia of 100 Women in Mission. New York: Women's Division, General Board of Global Ministries, UMC, 1986.

Vickers, John A., ed. *A Dictionary of Methodism in Britain and Ireland*. Peterborough, UK: Epworth Press, 2000.

II. GENERAL HISTORIES

A. World Methodism

Born, Ethel W. *From Memory to Hope: A Narrative History of the Areas of the World Federation of Methodist Women*. Ferrum, Va.: Ferrum College, 2000.

Keller, Rosemary Skinner, et al., eds. *Methodist Women, A World Sisterhood: A History of the World Federation of Methodist Women*. [Cincinnati, Ohio]: World Federation of Methodist Women, 1986.

Yrigoyen, Charles, Jr., ed. *The Global Impact of the Wesleyan Traditions and Their Related Movements*. Lanham, Maryland: Scarecrow Press, 2002.

B. Great Britain and Ireland

Ambler, R. W. *Ranters, Revivalists & Reformers: Primitive Methodism and Rural Society, South Lincolnshire, 1817–1875*. Hull: Hull University Press, 1989.

Baxter, Matthew. *Memorials of Free Methodism*. London: W. Reed, 1865.

Beckerlegge, Oliver A. *The United Methodist Free Churches*. London: Epworth Press, 1957.

Bett, Henry. *The Spirit of Methodism*. London: Epworth Press, 1937.

Bourne, Frederick W. *The Bible Christians*. London: Bible Christian Reading Room, 1905.

Brake, G. Thompson. *Policy and Politics in British Methodism, 1932–1982*. London: B. Edsall, 1985.

Carwardine, Richard. *Trans-Atlantic Revivalism: Popular Evangelicalism in Britain and America, 1790–1865*. Westport, Conn.: Greenwood Press, 1978.

Chilcote, Paul Wesley. *Her Own Story: Autobiographical Portraits of Early Methodist Women*. Nashville: Kingswood Books, 2001.

——. *John Wesley and the Women Preachers of Early Methodism.* ATLA Monograph Series No. 25. Metuchen, N.J.: Scarecrow Press, 1991.

Church, Leslie F. *The Early Methodist People.* London: Epworth Press, 1948.

——. *More About the Early Methodist People.* London: Epworth Press, 1949.

Cole, R. Lee. *History of Methodism in Ireland 1860–1960.* Belfast: 1960.

Cooney, D. Levistone. *The Methodists in Ireland, A Short History.* Blackrock, Co. Dublin: 2001.

Crookshank, C. H. *A History of Methodism in Ireland.* Belfast: R. S. Allen, 1885–1888.

Cumbers, Frank H. *The Book Room: The Story of the Methodist Publishing House and Epworth Press.* London: Epworth Press, 1956.

Davies, Rupert E. *Methodism.* 2nd revised edition. London: Epworth Press, 1985.

——. *The Testing of the Churches, 1932–1982: A Symposium.* London: Epworth Press, 1982.

—— and Gordon Rupp, eds. *A History of the Methodist Church in Great Britain.* 4 vols. London: Epworth Press, 1975–1987.

Dolby, George W. *The Architectural Expression of Methodism: The First Hundred Years.* London: Epworth Press, 1964.

Dreyer, Frederick. *The Genesis of Methodism.* Bethlehem, Pa.: Lehigh University Press, 1999.

Graham, E. Dorothy. *Chosen by God: The Female Itinerants of Early Primitive Methodism.* Birmingham: By the author, 1986.

Hempton, David. *Methodism and Politics in British Society, 1750–1850.* Stanford, Calif.: Stanford University Press, 1984.

——. *The Religion of the People: Methodism and Popular Religion c. 1750–1900.* London: Routledge, 1996.

Jeffery, Frederick. *Irish Methodism: An Historical Account of its Tradition, Theology and Influences.* Belfast: Epworth House, 1964.

Jenkins, David E. *Calvinistic Methodist Holy Orders.* Carnarvon: 1911.

Kendall, H. B. *The Origin and History of the Primitive Methodist Church.* London: Robert Bryant, 1906.

Kent, John. *The Age of Disunity.* London: Epworth Press, 1966.

——. *Holding the Fort: Studies in Victorian Revivalism.* London: Epworth Press, 1978.

——. *Wesley and the Wesleyans: Religion in Eighteenth-Century England.* Cambridge: Cambridge University Press, 2002.

Kirsop, Joseph. *Historic Sketches of Free Methodism.* London: Andrew Crombie, 1885.

Lander, John K. *Itinerant Temples: Tent Methodism, 1814–1832*. Carlisle, UK: Paternoster Press, 2003.

Moore, Robert. *Pit-men, Preachers & Politics: The Effects of Methodism in a Durham Mining Community*. Cambridge: Cambridge University Press, 1974.

Petty, John. *A History of the Primitive Methodist Connexion from its Origins to the Conference of 1860*. London: J. Dickinson, 1860.

Packer, George (ed.). *The Centenary of the Methodist New Connexion 1797–1897*. London: G. Burroughs, 1897.

Pyke, Richard. *The Early Bible Christians*. London: Epworth Press, 1941.

Semmel, Bernard. *The Methodist Revolution*. New York: Basic Books, 1973.

Shaw, Thomas. *The Bible Christians 1815–1907*. London: Epworth Press, 1965.

Swift, Wesley F. *Methodism in Scotland: The First Hundred Years*. London: Epworth Press, 1947.

Tabraham, Barrie. *The Making of Methodism*. Peterborough, UK: Epworth Press, 1995.

Taggart, Norman E. *The Irish in World Methodism, 1760–1900*. London: Epworth Press, 1986.

Turner, John Munsey. *Conflict and Reconciliation: Studies in Methodism and Ecumenism in England, 1740–1982*. London: Epworth Press, 1985.

———. *John Wesley: The Evangelical Revival and the Rise of Methodism in England*. Peterborough, UK: Epworth Press, 2002.

———. *Modern Methodism in England, 1932–1998*. Peterborough, UK: Epworth Press, 1998.

Valenze, Debora M. *Prophetic Sons and Daughters: Female Preaching and Popular Religion in Industrial England*. Princeton, N.J.: Princeton University Press, 1985.

van Noppen, Jean-Pierre. *Transforming Words: The Early Methodist Revival from a Discourse Perspective*. Bern, Switzerland: Peter Lang, 1999.

Warner, Wellman J. *The Wesleyan Movement in the Industrial Revolution*. New York: Russell, 1967. Reprint of 1930 edition.

Watson, David L. *The Early Methodist Class Meeting: Its Origins and Significance*. Nashville: Discipleship Resources, 1985.

Wearmouth, Robert F. *Methodism and the Working-Class Movements in England, 1800–1850*. Clifton, N.J.: Augustus M. Kelley Publishers, 1972. Reprint of 1937 edition.

Werner, Julia S. *The Primitive Methodist Connexion: Its Background and Early History*. Madison, Wis.: University of Wisconsin Press, 1984.

Wickes, Michael J. L. *The West Country Preachers: a new history of the Bible Christian Church (1815–1907)*. London: Appledore, 1987.

C. North America

1. Canada

Chown, S. D. *The Story of Church Union in Canada*. Toronto: Ryerson, 1930.

Clark, S. D. *Church and Sect in Canada*. Toronto: University of Toronto Press, 1948.

Clifford, N. Keith. *The Resistance to Church Union in Canada, 1904–1939*. Vancouver: University of British Columbia Press, 1985.

French, Goldwin S. *Parsons and Politics: The Role of the Wesleyan Methodists in Upper Canada and the Maritimes from 1850 to 1855*. Toronto: Ryerson, 1962.

Grant, John Webster. *The Canadian Experience of Church Union*. London: Lutterworth, 1967.

———. *The Church in the Canadian Era*. Toronto: McGraw-Hill Ryerson, 1972.

———, ed. *The Churches and the Canadian Experience*. Toronto: Ryerson, 1963.

Moir, John S. *Church and State and Canada West*. Toronto: University of Toronto Press, 1959.

———. *The Church in the British Era*. Toronto: McGraw-Hill Ryerson, 1972.

Morrow, E. Lloyd. *Church Union in Canada: Its History, Motives, Doctrine, and Government*. Toronto: Thomas Allen, 1923.

Muir, Elizabeth Gillan. *Petticoats in the Pulpit: The Story of Early Nineteenth-Century Methodist Women Preachers in Upper Canada*. Toronto: United Church Publishing House, 1991.

Playter, George F. *The History of Methodism in Canada*. Toronto: A. Green, 1862.

Ryerson, Egerton. *Canadian Methodism; its Epochs and Characteristics*. Toronto: William Briggs, 1882.

Sanderson, Joseph E. *The First Century of Methodism in Canada*. 2 vols. Toronto: William Briggs, 1908.

Semple, Neil. *The Impact of Urbanization on the Methodist Church in Central Canada, 1854–1884*. Doctoral dissertation, University of Toronto, 1979.

———. *The Lord's Dominion: The History of Canadian Methodism*. Montreal: McGill-Queens University Press, 1996.

Van Die, Marguerite. *An Evangelical Mind: Nathanael Burwash and the Methodist Tradition in Canada, 1839–1918*. Montreal: McGill-Queen's University Press, 1989.

2. United States

Abbey, Merrill R. *The Epic of United Methodist Preaching: A Profile in American Social History*. Lanham, Md.: University Press of America, 1984.

Acornley, John H. *A History of the Primitive Methodist Church in the United States of America*. Fall River, Mass.: N.W. Matthews, 1909.

Andersen, Arlo W. *The Salt of the Earth: A History of Norwegian-Danish Methodism in America*. Nashville: Parthenon Press, 1962.

Andrews, Dee. *Religion and the Revolution: The Rise of the Methodists in the Middle Atlantic, 1760–1800*. Princeton, N.J.: Princeton University Press.

Baker, Frank. *From Wesley to Asbury: Studies in Early American Methodism*. Durham, N.C.: Duke University Press, 1976.

Bartelman, Frank. *Azuza Street, 1907*. South Plainfield, N.J.: Bridge Publications, 1980.

Behney, J. Bruce, and Paul H. Eller. *The History of the Evangelical United Brethren*. Nashville: Abingdon Press, 1979.

Bradley, David H. *A History of the A.M.E. Zion Church, 1796–1968*. 2 vols. Nashville: AME Zion Publishing House, 1956–1960.

Bucke, Emory S., ed. *History of American Methodism*. 3 vols. Nashville: Abingdon Press, 1964.

Campbell, James T. *Songs of Zion: The African Methodist Episcopal Church in the United States and South Africa*. Oxford: Oxford University Press, 1995.

Case, Riley B. *Evangelical and Methodist: A Popular History*. Nashville: Abingdon Press, 2004.

Dayton, Donald W. *The Theological Roots of Pentecostalism*. Grand Rapids, Mich.: Francis Asbury Press of Zondervan Publishing House, 1987.

Dougherty, Mary Agnes. *My Calling to Fulfill: Deaconesses in the United Methodist Tradition*. New York: General Board of Global Ministries, 1997.

Douglass, Paul F. *The Story of German Methodism: Biography of an Immigrant Soul*. New York: Methodist Book Concern, 1939.

Drinkhouse, Edward J. *History of Methodist Reform, Synoptical of General Methodism 1703–1789, with special and comprehensive reference to its most salient exhibition in the History of the Methodist Protestant Church*. 2 vols. Baltimore, Md.: Board of Publication of the Methodist Protestant Church, 1899.

Forbes, Bruce D. "'And Obey God, etc.': Methodism and American Indians." *Methodist History* 23 (October 1984): 3–24.

Garber, Paul Neff. *The Methodist Meeting House*. New York: Board of Missions and Church Extension, The Methodist Church, 1941.

Gifford, Carolyn D., ed. *The American Deaconess Movement in the Early Twentieth Century*. New York: Garland Publishing, 1986.

———, ed. *The Debate in the Methodist Episcopal Church Over Laity Rights for Women*. New York: Garland Publishing, 1986.

———, ed. *The Defense of Women's Right to Ordination in the Methodist Episcopal Church*. New York: Garland Publishing, 1986.

González, Justo L., ed. *Each in Our Own Tongue: A History of Hispanic United Methodism*. Nashville: Abingdon Press, 1991.

Gorrell, Donald K., ed. *Woman's Rightful Place: Women in United Methodist History*. Dayton, Ohio: United Theological Seminary, 1980.

Gregg, Howard D. *History of the African Methodist Episcopal Church: The Black Church in Action*. Nashville: AME Church Sunday School Union, 1980.

Guillermo, Artemio R., ed. *Churches Aflame: Asian Americans and United Methodism*. Nashville: Abingdon Press, 1991.

Hatch, Nathan O. *The Democratization of American Christianity*. New Haven, Conn.: Yale University Press, 1989.

—— and John H. Wigger. *Methodism and the Shaping of American Culture*. Nashville: Kingswood Books, 2001.

Holsclaw, David F. *The Decline of Disciplined Christian Fellowship: The Methodist Class Meeting in Nineteenth-Century America*. Doctoral dissertation, University of California, Davis, 1979; Ann Arbor, Mich.: University Microfilms International, 1979.

Keller, Rosemary Skinner, ed. *Spirituality and Social Responsibility: Vocational Vision of Women in the United Methodist Tradition*. Nashville: Abingdon Press, 1993.

——, Hilah F. Thomas, and Louise L. Queen, eds. *Women in New Worlds: Historical Perspectives on the Wesleyan Tradition*. 2 vols. Nashville: Abingdon Press, 1981–1982.

Kirby, James E., Russell E. Richey, and Kenneth E. Rowe. *The Methodists*. Westport, Conn.: Greenwood Press, 1996.

Knotts, Alice G. *Fellowship of Love: Methodist Women Changing American Racial Attitudes, 1920–1968*. Nashville: Abingdon Press, 1996.

Lakey, Othal L. *The History of the C.M.E. Church*. Memphis, Tenn.: The CME Publishing House, 1985.

Lee, Jesse. *A Short History of the Methodists*. Rutland, Vt.: Academy Books, 1974. Reprint of 1810 edition.

Lyerly, Cynthia Lynn. *Methodism and the Southern Mind, 1770–1810*. Oxford: Oxford University Press, 1998.

McClain, William B. *Black People in the Methodist Church: Whither Thou Goest?* Nashville: Abingdon Press, 1984.

McEllhenney, John G., ed. *United Methodism in America: A Compact History*. Nashville: Abingdon Press, 1992.

McLeister, Ira Ford. *Conscience and Commitment: The History of the Wesleyan Methodist Church of America*. 4th revised edition. Wesleyan History Series, vol.1. Marion, Ind.: Wesley Press, 1976.

Marston, Leslie Ray. *From Age to Age A Living Witness: A Historical Interpretation of Free Methodism's First Hundred Years*. Winona Lake, Ind.: Light and Life Press, 1960.

Maynard, Edwin H. *Keeping Up with a Revolution: The Story of United Methodist Communications, 1940–1990.* Nashville: United Methodist Communications, 1990.

Ness, John H., Jr. *One Hundred Fifty Years: A History of Publishing in the Evangelical United Brethren Church.* Nashville: Abingdon Press, 1966.

Noley, Homer, ed. *First White Frost: Native Americans and United Methodism.* Nashville: Abingdon Press, 1991.

Norwood, Frederick A. *The Story of American Methodism: A History of the United Methodists and Their Relations.* Nashville: Abingdon Press, 1974.

———, ed. *Sourcebook of American Methodism.* Nashville: Abingdon Press, 1983.

Pilkington, James P. *The Methodist Publishing House: A History.* vol. 1. Nashville: Abingdon Press, 1968. Continued by Walter N. Vernon, *The History of The United Methodist Publishing House*, vol. 2. Nashville: Abingdon Press, 1988.

Richardson, Harry V. *Dark Salvation: The Story of Methodism as it Developed among Blacks in America.* New York: Doubleday, 1976.

Richey, Russell E. *Early American Methodism.* Bloomington, Ind.: Indiana University Press, 1991.

——— and Bruce Mullins, eds. *Reimagining Denominationalism: Interpretive Essays.* Nashville: Kingswood Books, 1985.

——— and Kenneth E. Rowe, eds. *Rethinking Methodist History: A Bicentennial Historical Consultation.* Nashville: Kingswood Books, 1985.

———, Kenneth E. Rowe, and Jean Miller Schmidt, eds. *The Methodist Experience in America: A Sourcebook.* Nashville: Abingdon Press, 2000.

———, Kenneth E. Rowe, and Jean Miller Schmidt, eds. *Perspectives on American Methodism: Interpretive Essays.* Nashville: Kingswood Books, 1993.

Schmidt, Jean Miller. *Grace Sufficient: A History of Women in American Methodism, 1760–1939.* Nashville: Abingdon Press, 1999.

Schneider, A. Gregory. *The Way of the Cross Leads Home: Social Religion and Domestic Ideology in 19th Century Methodist Evangelicalism.* Bloomington, Ind.: Indiana Univeristy Press, 1993.

Shockley, Grant S., ed. *Heritage and Hope: The African American Presence in United Methodism.* Nashville: Abingdon Press, 1991.

Sledge, Robert Watson. *Hands on the Ark: The Struggle for Change in the Methodist Episcopal Church, South, 1914–1939.* Lake Junaluska, N.C.: General Commission on Archives and History, UMC, 1975.

Smith, Timothy L. *Called Unto Holiness: The Story of the Nazarenes, the Formative Years.* Kansas City, Mo.: Nazarene Publishing House, 1962.

Sutton, William R. *Journeymen for Jesus: Evangelical Artisans Confront Capitalism in Jacksonian Baltimore.* State College, Pa.: Pennsylvania State University Press, 1998.

Sweet, William W. *Methodism in American History*. Revised edition. Nashville: Abingdon Press, 1953. First published in 1933.

——. *Religion on the American Frontier, 1783–1940: The Methodists, a Collection of Source Materials*. New York: Cooper Square, 1964. Reprint of 1946 edition.

Thomas, Paul W. *The Days of our Pilgrimage: The History of the Pilgrim Holiness Church*. Wesleyan History Series, vol. 2. Marion, Ind.: Wesley Press, 1976.

Washburn, Paul. *An Unfinished Church: A Brief History of the Union of the Evangelical United Brethren Church and the Methodist Church*. Nashville: Abingdon Press, 1985.

Wigger, John H. *Taking Heaven by Storm: Methodism and the Rise of Popular Christianity in America*. Oxford: Oxford University Press, 1998.

Williams, William H. *The Garden of Methodism: The Delmarva Peninsula, 1769–1820*. Wilmington, Del.: Scholarly Resources Inc., 1984.

D. Africa

Bartels, Francis L. *The Roots of Ghana Methodism*. Cambridge: Cambridge University Press, 1965.

Cochrane, James R. *Servants of Power: The Role of English-speaking Churches in South Africa, 1903–1930; Toward a Critical Theology via an Historical Analysis of the Anglican and Methodist Churches*. Johannesburg: Ravan Press, 1987.

Elliott, Sheila L. *Women's religious associations and social change in South Africa: a study of Methodist women's organizations*. Doctoral dissertation, University of South Carolina, 1996.

Garrett, A. E. F. *South African Methodism: Her Missionary Witness*. Cape Town: Methodist Publishing House, 1965.

Hastings, Adrian. *The Church in Africa: 1450–1950*. New York: Oxford University Press, 1994.

Isichei, Elizabeth. *A History of Christianity in Africa*. Grand Rapids, Mich.: Wm. B. Eerdmans, 1995.

Johnson, Walton R. *Worship and Freedom: A Black American Church in Zambia*. New York: Africana Publishing, 1977.

Kurewa, John Wesley. *The Church in Mission: A Short History of The United Methodist Church in Zimbabwe, 1897–1997*. Nashville: Abingdon Press, 1997.

Mears, W. Gordon. *Methodism in the Cape: An Outline*. Cape Town: Methodist Publishing House, 1973.

Muzorewa, Gwinyai H., Patrick Matsikenyiri, and Cheryl W. Reames. *Africa: Visions of Hope*. Nashville: Graded Press, 1991.

Nthamburi, Rosemary K. *The Impact of the Methodist Church in Kenya in the Nineteenth Century*. Claremont, Calif.: Claremont Graduate School, 1978. M.A. Thesis.

Nthamburi, Zablon. *A History of the Methodist Church in Kenya*. Nairobi: Uzima Press, 1982.

Oosthuizen, Constance M. *Conquerors through Christ: the untold story of the Methodist deaconess in South Africa*. Port Shepstone [South Africa?]: Deaconess Order of the Methodist Church of Southern Africa, 1990.

Reid, Alexander J. *Congo Drumbeat: History of the First Half Century in the Establishment of the Methodist Church among the Atetela of Central Congo*. New York: World Outlook Press, 1964.

Southon, Arthur E. *Gold Coast Methodism*. London: Cargate Press, 1934.

E. Asia/Australasia

Baker, Richard T. *Ten Thousand Years: The Story of Methodism's First Century in China*. New York: Board of Missions of The Methodist Church, 1947.

Basis of Union, as approved by The Congregational Union of Australia, The Methodist Church of Australasia and the Presbyterian Church of Australia for the formation of the Uniting Church in Australia. Melbourne, Vic.: Uniting Church Press, 1992 [1971].

Benson, C. Irving. *A Century of Victorian Methodism*. Melbourne: Spectator, 1935.

Breward, Ian. *A History of the Australian Churches*. St. Leonards, NSW: Allen & Unwin, 1993.

Colwell, James. *The Illustrated History of Methodism: Australia, New South Wales, and Polynesia*. Sydney: W. Brooks, 1904.

Cunningham, Floyd T. *Holiness Abroad: Nazarene Missions in Asia*. Lanham, MD: Scarecrow Press, 2003.

Davidson, Allan. *Christianity in Aotearoa*. Wellington, New Zealand: Education for Ministry, 1991.

Deats, Richard L. *The Story of Methodism in the Philippines*. Manila: Union Theological Seminary, 1964.

Emilsen, William, and Susan Emilsen (eds). *The Uniting Church in Australia: the First 25 Years*. Armadale, Vic., Australia: Circa, 2003.

Ernst, Manfred. *Winds of Change; Rapidly Growing Religious Groups in the Pacific Islands*. Suva: Pacific Conference of Churches, 1994.

Findlay, G. G. and Holdsworth, W. W. (eds). *The History of the Wesleyan Methodist Missionary Society*. Vol. III. London: Epworth Press, 1921.

Forman, Charles W. *The Island Churches of the South Pacific; Emergence in the Twentieth Century*. Maryknoll: Orbis Books, 1982.

Garrett, John. *Footsteps in the Sea; Christianity in Oceania to World War II*. Suva: Institute of Pacific Studies, 1992; Geneva: World Council of Churches,1992.

———. *To Live Among the Stars: Christian Origins in Oceania*. Geneva, Suva: World Council of Churches and the Institute of Pacific Studies, University of the South Pacific, 1982.

Grayson, James H. *Korea: A Religious History*. New York: Oxford University Press, 1989.

Hames, E. W. *Out of the Common Way* and *Coming of Age*. Auckland, New Zealand: Wesley Historical Society of New Zealand, 1972.

Harper, Marvin H. *The Methodist Episcopal Church in India*. Lucknow: Lucknow Publishing House, 1936.

Harris, John. *One Blood: 200 years of Aboriginal Encounter with Christianity: a Story of Hope*. Sutherland, NSW: Albatross Books, 1990.

Hollister, John N. *The Centenary of the Methodist Church in Southern Asia*. Lucknow: Lucknow Publishing House, 1956.

Howe, Renate and Swain, Shurlee. *The Challenge of the City: the Centenary History of Wesley Central Mission, 1893–1993*. South Melbourne, Vic.: Hyland House, 1993.

Hunt, Arnold D. *This Side of Heaven: a History of Methodism in South Australia*. Adelaide: Lutheran Publishing House, 1985.

Krummel, John W. *The Methodist Protestant Church in Japan*. 2 parts. Tokyo: Aoyama Gakuin University, 1982–1983.

Lacy, Walter N. *A Hundred Years of China Methodism*. Nashville: Abingdon-Cokesbury, 1948.

Morley, William. *The History of Methodism in New Zealand*. Wellington, New Zealand: McKee & Co., 1900.

Walker, Alan. *Heritage Without End: A Story to Tell to the Nation*. Melbourne: Methodist Church of Australia, 1953.

Wood, A. Harold. *Overseas Missions of the Australian Methodist Church*. 5 vols.. Melbourne: Aldersgate, 1975–87.

Wright, Don and Eric Clancy. *The Methodists: a History of Methodism in New South Wales*. St. Leonard, NSW: Allen & Unwin, 1993.

F. Central/South America

Bastian, Jean-Pierre. *Los Disidentes: Sociedades protestantes y revolución en México, 1872–1911*. México, D.F.: Fondo de Cultura Económica, Colegio de México, 1989.

———. *Protestantismo y sociedad en México*. México, D.F.: CUPSA, 1984.

Díaz Acosta, Juan. *Historia de la Iglesia Evangélica Unida de Puerto Rico: Obra Evangélica para el Cincuentenario en Puerto Rico, 1899–1949*. San Juan, Puerto Rico: Iglsia Evangélica Unida de Puerto Rico, 1949.

Duque Zúñiga, José, ed. *La Tradición Protestante en la Teología Latinoamericana*. San José, Costa Rica: DEI, 1983.

For Ever Beginning: Two Hundred Years of Methodism in the Western Area. Kingston, Jamaica: Literature Department of the Methodist Church, Jamaica District, 1960.

González, Justo L. *The Development of Christianity in the Latin Caribbean*. Grand Rapids, Mich.: Wm. B. Eerdmans, 1969.

Kindling of the Flame: How the Methodist Church Expanded in the Caribbean. Grand Rapids, Mich.: Wm. B. Eerdmans, 1969.

Míguez Bonino, José, et al. *Luta pela vida e evangelização: A Tradição metodista na teologia latin-americana*. São Paulo: Ediçoes Paulinas, 1985.

Neblett, Sterling A. *Historia de la Iglesia Metodista en Cuba*. Buenos Aires: El Evangelista Cubano, 1973.

———. *Methodism's First Fifty Years in Cuba*. Macon, Ga.: Wesleyan College, 1966.

Pérez, Carlos. *Un Resumen de los Setenta Años de Labor de la Iglesia Metodista en Cuba, 1898–1968*. Miami: s.n., 1983.

Sánchez, Gildo. *Un Jirón de Historia Metodista Unida: Testimonio de un superintendente de distrito en Puerto Rico durante su incumbencia*. San Juan, PR: s.n., 1981.

G. Europe

Andersen, Arlow W. *The Salt of the Earth: A History of Norwegian-Danish Methodism in America*. Nashville: Norwegian-Danish Historical Society. 1962.

Barclay, Wade Crawford. *History of Methodist Missions, The Methodist Episcopal Church 1845–1939, Volume III, Widening Horizons 1845–95*. New York: The Board of Missions of The Methodist Church, 1957.

Copplestone, J. Tremayne. *History of Methodist Missions, Volume IV, Twentieth-Century Perspectives (The Methodist Episcopal Church, 1896–1939)*. New York: The Board of Global Ministries, The United Methodist Church, 1973.

Douglass, Paul F. *The Story of German Methodism: Biography of an Immigrant Soul*. Cincinnati: The Methodist Book Concern, 1939.

Findlay, G. G. and W. W. Holdsworth. *The History of the Wesleyan Methodist Missionary Society*. Volume IV. London: Epworth Press, 1922.

Garber, Paul Neff. *The Methodists of Continental Europe*. New York: Board of Missions and Church Extension, The Methodist Church, 1949.

Hagen, Odd. *Preludes to Methodism in Northern Europe*. Oslo: Norsk Forlags-selskap, 1961.

Hassing, Arne. *Religion and Power: The Case of Methodism in Norway*. Lake Junaluska, NC: General Commission on Archives and History, The United Methodist Church, 1980.

Kimbrough, S. T. Jr., ed. *Methodism in Russia & the Baltic States. History and Renewal*. Nashville: Abingdon Press, 1995.

Kissack, Reginald. *Methodists in Italy*. London: Cargate Press, 1960.

Nauser, Wilhelm. *Be Eager to Maintain the Unity of the Spirit Through the Bond of Peace, A Short History of the Geneva Area of The United Methodist Church*. Cincinnati, Ohio: General Board of Global Ministries, UMC, 1985.

Short, Roy H. *History of Methodism in Europe*. Nashville: Office of the Secretary of the Council of Bishops, UMC, 1980.

Sommer, C. Ernst, and Karl Steckel, eds. *Geschichte der Evangelisch-methodistischen KircheWeg, Wesen und Aftrag des Methodismus unter besonderer Berücksichtigung der deutschsprachigen Länder Europas*. Stuttgart: Christliches Verlagshaus GmbH, 1982.

Stephens, Peter. *Methodism in Europe*. Cincinnati, Ohio: General Board of Global Ministries, UMC, 1981.

Streiff, Patrick Ph. *Methodism in Europe, 19th and 20th Century*. Tallinn, Estonia: Baltic Methodist Theological Seminary, 2004.

Van den Berg, Johannes and W. Stephen Gunter. *John Wesley and the Netherlands*. Nashville: Kingswood Books, 2002.

Weyer, Michel, ed. *Der kontinentaleuoropäsche Methoidsmus zwischen den beiden Weltkriegen*. Stuttgart: Christliches Verlagshaus, 1990.

III. BIOGRAPHIES AND AUTOBIOGRAPHIES

Jacob Albright

Miller, George. *Jacob Albright; the First Biography of the Founder of the Evangelical Association*. Translated by George Edward Epp. [S.l., s.n., 1959?].

Wilson, Robert S. *Jacob Albright: The Evangelical Pioneer*. Myerstown, Pa.: Church Center Press of Evangelical Congregational Church, 1940.

Richard Allen

Allen, Richard. *The Life Experiences and Gospel Labors of the Right Reverend Richard Allen*. Nashville: Abingdon Press, 1984. Reprint of the 1880 edition; first published in Philadelphia in 1833.

George, Carol V. R. *Segregated Sabbaths: Richard Allen and the Rise of the Independent Black Churches, 1760–1840*. NY: Oxford University Press, 1973.

Young J. Allen

Bennett, Adrian A. *Missionary Journalist in China: Young J. Allen and His Magazines, 1860–1883*. Athens, Ga.: University of Georgia Press, ca. 1983.

Jessie Daniel Ames

Hall, Jacquelyn Dowd. *Revolt against Chivalry: Jessie Daniel Ames and the Women's Campaign against Lynching*. New York: Columbia University Press, 1979.

James O. Andrew

Smith, George Gilman. *The Life and Letters of James Osgood Andrew*. Nashville: Southern Methodist Publishing House, 1883.

Henry Appenzeller

Davies, Daniel M. *The Life and Thought of Henry Gerhard Appenzeller (1858–1902), Missionary to Korea*. Lewiston, N.Y.: E. Mellen Press, ca. 1988.

Jacobus Arminius

The Works of James Arminius. Translated by James Nichols and William Nichols; introduction by Carl Bangs. 3 vols. Kansas City, Mo.: Beacon Hill Press, 1986.

Francis Asbury

Asbury, Francis. *Journal and Letters*. Edited by Elmer T. Clark. 3 vols. Nashville: Abingdon Press, 1958.
Rudolph, L. C. *Francis Asbury*. Nashville: Abingdon Press, 1983.
Salter, Darius L. *America's Bishop: The Life of Francis Asbury*. Nappanee, Ind.: Francis Asbury Press of Evangel Publishing House, 2003.
Vickers, John A. *Francis Asbury*. Peterborough [England]: Foundery Press, 1993.

Hannah Ball

McQuaid, Ina DeBord. *Miss Hannah Ball, a Lady of High Wycombe*. New York: Vantage Press, 1964.

Nathan Bangs

Herrmann, Richard E. *Nathan Bangs: Apologist for American Methodism*. Thesis, Emory University, 1973.
Stevens, Abel. *Life and Times of Nathan Bangs, D.D.* New York: Carlton & Porter, ca. 1863.

Susan Bauernfeind

Messerschmidt, Lowell. *Bauern-Sensei: The Story of Susan Bauernfeind, Pioneer Missionary to Japan*. Lima, Ohio: Fairway Press, 1991.

Belle Harris Bennett

MacDonell, Mrs. Robert W. *Belle Harris Bennett: Her Life Work*. New York: Garland Publishing, 1987. Reprint of the 1928 edition.
Stapleton, Carolyn L. "Belle Harris Bennett: Model of Holistic Christianity" *Methodist History* 21 (April 1983): 131–142.

Mary McLeod Bethune

Holt, Rackham. *Mary McLeod Bethune: A Biography*. Garden City, N.Y.: Doubleday, 1964.
McCluskey, Audrey Thomas and Elaine M. Smith, ed. *Mary McLeod Bethune: Building a Better World: Essays and Selected Documents*. Bloomington: Indiana University Press, 1999.

William Black

Betts, E. Arthur. *Bishop Black and His Preachers: The Story of Maritime Methodism to 1825*. Halifax, Nova Scotia: Maritime Conference Archives, Pine Hill Divinity Hall, 1984.
Maclean, John. *William Black: The Apostle of Methodism in the Maritime Provinces of Canada*. Halifax, Nova Scotia: Methodist Book Room, 1907.

Richard Boardman

Lockwood, John Prior. *The Western Pioneers, or, Memorials of the Lives and Labors of Richard Boardman and Joseph Pilmoor*. London: Wesleyan Conference Office, 1881.

Henry Boehm

Boehm, Henry. *The Patriarch of One Hundred Years, Being Reminiscences, Historical and Biographical of Rev. Henry Boehm*. edited by J. B. Wakeley. Willow Street, Pa.: Boehm's Chapel Society, 1985. Reprint of 1875 edition.

Martin Boehm

Sangrey, Abram W. *Martin Boehm, Pioneer Preacher in the Christian Faith and Practice*. [S.l.,s.n.], ca. 1976 (Ephrata, Pa.: Science Press).

Peter Böhler

Lockwood, John Prior. *Memorials of the Life of Peter Böhler*. London: Wesleyan Conference Office, 1868.

Catherine Booth

Booth Tucker, Frederick de L. *The Life of Catherine Booth: The Mother of the Salvation Army*. 2 vols. New York: Revell, ca. 1892.

William Booth

Bishop, Edward. *Blood and Fire; the Story of General William Booth and the Salvation Army*. London: Longmans, 1964.
Collier, Richard. *The General next to God: The Story of William Booth and the Salvation Army*. New York: Dutton, 1968.

Mary Bosanquet

Burge, Janet. *Women Preachers in Community: Sarah Ryan, Sarah Crosby, Mary Bosanquet*. Peterborough, England: Foundery Press, 1996.
Moore, Henry. *The Life of Mrs. Mary Fletcher*. Salem, Ohio: Schmul, reprint, 1997.

Hugh Bourne

Wilkinson, John T. *Hugh Bourne, 1772–1852*. London: Epworth Press, 1952.

Phineas Bresee

Brickley, Donald Paul. *Man of the Morning: The Life and Work of Phineas F. Bresee*. Kansas City, Mo.: Nazarene Publishing House, 1960.
Girvin, E.A. *Phineas F. Bresee, A Prince in Israel: A Biography*. Kansas City, Mo.: Nazarene Publishing House, 1981. Reprint of 1916 edition.

Edgar Sheffield Brightman

Egan, William Thomas. *Religious Experience in the Personalism of Edgar Sheffield Brightman*. Doctoral dissertation, Fordham University, 1972.

George Brown

Brown, George. *Recollections of Itinerant Life: Including Early Reminiscences*. Cincinnati, Ohio: R.W. Carroll, ca. 1866.

James Monroe Buckley

Mains, George Preston. *James Monroe Buckley*. New York: Methodist Book Concern, 1917.

Jabez Bunting

Bunting, Thomas P. and Rowe, G. Stringer. *The Life of Jabez Bunting* DD. London: T. Woomer, 1887.
Hempton, David. *The Religion of the People: Methodism and Popular Religion c.1750–1900*. London: Routledge, 1996.
Kent, John. *Jabez Bunting, the last Wesleyan*. London: Epworth Press, 1955.
Rigg, James H. *Jabez Bunting, a great Methodist leader*. London: C. H. Kelly, 1905.
Ward, W. R. (ed.). *The Early Correspondece of Jabez Bunting 1820–1829*. London: Royal Historical Society, 1972.
Ward, W. R. (ed.). *Early Victorian Methodism: The correspondence of Jabez Bunting 1830–1858*. Oxford: Oxford University Press, 1976.

Nathanael Burwash

Van Die, Marguerite. *An Evangelical Mind: Nathanael Burwash and the Methodist Tradition in Canada, 1839–1918*. Montreal: McGill-Queen's University Press, 1989.

William Butler

Butler, Clementina. *William Butler, the Founder of Two Missions of the Methodist Episcopal Church*. New York: Eaton & Mains; Cincinnati, Ohio: Jennings & Pye, 1902.

Warren Akin Candler

Bauman, Mark K. *Warren Akin Candler: The Conservative Idealist*. Metuchen, N.J.: Scarecrow Press, 1981.

Cannon, James, Jr.

Hohner, Robert A. *Prohibition and Politics: The Life of Bishop James Cannon, Jr.* Columbia, South Carolina: University of South Carolina Press, 1999.

Cannon, William R.

Cannon, William R. *A Magnificent Obsession: The Autobiography of William Ragsdale Cannon*. Nashville: Abingdon Press, 1999.

William Capers

Reily, Duncan. *William Capers: An Evaluation of His Life and Thought*. Thesis, Emory University, 1972.
Wightman, William M. *Life of William Capers*. Nashville: Southern Methodist Publishing House, 1858.

William Case

Carroll, John. *Case and His Contemporaries; or, The Canadian Itinerants' Memorial*. 5 vols. Toronto: S. Rose, 1866–1877.

Samuel Dwight Chown

Schwarz, Edward Richard. *Samuel Dwight Chown: An Architect of Canadian Church Union*. Doctoral dissertation, Boston University Graduate School, 1961.
———. "Samuel Dwight Chown and the Methodist Contribution to Canadian Church Union." *Canadian Journal of Theology* 11 (1965): 134–138.

Adam Clarke

Clarke, Adam. *An Account of the Infancy, Religious, and Literary Life of Adam Clarke*. 3 vols. London: T. S. Clarke, 1833.

Hare, John Middleton. *The Life and Labours of Adam Clarke, LL.D.* London: J. & D. A. Darling, 1849.

William Clowes

Garner, William. *The Life of the Venerable William Clowes*. London: William Lister, 1868.

Wilkinson, John T. *William Clowes 1780–1851*. London: Epworth Press, 1951.

Thomas Coke

Davey, Cyril. *Mad About Mission: The Story of Thomas Coke: Founder of the Methodist Overseas Mission*. London: Marshalls, 1985.

Vickers, John A. *Thomas Coke, Apostle of Methodism*. Nashville: Abingdon Press, 1969.

James Cone

Cone, James H. *My Soul Looks Back*. Nashville: Abingdon Press, 1982.

Ezekiel Cooper

Phoebus, George A. *Beams of Light on Early Methodism in America; Chiefly drawn from the diary, letters, manuscripts, documents, and original tracts of the Rev. Ezekiel Cooper*. New York: Phillips and Hunt, 1887.

Scherer, Lester B. *Ezekiel Cooper, 1763–1847: An Early American Methodist Leader*. Nashville: Commission on Archives and History, UMC, 1968.

Melville Cox

Cox, Melville. *Remains of Melville B. Cox, Late Missionary to Liberia*. New York: T. Mason & G. Lane, 1839.

Guptill, Roger S. *Though Thousands Fall; The Story of Melville B. Cox*. New York: Methodist Book Concern, ca. 1932.

Fanny Crosby

Crosby, Fanny. *Fanny Crosby's Story of Ninety-four Years, retold by S. Trevena Jackson*. New York: Fleming H. Revell, 1915.

Ruffin, Bernard. *Fanny Crosby*. Philadelphia, Pa.: United Church Press, 1976.

Thomas Crosby

Smith, Oswald J. *Men of God: David Brainer, John Fletcher, Thomas Crosby, George Whitefield*. London: Marshall, Morgan, & Scott, 1971.

Sarah Dickey

Griffith, Helen. *Dauntless in Mississippi: The Life of Sarah Dickey, 1838–1904*. South Hadley, Mass.: Dinosaur Press, 1966.

John Dickins

Cooper, Ezekiel. *A Funeral Discourse on the Death of that Eminent Man, the Late Reverend John Dickins*. Philadelphia, Pa.: Printed by H. Maxwell for Asbury Dickins, 1799.

Lorenzo Dow and Peggy Dow

Dow, Peggy. *Vicissitudes in the Wilderness; Exemplified, in the Journal of Peggy Dow*. Norwich, Conn.: Printed by William Faulkner, 1833.

Dow, Lorenzo. *The Life, Travels, Labors, and Writings of Lorenzo Dow*. New York: C. M. Saxton, 1859.

Sellers, Charles Coleman. *Lorenzo Dow, the Bearer of the Word*. New York: Minton, Balch, 1928.

Philip Embury

Lapp, Eula C. *To Their Heirs Forever*. [Picton, Ontario: Printed by the Picton Gazette Publishing, 1970].

John Emory

Emory, Robert. *The Life of the Rev. John Emory, D.D.* New York: George Lane, 1841.

Donald English

Hoare, Brian & Randall, Ian. *More than a Methodist: the life and ministry of Donald English.* Carlisle: Paternoster, 2003.

Wilbur Fisk

Fisk, Wilbur. *Travels on the Continent of Europe.* New York: Harper & Brothers, 1838.

Williamson, Douglas James. *The Ecclesiastical Career of Wilbur Fisk.* Doctoral dissertation, Boston University, 1988.

Fletcher, John William

Streiff, Patrick. *Reluctant Saint: A Theological Biography of Fletcher of Madeley.* Peterborough, UK: Epworth Press, 2001.

Wood, Laurence W. *The Meaning of Pentecost in Early Methodism: Rediscovering John Fletcher as Wesley's Vindicator and Designated Successor.* Lanham, Md: Scarecrow Press, 2002.

Nannie B. Gaines

Robins-Moury, Dorothy. "Not a Foreigner, but a Sensei—a Teacher: Nannie B. Gaines of Hiroshima." In *Women's Work for Women: Missions and Social Change in Asia,* Leslie A. Flemming, ed. Boulder, Colo.: Westview Press, 1989.

Mary Porter Gamewell

Gamewell, Mary Porter. *China Old and New.* New York: Missionary Society of the MEC, 1906.

Tuttle, A. H. *Mary Porter Gamewell and Her Story of the Siege in Peking.* New York: Garland Publishing, 1987. Reprint of the 1907 edition.

Catherine Garrettson

Lobody, Diane. *Lost in the Ocean of Love: The Mystical Writings of Catherine Livingston Garrettson.* Doctoral dissertation, Drew University, 1990.

Freeborn Garrettson

Garrettson, Freeborn. *American Methodist Pioneer; The Life and Journals of the Rev. Freeborn Garrettson, 1752–1827.* Edited by Robert Drew Simpson. Madison, N.J.: Drew University Library, 1983.

Philip Gatch

Gatch, Philip. *Sketch of Rev. Philip Gatch / prepared by John McLean*. Cincinnati, Ohio: Swormstedt & Poe, 1856.

Enoch George

Fry, Benjamin St. James. *The Life of Rev. Enoch George*. New York: Carlton & Porter, 1852.

Frederick Pratt Green

Braley, Bernard. *Serving God and God's creatures: A memorial volume to celebrate the life of Frederick Pratt Green*. London, 2001.

William Grimshaw

Cragg, G. G. *Grimshaw of Haworth, a Study in Eighteenth Century Evangelism*. London: Canterbury, 1947.
Baker, Frank, *William Grimshaw 1708–1763*. London: Epworth Press, 1963.

L. L. Hamline

Palmer, Walter Clarke. *Life and Letters of Leonidas L. Hamline*. New York: Carlton & Porter, 1866.

William Hanby

Shoemaker, Dacia Custer. *Choose You This Day: The Legacy of the Hanbys*. Westerville, Ohio: Westerville Historical Society, ca. 1983.

John Hannah

Dixon, James. *A Man Greatly Beloved: A Sermon Preached . . . on the Occasion of the Death of Dr. Hannah*. London: Hamilton, Adams, 1868.

Georgia Harkness

Keller, Rosemary Skinner. *Georgia Harkness: For Such a Time as This*. Nashville: Abingdon Press, 1992.

Howell Harris

Hughes, H. J. *The Life of Howell Harris*. Hanley, England: Tentmaker Publications, 1996.

Nuttall, Geoffrey F. *Howell Haris: the last enthusiast*. Cardiff: University of Wales Press, 1965.

Roberts, Griffith T. *Howell Harris*. London: Epworth Press, 1951.

Schlenther, Boys Stanley and White, Eryn Mant. *Calendar of the Trevecka Letters*. Aberystwyth: 2003.

Tudur, Geraint. *Howell Harris: From Conversion to Separation, 1735–1750*. Cardiff: University of Wales Press, 2000.

Joseph Hartzell

Swartz, Barbara Myers. *The Lord's Carpetbagger: A Biography of Joseph Crane Hartzell*. Doctoral dissertation, State University of New York at Stony Brook, 1972.

Gilbert Haven

Gravely, Will B. *Gilbert Haven, Methodist Abolitionist: A Study in Race, Religion and Reform, 1850–1880*. Nashville: Abingdon Press, 1973.

Atticus Greene Haygood

Mann, Harold W. *Atticus Greene Haygood: Methodist Bishop, Editor, and Educator*. Athens, Ga.: University of Georgia Press, 1965.

Laura Askew Haygood

Brown, Oswald Eugene, and Anna Muse Brown, ed. *Life and Letters of Laura Askew Haygood*. Nashville: Publishing House of the MECS, 1904.

Barbara Heck

Caddell, Garwood Lincoln. *Barbara Heck: Pioneer Methodist*. [Cleveland, Tenn.: Pathway Press, 1961].

Elijah Hedding

Clark, D. W. *Life and Times of Rev. Elijah Hedding*. New York: Carlton & Phillips, 1855.

Olaf Hedstrom

Whyman, Henry C. *The Hedstroms and the Bethelship Saga*. Carbondale, Ill.: Southern Illinois University Press, 1992.

Sophia Hopkey

Ethridge, Willie Snow. *Strange Fires: the True Story of John Wesley's Love Affair in Georgia*. New York: Vanguard Press, 1971.

Harry Hosier

Smith, Warren T. *Harry Hosier, Circuit Rider*. Nashville: Discipleship Resources, 1981.

Wilbert F. Howard

Lofthouse, W. F. et al. *Wilbert F. Howard, Appreciations of the Man*. London: Epworth Press, 1954.

Hugh Price Hughes

Hughes, Dorothea Price. *The Life of Hugh Price Hughes*. New York: A.C. Armstrong, 1904.

Walters, Arthur. *Hugh Price Hughes, Pioneer and Reformer*. London: Robert Culley, 1907.

Selina, Countess of Huntingdon

Gentry, Peter W. *The Countess of Huntingdon*. Peterborough: Foundery Press, 1994.

Welch, Edwin. *Spiritual pilgrim: a reassessment of the life of the Countess of Huntingdon*. Cardiff: University of Wales Press, 1995.

John Inskip and Martha Inskip

Breeze, Lawrence E. "The Inskips: Union in Holiness." *Methodist History* 13 (July 1975): 25–45.

Brown, Kenneth O. "'The World-Wide Evangelist'—the Life and Work of Martha Inskip." *Methodist History* 21 (July 1983): 179–191.

McDonald, William, and John E. Searles. *The Life of Rev. John S. Inskip*. New York: Garland Publishing, 1985. Reprint of 1885 edition.

Thomas Jackson

Rupp, E. Gordon. *Thomas Jackson, Methodist Patriarch*. London: Epworth Press, 1954.

E. Stanley Jones

Alphonse, Martin Paul. *The Evangelistic Enterprise of E. Stanley Jones: A Missiological Review*. Thesis, Fuller Theological Seminary, 1986.

Jones, E. Stanley. *A Song of Ascents: A Spiritual Autobiography*. Nashville: Abingdon Press, 1968.

Peter Jones

Smith, Donald B. *Sacred Feathers: The Rev. Peter Jones (Kah-Ke-Wa-Quo-Na-By) and the Mississauga Indians*. Lincoln, Neb.: University of Nebraska Press, 1987.

Daniel Kidder

Kidder, Daniel P. *Sketches of Residence and Travel in Brazil*. 2 vols. Philadelphia, Pa.: Sorin & Ball, 1845.

Strobridge, G. E. *Biography of the Rev. Daniel Parish Kidder*. New York: Hunt & Eaton, 1894.

Alexander Kilham

Blackwell, John. *The Life of the Rev. Alexander Kilham*. London: R. Groombridge, 1838.

Helen Kim

Kim, Helen. *Grace Sufficient: The Story of Helen Kim*. Nashville: The Upper Room, 1964.

Walter Lambuth

Pinson, William W. *Walter Russell Lambuth: Prophet and Pioneer*. Nashville: Cokesbury Press, 1924.

Isaac Lane

Lane, Isaac. *Autobiography of Bishop Isaac Lane, LL.D.* Nashville: Publishing House of the MECS, 1916.

Jarena Lee

Lee, Jarena. "The Life and Religious Experience of Jarena Lee." In *Sisters of the Spirit*, edited by William L. Andrews, 25–48. Bloomington, Ind.: Indiana University Press, 1986.
Spiritual Narratives: Maria W. Stewart, Jarena Lee, Julia A. Foote and Virginia W. Broughton, with an introduction by Sue E. Houchins. New York: Oxford University Press, 1991.

Jason Lee

Brosnan, Cornelius J. *Jason Lee: Prophet of the New Oregon.* New York: Macmillan, 1932.
Loewenberg, Robert J. *Equality on the Oregon Frontier: Jason Lee and the Methodist Mission, 1834–1843.* Seattle, Wash.: University of Washington Press, 1976.

Jesse Lee

Lee, Jesse. *Memoir of the Rev. Jesse Lee, with Extracts from His Journals.* Edited by Minton Thrift. New York: Ayer, 1969. Reprint of the 1823 edition.

Luther Lee

Lee, Luther. *Autobiography of the Rev. Luther Lee.* New York: Garland Publishing, 1984. Reprint of the 1882 edition.

John Scott Lidgett

Davies, Rupert E. (ed.). *John Scott Lidgett: A Symposium.* London: Epworth Press, 1957.
Turberfield, Alan. *John Scott Lidgett, Archbishop of British Methodism?* Peterborough: Epworth Press, 2003.

James K. Mathews

Mathews, James K. *Global Odyssey: The Autobiography of James K. Mathews.* Nashville: Abingdon Press, 2000.

John McClintock, Jr.

Crooks, George R. *Life and Letters of the Rev. John M'Clintock.* New York: Nelson & Phillips, 1876.

Francis John McConnell

McConnell, Francis John. *By the Way: An Autobiography.* New York: Abingdon-Cokesbury Press, ca. 1952.

George McDougall

Nix, James Ernest. *Mission Among the Buffalo: The Labours of the Reverends George M. and John C. McDougall in the Canadian Northwest, 1860–1876.* Toronto: Ryerson Press, 1960.

William McKendree

Fry, Benjamin St. James, *The Life of Reverend William McKendree.* New York: Carlton & Porter, ca. 1852.
Paine, Robert. *Life and Times of William McKendree.* 2 vols. Nashville: Southern Methodist Publishing House, 1869.

Lucy Rider Meyer

Horton, Isabelle. *High Adventure: Life of Lucy Rider Meyer.* New York: Garland Publishing, 1987. Reprint of 1928 edition.

Carl Michalson

Thompson, Henry O. *The Contribution of Carl Michalson to Modern Theology: Studies in Interpretation and Application.* Lewiston, N.Y.: E. Mellen Press, ca. 1991.

John Miley

Gootblatt, George. *John Miley and the Status of Science at Drew Theological Seminary, 1868–1895*. Thesis, Drew Theological Seminary, 1978.

John R. Mott

Hopkins, C. Howard. *John R. Mott, 1865–1955: A Biography*. Grand Rapids, Mich.: Wm. B. Eerdmans Publishing, 1979.

Grace Murray

Valentine, Simon R. *John Bennet and the Origins of Methodism and the Evangelical Revival in England*. Lanham, Md.: Scarecrow, 1997.

Christian Newcomer

Newcomer, Christian. *Christian Newcomer, His Life, Journal, and Achievements*. Edited by Samuel S. Hough. Dayton, Ohio: Board of Admin., UB, ca. 1941.
Robertson, John Dallas. *Christian Newcomer (1749–1830)*. Doctoral dissertation, George Washington University, 1973.

Frank Mason North

Lacy, Creighton. *Frank Mason North, His Social and Ecumenical Mission*. Nashville: Abingdon Press, 1967.

William O'Bryan

Thorne, S. L. *William O'Bryan, Founder of the Bible Christians: the man and his work*. Plymouth, England: J. C. Holland, 1878.

James O'Kelly

Kilgore, Charles Franklin. *The James O'Kelly Schism in the Methodist Episcopal Church*. Thesis, Emory University, 1963.
MacClenny, Wilbur E. *The Life of Rev. James O'Kelly and the Early History of the Christian Church in the South*. Raleigh, N.C.: Edwards & Broughton Printing, 1910.

Anna Oliver

Oliver, Anna. *Test Case on the Ordination of Women.* New York: William N. Jennings, 1880.

Rowe, Kenneth E. "Ordination of Women, Round One: Anna Oliver and the Methodist General Conference of 1880." *Methodist History* 12 (April 1974): 60–72.

Philip William Otterbein

Core, Arthur C., ed. *Philip William Otterbein, Pastor, Ecumenist.* Dayton, Ohio: Board of Publication, The Evangelical United Brethren Church, 1968.

O'Malley, J. Steven. *Pilgrimage of Faith: The Legacy of the Otterbeins.* Metuchen, N.J.: Scarecrow Press, 1973.

Albert Outler

Outler, Albert C. *Oral Memoirs of Albert Cook Outler.* [H. Wayne Pipkin, interviewer] [Waco,TX]: Baylor University, Program for Oral History, 1974.

G. Bromley Oxnam

Miller, Robert M. *Bishop G. Bromley Oxnam: Paladin of Liberal Protestantism.* Nashville: Abingdon Press, 1990.

Phoebe Palmer

Wheatley, Richard. *The Life and Letters of Mrs. Phoebe Palmer.* New York: Garland Publishing, 1984. Reprint of the 1876 edition.

White, Charles E. *The Beauty of Holiness: Phoebe Palmer as Theologian, Revivalist, Feminist, and Humanitarian.* Grand Rapids, Mich.: Francis Asbury Press of Zondervan Publishing House, 1986.

Sarah Lankford Palmer

Brown, Kenneth O., comp. *Sarah A. Lankford Palmer: A Daughter of the King.* Hazelton, Pa.: Holiness Archives, 2001.

Roche, John A. *The Life of Mrs. Sarah A. Lankford Palmer.* Salem, Ohio: Allegheny Pub., 1989. Reprint of 1898 edition.

Daniel Payne

Payne, Daniel Alexander. *Recollections of Seventy Years.* New York: Arno Press, 1968. Reprint of 1888 edition.

Arthur Samuel Peake

Howard, W. F. (ed.). *A. S. Peake: Recollections and Appreciations.* London: 1938.

Peake, L. S. *Arthur Samuel Peake: a Memoir.* London: Hodder and Stoughton, 1930.

Wilkinson, John T. *Arthur Samuel Peake.* London: Epworth Press, 1971.

Vincent Perronet

Batty, Margaret. *Vincent Perronet, 1693–1785, "The Archbishop of the Methodists."* Emsworth, England: WMHS Publications, 2002.

Joseph Pilmore

Johnson, Michael Dewitt. *The History and Theology of Joseph Pilmore.* Thesis, Northwestern University, 1976.

Pilmore, Joseph. *The Journal of Joseph Pilmore, Methodist Itinerant, for the years August 1, 1769 to January 2, 1774.* With a biographical sketch by Frank B. Stanger. Edited by Frederick E. Maser and Howard T. Maag. Philadelphia, Pa.: Historical Society of the Philadelphia Annual Conference, UMC, 1969.

W. B. Pope

Moss, R. Waddy. *The Rev. W.B. Pope, D.D., Theologian and Saint.* London: Robert Culley, 1909.

W. Morley Punshon

Dawson, Joseph. *William Morley Punshon, the orator of Methodism.* London: C. H. Kelly, 1906.

Macdonald, F. W. *The Life of William Morley Punshon.* London: Hodder and Stoughton, 1887.

McCullagh, Thomas. *The Rev. W. M. Punshon.* London: Wesleyan Conference Office, 1881.

Harris Franklin Rall

McCutcheon, William John. *Essays in American Theology: The Life and Thought of Harris Franklin Rall.* New York: Philosophical Library, 1973.

Thomas Rankin

Rankin, Thomas. *The Diary of Thomas Rankin: One of the Helpers of John Wesley.* Lake Junaluska, N.C.: Commission on Archives and History, UMC, 1975.

Reverdy Ransom

Morris, Calvin Sylvester. *Reverdy C. Ransom: A Pioneer Black Social Gospeler.* Doctoral dissertation, Boston University, 1982.
Ransom, Reverdy. *The Pilgrimage of Harriet Ransom's Son.* Nashville: Sunday School Union, 1949.

James H. Rigg

Telford, John. *James Harrison Rigg.* London: Robert Culley, 1912.
Smith, John T. *Methodism and Education, 1849–1912: J.H. Rigg, Romanism and Wesleyan Schools.* Oxford: Oxford University Press, 1998.

B. T. Roberts

Roberts, Benson Howard. *Benjamin Titus Roberts: A Biography.* North Chili, N.Y.: "The Earnest Christian" Office, 1900.
Zahniser, Clarence Howard. *Earnest Christian: Life and Works of Benjamin Titus Roberts.* [S.l., 1957].

Harold Roberts

Lenton, John H. *Harold Roberts.* Peterborough, England: Foundery Press, 1995.

Oral Roberts

Harrell, David E., Jr. *Oral Roberts: An American Life.* Bloomington, Ind.: Indiana University Press, 1985.

Martin Ruter

Gross, John Owen. *Martin Ruter: Pioneer in Methodist Education*. [Nashville]: Division of Educational Institutions, Board of Education, MC, ca. 1956.

Smith, Ernest Ashton. *Martin Ruter*. New York: The Methodist Book Concern, ca. 1915.

Adolphus Egerton Ryerson

Ryerson, Egerton. *"The Story of My Life."* Toronto: W. Briggs, 1883.

Sissons, Charles Bruce. *Egerton Ryerson: His Life and Letters*. 2 vols. Toronto: Clarke, Irwin, 1937–1947.

William E. Sangster

Sangster, Paul. *Doctor Sangster*. London: Epworth Press, 1962.

Ira Sankey

Sankey, Ira David. *My Life and the Story of the Gospel Hymns and of Sacred Songs and Solos*. New York: Harper, ca. 1907.

Orange Scott

Matlack, Lucius C. *The Life of Rev. Orange Scott*. New York: Ayer, 1971. Reprint of the 1847 edition.

John Seybert

Spreng, Samuel Peter. *The Life and Labors of John Seybert*. Cleveland, Ohio: Lauer & Mattill, 1888.

Anna Howard Shaw

Carpenter, Alma Lee. *Anna Howard Shaw: A Voice for Women*. [S.l.: s.n.], 1994.

Linkugel, Wil A., and Martha Solomon. *Anna Howard Shaw: Suffrage Orator and Social Reformer*. Westport, Conn.: Greenwood Press, 1990.

Shaw, Anna H. *The Story of a Pioneer*. New York: Kraus Reprint, 1972. Reprint of the 1915 edition.

Asa Shinn

Cooke, C. *Discourse on the Life and Death of the Rev. Asa Shinn*. Pittsburgh: W. S. Haven, 1853.

Matthew Simpson

Clark, Robert Donald. *The Life of Matthew Simpson*. New York: Macmillan, 1956.

Amanda Berry Smith

Smith, Amanda B. *An Autobiography: The Story of the Lord's Dealings with Mrs. Amanda Smith, the Colored Evangelist*. With an introduction by Jualynne E. Dodson. New York: Oxford University Press, 1988.

Nicholas Snethen

Feeman, Harlan Luther. *Francis Asbury's Silver Trumpet; Nicholas Snethen: Non-Partisan Church Statesman and Preacher of the Gospel, 1769–1845*. Nashville, 1950.

Ralph W. Sockman

Hibbard, Robert Bruce. *The Life and Ministry of Ralph Washington Sockman*. Doctoral dissertation, Boston University, 1957.

Donald Soper

Thompson, Douglas. *Donald Soper*. Nutfield, England: Denholm House Press, 1971.
Purcell, William. *Odd Man Out: A Biography of Lord Soper of Kingsway*. London: Mowbray, 1983.
Frost, Brian. *Goodwill on Fire*. London: Hodder and Stoughton, 1996.

Joshua Soule

DuBose, Horace M. *Life of Joshua Soule*. Nashville: Publishing House of the MECS, 1911.

John Springer and Helen Springer

Springer, Helen. *Camp Fires in the Congo*. Boston, Mass.: Central Committee on the United Study of Foreign Missions, 1936.

Springer, John. *I Love the Trail: A Sketch of the Life of Helen Emily Springer*. Nashville: Congo Book Concern, 1952.

Springer, John. *Pioneering in the Congo*. N.Y.: Methodist Book Concern, ca. 1916.

Thomas Bowman Stephenson

Bradfield, William. *The Life of Thomas Bowman Stephenson*. London: C. H. Kelly, 1913.

Barritt, Gordon E. *Thomas Bowman Stephenson*. Peterborough, England: Foundery Press, 1996.

Robert Strawbridge

Maser, Frederick E. *Robert Strawbridge: First American Methodist Circuit Rider*. New Windsor, Md.: Strawbridge Shrine Association, 1983.

Clara Swain

Swain, Clara A. *A Glimpse of India, being a Collection of Extracts from the Letters of Dr. Clara A. Swain, First Medical Missionary to India of the Woman's Foreign Missionary Society of the Methodist Episcopal Church in America*. New York: Garland Publishing, 1987. Reprint of the 1909 edition.

William Warren Sweet

Ash, James L. *Protestantism and the American University: An Intellectual Biography of William Warren Sweet*. Dallas, Texas: SMU Press, ca. 1982.

William Taylor

Taylor, William. *Story of My Life*. Edited by John Clark Ridpath. 2 vols. Freeport, N.Y.: Books for Libraries Press, 1972. Reprint of 1895 edition.

Isabella Thoburn

Gesling, Linda Joyce. *Gender, Ministry, and Mission: The Lives of James and Isabella Thoburn, Brother and Sister in Methodist Service*. Doctoral dissertation, Northwestern University, 1996.

Thoburn, James M. *Life of Isabella Thoburn*. New York: Garland Publishing, 1987. Reprint of the 1903 edition.

James M. Thoburn

Oldham, W. F. *Thoburn—Called of God*. New York: The Methodist Book Concern, 1918.
Thoburn, J. M. *My Missionary Apprenticeship*. New York: Phillips & Hunt, 1884.

Dorothy Rogers Tilly

Shankman, Arnold. "Dorothy Tilly, Civil Rights, and The Methodist Church." *Methodist History* 18 (January 1980): 95–108.

Charles Albert Tindley

Jones, Ralph H. *Charles Albert Tindley, Prince of Preachers*. Nashville: Abingdon Press, ca. 1982.

Harriet Tubman

Bradford, Sarah Hopkins. *Harriet Tubman, the Moses of Her People*. New York: Corinth Books, 1969. Reprint of 1869 edition.

Henry McNeal Turner

Angell, Stephen. *Bishop Henry McNeal Turner and African American Religion in the South*. Knoxville, Tenn.: University of Tennessee Press, 1992.

Margaret Newton Van Cott

Foster, John O. *Life and Labors of Mrs. Maggie Newton Van Cott*. Cincinnati, Ohio: Hitchcock & Walden, 1872.

James Varick

Wheeler, B.F. *The Varick Family*. [Mobile, AL]: B. F. Wheeler, 1990. Reprint of 1907 edition.

John H. Vincent

Vincent, Leon H. *John Heyl Vincent: A Biographical Sketch.* New York: Macmillan, 1925.

Alan Walker

Don Wright, *Alan Walker: Conscience of the Nation.* Adelaide, Australia: Open Book Publishers, 1997.

Harry F. Ward

Duke, David Nelson. *In the Trenches with Jesus and Marx: Harry F. Ward and the Struggle for Social Justice.* Tuscaloosa, Ala.: University of Alabama Press, 2003.
Link, Eugene P. *Labor-Religion Prophet: The Times and Life of Harry F. Ward.* Boulder, Colo.: Westview Press, 1984.

Thomas Ware

Phinney, William R., Kenneth E. Rowe, and Robert B. Steelman, eds. *Thomas Ware, A Spectator at the Christmas Conference.* Rutland, Vt.: Academy Books, 1984.
Ware, Thomas. *Sketches of the Life and Travels of Rev. Thomas Ware, who has been an Itinerant Methodist Preacher for more than Fifty Years.* Kingsport, Tenn.: Holston Conference Task Force on Observance of the Bicentennial of American Methodism, 1984. Reprint of the 1842 edition.

Leslie Weatherhead

Weatherhead, A. Kingsley. *Leslie Weatherhead: A Personal Portrait.* Nashville: Abingdon Press, [1975].

Thomas Webb

Bates, E. Ralph. *Captain Thomas Webb: Anglo-American Methodist Hero.* London: Pinhorns for the WMHS, British Section, 1975.

Charles Wesley

See pages 394–402

John Wesley

See pages 394–402

Samuel Wesley

See pages 394–402

Susanna Wesley

See pages 394–402

Richard Whatcoat

Bradley, Sidney. *The Life of Bishop Richard Whatcoat.* Louisville, Ky.: Pentecostal, ca. 1936.
Fry, Benjamin St. James. *The Life of Rev. Richard Whatcoat.* New York: Carlton & Phillips, 1854.

George Whitefield

Stout, Harry S. *The Divine Dramatist: George Whitefield and the Rise of Modern Evangelism.* Grand Rapids, Mich.: W.B. Eerdmans, 1991.
Whitefield, George. *An Authentic Memoir of the Life of the Late Rev. George Whitefield.* London: Printed by E. Justins, 1803.

Frances Willard

Bordin, Ruth. *Frances Willard: A Biography.* Chapel Hill, N.C.: University of North Carolina Press, 1986.
Gifford, Carolyn DeSwarte. *Writing Out My Heart: Selections From the Journal of Frances E. Willard, 1855–96.* Urbana: University of Illinois Press, 1995.
Willard, Frances. *Glimpses of Fifty Years: The Autobiography of an American Woman.* New York: Hacker Art Books, 1970. Reprint of the 1880 edition.

Jennie Fowler Willing

Brown, Joanne E. C. *Jennie Fowler Willing: Methodist Churchwoman and Reformer.* Doctoral dissertation, Boston University, 1983.

Annie Turner Wittenmyer

Sillanpa, Tom. *Annie Wittenmyer, God's Angel*. Hamilton, Ill.: Hamilton Press, 1972.

Enoch Wood

Cummings, Arthur D. *A Portrait in Pottery*. London: Epworth Press, 1962.

James Shaver Woodsworth

McNaught, Kenneth. *A Prophet in Politics; A Biography of J. S. Woodsworth*. Toronto: University of Toronto Press, [1959].

Milton Wright

Elliott, Daryl M. *Bishop Milton Wright and the Quest for Christian America*. Doctoral dissertation, Drew University, 1992.

IV. TOPICAL STUDIES

A. Evangelism

Brown, Kenneth O. *Holy Ground: A Study of the American Camp Meeting*. New York: Garland Publishing, Inc., 1993.

Collins, Kenneth J. and John R. Tyson, eds. *Conversion in the Wesleyan Tradition*. Nashville: Abingdon Press, 2001.

Johnson, Charles A. *The Frontier Camp Meeting*. Dallas, Texas: Southern Methodist University Press, 1955.

Jones, Scott J. *The Evangelistic Love of God and Neighbor*. Nashville: Abingdon Press, 2003.

Logan, James C. *Theology and Evangelism in the Wesleyan Heritage*. Nashville: Kingswood Books, 1994.

Outler, Albert C. *Evangelism in the Wesleyan Spirit*. Nashville: Discipleship Resources, 1971.

Tuttle, Robert G., Jr. *On Giant Shoulders: The History, Role and Influence of the Evangelist in the Movement called Methodism*. Nashville: Discipleship Resources, 1984.

Weiss, Ellen. *City in the Woods: The Life and Design of an American Camp Meeting*. New York: Oxford University Press, 1987.

B. Holiness

Caldwell, Wayne E., ed. *Reformers and Revivalists*. Wesleyan History Series, vol. 3. Indianapolis, Ind.: Wesley Press, 1992.

Dayton, Donald W. *Discovering an Evangelical Heritage*. Peabody, Mass.: Hendrickson Publishers, 1988. Reprint of the 1976 edition.

———. *The Theological Roots of Pentecostalism*. Metuchen, N.J.: Scarecrow Press, 1987.

Dieter, Melvin E. *The Holiness Revival of the Nineteenth Century*. Metuchen, N.J.: Scarecrow Press, 1980.

Kreutziger, Sarah S. *Going on to Perfection: The Contributions of the Wesleyan Doctrine of Entire Sanctification to the Value Base of American Professional Social Work through the Eyes of Nineteenth-Century Evangelical Women Reformers*. Doctoral dissertation, Tulane University, 1991.

Synan, Vinson. *The Holiness-Pentecostal Movement*. Grand Rapids, Mich.: Wm. B. Eerdmans, 1972.

C. Missions

Baker, Frances J. *The Story of the Woman's Foreign Missionary Society of the Methodist Episcopal Church, 1869–1895*. New York: Garland Publishing, 1987. Reprint of the 1896 edition.

Barclay, Wade C. *History of Methodist Missions*. 4 vols. New York: Board of Missions, The Methodist Church, 1949–1957.

Born, Ethel W. *By My Spirit: The Story of Methodist Protestant Women in Mission, 1879–1939*. New York: Women's Division, General Board of Global Ministries, UMC, 1990.

Grant, John Webster. *Moon of Wintertime: Missionaries and the Indians of Canada in Encounter since 1534*. Toronto: University of Toronto Press, 1984.

Myers, Sarah Joyce. *Southern Methodist Women Leaders and Church Missions, 1878–1910*. Doctoral dissertation, Emory University, 1990.

O'Malley, J. Steven. *"On the Journey Home": The History of Mission of the Evangelical United Brethren Church, 1946–1968*. New York: General Board of Global Ministries, 2003.

Reber, Audrie. *Women United in Mission: A History of the Woman's Society of World Service of the Evangelical United Brethren Church, 1946–1968*. Dayton, Ohio: Otterbein Press, 1969.

Robert, Dana Lee. *American Women in Mission: A Social History of Their Thought and Practice*. Macon, Ga.: Mercer University Press, 1996.

To a Higher Glory: The Growth and Development of Black Women Organized for Mission in The Methodist Church 1940–1968. Cincinnati, Ohio: Board of Global Ministries, UMC, 1978.

D. Social Reform

Cameron, Richard M. *Methodism and Society in Historical Perspective.* Nashville: Abingdon Press, 1961.

Dunnam, Maxie D. and H. Newton Malony. *Staying the Course: Supporting the Church's Position on Homosexuality.* Nashville: Abingdon Press, 2003.

Gorrell, Donald K. *The Age of Social Responsibility: The Social Gospel in the Progressive Era, 1900–1920.* Macon, Ga.: Mercer University Press, 1988.

——. "The Social Creed and Methodism through Eighty Years." *Methodist History* 26 (July 1988): 213–228.

Hardesty, Nancy A. *Women Called to Witness: Evangelical Feminism in the 19th Century.* Nashville: Abingdon Press, 1984.

Heitzenrater, Richard P., ed. *The Poor and the People Called Methodists.* Nashville: Kingswood Books, 2002.

Keller, Rosemary Skinner, ed. *Spirituality and Social Responsibility: The Vocational Vision of Women in the Methodist Tradition.* Nashville: Abingdon Press, 1993.

Knotts, Alice G. *Bound by the Spirit, Found on the Journey: The Methodist Women's Campaign for Southern Civil Rights 1940–1968.* Doctoral dissertation, Iliff School of Theology/University of Denver, 1989.

McDowell, John Patrick. *The Social Gospel in the South: The Woman's Home Mission Movement in the Methodist Episcopal Church, South, 1886–1939.* Baton Rouge, La.: Louisiana State University Press, 1982.

Muelder, Walter G. *Methodism and Society in the Twentieth Century.* Nashville: Abingdon Press, 1961.

Stevens, Thelma. *Legacy for the Future: The History of Christian Social Relations in the Woman's Division of Christian Service, 1940–1968.* Cincinnati, Ohio: Women's Division, General Board of Global Ministries, UMC, 1978.

E. Sunday Schools

Boylan, Anne M. *Sunday School: The Formation of an American Institution, 1790–1880.* New Haven, Conn.: Yale University Press, ca. 1988.

Brown, W. L. *The Sunday School Movement in the Methodist Church in Canada, 1875–1925.* Th.M. Thesis, University of Toronto, 1959.

Lynn, Robert W. *The Big Little School: Two Hundred Years of the Sunday School.* Birmingham, Ala.: Religious Education Press, ca. 1980.

Meir, John Kenneth. *The Origin and Development of the Sunday School Movement in England from 1780 to 1880.* Thesis, University of Edinburgh, 1954.

V. THEOLOGY AND DOCTRINE

A. John and Charles Wesley

1. Bibliographies

Baker, Frank. "Unfolding John Wesley: A Survey of Twenty Years Study in Wesley's Thought." *Quarterly Review* 1 (1980): 44–58.

———. *A Union Catalogue of the Publications of John and Charles Wesley.* Stone Mountain, Ga.: George Zimmerman, 1991.

Bowmer, John C. "Twenty-five Years (1943–68): Methodist Studies." *Proceedings of the Wesley Historical Society* 37 (1969): 61–66.

Green, Richard. *The Works of John and Charles Wesley.* 2nd rev. ed. New York: AMS Press, 1976.

Heitzenrater, Richard P. "The Present State of Wesley Studies." *Methodist History* 22 (1984): 221–231.

Jarboe, Betty. *John and Charles Wesley: A Bibliography.* Metuchen, N.J.: Scarecrow Press, 1987.

2. Basic Texts

Albin, Thomas A. and Oliver A. Beckerlegge, eds. *Charles Wesley's Earliest Sermons.* London: Wesley Historical Society, 1987.

Burtner, Robert W. and Robert E. Chiles, eds. *John Wesley's Theology: A Collection from His Works.* Nashville: Abingdon Press, 1982.

Curnock, Nehemiah, ed. *The Journal of the Rev. John Wesley.* 8 vols. London: Epworth Press, 1909–1916.

Jackson, Thomas, ed. *The Journal of the Rev. Charles Wesley.* 2 vols. Grand Rapids, Mich.: Baker Book House, 1980.

———, ed. *The Works of John Wesley.* 14 vols. Reprint of 1872 edition. Grand Rapids, Mich.: Baker Book House, 1979.

Jarboe, Betty, comp. *Wesley Quotations: Excerpts from the Writings of John Wesley and other Family Members.* Metuchen, N.J.: Scarecrow Press, 1990.

Jay, Elisabeth, ed. *The Journal of John Wesley: A Selection.* New York: Oxford University Press, 1987.

Kimbrough, S. T., Jr. and Oliver A. Beckerlegge, eds. *The Unpublished Poetical Writings of Charles Wesley.* 3 vols. Nashville: Kingswood Books, 1988–1992.

Newport, Kenneth G. C. *The Sermons of Charles Wesley: A Critical Edition with Introduction and Notes.* Oxford: Oxford University Press, 2001.

Osborn, George, ed. *Poetical Works of John and Charles Wesley.* 13 vols. London: Wesleyan-Methodist Conference Office, 1868–1872.

Outler, Albert C. and Richard P. Heitzenrater, eds. *John Wesley's Sermons: An Anthology.* Nashville: Abingdon Press, 1991.

Outler, Albert C., ed. *John Wesley*. The Library of Protestant Thought. New York: Oxford University Press, 1964.

Telford, John, ed. *The Letters of the Rev. John Wesley*. 8 vols. London: Epworth Press, 1931.

Tyson, John R., ed. *Charles Wesley: A Reader*. New York: Oxford University Press, 1989.

Wallace, Charles, Jr. *Susanna Wesley: The Complete Writings*. Oxford: Oxford University Press, 1997.

Watson, Philip S., ed. *The Message of the Wesleys: A Reader*. Grand Rapids, Mich.: Zondervan Publishing House, 1984.

Whaling, Frank, ed. *John and Charles Wesley: Selected Prayers, Hymns, Journal Notes, Sermons, Letters and Treatises*. Classics of Western Spirituality. Ramsey, N.J.: Paulist Press, 1981.

Wesley, Charles. *Hymns for our Lord's Resurrection*. Facsimile of 1746 edition with introduction and notes by Oliver A. Beckerlegge. Madison, N.J.: The Charles Wesley Society, 1992.

——. *Hymns for the Nativity of Our Lord*. Facsimile of 1745 edition with introduction with introduction and notes by Frank Baker. Madison, N.J.: The Charles Wesley Society, 1991.

——. *Hymns on the Great Festivals and Other Occasions*. Facsimile of 1746 edition with introduction by Carlton R. Young, et al. Madison, N.J.: The Charles Wesley Society, 1996.

——. *Hymns on the Trinity*. Facsimile of 1767 edition with introduction by Wilma J. Quantrille. Madison, N.J.: The Charles Wesley Society, 1998.

—— and John Wesley. *Hymns for Ascension-Day and Hymns for Whitsunday*. Facsimile of 1746 edition with introduction and notes by S. T. Kimbrough, Jr. and Oliver A. Beckerlegge. Madison, N.J.: The Charles Wesley Society, 1994.

Wesley, John. *A Plain Account of Christian Perfection*. London: Epworth Press, 1990.

——. *Explanatory Notes Upon the New Testament*. Grand Rapids, Mich.: Baker Book House, 1987.

——. *Explanatory Notes Upon the Old Testament*. 3 vols. Bristol, England: William Pine, 1765.

——. *Primitive Physick: Or an Easy and Natural Method of Curing Most Diseases*. 22nd edition. Philadelphia, Pa.: Hall, 1791.

——. *The Sunday Service of the Methodists in North America*. London: Strahan, 1784.

——. *The Works of John Wesley*. Bicentennial Edition. Projected 35 vols. Nashville: Abingdon Press, 1978–.

—— and Charles Wesley. *Hymns on the Lord's Supper*. Facsimile of 1745 edition with introduction by Geoffrey Wainwright. Madison, N.J.: The Charles Wesley Society, 1995.

3. Life and Thought

Abelove, Henry D. *The Evangelist of Desire: John Wesley and the Methodists.* Stanford, Calif.: Stanford University Press, 1990.

Ayling, Stanley E. *John Wesley.* London: Collins, 1979.

Baker, Eric. *A Herald of the Evangelical Revival: A Critical Inquiry into the Relation of William Law and John Wesley.* London: Epworth Press, 1948.

Baker, Frank. *Charles Wesley, As Revealed by His Letters.* London: Epworth Press, 1948.

—— *Charles Wesley's Verse: An Introduction.* 2nd edition. London: Epworth Press, 1988.

——. *John Wesley and the Church of England.* Nashville: Abingdon Press, 1970.

Berg, Johannes van den and W. Stephen Gunter. *John Wesley and the Netherlands.* Nashville: Kingswood Books, 2002.

Borgen, Ole Edvard. *John Wesley on the Sacraments: A Theological Study.* Nashville: Abingdon Press, 1972.

Brailsford, Mabel R. *Susanna Wesley: the Mother of Methodism.* London: Epworth Press, 1938.

——. *A Tale of Two Brothers: John and Charles Wesley.* London: Rupert Hart-Davis, 1954.

Brantley, Richard E. *Locke, Wesley, and the Method of English Romanticism.* Gainesville, Fla.: University Presses of Florida, 1984.

Brown, Earl Kent. *Women of Mr. Wesley's Methodism.* New York: Edwin Mellen Press, 1983.

Campbell, Ted A. *John Wesley and Christian Antiquity: Religious Vision and Cultural Change.* Nashville: Kingswood Books, 1991.

Cannon, William R. *The Theology of John Wesley, with Special Reference to the Doctrine of Justification.* Lanham, Md.: University Press of America, 1984.

Cell, George C. *The Rediscovery of John Wesley.* Lanham, Md.: University Press of America, 1984.

Chilcote, Paul Wesley. *Recapturing the Wesleys' Vision: An Introduction to the Faith of John and Charles Wesley.* Downers Grove, Ill.: InterVarsity Press, 2004.

Chiles, Robert E. *Scriptural Christianity: A Call to John Wesley's Disciples.* Grand Rapids, Mich.: Zondervan, 1984.

Clapper, Gregory S. *John Wesley on Religious Affections: His Views on Experience and Emotion and their Role in the Christian Life and Theology.* Metuchen, N.J.: Scarecrow Press, 1989.

Clifford, Alan Charles. *Atonement and Justification: English Evangelical Theology, 1640–1790.* Oxford: Clarendon Press, 1990.

Coe, Bufford W. *John Wesley and Marriage.* Bethlehem, Pa.: Lehigh University Press, 1996.

Collins, Kenneth J. *A Faithful Witness: John Wesley's Homiletical Theology.* Wilmore, Ky.: Wesley Heritage Press, 1993.

——. *John Wesley: A Theological Journey.* Nashville: Abingdon Press, 2003.

——. "John Wesley's Assessment of Christian Mysticism." *Lexington Theological Quarterly* 27:57–92.

——. *A Real Christian: The Life of John Wesley.* Nashville: Abingdon Press, 1999.

——. *The Scripture Way of Salvation: The Heart of John Wesley's Theology.* Nashville: Abingdon Press, 1997.

——. *Wesley on Salvation: A Study in the Standard Sermons.* Grand Rapids, Mich.: Zondervan, 1989.

Coppedge, Allan. *John Wesley in Theological Debate.* Wilmore, Ky.: Wesley Heritage Press, 1988.

Cox, Leo George. *John Wesley's Concept of Perfection.* Kansas City, Mo.: Beacon Hill Press, 1964.

Cushman, Robert Earl. *John Wesley's Experimental Divinity: Studies in Methodist Doctrinal Standards.* Nashville: Kingswood Press, 1981.

Dallimore, Arnold A. *A Heart Set Free: The Life of Charles Wesley.* Westchester, Ill.: Crossway Books, 1988.

Deschner, John. *Wesley's Christology: An Interpretation.* Dallas, Texas: Southern Methodist University Press, 1985.

Dorr, Donal J. "Total Corruption and the Wesleyan Tradition." *Irish Theological Quarterly* 31: 303–321.

——. "Wesley's Teaching on the Nature of Holiness." *London Quarterly and Holborn Review* 190: 234–239.

Doughty, William Lamplough. *John Wesley: His Conferences and His Preachers.* London: Epworth Press, 1944.

Dowley, T. E. *Through Wesley's England.* Nashville: Abingdon Press, 1988.

Eayrs, George. *John Wesley, Christian Philosopher and Church Founder.* London: Epworth Press, 1926.

Edwards, Maldwyn. *After Wesley; a Study of the Social and Political Influence of Methodism in the Middle Period (1791–1849).* London: Epworth Press, 1935.

——. *Family Circle: A Study of the Epworth Household in Relation to John and Charles Wesley.* London: Epworth Press, 1949.

——. *John Wesley & the Eighteenth Century: A Study of His Social and Political Influence.* London: Epworth Press, 1955.

——. *My Dear Sister: The Story of John Wesley and the Women in His Life.* Manchester, England: Penwork, 1980.

——. *Sons to Samuel.* London: Epworth Press, 1961.

——. *The Wesley Family and Their Epworth Home.* Manchester, England: Penwork, 1972.

English, John C. *The Heart Renewed: John Wesley's Doctrine of Christian Initiation.* Macon, Ga.: Wesleyan College, 1967.

Gill, Frederick C. *Charles Wesley, the First Methodist.* London: Lutterworth Press, 1964.

———. *In the Steps of John Wesley.* London: Lutterworth Press, 1962.

Green, John Brazier. *John Wesley and William Law.* London: Epworth Press, 1945.

Green, V. H. H. *John Wesley.* Lanham, Md.: University Press of America, 1987.

Gunter, W. Stephen. *The Limits of "Love Divine": John Wesley's Response to Antinomianism and Enthusiasm.* Nashville: Kingswood Books, 1989.

———. et al. *Wesley and the Quadrilateral: Renewing the Conversation.* Nashville: Abingdon Press, 1997.

Harper, Steve. *Devotional Life in the Wesleyan Tradition.* Nashville: The Upper Room, 1983.

———. *John Wesley's Message for Today.* Grand Rapids, Mich.: Zondervan, 1983.

Hattersley, Roy. *A Brand from the Burning: The Life of John Wesley.* London: Little, Brown, 2002.

Heitzenrater, Richard P. *The Elusive Mr. Wesley.* 2 vols. Nashville: Abingdon Press, 1984.

———. *Wesley and the People Called Methodists.* Nashville: Abingdon Press, 1995.

Herbert, Thomas Walter. *John Wesley as Editor and Author.* Princeton, N.J.: Princeton University Press, 1940.

Hildebrandt, Franz. *From Luther to Wesley.* London: Lutterworth Press, 1951.

Hulley, Leonard D. *To Be and To Do: Exploring Wesley's Thought on Ethical Behavior.* Pretoria, South Africa: University of South Africa, 1988.

Hynson, Leon O. *To Reform the Nation: Theological Foundations of Wesley's Ethics.* Grand Rapids, Mich.: Zondervan Publishing House, 1984.

Jeffery, Thomas R. *John Wesley's Religious Quest.* New York: Vantage Press, 1960.

Jennings, Theodore W., Jr. *Good News to the Poor: John Wesley's Evangelical Economics.* Nashville: Abingdon Press, 1990.

Jones, Scott. *John Wesley's Concept and Use of Scripture.* Ann Arbor, Mich.: University Microfilms International, 1992.

Kallstand, Thorvald. *John Wesley and the Bible: A Psychological Study.* Bjarnum, Sweden: Bjarnums Tryckeri, 1974.

———. "John Wesley Och Mystien." *Teologisk Forum* 2.2:7–42.

Kimbrough, S. T., Jr., ed. *Charles Wesley: Poet and Theologian.* Nashville: Kingswood Books, 1992.

———, ed. *Orthodox and Wesleyan Spirituality.* Crestwood, N.Y.: St. Vladimir's Seminary Press, 2002.

Knickerbocker, Waldo E., Jr. "Arminian Anglicanism and John and Charles Wesley." *Memphis Theological Seminary Journal* 29:79–97.

Knox, Ronald A. *Enthusiasm: A Chapter in the History of Religion with Special Reference to the XVII and XVIII Centuries.* Oxford: Clarendon Press, 1950.

Koerber, Carolo J. *The Theology of Conversion According to John Wesley.* Rome: Neo-Eboraci, 1967.

Lawton, George. *John Wesley's English: A Study of His Literary Style.* London: Allen and Unwin, 1962.

Lee, Umphrey. *John Wesley and Modern Religion.* Nashville: Cokesbury, 1936.

——. *The Lord's Horseman: John Wesley the Man.* Nashville: Abingdon Press, 1954.

Lessmann, Thomas. *Rolle and Bedeutung des Heiligen Geistes in der Theologie John Wesley.* Stuttgart: Christliches Verlagshaus, 1987.

Lindstrom, Harald. *Wesley and Sanctification: A Study in the Doctrine of Salvation.* Grand Rapids, Mich.: Zondervan Publishing House, 1982.

McConnell, Francis J. *John Wesley.* New York: Abingdon Press, 1939.

McGonigle, Herbert. *The Arminianism of John Wesley.* Derbys, England: Moorley's Bookshop, 1988.

——. *John Wesley and the Moravians.* Ilkeston, England: Moorley's Bookshop, 1993.

Maddox, Randy L., ed. *Aldersgate Reconsidered.* Nashville: Abingdon Press, 1990.

——. "Reading Wesley as a Theologian." *Wesleyan Theological Journal* 30 (Spring, 1995):7–54.

——. *Responsible Grace: John Wesley's Practical Theology.* Nashville: Kingswood Books, 1994.

Marquardt, Manfred. *John Wesley's Social Ethics: Praxis and Principles.* Nashville: Abingdon Press, 1992.

Marshall, I. Howard. "Sanctification in the Teaching of John Wesley and John Calvin." *Evangelical Quarterly* 34:75–82.

Maser, Frederick E. *The Story of John Wesley's Sisters, or Seven Sisters in Search of Love.* Rutland, Vt.: Academy Books, 1988.

——. "The Unknown John Wesley." *Drew Gateway* 49, 2:1–28.

Mickey, Paul. *Essentials of Wesleyan Theology.* Grand Rapids, Mich.: Zondervan Publishing House, 1980.

Monk, Robert C. *John Wesley: His Puritan Heritage.* Nashville: Abingdon Press, 1966.

Moore, Robert Louis. *John Wesley and Authority: A Psychological Perspective.* Missoula, Mont.: Scholars Press, 1979.

Nagler, Alfred W. *Pietism and Methodism.* Nashville: Methodist Publishing House, 1918.

Naglee, David I. *From Everlasting to Everlasting: John Wesley on Eternity and Time.* 2 vols. New York: Peter Lang, 1991–1992.

Oden, Thomas C. *John Wesley's Scriptural Christianity: A Plain Exposition of His Teaching on Christian Doctrine.* Grand Rapids, Mich.: Zondervan Publishing House, 1994.

Outler, Albert C. *Evangelism in the Wesleyan Spirit.* Nashville: Tidings, 1971.

———. *Theology in the Wesleyan Spirit.* Nashville: Discipleship Resources, 1975.

———. *The Wesleyan Theological Heritage: Essays of Albert C. Outler.* Edited by Thomas C. Oden and Leicester R. Longden. Grand Rapids, Mich.: Zondervan Publishing House, 1991.

Piette, Maximin. *John Wesley in the Evolution of Protestantism.* New York: Sheed and Ward, 1937.

Pollack, Jonn. *John Wesley: Servant of God.* Wheaton, Ill.: Victor Books, 1989.

Pubney, John. *John Wesley and His World.* New York: Charles Scribner's Sons, 1978.

Rack, Henry D. *Reasonable Enthusiast: John Wesley and the Rise of Methodism.* London: Epworth Press, 1989.

Rakestraw, Robert. *The Concept of Grace in the Ethics of John Wesley.* Ann Arbor, Mich.: University Microfilms International, 1985.

Rattenbury, J. Ernest. *The Conversion of the Wesleys; a Critical Study.* London: Epworth Press, 1938.

———. *Wesley's Legacy to the World: Six Studies in the Permanent Values of the Evangelical Revival.* Nashville: Cokesbury, 1928.

Rogal, Samuel J. *John Wesley's London: A Guidebook.* Lewiston, N.Y.: The Edwin Mellen Press, 1988.

———. *Susanna Annesley Wesley (1669–1742): A Biography of Strength and Love.* Bristol, Ind.: Wyndham Hall Press, 2001.

Rowe, Kenneth E., ed. *The Place of Wesley in the Christian Tradition.* Revised edition. Metuchen, N.J.: Scarecrow Press, 1980.

Sangster, William E. *The Path to Perfection: An Examination and Restatement of John Wesley's Doctrine of Christian Perfection.* London: Epworth Press, 1984.

Schmidt, Martin. *John Wesley: A Theological Biography.* 3 vols. Nashville: Abingdon Press, 1962–1973.

Simon, John Smith. *John Wesley and the Advance of Methodism.* London: Epworth Press, 1925.

———. *John Wesley and the Methodist Societies.* London: Epworth Press, 1923.

———. *John Wesley and the Religious Societies.* London: Epworth Press, 1921.

———. *John Wesley, the Last Phase.* London: Epworth Press, 1934.

———. *John Wesley, the Master Builder, 1757–72.* London: Epworth Press, 1927.

Smith, Warren Thomas. *John Wesley and Slavery*. Nashville: Abingdon Press, 1986.

Snowden, Rita Frances. *Such a Woman; the Story of Susanna Wesley*. Nashville: Upper Room, 1962.

Southey, Robert. *The Life of Wesley and the Rise and Progress of Methodism*. Charles Cuthbert Southey, editor. 3rd edition. 2 vols. London: Longman, Brown, Green, and Longman, 1846.

Stacey, John, ed. *John Wesley: Contemporary Perspectives*. London: Epworth Press, 1988.

Starkey, Lycurgus M. *The Work of the Holy Spirit: A Study in Wesleyan Theology*. Nashville: Abingdon Press, 1962.

Stone, Ronald H. *John Wesley's Life and Ethics*. Nashville: Abingdon Press, 2001.

Thorsen, Donald A. *The Wesleyan Quadrilateral: Scripture, Tradition, Reason & Experience as a Model of Evangelical Theology*. Grand Rapids, Mich.: Zondervan Publishing House, 1990.

Todd, John M. *John Wesley and the Catholic Church*. London: Hodder and Stoughton, 1958.

Tomkins, Stephen. *John Wesley: A Biography*. Grand Rapids, Mich.: Eerdmans, 2003.

Tuttle, Robert G., Jr. *John Wesley: His Life and Thought*. Grand Rapids, Mich.: Zondervan Publishing House, 1978.

——. *Mysticism in the Wesleyan Tradition*. Grand Rapids, Mich.: Zondervan Publishing House, 1989.

Tyerman, Luke. *Life and Times of the Rev. John Wesley, Founder of the Methodists*. 3 vols. London: Hodder and Stoughton, 1871.

Tyson, John R., Jr. *Charles Wesley and Sanctification: A Biographical and Theological Study*. Grand Rapids, Mich.: Zondervan Publishing House, 1986.

Villiamy, Colwyn Edward. *John Wesley*. 3rd edition. London: Epworth Press, 1954.

Waller, Ralph. *John Wesley: A Personal Portrait*. New York: Continuum International, 2003.

Weber, Theodore R. *Politics in the Order of Salvation: Transforming Wesleyan Political Ethics*. Nashville: Kingswood Books, 2001.

Weems, Lovett Hayes. *The Gospel According to Wesley: A Summary of John Wesley's Message*. Nashville: Discipleship Resources, 1982.

Weyer, Michel. *Die Bedeutung von Wesleys Lehrpredigten fur die Methodisten*. Stuttgart: Christliches Verlagshaus, 1987.

Wood, A. Skevington. *The Burning Heart: John Wesley, Evangelist*. Exeter, England: Paternoster Press, 1967.

Wynkoop, Mildred Bangs. *John Wesley: Christian Revolutionary*. Kansas City, Mo.: Beacon Hill Press, 1970.

Yrigoyen, Charles, Jr. *John Wesley: Holiness of Heart and Life.* Nashville: Abingdon Press, 1999.

———. *Praising the God of Grace: The Theology of Charles Wesley's Hymns.* Nashville: Abingdon Press, 2005.

B. History of Doctrine

Campbell, Ted A. *Methodist Doctrine: The Essentials.* Nashville: Abingdon Press, 1999.

Chilcote, Paul Wesley. *Wesleyan Tradition: A Paradigm for Renewal.* Nashville: Abingdon Press, 2002.

Chiles, Robert E. *Theological Transition in American Methodism.* Lanham, Md.: University Press of America, 1984.

Deats, Paul and Carol Robb, eds. *The Boston Personalist Tradition in Philosophy, Social Ethics, and Theology.* Macon, Ga.: Mercer University Press, 1986.

Dunlap, E. Dale. *Methodist Theology in Great Britain in the 19th Century.* Ann Arbor, Mich.: University Microfilms, 1968.

Holifield, E. Brooks. *The Gentlemen Theologians: American Theology in Southern Culture.* Durham, N.C.: Duke University Press, 1978.

Johnson, Robert K. et al., eds. *Grace Upon Grace: Essays in Honor of Thomas A. Langford.* Nashville: Abingdon Press, 1999.

Jones, Scott J., *United Methodist Doctrine: The Extreme Center.* Nashville: Abingdon Press, 2002.

Langford, Thomas A., ed. *Doctrine and Theology in the United Methodist Church.* Nashville: Kingswood Books, 1990.

———. *Practical Divinity: Theology in the Wesleyan Tradition.* Nashville: Abingdon Press, 1983.

———, comp. *Wesleyan Theology: A Sourcebook.* Durham, N.C.: Labyrinth Press, 1984.

Lodahl, Michael. *God of Nature and Grace: Reading the World in a Wesleyan Way.* Nashville: Kingswood Books, 2003.

Maddox, Randy L., ed. *Rethinking Wesley's Theology for Contemporary Methodism.* Nashville: Abingdon Press, 1998.

Meeks, M. Douglas. *Trinity, Community, and Power: Mapping Trajectories in Wesleyan Theology.* Nashville: Kingswood Books, 2000.

Messer, Donald E. and William J. Abraham. *Unity, Liberty and Charity: Building Bridges Under Icy Waters.* Nashville: Abingdon Press, 1996.

Naumann, William H. *Theology and German-American Evangelicalism: the Role of Theology in the Church of the United Brethren in Christ and the Evangelical Association.* Ann Arbor, Mich.: University Microfilms International, 1966.

Norwood, Frederick A., ed. *The Methodist Discipline of 1798, including the annotations of Thomas Coke and Francis Asbury.* Rutland, Vt.: Academy Books, 1979.

Oden, Thomas C. *Doctrinal Standards in the Wesleyan Tradition.* Grand Rapids, Mich.: Zondervan Publishing House, 1988.

Peters, John L. *Christian Perfection and American Methodism.* Nashville: Abingdon Press, 1956.

Rieger, Joerg and John J. Vincent, eds. *Methodist and Radical: Rejuvenating a Tradition.* Nashville: Kingswood Books, 2003.

Runyon, Theodore H., ed. *Wesleyan Theology Today: A Bicentennial Theological Consultation.* Nashville: Kingswood Books, 1985.

Scott, Leland. "Methodist Theology in America in the 19th Century." *Religion in Life* 25 (Winter, 1955–1956): 87–98.

Shipley, David C. "The Development of Theology in American Methodism in the 19th Century." *London Quarterly and Holborn Review* 184 (1959): 249–264.

Stoeffler, F. Ernest. "Pietism, the Wesleys and Methodist Beginnings in America." In his *Continental Pietism and Early American Christianity,* 184–221. Grand Rapids, Mich.: Wm. B. Eerdmans, 1976.

Stone, Bryan P. and Thomas Jay Oord. *Thy Nature & Thy Name is Love: Wesleyan and Process Theologies in Dialogue.* Nashville: Kingswood Books, 2001.

Yrigoyen, Charles, Jr. *Belief Matters: United Methodism's Doctrinal Standards.* Nashville: Abingdon Press, 2001.

C. Representative Methodist Theologians

Arthur, William. *The Tongue of Fire; or, The True Power of Christianity.* London: Hamilton, Adams, 1856.

Bangs, Nathan. *The Errors of Hokinsianism Detected and Exposed.* New York: John C. Totten, 1815.

Banks, John A. *A Manual of Christian Doctrine.* London: T. Woolmer, 1887.

Biblical Theology. Papers from the First (1959) Oxford Institute of Methodist Theological Studies. Published in *London Quarterly and Holborn Review* 184 (1959): 162–274.

Bowne, Borden P. *Personalism.* Boston, Mass.: Houghton Mifflin, 1908.

Brightman, Edgar S. *A Philosophy of Religion.* New York: Prentice-Hall, 1940.

Chopp, Rebecca S. *The Power to Speak: Feminism, Language, God.* New York: Crossroad, 1989.

Cobb, John B., Jr. *A Christian Natural Theology: Based on the Thought of Alfred North Whitehead.* Philadelphia, Pa.: Westminster Press, 1965.

———. *Grace and Responsibility: A Wesleyan Theology for Today.* Nashville: Abingdon Press, 1995.

—— and D. R. Griffin. *Process Theology: An Introductory Exposition.* Philadelphia, Pa.: Westminister Press, 1976.

Cone, James H. *A Black Theology of Liberation.* Philadelphia, Pa.: J. B. Lippincott, 1970.

——. *For My People: Black Theology and the Black Church.* Maryknoll, N.Y.: Orbis Books, 1984.

——. *Soul Looks Back.* Nashville: Abingdon Press, 1982.

Cushman, Robert E. *Faith Seeking Understanding.* Durham, N.C.: Duke University Press, 1981.

DeWolf, L. Harold. *A Theology of the Living Church.* New York: Harper & Brothers, 1953.

Faulkner, John A. *Modernism and the Christian Faith.* Methodist Book Concern, 1921.

Fisk, Wilbur. *Calvinistic Controversy.* New York: Mason and Lane, 1837.

Fletcher, John W. *Works.* 4 vols. New York: Waugh and Mason for the Methodist Episcopal Church, 1833.

Foster, Randolph S. *Nature and Blessedness of Christian Purity.* New York: Harper and Row, 1851.

——. *Philosophy of Christian Experience.* New York: Hunt & Eaton, 1891.

Gamertsfelder, Solomon J. *Systematic Theology.* Cleveland, Ohio: C. Hauser, 1913.

González, Justo L. *Manana: Christian Theology from a Hispanic Perspective.* Nashville: Abingdon Press, 1990.

Harkness, Georgia. *Understanding the Christian Faith.* New York: Abingdon-Cokesbury, 1947.

Jennings, Theodore W., Jr. *Loyalty to God: The Apostles' Creed in Life and Liturgy.* Nashville: Abingdon Press, 1992.

Jones, E. Stanley. *The Christ of the Indian Road.* New York: Abingdon Press, 1925.

Jones, Major J. *Black Awareness: A Theology of Hope.* Nashville: Abingdon Press, 1971.

Kirkpatrick, Dow, ed. *The Doctrine of the Church.* Papers from the Second (1962) Oxford Institute of Methodist Theological Studies. Nashville: Abingdon Press, 1964.

——. *The Finality of Christ.* Papers from the Third (1965) Oxford Institute of Methodist Theological Studies. Nashville: Abingdon Press, 1966.

——. *The Holy Spirit.* Papers from the Fifth (1973) Oxford Institiute of Methodist Theological Studies. Nashville: Abingdon Press, 1974.

——. *The Living God.* Papers from the Fourth (1969) Oxford Institute of Methodist Theological Studies. Nashville: Abingdon Press, 1971.

Klaiber, Walter and Manfred Marquardt. *Living Grace: An Outline of United Methodist Theology.* Nashville: Abingdon Press, 2001.

Knudson, Albert C. *The Doctrine of God.* New York: Abingdon Press, 1930.

——. *The Doctrine of Redemption*. Nashville: Cokesbury, 1933.

Langford, Thomas A. *God Made Known*. Nashville: Abingdon Press, 1992.

——. *Methodist Theology*. Peterborough, UK: Epworth Press, 1998.

Lee, Luther. *Elements of Theology; or, An Exposition of the Divine Origin, Doctrine, Morals and Institutions of Christianity*. New York: Miller, Orton & Mulligan, 1856.

Lewis Edwin. *A Christian Manifesto*. Nashville: Cokesbury, 1934.

McConnell, Francis J. *The Christlike God: A Survey of the Divine Attributes from the Christian Point of View*. New York: Abingdon Press, 1927.

Meeks, M. Douglas, ed. *The Future of the Methodist Theological Traditions*. Papers from the Seventh (1982) Oxford Institute of Methodist Theological Studies. Nashville: Abingdon Press, 1985.

——. *God the Economist: The Doctrine of God and Political Economy*. Minneapolis, Minn.: Fortress Press, 1989.

——, ed. *What Should Methodists Teach? Wesleyan Tradition and Modern Diversity*. Papers from the Eighth (1987) Oxford Institute of Methodist Theological Studies. Nashville: Abingdon Press, 1990.

Michalson, Carl. *The Hinge of History: An Existentialist Approach to the Christian Faith*. New York: Charles Scribner's Sons, 1959.

Miguez Bonino, Jose. *Doing Theology in a Revolutionary Situation*. Philadelphia, Pa.: Fortress Books, 1975.

Miley, John. *Systematic Theology*. 2 vols. New York: Hunt & Eaton, 1892–1894.

Oden, Thomas C. *Agenda for Theology: Recovering Christian Roots*. San Francisco, Calif.: Harper, 1979.

——. *Systematic Theology*. 3 vols. San Francisco, Calif.: Harper and Row, 1987–1992. Vol. 1: *The Living God*; Vol. 2: *The Word of Life*; Vol. 3: *Life in the Spirit*.

——. *To Will and To Work: The Transforming Power of Grace*. Nashville: Abingdon Press, 1993.

Ogden, Schubert M. *Christ Without Myth: A Study Based on the Theology of Rudolph Bultmann*. New York: Harper, 1961.

——. *On Theology*. San Francisco, Calif.: Harper & Row, 1986.

Olin, Curtis A. *The Christian Faith*. New York: Eaton & Mains, 1905.

Palmer, Phoebe. *The Way of Holiness*. New York: Palmer and Hughes, 1850.

Parker, Franklin N. *What We Believe: Studies in Christian Doctrine*. Nashville: Publishing House of the Methodist Episcopal Church, South, 1923.

Pope, William B. *A Compendium of Christian Theology*. 2nd edition. 3 vols. New York: Phillips & Hunt, 1881.

Rall, Harris Franklin. *A Faith for Today*. Nashville: Cokesbury, 1936.

——. *Religion as Salvation*. Nashville: Abingdon-Cokesbury, 1953.

Raymond, Miner. *Systematic Theology*. 3 vols. New York: Nelson & Phillips, 1877.

Rishell, Charles W. *The Higher Criticism; an Outline of Modern Biblical Study.* Cincinnati, Ohio: Cranston & Stowe, 1893.

Roberts, Benjamin Titus. *Why Another Sect. . . .* Rochester, N.Y.: The Earnest Christian Publishing House, 1879.

Rowe, Gilbert T. *The Meaning of Methodism.* Nashville: Cokesbury, 1926.

Runyon, Theodore H., ed. *Sanctification and Liberation: A Reexamination in the Light of the Wesleyan Tradition.* Papers from the Sixth (1977) Oxford Institute of Methodist Theological Studies. Nashville: Abingdon Press, 1981.

——. *The New Creation: John Wesley's Theology Today.* Nashville: Abingdon Press, 1998.

Sheldon, Henry C. *System of Christian Doctrine.* Revised edition. New York: Harper & Brothers, 1886.

Smith, George. *Elements of Divinity: A Series of Lectures on Biblical Science, Theology, Church History & Homiletics, Designed for Candidates for the Ministry, and other Students of the Bible.* Revised by T. O. Summers. Nashville: Southern Methodist Publishing House, 1860.

Steele, Daniel. *A Defense of Christian Perfection.* New York: Hunt & Eaton, 1896.

Summers, Thomas O. *Systematic Theology.* Edited by John Tigert. 2 vols. Nashville: Publishing House of the Methodist Episcopal Church, South, 1888.

Terry, Milton S. *Biblical Dogmatics.* New York: Eaton & Mains, 1907.

Turner, George A. *The More Excellent Way: The Scriptural Basis of the Wesleyan Message.* Winona Lake, Ind.: Light and Life Press, 1952.

Wainwright, Geoffrey. *Doxology: The Praise of God in Worship, Doctrine and Life; A Systematic Theology.* New York: Oxford University Press, 1980.

Watson, David L. *God Does Not Foreclose: The Universal Promise of Salvation.* Nashville: Abingdon Press, 1990.

Watson, Richard. *Theological Institutes.* 2 vols. New York: N. Bangs and J. Emory for the Methodist Episcopal Church, 1826.

Whedon, Daniel D. *The Freedom of the Will as Basis of Human Responsibility and a Divine Government.* New York: Carlton & Porter, 1864.

VI. WORSHIP, THE SACRAMENTS, AND HYMNODY

Hymnals and books of worship have been published by the various Methodist churches during their histories. These volumes illustrate their liturgical practices and hymnody.

Allen, Richard. *A Collection of Hymns and Spiritual Songs.* Reprint of 1801 edition. Nashville: African Methodist Episcopal Church Sunday School Union, 1987.

Berger, Teresa. *Theologie in Hymnen? Zum Verhaltnis von Theologie und Doxologie am Beispiel der "Collection of Hymns for the Use of the People Called Methodists."* Altenberg, Germany: Telos Verlag, 1989.

Bowmer, John C. *The Sacrament of the Lord's Supper in Early Methodism.* London: Dacre, 1951.

Davies, Horton. *Worship and Theology in England: From Watts and Wesley to Maurice, 1690–1850.* Princeton, N.J.: Princeton University Press, 1961.

Felton, Gayle Carlton. *This Gift of Water: The Theology and Practice of Baptism Among Methodists in America.* Nashville: Abingdon Press, 1992.

Holland, Bernard. *Baptism in Early Methodism.* London: Epworth Press, 1970.

Job, Rueben. *A Wesleyan Spiritual Reader.* Nashville: Abingdon Press, 1997.

Kimbrough, S. T., Jr. *Lost in Wonder: Charles Wesley, the Meaning of His Hymns Today.* Nashville: The Upper Room, 1987.

Knight, Henry H., III. *The Presence of God in the Christian Life: A Contemporary Understanding of John Wesley's Means of Grace.* Metuchen, N.J.: Scarecrow Press, 1992.

Lawson, John. *The Wesley Hymns as a Guide to Scriptural Teaching.* Grand Rapids, Mich.: Zondervan Publishing House, 1987.

Lorenz, Ellen Jane. *Glory Hallelujah: The Story of the Camp Meeting Spiritual.* Nashville: Abingdon Press, 1980.

Rattenbury, John E. *The Eucharistic Hymns of John and Charles Wesley.* London: Epworth Press, 1948.

———. *The Evangelical Doctrines of Charles Wesley's Hymns.* London: Epworth Press, 1941.

Rogal, Samuel J., comp. *Guide to the Hymns and Tunes of American Methodism.* New York: Greenwood Press, 1986.

Ruth, Lester. *A Little Heaven Below: Worship at Early Methodist Quarterly Meetings.* Nashville: Abingdon Press, 2000.

Sanders, Paul S. "The Sacraments in Early American Methodism." *Church History* 26 (1957): 355–371.

Sizer, Sandra. *Gospel Hymns and Social Religion: The Rhetoric of Nineteenth-Century Revivalism.* Philadelphia: Temple University Press, 1978.

Spencer, Jon Michael. *Protest and Praise: Sacred Music of Black Religion.* Minneapolis, Minn.: Fortress Press, 1990.

Staples, Rob L. *Outward Sign and Inward Grace: The Place of Sacraments in Wesleyan Spirituality.* Kansas City, Mo.: Beacon Hill Press, 1991.

Stookey, Laurence H. *Baptism: Christ's Act in the Church.* Nashville: Abingdon Press, 1982.

———. *Eucharist: Christ's Feast with the Church.* Nashville: Abingdon Press, 1993.

Tucker, Karen B. Westerfield. *American Methodist Worship.* Oxford: Oxford University Press, 2001.

Wainwright, Geoffrey. *Eucharist and Eschatology.* New York: Oxford University Press, 1982.

Wakefield, Gordon S. *Methodist Spirituality.* Peterborough, UK: Epworth Press, 1999.

Warren, James I., Jr. *O For A Thousand Tongues: The History, Nature, and Influence of Music in the Methodist Tradition.* Grand Rapids, Mich.: Zondervan, 1988.

White, James F. *Sacraments as God's Self-Giving.* Nashville: Abingdon Press, 1983.

———. *Protestant Worship: Traditions in Transition.* Louisville, Ky.: Westminster/John Knox, 1989.

Willimon, William H. *Remember Who You Are: Baptism, a Model for Christian Life.* Nashville: The Upper Room, 1980.

———. *Sunday Dinner: The Lord's Supper and the Christian Life.* Nashville: The Upper Room, 1981.

Yoder, Don. *Pennsylvania Spirituals.* Lancaster, Pa.: Pennsylvania Folklore Society, 1961.

VII. CHURCH ORGANIZATION

Books of Discipline and organizational manuals of the various Methodist churches have been published regularly during their histories. These volumes describe their polity, for example, *The Book of Discipline of The United Methodist Church.* Nashville: United Methodist Publishing House, 2005.

Bowmer, John C. *Pastor and People: A Study of Church and Ministry in Wesleyan Methodism.* London: Epworth Press, 1975.

Campbell, Dennis. *The Yoke of Obedience: The Meaning of Ordination in Methodism.* Nashville: Abingdon, 1988.

Edwards, Maldwyn. *Laymen and Methodist Beginnings Throughout the World.* Nashville: Methodist Evangelistic Materials, 1963.

Frank, Thomas Edward. *Polity, Practice, and the Mission of The United Methodist Church.* Nashville: Abingdon Press, 1997.

Gerdes, Egon W. *Informed Ministry: Theological Reflections on the Practice of Ministry in Methodism.* Zurich: Publishing House of the United Methodist Church, 1976.

Holifield, E. Brooks. *A History of Pastoral Care in America: From Salvation to Self-Realization.* Nashville: Abingdon Press, 1983.

Kirby, James E. *The Episcopacy in American Methodism.* Nashville: Kingswood Press, 2000.

Mathews, James K. *Set Apart to Serve: The Meaning and Role of Episcopacy in the Wesleyan Tradition.* Nashville: Abingdon Press, 1985.

Moede, Gerald F. *The Office of Bishop in Methodism: Its History and Development.* New York: Abingdon Press, 1964.

Norwood, Frederick A. "The Shaping of Methodist Ministry." *Religion in Life* 43 (Autumn 1974): 337–351.

———. *Church Membership in the Methodist Tradition.* Nashville: Abingdon Press, 1958.

Oden, Thomas C. *Ministry Through Word and Sacrament.* New York: Crossroad, 1988.

———. *Pastoral Theology: Essentials of Ministry.* San Francisco, Calif.: Harper and Row, 1983.

Richey, Russell E. *The Methodist Conference in America: A History.* Nashville: Kingswood Books, 1996.

——— and Thomas Edward Frank. *Episcopacy in the Methodist Tradition: Perspectives and Proposals.* Nashville: Abingdon Press, 2004.

Robbins, Bruce W. *A World Parish? Hopes and Challenges of The United Methodist Church in a Global Setting.* Nashville: Abingdon Press, 2004.

Sherman, David. *History of the Revisions of the Discipline of the Methodist Episcopal Church.* New York: Hunt & Eaton, 1880.

Short, Roy H. *The Episcopal Leadership Role in United Methodism.* Nashville: Abingdon Press, 1985.

———. *History of the Council of Bishops of The United Methodist Church, 1939–1979.* Nashville: Abingdon Press, 1980.

Tigert, John J. *Constitutional History of American Episcopal Methodism.* 6th edition, revised and enlarged. Nashville: Publishing House of the Methodist Episcopal Church, South, 1916.

Tuell, Jack M. *The Organization of The United Methodist Church.* Revised edition. Nashville: Abingdon Press, 2002.

Wilson, Robert L. and Steve Harper. *Faith and Form: A Unity of Theology and Polity in the United Methodist Tradition.* Grand Rapids, Mich.: Zondervan, 1988.

VIII. PERIODICALS

A.M.E. Church Review. Published quarterly by the African Methodist Episcopal Church.

A.M.E. Zion Quarterly Review. Published quarterly by the African Methodist Episcopal Zion Church.

The Charles Wesley Society Newsletter. Published biannually by the Charles Wesley Society.

Christian Index. Published monthly by the Christian Methodist Episcopal Church.

Herald of Holiness. Published monthly by the Church of the Nazarene.

Historical Bulletin. Published quarterly by the World Methodist Historical Society.

Light and Life. Published monthly by the Free Methodist Church.

Methodist History. Published quarterly by the General Commission on Archives and History of The United Methodist Church.

Proceedings of the Wesley Historical Society. Published three times a year by The Wesley Historical Society in Great Britain.

Wesleyan Theological Journal. Published biannually by the Wesleyan Theological Society.

About the Contributors

Frank Baker was professor emeritus of English church history at Duke University, Durham, North Carolina, and the first textual editor of *The Bicentennial Edition of the Works of John Wesley.*

John D. Beasley is an author and local historian who lives in London, England.

Oliver A. Beckerlegge was an historian of the Methodist Reform movement and the United Methodist Free Churches who lived in York, England.

Charles W. Brockwell, Jr. is adjunct professor of Methodist studies at Louisville Presbyterian Theological Seminary, Louisville, Kentucky.

Joanne Carlson Brown is an adjunct professor in the School of Theology and Ministry, Seattle University, Seattle, Washington.

Kenneth O. Brown is a researcher and scholar of the American holiness and camp-meeting movements.

Barbara E. Campbell is a retired assistant general secretary in administration, Women's Division, General Board of Global Ministries, The United Methodist Church.

David J. Carter is research associate in religious studies at the Open University and lives in Carshalton, England.

Philip L. Carter is music adviser to the Methodist New Room, Bristol, England.

Kenneth J. Collins is professor of Wesley studies and historical theology at Asbury Theological Seminary, Wilmore, Kentucky.

Dudley A. L. Cooney is an historian of Irish Methodism who lives in Levistone, Glenageary, County Dublin, Ireland.

Dennis C. Dickerson is professor of history at Vanderbilt University, Nashville, Tennessee, and historiographer of the African Methodist Episcopal Church.

Melvin E. Dieter is professor emeritus of church history and historical theology, Asbury Theological Seminary, Wilmore, Kentucky.

Mary Agnes Dougherty is a researcher and writer living in California who has done extensive work on the history of the Methodist deaconess movement.

Daryl M. Elliot is a pastor and superintendent in the Church of the United Brethren in Christ, Huntington, Indiana.

John C. English is professor emeritus of history at Baker University, Baldwin City, Kansas.

Gayle Carlton Felton is a consultant/writer for worship resources, the General Board of Discipleship, The United Methodist Church, living in North Carolina.

Bruce David Forbes is professor of religious studies at Morningside College, Sioux City, Iowa.

Peter S. Forsaith is coordinator of the Methodist Studies Unit in the Wesley Centre at Oxford Brookes University, Oxford, England.

Donald K. Gorrell is professor emeritus of church history at United Theological Seminary, Dayton, Ohio.

E. Dorothy Graham is general secretary of the Wesley Historical Society and lives in Birmingham, England.

Kenneth G. Greet is former secretary of the British Methodist Conference.

Frank Hanson is a retired Methodist presbyter, who, in addition to three parish appointments, has also been director of the New Zealand Methodist Education Division and Principal of Trinity Methodist Theological College.

John A. Hargreaves is an historian and Methodist local preacher in the Halifax Circuit, England.

Richard P. Heitzenrater is William Kellon Quick Professor of Church History and Wesley Studies at Duke University, Durham, North Carolina.

William D. Horton is a retired tutor in pastoral theology at Wesley College, Bristol, England.

Alice G. Knotts is a local church pastor in the Oregon–Idaho Annual Conference of The United Methodist Church living in Phoenix, Oregon.

William Leary was a British Methodist minister and historian.

John H. Lenton is convener of the British Archives and History Committee and lives in Wellington, Salop, England.

Robin W. Lovin is Care M. Maguire Professor of Christian Ethics at Perkins School of Theology, Southern Methodist University, Dallas, Texas.

Lawrence D. McIntosh, an Australian, did his doctoral work in Wesley studies at Drew University, served as a theological librarian, and has authored and edited numerous publications.

Timothy S. A. Macquiban is principal of Sarum College, Salisbury, Wiltshire, England.

Frederick E. Maser was the former executive secretary of the World Methodist Historical Society and a researcher/writer of Wesleyan and Methodist history.

John G. McEllhenney is a retired United Methodist pastor and adjunct professor of Methodist Studies at Eastern Baptist Theological Seminary, Philadelphia, Pennsylvania.

Robert C. Monk is professor emeritus of religion at McMurry University, Abilene, Texas.

John A. Newton is associate tutor in church history at Wesley College, Bristol, England.

Zablon Nthamburi was the presiding bishop of the Methodist Church in Kenya, where he now teaches, and is the former president of the World Methodist Historical Society.

J. Steven O'Malley is John T. Seamands Professor of Methodist Holiness History at Asbury Theological Seminary, Wilmore, Kentucky.

L. Dale Patterson is archivist/records administrator of the General Commission on Archives and History, The United Methodist Church, Madison, New Jersey.

Dana L. Robert is Truman Collins Professor of World Mission at Boston University School of Theology, Boston, Massachusetts.

Cyril S. Rodd is a retired lecturer in biblical studies at Southlands College, London, England.

Samuel J. Rogal is emeritus chair of the division of humanities and fine arts at Illinois Valley Community College, Oglesby, Illinois.

E. Alan Rose is editor of the Wesley Historical Society's *Proceedings* and lives in Mottram, England.

Kenneth E. Rowe is emeritus Methodist research librarian and professor emeritus of church history at Drew University, Madison, New Jersey.

Edwin A. Schell is the retired archivist of the Lovely Lane Museum, Baltimore, Maryland.

Thomas Shaw is a researcher and author specializing in Cornish Methodism who lives in Perranporth, Cornwall, England.

Dale H. Simmons is provost and vice president for academic affairs, Judson College, Elgin, Illinois.

Robert Drew Simpson is a retired United Methodist clergyman and an assistant archivist with the General Commission on Archives and History, The United Methodist Church, Madison, New Jersey.

K. James Stein is senior scholar and Jubilee professor emeritus of church history at Garrett-Evangelical Theological Seminary, Evanston, Illinois.

Patrick Ph. Streiff is lecturer in modern church history at the University of Lausanne, Switzerland.

Douglas M. Strong is professor of the history of Christianity at Wesley Theological Seminary, Washington, D.C.

Edwin E. Sylvest is associate professor of the history of Christianity at Perkins School of Theology, Southern Methodist University, Dallas, Texas.

Norman W. Taggart is a specialist in the history of Methodism in Ireland and lives in Coleraine, Ireland.

Geraint Tudur is senior lecturer in church history at the University of South Wales, Bangor, Wales.

Eteuati L. Tuioti is lecturer in church history and Methodist studies at Piula Theological College, Apia, Samoa.

John Munsey Turner is retired tutor in church history at Queen's College, Birmingham, England.

John A. Vickers is retired senior lecturer in religious studies at the College of Education, Bognor Regis, Sussex, England, and editor of *A Dictionary of Methodism in Britain and Ireland*.

Gordon S. Wakefield is retired connexional editor of the British Methodist Publishing House.

Charles Wallace, Jr. is university chaplain and associate professor of religion at Willamette University, Salem, Oregon.

Susan E. Warrick is the former assistant general secretary of the General Commission on Archives and History, The United Methodist Church, Madison, New Jersey. She lives in Oakton, Virginia.

Pauline M. Webb is an author, editor, and broadcaster who lives in London, England.

Marilyn Färdig Whiteley is an independent scholar specializing in the study of Canadian Methodist women and living in Guelph, Ontario, Canada.

Robert J. Williams is senior pastor at St. Andrew's United Methodist Church, Cherry Hill, New Jersey, and Visiting Professor of United Methodist Studies at Princeton Theological Seminary, Princeton, New Jersey.

Philip Wingeier-Rayo is missionary-in-residence and assistant professor of religion at Pfeiffer University, Misenheimer, North Carolina, and has served as a missionary in Nicaragua, Cuba, and Mexico.

Charles Yrigoyen, Jr. is general secretary of the General Commission on Archives and History, The United Methodist Church, Madison, New Jersey, and editor of *Methodist History*.

LaVergne, TN USA
10 October 2010
200238LV00004B/69/P